Becoming a Personal

Support Worker

Lynelle A. Hamilton

Toronto

To my mother Velma Williams, aunt May Denton, and uncle Robert Hamilton, who taught me the value of caring.

To Olivia Wilson, who proved every day that competent and caring support was an attainable goal, not simply an ideal.

To my husband Kerry, daughter Alex, and sister-in-law Cynthia, without whose support this book would not have been completed.

Canadian Cataloguing in Publication Data

Hamilton, Lynelle A. (Lynelle Anne), 1956 -
    Becoming a Personal Support Worker

Includes index.
ISBN 0-13-081260-9

1. Home care services.   2. Home health aides.   I. Title.

RA645.3.H35 2001   362.1'4   C00-931784-8

ISBN 0-13-081260-9

Vice President, Editorial Director: Michael Young
Acquisitions Editor: Samantha Scully
Director of Marketing: Tim Collins
Developmental Editor: Maurice Esses
Production Editor: Jennifer Therriault
Copy Editor: Edie Franks
Production Coordinator: Janette Lush
Page Layout: Prime Imaging and Typography
Art Director: Mary Opper
Interior Design: Anthony Leung
Illustrator: Jackie Wald
Cover Design: Anthony Leung
Cover Image: Peter Samuels/Tony Stone Images

3 4 5 05 04 03 02

Printed and bound in USA

Toronto

Brief Contents

Table of Contents

List of Procedures

Preface

A Canadian Text

We have *always* needed a Canadian text for support workers. I am immensely pleased to have been asked to write this text. Finally, we now have a Canadian book that covers the unique ways in which we across the country provide support services in our multi-cultural society.

Content

Support services are by nature diverse. Services vary from province to province. And support workers help people of all ages, people who have a wide range of conditions and needs, and people who live and work in a variety of settings.

To address this diversity, *Becoming a Personal Support Worker* incorporates the following important characteristics:

- It covers the entire spectrum of support work, from community to facility services. Students no longer need two texts to address the range of settings in which they may work.
- It reflects the current view that support work involves social and emotional support as well as physical assistance.
- It emphasises multicultural issues that worker should consider
- It reflects the current range of client needs. The book prepares support workers to work with people of all ages who need support. It also demonstrates how to meet the needs of adults with impairments who direct their own care. And the book includes chapters on cognitive impairment, mental health, medications, abuse, and child care.
- It includes information on employability and guidance on obtaining employment in the field.

Organization

Becoming a Personal Support Worker is organized into 27 chapters, grouped into 6 main parts. Part One (The Role of the Support Worker) consists of 5 chapters that examine the roles and functions of personal support workers and the various settings in which they can work. Chapter 3, on ethics, encourages students to consider how they provide support. Part Two (The Client) consists of 2 chapters that focus on the client setting and the client-worker relationship.

Parts Three, Four, and Five provide the information and skills that support workers require to perform their duties competently. Part Three (Fundamental Skills) consists of 5 chapters that address important aspects of communication, safety, time management, problem solving, and care planning. Part Four (Assisting With Routine Activities) consists of 8 chapters that focus on the skills commonly used in support work. Part Five (Assisting in Special Situations) consists of 5 chapters that focus on the skills used to support clients with complex needs.

Part Six (Gaining Employment) consists of 2 chapters that provide the student with information and skills necessary to gain employment.

Features

A special effort has been made to incorporate special features in the book to facilitate the learning and application of the material:

- An introductory section entitled **How To Use This Book** provides valuable guidance to the student.
- The entire book is written in an informal style that is **easy to read**.
- Each chapter opens with a set of **Learning Objectives**, a **Chapter at a Glance** section, and a list of **Terms You'll Use** with their definitions.
- **Key Terms** are defined at the beginning of each chapter, boldfaced in the body of the text, and collated with their definitions in a **Glossary** at the back of the book.
- **Procedures** are highlighted throughout the book. For convenience, a **List of Procedures** is presented near the front of the book.
- **Stop and Reflect Boxes** throughout the book pose questions that encourage students to relate the material being discussed to their own personal experiences.
- **Case Example Boxes** throughout the book present realistic situations that students are likely to face when they begin working in the field.
- **Multicultural issues** are addressed wherever appropriate throughout the book. For convenience, the **Canadian Charter of Rights and Freedoms** is reproduced in an Appendix near the back of the book.
- **Questions for Review** at the end of each chapter test the student's factual recall of information and concepts.
- **Questions for Discussion** at the end of each chapter require students to apply their learning in realistic scenarios.
- An annotated list of **National and Provincial Long Term Care Associations** is provided in an Appendix near the back of the book.

Supplement

An *Instructor's Manual* is available to facilitate teaching. This Guide includes teaching suggestions, notes on the Stop and Reflect Boxes, answers to the Review Questions, answers to the Discussion Questions, and suggested class activities.

Acknowledgements

This text would not be as comprehensive as it is without the contributions of others. I am indebted to the following people who, in addition to sharing their health care expertise, also drew upon their experience as teachers to make contributions that strengthened the text:

- Elizabeth Sime, B.Sc.N, Dip. Gerontology, who reviewed the entire text and provided a great deal of information on many aspects of support.
- Brenda Smith, B.Sc.N, B.Ed., who contributed many physical procedures and medication administration techniques.
- Maryann Jefferies, B.Sc. P.T., M.A., who reviewed and contributed to the chapter on Mobility.

My thanks also go to the teachers of the Personal Support Worker Programmes of the York Region District School Board and the Simcoe County District School Board for their comments, suggestions, and support as this book evolved.

I am also grateful to the following instructors who provided formal reviews of part or all of the manuscript:

- Jan Chamberlain, Creative Career Systems Inc.
- Diana Miller, Centennial College of Applied Arts and Technology
- Ann Robinson, Career Canada College
- Glennyce Sinclair, Loyalist College of Applied Arts and Technology
- Susan D. Wilson, West Coast College of Health Care

I owe an additional thanks to Susan D. Wilson of the West Coast College of Health Care for checking the entire edited manuscript.

I'd also like to express my appreciation to the many people who provided photos or gave of their time to pose in photographs. Specifically, I'd like to thank Interface Personnel, Leisureworld Preferred Institute, Leisureworld Incorporated, Community Home Assistance to Seniors (CHATS), the CHATS' Day Program, Maple Health Centre, and Forget's Aurora IGA, and the following people: Marya Grad, Deb Messervey, Tim Valyear, Lynn Slaney, Jacqueline Carabott, Robert Harmon, Cynthia Brodeur, Alexandra Hamilton-Brodeur, Faye Gardner, A. Kuminthini Ponniah, Esme Cyrus, Marylou B. Marqueses, Hyacnth Daley as well as clients of CHATS and CHATS' Day Program.

Finally, I would like to express my appreciation to those Personal Support Worker students who gave me feedback and suggestions. Student input helped me keep the text focussed on what really matters.

How to Use this Text

Scope of this Text

This text is intended to provide a reference for you, as you develop skills in providing personal support. It is *not* intended to replace a course or program, nor will it provide all of the information you'll need as you work in the field. It is a companion to the classroom sessions in which you'll participate. At the conclusion of the course or program, it can serve as a reference for many years. We also hope that it will encourage you to go on and read more about topics that interest you.

You may find that you may not be able to use all of the information and/or skills described in this text. Your employer may not allow you to do certain tasks, or you simply may not have clients who require you to use all your skills. *Your practice should always be within the bounds set by your employer and your client's needs.*

Using the Information

Keep in mind that knowledge and skill often become stale if not used for a period of time. Before you use any skill, ask yourself the following questions:

Am I *competent?* Can I perform the skill properly?
Am I *current?* Have I used this skill recently?
Am I *comfortable* performing the skill?

Only proceed if the answer to all three questions is yes. If you need to review the procedure or information, do so. Ask a teacher, supervisor, or a skilled colleague to go over the information with you. If you need to practise, ask a colleague to assist you. Review and practise until you feel comfortable.

How the Text is Organized

In each chapter, you'll find:

- Objectives: the things you'll learn by reading the chapter;
- Key words introduced in the chapter;
- Information and/or procedures;
- Case studies, examples, biographies;
- Questions for review; and
- Questions for discussion.

Suggestions for Using this Text

As an adult learner, you probably want to learn information and skills that are useful to you. Keeping this in mind, try the following to get the most out of the textbook.

Read the chapter before you discuss the topic in class. Reading the chapter beforehand prepares you to take full advantage of the teacher's presentation, take part in the class discussions, as well as get answers to your questions about the topic. The text is broken down into chapters which will relate to one or more classes. If you're not sure which chapter you should read, ask your teacher.

Review the chapter first, making note of the question boxes, headings, and key words. Relate your answers, the headings, and key words to your work and your learning needs. Does the chapter contain information which helps you to better understand or meet a client's need? Is there information that you already know and use? This process helps you to connect the information in the text with your own work.

Identify the questions you have with regard to the chapter. You may want to make a written list of the questions as you go along.

Read the chapter. Have you ever heard the advice, "Spread the butter thickest where it will do the most good"? In this context, it means to spend more time on the information which is new to you, or answers questions you have. Spend less time on the information with which you are already familiar.

As you read, relate the information to the clients with whom you work and to the settings in which you work. Many times, the information in the text will remind you of a client or a situation. Thinking of the information in connection with your client will help you to retain the information. The question boxes will help you to connect the information to your work. The case studies in each chapter also give you an opportunity to see the information applied in a "real" setting.

Make notes or highlight information you want to remember. Many students find that making written notes best helps them to remember information, particularly if they put the information into their own words as they make the notes. Some students prefer to underline or highlight information in the text. Experiment to see which method works best for you.

Complete the review questions at the end of the chapter. This review makes you connect the information to your own experiences and helps you to retain the information. Once you are finished, compare your answers to those in the text. Review material you found difficult.

Discuss the chapter with classmates or colleagues. This activity has many benefits. You can share information with each other, thus helping each other to understand difficult parts. Also, as you put the information into your own words, you, once again, are connecting the information to your own experience.

Apply the reading to class discussions.   Use the information to participate in class discussions, case studies, and other activities.

Ask questions in class.   Sometimes, it's hard to "get" a concept or to understand information. This happens to everyone. We all have topics that are harder for us to understand as well as topics that come more easily to us. Don't be afraid to ask questions. Chances are that you are not the only person who has that question.

Apply the information you learn.   Make a point to apply the information and concepts you learn to your work. Remember, you retain, on average:

> 10% of what you read
> 20% of what you hear
> 30% of what you see
> 50% of what you see *and* hear
> 70% of what you say
> 90% of what you say *and* do

PART ONE

THE ROLE OF THE SUPPORT WORKER

Source: Interface Personnel.

What Is Personal Support?

Terms You'll Use

Acute Care Facility   A setting in which a person receives treatment for a specific medical condition on a short-term basis. This is another term for a hospital.

Assisted Living   A setting in which clients live in their own apartments or town-houses but receive services from an agency in the building. Assisted living is also called supportive housing or assisted housing.

Attendant   A person who assists a client with physical disabilities where the client directs his or her own care.

Caregiver   A person who assists the client. Caregivers can include people who are not paid (e.g., family, friends, neighbours, and volunteers) as well as those who are paid (e.g., support workers or companions).

⏭

Client   A person who uses community support services. Throughout this text, we will use the term *client* to refer to *clients, residents,* and *consumers.*

Community   A setting in which a person lives in her or his own home (house or apartment) without support services located in the same building.

Consumer   In this book, we use the term to describe a person with temporary or permanent disability who uses support services.

Facility   A setting in which a person lives that has shared dining and recreational facilities. In facilities, the person receives support from services housed in the same building. Throughout this text, the term *facility* will refer to *long-term care facilities, retirement homes,* and *rest homes.*

Long-Term Care Facilities   A setting in which a person lives and receives assistance with routine activities of living as well as some nursing care.

Patient   A person who is in an acute care facility (hospital).

Resident   A person who lives in a long-term care facility, retirement, or rest home.

Retirement Homes or Rest Homes   Settings in which older adults live where some laundry and homemaking services are provided.

Support Worker   A worker who provides personal support. Support Worker may or may not be the title of the program you are taking. Different provinces have different titles to describe the worker who provides personal support.

How would you define personal support?

_____

_____

What types of activities do you think personal support includes?

_____

_____

If you had to describe the typical person who would need personal support, what would you say? How old would the person be? Would they be male or female? What other characteristics would the typical person have?

_____

_____

Compare your answers with those of your colleagues or other students.

Did you find that your answers were different than those other people had? You likely identified some things that were the same and some that were different. That's because the personal support activities needed can vary a great deal from person to person.

The Purpose of Personal Support

The purpose of support work is to assist *clients* to accomplish the tasks of everyday living so that they can get on with their lives. As you saw earlier, support means different things to different people. Consider the following examples.

CASE EXAMPLE 1-1

Allison Grey is 42. Since her stroke at age 29, she uses personal support services to help her get up, wash, dress, and eat before she goes to work. She uses a wheelchair to get about, as her right leg is weak. She advises her attendant as to how she wants things done.

CASE EXAMPLE 1-2

Gary Fulton is 88. He has Alzheimer Disease and lives in a long-term care facility. He is able to get dressed by himself if his support worker hands him his clothes in the order he needs to put them on. | *He often forgets where he is and becomes frightened. Staff members spend a great deal of time comforting and reassuring him, as well as making sure that he is safe.*

CASE EXAMPLE 1-3

Sue and Jim Corbin recently had triplets. They also have a five-year-old daughter. Sue had a Caesarian section and is still quite weak. Sue and Jim prefer to provide most care to the newborns and prefer that the support worker assist Sue with bathing and | *dressing, help in the care of their older daughter, help with laundry, and perform household chores so that Sue and Jim can spend as much time as possible with their children.*

As you can see from the examples, support means many things to many people. Furthermore, even though the same kind of support might be provided (for example, assistance with dressing), how it is provided may be very different, depending upon the person's needs and preferences. For example, both Allison Grey and Gary Fulton require assistance in order to get dressed. However, the way in which the support worker assists them is very different. Allison Grey guides her support worker in doing what she needs done while Gary Fulton relies on his support worker to guide him.

Clients can be assisted by *attendants, caregivers,* and *support workers.* **Clients** are people who use community support services. **Attendants** are people who assist clients with physical disabilities who direct their own care. **Caregivers** include people who assist the client but are not paid (volunteers, family, friends, and neighbours) and those that are paid (support workers). **Support workers** are those who provide personal support to clients.

Despite the differences in *how* it is carried out, personal support can be divided into four general categories; home management, personal care, family responsibilities, and social and recreational activities.

Home Management

Home management refers to the many tasks that are involved in the running of a household such as shopping, house cleaning, and meal preparation (Photo 1-1). It is a significant part of personal support.

The specific tasks vary according to where the person lives and what other services and assistance he or she has. For example, some workers prepare a noon meal for a client whose family is able to do the shopping and housekeeping, but who can't be at home

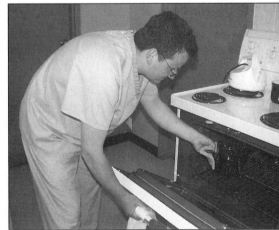

Photo 1-1 *Household tasks such as meal preparation are an essential component of personal support.*

when the client eats lunch. Other workers may shop for a client as well as prepare meals. Sometimes, the help that the worker provides seems unusual. Some workers in northern areas must melt snow in the winter to get drinking water for their clients! Other workers assist clients who have no running water in their homes or who heat their homes by means of a wood-burning stove.

Personal Care

Personal care refers to help with dressing, bathing, toileting, grooming, mobility, and other routine activities of living. Many clients will require some assistance with personal care (Photo 1-2). Some will require a great deal of help, others will require very little. Because personal care is so intimate, it is often the most challenging type of care to provide.

Family Responsibilities

Family responsibilities refer to things that the client is responsible to do as a husband or wife, a parent, or even as an adult child. Support workers may be asked to care for children, to prepare meals for the family, or to do the family's laundry (Photo 1-3). In keeping with the purpose of helping clients to do what they need to do, support workers are often asked to assist with or complete some things that are not directly related to the client's care.

Photo 1-2
Personal care helps your clients to look and feel their best.
Source: CHATS.

Photo 1-3 *Caring for a client's children may be a part of the support you are asked to provide. It should be seen as part of the support your client needs, not as an "extra" duty.*
Source: Interface Personnel.

Social and Recreational Activities

Social and recreational activities refer to activities for enjoyment and interaction with others, such as accompanying clients on outings or helping the client to do things with others or take part in activities. Support workers in assisted living settings or long-term care facilities might help clients plan a tea party or encourage residents to visit one another. Some support workers have been hired by clients to accompany them on a vacation.

Stop and Reflect 1-2

If you work in the field...

What kinds of support service do you provide?

_____

_____

Do your colleagues provide other types of support?

_____

_____

Does your employer provide all types of support services described in this text? If not, which ones are provided?

_____

_____

If you are new to the field or do not work in the field...

Find out who provides support services in your community. What services do these agencies provide?

_____

_____

Do all agencies provide the same types of services?

_____

_____

Do any agencies specialize in providing one type of service (for example, homemaking) or serve only one type of client (for example, older adults)?

_____

_____

Short-Term and Long-Term Support

Not all support work is provided on a long-term basis. Some services are provided for a short period of time. Examples of situations in which you might be asked to provide short-term support include:

- Assisting a person who is recovering from an illness, an operation, or an accident.
- Assisting a new mother.
- Assisting a person while their primary *caregiver* (spouse or family member) is away.
- Assisting a person who has moved from a *long-term care facility* to a more independent living arrangement.

Stop and Reflect 1-3

Have you ever had help on a short-term basis? Perhaps someone came to help when you or your spouse had a child. Maybe you had help if you had an operation and were recovering. Perhaps you were ill and had someone help you out for a bit.

How did you feel about needing help?

_____

_____

How did you feel about having that person who was helping you in your home?

_____

_____

How did you feel when the person no longer came to help you?

_____

_____

Would you have felt differently if you had to have help for a long period of time? If so, how?

_____

_____

Did you have mixed feelings about the support you had? Perhaps you appreciated the help but at the same time you were uncomfortable with having someone else in your home. Perhaps the person was very nice but did not do things the way you would do them.

When the person left, you might have been a bit sad and a bit glad. Compare this to how you might have felt if you needed the help for a much longer period of time. Chances are, you'd feel differently about longer-term support.

Needing support for a short time is different than needing it for a long period of time. Short-term support is often seen as meaning that the person will recover and be able to go back to a previous lifestyle after a while, or that the person will be able to move on to a new, more exciting phase in life.

Assisting a client on a short-term basis requires you to quickly learn your client's preferences and the basic information you need to assist. You'll also have to adapt to changes in routine as your client's condition improves. When the client no longer needs you, you may find yourself feeling a little sad that you didn't get to know him or her better. This is perfectly normal.

Needing long-term support can make a person feel dependent, frustrated, and very sad. It may take time for the person to adjust to the change in lifestyle and to begin to see the support needed as something that helps them to get on with life.

As a support worker, you always want to assist your client in a way that makes the person feel valued and that their needs and preferences are respected (Photo 1-4). Working with a client who has just begun to use long-term support will require you to be particularly sensitive to the effect that needing your help has on the client. You'll also have to be particularly flexible as you learn about your client's ways of doing things. You'll have to adapt your approach to support each individual client.

Photo 1-4
Provide assistance in a way that respects your clients needs and preferences.
Source: CHATS.

Personal Support as a Career

Although this type of work has been done for decades, personal support work is a relatively new career in Canada. Support work has its roots in the heath care aide and homemaker training programs developed in the late 1970s and early 1980s. In many areas, support workers now require a provincially recognized certificate to work in most settings. However, support workers who assist adults with physical disabilities where the client directs their own care are often trained by their employer and may not be required to take a provincial training program.

Personal support training programs differ from province to province. Some provinces have one program that prepares workers to work in both community and facility settings. Others have separate training programs for facility and community support workers. Table 1-1 illustrates selected training programs of selected provinces in 2000. It's important to note that there may be more than one training program

TABLE 1-1	Selected Training Programs Across Canada	
Province	**Community Support Work**	**Facility Support Work**
Alberta	Personal Care Attendant	
British Columbia	Home Support Attendant	Resident Care Attendant
Manitoba	Home Care Attendant	Health Care Aide
Nova Scotia	Continuing Care Assistant	
Ontario	Personal Support Worker	
Prince Edward Island	Primary Health Care Worker	
Saskatchewan	Home Care/Special Care Aide	
Western NW Territories	Homemaker/ Personal Care Attendant	Long-Term Care Aide

available in your province. As well, specific employers may prefer a particular training program or provide their own.

Although training programs across the country have much in common, the programs do vary from province to province. A certificate valid in one province may not be seen as equal to another province's certificate. However, many schools have experience in reviewing out-of-province certificates for equivalency.

Regulation and Personal Support

You may hear colleagues speak of *regulation* of support workers. Regulation is the way that each province determines which professions may perform certain activities that are considered to be too dangerous for most people to perform.

Many health professionals are *regulated*. Each province determines which professions must be regulated. Regulation usually involves at least these three things: identifying what education is required for the profession, establishing what activities may be done by the profession, and establishing a disciplinary procedure to handle complaints about members of the profession. Usually, a regulated profession establishes a *college* or *professional association* to carry out these duties. In order to work in the profession, a person must be a member of the appropriate college or association.

Support workers are *unregulated*. While a support worker may choose to belong to a provincial association, there is no requirement that he or she do so. Most importantly, the lack of regulation means that you, as a support worker, are responsible to make certain that your work is always within the bounds set by your training, your employer, and any legislation that applies to your work.

Who Uses Support Services?

There are several terms that describe people who use support services. **Consumers** are people with temporary or permanent disability. **Residents** are those who live in long-term care facilities, retirement homes, or rest homes. **Patients** are people who are being cared for in acute care facilities. This book uses the term clients to refer to consumers, residents, and patients.

As you might guess from the beginning of this chapter, clients come from all age groups. While it is true that most clients are older adults, a significant proportion are younger adults and children. A recent Statistics Canada study found that 1/3 of the clients of the provincial home care programs were children or adults under the age of 65. (Statistics Canada *Health Reports*, vol. 10, no. 1, Summer 1998.)

We can distinguish three main categories of clients. It's important to remember that a client may belong to more than one of these general categories described below. It's also important to remember that each client is an *individual* with specific needs and preferences. The support service you provide to a specific client depends as much upon who they are as it does upon their chronological age.

Photo 1-5 *Many – but not all – clients are older adults.*

Source: Interface Personnel.

Older Adults

Older adults account for nearly 2/3 of the community services and most of the *facility* support services used (Photo 1-5). Although many older adults use support services for a long period of time, some older adults use services on a short-term basis to recover from an injury or illness. Most older adults receive support services in their homes – only approximately seven percent live in a long-term care facility.

Adults with Physical Disabilities

Adults with disabilities make up approximately ten percent of the population over age 18. Most adults with physical disabilities use services on a long-term basis (Photo 1-6). Like an older adult, the adult with physical disabilities may require a different type of service on a short-term basis (for example, help while the person recovers from surgery or an illness). The vast majority of adults with disabilities live and receive services in their own home.

Services provided to adults with disabilities may be provided in a way that differs from those provided to older or younger clients. Adults with disabilities who work may require assistance getting ready for work, or they may require assistance at work. They may also require assistance to travel for work or pleasure.

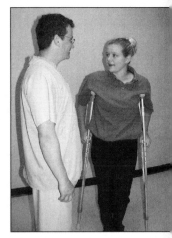

Photo 1-6
Most younger adults with a disability will use support services for many years.

Children

Most children who receive support services *directly* receive them because of the effects of a physical or developmental condition. Many children also receive rehabilitation services (services aimed at helping them to recover ability) and support workers may be asked to assist in certain activities related to the rehabilitation under the direction of the health professional who is working with the particular child. Some children receive support services at school and/or they are accompanied by a support worker on the way to and from school (Photo 1-7).

Children can also receive services indirectly because of a caregiving parent's illness or disability or because the family has had a new child or children.

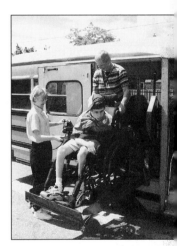

Photo 1-7
Children with disabilities may receive a variety of support services, both at home and at school.
Source: CHATS.

Settings

People who use support services have the right to participate fully in life. Support service is provided wherever the client is located – at home, at work, on the way to and from locations such as a mall or the movies, or in *facilities*. A **Community** setting is one in which a person lives in his or her own home without support services in the same building. **Assisted living** is a setting where clients live in their own apartments or townhouses but receive services from an agency in the building. This is also called supportive housing or assisted housing. **Facilities** are settings in which people share dining and recreational areas and receive support from services housed in the same building. In this text, the term facilities will be used to refer to retirement homes, long-term care facilities, rest homes, and acute care facilities. **Retirement homes** are settings in which older adults live where some laundry and homemaking services are provided. Personal care may or may not be available and residents are usually able to perform most routine activities of independent living. In general, care is not regulated to the same extent that it is in long-term care facilities. **Long-term care facilities** are those in which a person lives and receives assistance with routine activities and some nursing care. Each province has different names for these facilities, including nursing homes, board and care homes, special care homes, and homes for the aged. **Acute care facilities** are settings where people receive treatment for specific medical conditions on a short-term basis. Hospitals are examples of acute care facilities. Each setting is different, and how you carry out your duties will vary by the setting in which you work. In the next chapter, we will discuss the major types of settings in more detail.

Questions for Review

Answer each of the following. Then, check your answers with the text.

1. What are the four major categories of personal support work?

2. How is short-term support different from long-term support?

3. Do you need a provincially recognized certificate to work as a support worker in most provinces?

4. When might you be trained by your client?

5. How are patients and residents different?

6. What are the three main categories of clients?

Questions for Discussion

1. Talk to a person who uses support services. How does the person describe the services he or she receives? Does this person's definition match yours? In what ways is it similar? In what ways is it different?

2. Talk to a person who has been providing personal support for five years or more. According to that person, how has the career changed over that time?

3. Imagine that you have broken your leg and must wear a cast from toes to groin for six weeks. You can't walk even a short distance without crutches and, even then, getting around is difficult. You must use a wheelchair if you want to go out of your home. What help would you need? How do you think you would feel about needing this help? How would you feel about asking another person to provide it? Would your feelings be different if the person helping you was a family member, friend, or a personal support worker?

CHAPTER TWO

Work Settings

Terms You'll Use

Acute Care   The type of care provided in hospitals. Clients in an acute care setting are usually called patients.

Chronic Care   The type of care provided to people whose condition is stable, but who need more professional care than residents of long-term care facilities. Some provinces have separate buildings for chronic care facilities, others provide chronic care services in acute care centres.

Continuing Care   The type of care provided on a long-term basis. Continuing care can refer to long-term services provided in facilities or for people who live in their own homes.

Day Program   Programs that provide clients an opportunity to take part in activities and be with others in a secure setting. Some day programs offer rehabilitation services to help clients recover from illness or injury. Other programs are geared toward clients with specific conditions, such as clients who have dementia or who have had a stroke.

Group Home   A home in which a small number of people live; in most cases no more than eight people. The group home has round-the-clock staff members and they are usually located in residential neighbourhoods.

Home Care   Services provided to clients in their own homes through a provincially funded program. Different provinces include different services, although most include personal support as well as nursing, physiotherapy, and occupational therapy services.

Mental Health Facility   A facility designed to provide service to people with mental health concerns. Many such facilities provide both short-term and long-term services. Some mental health facilities are located in acute care settings whereas others are completely separate. Increasingly, mental health services are provided to clients who live in their own homes.

Multidisciplinary Teams   A support team made up of members from different professions or backgrounds.

Outreach Services   Services that are provided to clients in their own home, not in facilities, assisted living, or supportive housing.

Rehabilitation Centre   A facility that provides rehabilitation services to patients to help the patient recover from surgery, illness, or injury. Patients usually stay in rehabilitation centres for only a short period of time.

Respite Care   A type of service provided to a client and the client's caregiver, so that the caregiver can be relieved from the responsibilities of caring for the client and has the opportunity to take a break. Respite care is provided in the client's home and in many long-term care facilities. Respite care is also called *caregiver relief.*

The Canadian Health Care System

Canada has a nationwide system of health care. This system is governed by federal legislation, specifically the *Canada Health Act*. It requires each province to ensure that its residents have access to necessary health care, according to five criteria:

1. Universality. All residents of the province are entitled to public health insurance coverage.
2. Accessibility. No fees or other barriers prevent residents from receiving medically necessary services.
3. Comprehensiveness. All medically necessary services are covered by provincial health insurance.
4. Portability. People have coverage if they move from one province or territory to another within Canada.
5. Public Administration. The health insurance plan is administered by a not-for-profit, public organization.

Many people think of Canada's health care system as socialized medicine. It is not. It is a system of provincial insurance programs that cover the costs of necessary services. Hospital care, most physician services and some rehabilitation services, as well as long-term (or continuing) care services are covered under these provincial plans. However, provincial plans do vary according to exactly what is covered.

Extended Health Care

The *Canada Health Act* includes many extended health care services – the type of ongoing care that many personal support workers help provide. This care includes services provided to clients who live in their own homes as well as residents of approved long-term care facilities. There are three types of care discussed in this book, *acute care, chronic care,* and *continuing care.* **Acute care** is the type of care provided in hospitals while **chronic care** is provided to people whose conditions are stable but who need more care than people in long-term care facilities. **Continuing care** is provided on a long-term basis in facilities or in a client's home. Health Canada estimates that continuing care is the third-largest program funded under the *Canada Health Act* and that it is the fastest-growing of all types of health care covered by the Act. (Health Canada, *Reports of the Continuing Care Symposium,* 1995.)

Most provinces have a **home care program** whose purpose is to provide services to clients who live in their own homes. Clients who receive service from this program are assessed to identify their needs and to determine the services that the program will provide. These services are usually provided without charge to the client.

Each province has established specific types of long-term care facilities that may receive extended health care funds. In such facilities, medically necessary services are covered by the insurance program. However, residents in long-term care facilities may be required to pay part of the portion of the cost of their room and board. This payment by residents is often called a *copayment.*

The Variety of Settings

Support workers can work in a wide variety of settings and under many different employment arrangements. Some support workers work in more than one setting, while others work in only one. In this chapter, we will examine some of the more common settings in which you might work. We can identify the following nine types of work settings:

- Direct Employment by a Client
- Community Outreach, including Respite Care
- Day, Social, and Recreational Programs
- School or Work Support
- Assisted Living or Supportive Housing
- Retirement Homes
- Group Homes
- Long-Term Care Facilities
- Other Centres (including Chronic Care Centres, Rehabilitation Centres, and Acute Care Centres)

Each setting has different rules, regulations, and expectations of support workers. Furthermore, each facility or agency has its own policies and procedures. You will have to adapt your work habits to meet the expectations of your employer. If you work in more than one setting, you'll have to learn to adapt to the different procedures each uses. However, it's important to remember that no matter where you work, you must always perform your duties to the best of your ability. You owe your clients and yourself nothing less than your best.

Stop and Reflect

In what kinds of settings do support workers in your community work? Aside from being in different locations, how do these settings differ?

_____

_____

_____

If you work in the field, do you work in more than one type of setting? If so, is what you do – or how you do it – different in the different settings? In what ways?

_____

_____

_____

The Variety of Job Titles

As you read this chapter, you'll come across many different job titles. Each employer determines the title they will use for workers providing personal support. Moreover, your job title may not exactly match the title of the training program you are taking. For example, you may receive a certificate in *personal support*, yet work as a *homemaker* or *care aide*.

Direct Employment by a Client

Some clients prefer to employ support workers directly. There are a number of reasons why a client might hire a support worker. In some provinces, persons with disabilities may receive funding to employ support workers directly, rather than receiving services through an outreach agency. Some clients need to have support services at times when local agencies do not offer services. The client's needs may change or the times at which they need assistance may change from week to week. Others simply prefer to select, orient, and supervise the support worker themselves.

Sometimes, a client or family will hire a support worker to assist a client who lives in a retirement home or long-term care facility. This arrangement is often called *private-duty work*.

When you work directly for a client, the client is your supervisor. Like any other employer, the client determines what his or her needs are, the tasks you'll perform, and, often, when you'll need to perform them. The client may provide you with additional training or ask that you take additional training in order to provide the right support.

CASE EXAMPLE 2-1

Olivia has worked for her client for many years. Over time, her duties have changed. At first, she assisted her client with household tasks, usually for a few hours one day each week. When her client was recovering from a fractured ankle, Olivia was asked to increase her time to include shopping once a week and visiting three mornings a week to assist in exercises and other follow-up care.

Recently, Olivia's client has had an illness and is recuperating at home. Olivia now spends several nights with her client. She also drives the client to medical appointments three times each week. Olivia has arranged with her client to have time off during the day to visit her other clients.

Olivia is an employee of her client. Therefore, the client handles deductions and premium payments. As the client's needs have changed, she and Olivia have worked out a schedule that has allowed Olivia to meet her obligations to her other clients while still meeting this client's needs.

Terms of Employment

Working directly for a client can be very rewarding. However, you need to make sure that both you and the client agree on the terms of your employment: in particular, your wages, your hours of work, whether the hours will change from day to day, and how you will handle any problems that come up.

It's especially important to know if you or the client is responsible for submitting taxes and other benefit payments from your salary. Some clients act as employers, meaning that they deduct from your salary any taxes, Canada Pension Plan premiums, and Employment Insurance premiums required. When the client does this, they are responsible for sending the monies deducted to Revenue Canada.

Some clients prefer to hire you as a contractor. In most cases, this means that you are responsible for paying taxes and other premiums on your income. If you are considering taking a contract position, you should contact an accountant for advice.

Challenges

Working on Your Own

Some support workers who work directly for clients can feel alone. Because of the nature of the work arrangement, the support worker may have no one with whom to discuss problems or stresses that may arise related to the work. Be certain that you are comfortable working without the support of coworkers before you accept this type of position.

Resolving Problems

Because there is no agency to help you resolve any problems, it's important to work out with your client a way to resolve differences of opinion or disputes. You must make sure that you and your client are comfortable discussing issues or concerns, so that neither of you becomes frustrated with the arrangement.

Keeping Busy and Balancing Commitments

When you are directly employed by a client, you and your client will determine the amount of time that you will work. If you need additional work, it will be your responsibility to find it. You may choose to work for another client directly or to seek part-time employment through an agency. Whichever you choose, you will be responsible to make sure that you have enough work.

You will also be responsible to make sure that you can meet all the commitments you make (Photo 2-1). You must not lower your standard of service to a client because you have taken on too many obligations. Before you take on a new position, you should carefully consider its requirements to ensure that you can meet them along with your other obligations.

Be sure to discuss the time and location requirements with a new client so that you are well aware of the scope of the assignment before you take it on. For example, will you be required to stay with the client overnight? Travel with the client? Provide service at different times on different days? The answers to these questions will help you to determine whether you can fulfill the assignment if you accept it.

Photo 2-1
Support workers must be well-organized so as to be able to meet schedule commitments.

Community Outreach, Including Respite Care

Many support workers work for agencies that provide **outreach services** or services to clients in their own homes, not in facilities, assisted living, or supportive housing (Photo 2-2). The agencies may be not-for-profit or for-profit. Some agencies may provide service to individual clients who call them directly. Others may take referrals from a third party, such as a home care program or an insurance company. Some agencies do both.

Photo 2-2
Many support workers work through an agency. They receive assignments from the agency, not directly from clients.
Source: CHATS.

Support workers who work for agencies providing outreach may perform a wide variety of tasks. Some agencies offer many types of outreach, such as basic personal care, homemaking, new mother and child care, convalescent care, as well as assistance to the person who is dying. **Respite care** is another type of outreach in which the support worker relieves the client's caregiver in the client's home or in a long-term care facility. This allows the caregiver to take a break from their responsibilities while making sure that client is cared for. Support workers may be hired to provide service in one or more of the programs the agency offers.

Working for an agency that provides outreach can be very rewarding in many ways. On one hand, the opportunity to work with a single client at a time is attractive to many support workers. They enjoy having the opportunity to personalize their service as well as not having to juggle the needs of many clients at the same time. On the other hand, working with a number of different clients provides variety and the opportunity to get to know many people.

Terms of Employment

In most cases, support workers hired by agencies are hired as employees. The worker's time is scheduled by the agency. The agency also determines which worker is assigned to a particular client. This does not mean that the worker is not consulted about when he or she is available, or about the type of work he or she performs. In fact, the worker is consulted. However, the agency usually retains the right to make assignments. Many agencies will attempt to accommodate a worker's schedule where possible. Some agencies offer support workers full-time work. Other agencies offer only part-time or casual (occasional) assignments.

Most outreach agencies require support workers to have provincially recognized training. In addition, most agencies provide an orientation program to help new workers become familiar with the agency's philosophy, policies, and procedures. New workers may accompany an experienced worker for a visit or two to see how things are done. Agencies often provide additional training (often called *inservice training*) to help workers meet clients' needs.

In most cases, the support worker reports to a coordinator or supervisor. The worker may also take assignments from another person called a scheduler. In some agencies, the supervisor or coordinator also assigns the visits.

Following Agency Policies and Procedures

When you are hired by an agency, you'll be asked to follow the agency's policies and procedures for support work. These policies and procedures may change according to the type of service you are providing.

As well, an agency may provide a particular type of service to a particular type of client, but not provide that service to other clients. For example, an agency may allow support workers in respite care to set a client's hair on rollers, even if this is not done for clients receiving service through another program. Sometimes, the agency who refers the client sets out what can and cannot be done for that client.

It is up to you to be aware of your agency's policies and procedures and how they affect the type of service you are providing.

CASE EXAMPLE 2-2

Claire has been an employee of a small homemaking agency for over 10 years. She takes pride in doing her job well. Claire has four clients she sees each week. Two clients are referred by the local home care program and a third client receives service directly from the agency. Her fourth client receives respite care which helps the client's spouse to get some needed rest and relaxation.

Claire's duties vary with each client's needs and the requirements of the specific program. For example,

each home care client's service plan specifies the exact tasks that Claire is to perform during her visits. However, Claire has been asked to work out with her other two clients the tasks each client would like done, within the bounds of her training and agency policy.

Claire enjoys her work and the different people she meets. If she has a problem she cannot work out with the client, she discusses it with her supervisor. She relies upon her supervisor to assign her to clients whose needs match Claire's abilities.

Challenges

Isolation

The support worker does not have day-to-day contact with other support workers. The worker does, however, have the opportunity to speak with his or her supervisor to discuss concerns. Many agencies will arrange for a regular time for support workers to meet and share concerns. As well, most agencies set aside time for support workers who share the care of a client to meet to discuss issues related to that client.

Travel

Support workers in outreach must travel from one client's home to another throughout the day. Agencies try to schedule visits to keep travel to a minimum. Nonetheless, travel can be considerable, particularly in rural areas. It also can be hazardous in severe winter weather. Some agencies require support staff to have a driver's licence and reliable transportation. Agencies located in cities often expect workers to use public transit to get from client to client. It is your responsibility to be sure that you can travel to each client you are assigned.

Working with Personnel from Other Agencies

Many clients receiving outreach services also receive visits from other health professionals or agencies.

It is important to make sure that you know your responsibility with regard to the other members of the support team. You may, from time to time, be asked to take direction from a nurse or therapist also visiting the client, even though that person is not an employee of your agency. Sometimes, another member of the support team may assume that you can perform activities your agency actually forbids you to do. Always clarify your role with your supervisor prior to taking on any new tasks or responsibilities assigned by other members of the support team. In Chapter 5 we will discuss support teams in more detail.

Day, Social, and Recreational Programs

One relatively new area of employment is in day, social, and recreational programs. Support workers assisting clients in these settings often assist clients with recreational activities such as baking, crafts, and games, as well as assisting the clients with any personal care they may need (Photo 2-3). In some provinces, you will need additional training to work in this setting.

Photo 2-3
Support workers employed by day programs often conduct activities or other social events.
Source: CHATS.

Day programs provide support workers the opportunity to expand their skills in small group work and recreation. They offer the worker the opportunity to get to know clients (and, sometimes, the clients' families) over a period of time.

Terms of Employment

Support workers are generally considered to be employees of the day program. The program supervisor will schedule the support worker's time. The program supervisor is the person to whom the worker would go to resolve any work-related problems.

Working Closely with a Team

Support workers in day programs work closely with a team. This team usually consists of a program supervisor and other support workers. It may also include nurses, social workers, and therapists. The challenge of working in a team is also a benefit, as the team can easily work together to resolve concerns and assist each other.

Following Agency Policies and Procedures

Day programs, like outreach programs, have policies and procedures which the support worker must know and follow.

Challenges

Balancing Multiple Demands

There may be a number of clients taking part in the day program. Support workers have to be able to balance multiple demands upon their time. The worker must also be able to easily shift attention from one client to another as each client's needs require. The worker has to be able to set priorities, manage time well, and quickly solve problems.

School or Work Support

Some support workers find employment in schools or work sites. Generally, support workers in these settings provide personal care and other support to one or more clients in the setting. The specific personal support duties will vary with the employing agency, and may be affected by provincial legislation. The worker may or may not function as a member of a team.

Terms of Employment

The worker is usually employed by the organization (such as the school board or the agency for whom the client works) not the individual clients she or he assists.

Challenges

Following Agency Policies and Procedures

School or work support programs have policies and procedures which the support worker must know and follow.

Balancing Conflicting Demands

Sometimes the client's needs or preferences may conflict with the employer's policies. Support workers must develop skill in working through these problems.

Assisted Living or Supportive Housing

Support workers working in assisted living settings provide service to clients who live in an apartment block or condominium development. Each client has his or her own apartment or condominium unit. Support workers provide service to a number of clients each day. Clients who live in assisted living do not necessarily receive the same amount of service each day. Because all clients are located in the same area, it is easier than in other settings for the support worker to provide service when the client needs it.

Terms of Employment

Generally, support workers in assisted living settings are hired and scheduled by an agency. The agency schedules the worker's shifts. However, the individual workers in supportive housing often talk with the clients to identify the actual tasks they will do each day.

The support worker usually reports to a coordinator who is responsible for the services provided. The coordinator may be responsible for more than one supportive housing site. The coordinator may have an office at the site or may make regular visits to the site.

Like outreach programs, many assisted living programs require workers to have provincially recognized training. Many provide an orientation program and regular inservice training to their staff members.

Working As Part of a Team

Support workers in assisted living settings often work in teams to help a group of clients (Photo 2-4). This arrangement allows workers to share responsibilities. The support workers also work closely with the coordinator.

Photo 2-4 *Planning helps support workers work together to make certain that all clients receive service when they need it.*

Source: Leisureworld Preferred Institute/Leisureworld, Inc.

Sometimes, a supportive housing client receives nursing, therapy, or other services. When this happens, the support workers involved with the client must work with the client and the coordinator to identify any changes in the worker's routine.

Following Agency Policies and Procedures

Assisted living programs, like outreach programs, have policies and procedures which the support worker must know and follow.

Challenges

Balancing Multiple Demands

Because the support worker has to meet the needs of several clients each day, the worker has to be able to prioritize needs with clients, to solve problems, and to be flexible. For example, a support worker may make breakfast for one client. While the client eats, the worker may assist another client to dress. Once the second client is dressed, the worker may return to the first client to assist with a bath. If two clients have needs which they want met at the same time, the worker must work out a suitable arrangement with them.

Retirement Homes

Some support workers work in retirement homes. Retirement homes provide housekeeping, laundry, and meals to clients (often called residents) who live in the facility. Residents usually have their own bedroom, but they share the living and dining facilities with other residents (Photo 2-5). In some provinces, retirement homes are regulated.

It is important to remember that retirement homes are not long-term care facilities. The residents living in retirement homes are generally able to perform most routine activities of living on their own.

Photo 2-5
Residents of retirement homes usually have their own rooms, yet share common living areas, such as the sitting room in this photo.

Terms of Employment

Support workers are most often employed by the retirement home itself. However, some retirement home residents employ support workers to provide assistance. As we mentioned earlier in the chapter, this is often called *private-duty work*.

When employed by the retirement home, support workers may report to a director of client service, a guest services coordinator, or to the administrator of the home. When employed by a resident, the support worker would report directly to the resident.

Working as Part of a Team

Support workers in retirement homes work as a part of the team which may include a supervisor, an activity director, other support workers, as well as dietary, housekeeping, and laundry staff. Nurses or therapists may also form part of the team if a resident receives their services.

Following Agency Policies and Procedures

Retirement homes have policies and procedures that the support worker must know and follow. Some of these policies and procedures may be in place to meet provincial regulations. As in all other settings, it is important for you to know and follow the policies and procedures that apply to your work.

Challenges

Balancing Multiple Demands

Support workers in retirement homes are often responsible for assisting a number of residents. As in assisted living and day programs, here the support worker must be able to set priorities, solve problems, and be flexible in order to meet each resident's needs.

Group Homes

Group homes are small facilities, often located in residential neighbourhoods (Photo 2-6). In most cases, no more than eight people live in the home. Residents of a group home usually have their own bedrooms, but share living, dining, and other facilities. They often require supervision as well as assistance with routine activities of living. Staff members provide service twenty-four hours a day.

People of any age may live in a group home. However, most residents of group homes are younger adults or children who have physical or developmental disabilities or both.

Photo 2-6 *Group homes are designed to blend in with the neighbourhood. It's often impossible to tell a group home from any other home in the area.*

Terms of Employment

Support workers employed in group homes are usually employed by the organization operating the home. Terms of employment are very much like those for supportive housing. Support workers usually report to a supervisor or coordinator. The supervisor or coordinator may have an office in the group home, or may make regular visits to the home.

Challenges

The challenges of working in a group home are very much like those identified for assisted living – namely, the challenge of balancing multiple demands and the challenge of working as a team member.

CASE EXAMPLE 2-3

Cassie works in a group home for adults with cerebral palsy. Six people live in the bungalow located in a new housing development. The home looks like any other on the street. Two of the residents work part-time, one goes to community college, and three residents attend day programs.

Cassie works the 11 p.m. to 7 a.m. shift. She is usually the only person on duty. Her tasks include assisting two residents to bed just after 11 p.m. She is also responsible for assisting a resident to get up at 6 a.m. to get ready for school. Overnight, she assists residents as they require it. She may assist someone to use the commode, change an incontinent brief, or reposition a resident who cannot do so herself.

In slow periods, she does laundry and some cleaning, and makes up grocery lists for the day staff. Sometimes, the evening worker has told her about other tasks scheduled for the night. If so, Cassie fits them into her schedule.

Cassie has gotten to know the residents and looks forward to spending some time talking with those who happen to be up late when she's working. On some Friday nights, she is responsible for ordering the pizza that residents usually get at midnight.

Cassie spends a few minutes at the end of her shift filling in the day staff about any significant events that occurred overnight.

Long-Term Care Facilities

As we discussed in Chapter 1, residents of long-term care facilities receive assistance with routine activities of living as well as nursing care. Long-term care facilities are regulated by the province in which they are located. Provincial regulations vary, as do the names by which these facilities are known. Some of the more common names are *nursing homes, special care homes, board and care homes,* or *homes for the aged.*

Terms of Employment

Support workers in long-term care facilities may be called *personal care aides* or *health care aides.* They are normally hired by the facility.

Support workers in long-term care facilities are usually members of the Nursing Department and report to a charge nurse. The charge nurse, in turn, reports to a Director of Care or Director of Nursing. Some support workers work in Activity Departments and report to the Activity Director.

Most long-term care facilities require support workers to be available to work shifts. As a support worker, you may be required to be available to work day, evening, and night shifts.

Long-term care facilities usually require support workers to have provincially recognized training. In addition, they may require or provide additional training to help support workers meet specific resident needs. Most facilities provide orientation and inservice training to their staff.

Working as Part of a Team

Support workers in long-term care facilities work as a part of the team which includes their supervisor, the facility's pharmacist, the resident's doctor, nurses, the activity director, activity aides, dietary aides, housekeeping aides, and laundry aides, as well as clergy, families, and volunteers (Photo 2-7). Therapists may form part of the team, if the resident receives therapy. Teams in long-term care facilities are often called **multi-disciplinary teams**, as they bring together staff members from various disciplines to assist in the care of the resident.

Photo 2-7
The team is key to good support.

Source: Leisureworld Preferred Institute/ Leisureworld, Inc.

The high level of support that long-term care facility residents require means that the team must work very closely to provide good service. The team must share information and tasks and must problem-solve together daily.

Challenges

Needs of Residents

More and more, residents in long-term care facilities have complex care needs. Many residents may have dementia. Most residents move to long-term care facilities when they can no longer remain at home. Many residents must cope with the effects of their condition and the losses that they experienced when they had to leave their homes.

Making a Homelike Setting

A long-term care facility is a place where people live. However, most of us would not say that it's like our homes. Making the facility as much like home as possible is one of the most important challenges that support workers are expected to meet.

Balancing Multiple Demands

Support workers in long-term care facilities are responsible for assisting a number of residents with many tasks. The level of resident need means that demands are greater than in other facilities. The worker must work as efficiently as possible, yet be caring, kind, and gentle. Support workers must be able to set priorities, solve problems, and be flexible in order to meet each resident's needs.

CASE EXAMPLE 2-4

Karen Morris works in a long-term care facility in which 110 residents live. She works the day shift. Karen shares with another support worker the responsibility of caring for 22 residents in a unit of the home. She and her coworker help the residents get up, washed, and dressed and helps them get to breakfast each morning.

When she arrives, Karen attends the unit's morning report. She learns of any new residents and any changes in each resident's condition. She also goes over the shift duty roster to confirm her schedule. If she has any questions, she discusses them with the charge nurse. She then gets on with the duties of the day.

Many of Karen's residents have some type of dementia. Some do not always remember where they are and become very frightened when first awakened. Although she is very busy, Karen has to make sure that she approaches each person calmly and gently so that she does not make them more frightened.

In order to make the best use of her time, Karen has learned who can get themselves dressed and who needs help. She also knows who just needs a bit of time to adjust to the new day before getting out of bed. She plans her morning rounds to spend the time with the residents who need her most. She also works with her coworker to assist residents who need the help of more than one person.

Other Centres

Other centres have begun to hire support workers. They include:

- Chronic Care Centres
- Rehabilitation Centres
- Acute Care Centres
- Mental Health Facilities

People using these centres are often called *patients*. Patients do not usually stay in acute care centres or *rehabilitation centres* for a long period of time. **Mental health facilities** provide both long- and short-term services to patients with mental health concerns. However, patients in chronic care centres may live there for many months or years, much like residents of long-term care facilities. **Rehabilitation Centres** are facilities that provide services to help patients recover from surgery, illness, or injury. Patients in these centres have conditions which may change, or they may require professional services on a regular basis.

Some hospitals offer all three types of service in separate wings. A hospital may have a rehabilitation unit, a chronic care unit, a mental health unit, and an acute care as well as an emergency unit.

Some chronic care centres, rehabilitation centres, mental health facilities, and acute care centres have employed support workers for many years. Others have only recently hired support workers. Some of these centres do not hire support workers at all.

Terms of Employment

Support workers in chronic care centres, rehabilitation centres, and acute care centres may be called *health care aides* or *patient care attendants*. They are usually hired by the centre. The organization in which they work is often much like that of a long-term care facility, although it is usually larger and has more specialized services. For example, a hospital may employ support workers to assist patients in its medical unit, or new mothers on the maternity ward. Patients have medical or rehabilitation needs as well as needs for assistance with routine activities.

The role that the support worker fulfills may be much different than it would be in the long-term care facility. In chronic care centres, rehabilitation centres, and acute care centres support workers assist patients with routine activities of living while the patient is receiving other types of care. Support workers must be careful not to exceed the bounds of their training or legislation when assisting patients in these centres.

Most support workers are members of the Nursing Department and report to a Charge Nurse. The Charge Nurse reports to a Unit Director, the Director of Care, or Director of Nursing. In some centres, support workers may be hired to work in rehabilitation or other departments. In these situations, the worker reports to the department supervisor.

These centres usually require support workers to have provincially recognized training. Because not all provincial training programs include a great deal of training in this area, many centres require or provide additional training to help support workers meet the centre's needs. In addition, most centres provide orientation and inservice training to their staff.

Working as Part of a Team

Support workers work as a part of a team that includes physicians, pharmacist, other nursing staff, rehabilitation staff, dietary staff, housekeeping staff, as well as clergy, families, and volunteers. Because most patients' conditions are changing, this team has to work very closely to make sure that appropriate care is given and that the appropriate person provides the needed care. The team must share information and tasks and problem-solve together daily.

Challenges

Patient Need

Patients have complex care needs which may change rapidly. Usually, the patient is coping with an illness or condition which has changed their life, if only for a little while. Furthermore, the patient is in unfamiliar surroundings. All these things can make it difficult for the patient to cope. The patient may become frustrated or irritated at things. You must be able to appreciate the patient's perspective. You must be able to put yourself in the patient's shoes, so to speak, and provide care as you would like it to be provided to you.

Balancing Multiple Demands

Support workers in centres are responsible for assisting many patients with many tasks. Patients' conditions may change rapidly. Their need for support may change from day to day. Emergencies may disrupt the normal workflow of the unit or cause other members of the team to be called away. Support workers must be able to set priorities, solve problems, and be flexible in order to meet each patient's needs.

Respecting the Scope of Your Role

Many patients will have needs that the support worker is not trained or permitted to meet. Sometimes, the worker is very familiar with what needs to be done. However, the worker should never exceed the bounds of his or her role, no matter how seemingly simple or familiar the task. Support workers must report to their supervisor as soon as possible about any needs for care that lie beyond the scope of their training or their role.

Which Setting Is Best for You?

No one setting is the *best* setting. Each has its benefits and challenges. The one that's right for you depends upon what you want to do. Many factors should be considered when you seek employment (Figure 2-1).

- Does the type of work interest me? Am I excited by the job?
- Can I perform the tasks required? Do I have all the training I'll need?
- Do I like working with people in that kind of work setting?

Figure 2-1 *Many Factors Determine Which Setting Is Best for You*

- Can I get to the work site? Can I travel from client to client if the job requires it? Do I *like* the amount of travel required?
- Am I comfortable with the agency or client who is hiring me? Will I be proud to work for them?
- Are the wages and benefits (if any) competitive?
- Is there an opportunity to learn additional skills and take on different responsibilities if I would like to?

Employers may differ in the type of working arrangements, wages, policies, and procedures. One employer may offer things another does not. It is up to you to find out what each employer offers in order to determine which setting and which employer is best for you.

Questions for Review

1. What are the five requirements set out by the *Canada Health Act* to ensure that everyone has access to necessary health care?

2. List the nine major types of settings in which support workers may work.

3. What are two of the challenges in working directly for a client?

4. In which settings might you need additional training?

5. In which settings do you work as part of a team?

6. How might working in an acute care centre be different than working in a long-term care facility?

7. What must you have in order to work in *most* settings?
   a) A reliable car
   b) The ability to be flexible and to problem-solve
   c) A uniform
   d) Thorough knowledge of the agency's history

Questions for Discussion

1. In which setting do you prefer to work? Why? Compare your preferences with your colleagues or classmates.

2. What agencies in your community offer the types of support discussed in this chapter? With three other classmates or colleagues, draw up a list of the agencies. Compare your answers to those of other groups.

3. You have recently been offered employment by a community agency offering respite care and outreach services to a rural community near where you live. What factors should you consider in deciding whether or not to take position offered by the agency? What characteristics would be positive factors for you? What characteristics would be difficult for you to accept?

CHAPTER THREE

Ethics and Personal Support

Learning Objectives

Through reading this chapter, you'll be able to:

1. Define the term ethics.
2. Describe the personal ethics you use in everyday life.
3. List and discuss six important principles of the ethics that apply to providing personal support.

Chapter At A Glance

What Are Ethics?

The Ethics of Personal Support

Terms You'll Use

Autonomy   Each person's right to have his or her decisions respected.

Beneficence   The obligation to prevent or remove what is bad and to promote what is good.

Confidentiality   The obligation to keep the client's personal information private.

Ethics   The principles that guide how people behave.

Nonmaleficence   The obligation to do no harm to another person.

What Are Ethics?

Stop and Reflect 3-1

Imagine that you are going to a friend's house. On the sidewalk, just steps away from her home, you find a $20 bill. You put it in your pocket.

When you get to your friend's house, her neighbour is there. This neighbour has not been nice to you in the past. Today, she is upset and barely notices that you have arrived. Your friend tells you that this neighbour has lost $20—money she needed to help pay her telephone bill.

What do you do?

_____

_____

_____

Why?

_____

_____

_____

Did you find yourself thinking of the 'right' thing to do? If so, you've relied upon your **ethics** — the principles that guide behaviour. We all have them, although we may not all have exactly the same ones. Sometimes, ethics are called *morals* or *precepts*.

Personal Ethics

> *What you do not want done to yourself, do not do unto others.*
>
> — Confucius

Each of us has personal ethics—the principles that guide how we behave in everyday life. The principle expressed by Confucius is one of the most common—treat others as you'd like to be treated. There are many others.

We can become so used to these principles that we use them without thinking. Sometimes, when we feel bad about something we did, we realize that we have gone against a principle in which we believe.

SR *Stop and Reflect 3-2*

What principles do you try to live by?

_____

_____

Are you always aware of these principles?

_____

_____

Have you ever done something that went against your principles? Did you know it at the time? How? What did you do about it?

_____

_____

_____

Compare your answers with those of your colleagues. In what ways are your answers similar? Different? Did you find that you and a colleague called a principle by different names, but you both meant the same thing?

Common Personal Ethics

Many of us might say that we live by the Golden Rule–to treat others as we'd like to be treated. What, though, does that mean? The following principles might be included:

Honesty   To not lie or mislead.

Integrity   To mean what we say, say what we mean, and do what we say we will do.

Caring   To have concern for other people, their feelings, and their needs.

Fairness   To do what we feel is right and just in a situation.

Consistency   To apply the same standard to all; to not have a double standard, nor to change how we apply a standard.

Acceptance   To respect each person as an individual, despite differences in appearance, background, situation, or behaviour.

While they might appear clear, the way in which we use each of these principles is sometimes a bit complicated. For instance, imagine that your best friend has just had her hair cut (Figure 3-1). Your friend asks you how you like it. From how your friend looks at you, you know that she wants you to approve. You think that the style is all wrong for her. What do you say? Complete honesty may hurt your friend. Yet, you may not want to lie just to make her feel good. How do you balance these principles?

Figure 3-1   *Balancing the principles of personal ethics. How would you answer her?*

The Ethics of Personal Support

Health care and human service workers have codes of ethics which relate to the performance of their duties. These ethics are in many ways similar to the ones we have for ourselves. Most are extensions of those personal ethics, applied to common work situations. Most codes of ethics reflect the personal ethics described above. The ethics of personal support include the following six important principles:

1. Confidentiality

Confidentiality is one of the most fundamental concepts of personal support ethics. **Confidentiality** refers to your obligation to keep the client's personal information private.

Support workers often spend a great deal of time with clients. They get to know the client and, often, the client's family and friends. As a result, the support worker usually learns a great deal of personal information that the client wouldn't share with most other people.

As a support worker, you have an obligation not to share this information with others. There is one exception to this rule: you must share information that is essential to the client's health or well-being with your supervisor.

 Stop and Reflect 3-3

You are a support worker assigned to Mrs. Cabriole. Mrs. Cabriole does not speak a great deal of English. You have been assigned extra hours as her family is on vacation for the next four weeks and cannot visit her as they normally would.

While you are tidying her kitchen, you accidentally drop her mail on the floor. As you pick it up, you notice a disconnection notice for Mrs. Cabriole's telephone. It says that if the bill is not paid this week, the service will be disconnected. You know that Mrs. Cabriole needs to have her phone in case of an emergency. You also know that her family pays her bills.

What do you do?

_____

_____

_____

_____

In this case, you should contact your supervisor to advise her or him of the situation. It would *not* be appropriate to share this information with a coworker or anyone else.

At times, you may share the care of a client with another support worker. Then, you may have a legitimate need to discuss client care with the coworker, particularly if the client has complex needs. Even so, you must not do so in a way that allows the information to be overheard by unauthorized persons. It is never appropriate to discuss client concerns in public areas such as in a lunch room or in a store.

It is best to use your agency's staff conference room or other private room to meet. If you work in the community, ask your supervisor to arrange for a meeting with you and your coworker so that the information may be shared in private.

Confidentiality also applies to any written information you may have about the client, such as a referral form, a duty roster, or any other item which includes personal information about the client or their needs. You must be extremely careful not to allow unauthorized people to see this information. In most cases, your agency will have guidelines about what written information you may have and how it must be kept. Be sure to follow those guidelines.

Maintaining confidentiality is more difficult when you have known the client before he or she became a client—perhaps because the client is a relative of a friend or was a neighbour of yours. In these situations, you must be particularly cautious of what you say to others, so as not to share information you have gained through your work. Responding to the simplest questions can be difficult. Consider what you would say in this situation.

Stop and Reflect 3-4

You have just finished your shift at the long-term care facility and are at the post office. One of your neighbours sees you and inquires about a resident who used to live across the street from you both. She asks whether the resident is happy living in the home and if she and her roommate are now getting along.

What do you say?

_____

_____

_____

There are two issues here. First, you are in a public place where you could be overheard. Second, some of the information your neighbour is asking for is information you have gained through your professional relationship with the client. In order to avoid a breach of confidentiality, you might ask your neighbour to wait until you are both outside and away from others, and then you might suggest that your neighbour visit the resident.

2. Respect for a Person's Right to Make Decisions and Take Risks

Respecting a person's right to make decisions and take risks is also called respecting the person's **autonomy**. We all have the right to make decisions that affect our lives. Most of us, at one time or another, have made a decision with which our close friends or family did not agree. Sometimes, we ourselves have disagreed with a decision a friend or family member has made. When these differences of opinion happen, the person making the decision can feel as though they do not have the right to make the decision after all. The person can become angry. Consider the following situation.

 Stop and Reflect 3-5

After thinking about it for a while, you have made the decision to return to school to become a personal support worker. Your closest friend thinks that this is not a good idea. She says that you have too much to do already and that your family will be neglected. She also tells you that you are doing fine as you are now, so you shouldn't change anything. She points out that you will not earn any more money and may have to work night shifts.

How do you feel about your friend's comments?

_____

_____   ▶▶

What would you say to her?

_____

_____

_____

Would you rethink your decision?

_____

_____

_____

Like you, clients have the right to make decisions about things that affect their lives. It is your responsibility not to attempt to influence your client's decisions simply because you don't think that the client's choice is a good one.

In some situations, it's pretty easy to apply this principle. For example, your client may prefer a particular brand of canned corn. It may happen to be one you don't feel is as good as another. However, it's likely that you'll respect the client's right to select the brand that he or she prefers. You would likely not even say anything to the client about it.

It becomes more difficult when the client's choice seems to be risky. For example, how would you feel if your client asked you to purchase something you know he or she is not allowed to eat? Would you react differently than you might to the choice of canned corn?

Respecting a person's right to make decisions becomes much more difficult when the client has a condition (such as a dementia) which affects his or her ability to make decisions. In these cases, you will have to work closely with the support team to identify what decisions the client can safely make and what decisions the client cannot.

3. The Obligation to Do No Harm

The obligation to do no harm is called **nonmaleficence**. As a support worker, you must not do things which would cause your client harm. This seems pretty clear and, in most cases, it is. However, this principle also includes not doing harm unintentionally if you should have known that the activity would cause harm. For example, running a client's bath without checking the temperature of the water could cause harm if the water was too hot. As a support worker, you should know to check the water temperature before the client gets into the tub.

The obligation to do no harm requires that you know the correct procedure for doing the tasks you are assigned to do. You must also be aware of how to safely use different types of household equipment, in order to avoid damaging the client's property.

4. The Obligation to Prevent or Remove What Is Bad and to Promote What Is Good

The obligation to prevent or remove what is bad and to promote what is good is called **beneficence**. As a support worker, you are obliged to do your best to promote the client's well-being. However, you must balance this principle with the need to respect the client's right to make decisions and take risks. Sometimes, clients make decisions which are based on priorities that others around them do not share. The client weighs the risk with the benefit and makes a decision.

Sometimes a decision or situation may seem to you to be too risky. Before you say anything, you must always ask yourself if excessive harm will be caused by not acting, or whether you will simply be uncomfortable with the situation. You may want to talk over the situation with your supervisor. Consider the following situation.

Stop and Reflect 3-6

Your client lives alone in a two-story house. He has had several falls, all related to a balance problem. The last time, he could not get up and lay on the floor for 14 hours before someone found him. He wants very much to stay in his own home, yet he will not allow more help. He also won't let his family rearrange his furnishings so that all he needs would be on the ground floor. Today, you arrived to find him at the foot of the stairs, bruised and unable to get up. He was taken to hospital, checked over, and released.

How do you feel about the risks your client is taking?

_____

_____

Would you feel better if he moved or rearranged the furnishings in his home?

_____

What, if anything, would you say to him about this situation?

_____

_____

_____

Compare your answers with those of your colleagues.

Did you find that you wanted the client to be safe? Perhaps you wanted to protect him from the harm that might come from living the way he does. Yet, you must balance your feelings with respect for his right to make choices and take risks. As with other ethical problems, you might want to discuss your thoughts and feelings with your supervisor.

5. The Obligation Not to Take Advantage of a Person

We take advantage of a person when we use our power over them to make the person do something we want. Your client may see you as being more powerful, simply because you are coming to help. Like the obligation to do no harm, the obligation not to take advantage of a person seems pretty clear. Most of us would not *intentionally* use our position to make someone do something. Sometimes, though, we may use this power unintentionally. Consider the following situation.

Stop and Reflect 3-7

You have been assigned to a new client, Mrs. Green. She is quite capable, alert, and oriented. A recently fractured hip has meant that she needs some help with her homemaking and getting around.

As you're helping Mrs. Green dry off after her bath, she asks you to get her body lotion. As you hand her the Avon lotion, she remarks that the bottle is almost empty and that she has to remember to order more. "Some neighbour sells it," she tells you, "I don't really know her, but she lives a few houses down." She also says she buys some stocking stuffers (cologne and other things) from the catalogue because it's "easier than going to the store."

You sell Avon. While you don't make a lot of money at it, it helps pay for the incidentals.
Do you tell Mrs. Green you sell Avon?

_____

Why or why not?

_____

_____

_____

Would you take an order for Avon from her?

_____

Compare your answers with those of your colleagues.

Would you be taking advantage of Mrs. Green by telling her you sell Avon? By taking an order from her? Deciding whether or not you should tell her probably wasn't as easy as you thought.

Sometimes you can figure out if something is not a good idea by looking at it from the client's point of view. For example, would Mrs. Green possibly feel obligated to buy Avon from you? Would she feel that your relationship with her would be different if she chose *not* to buy Avon from you? If the answer to these questions is yes, you should not tell her you sell the products. In such situations, you should also make sure that you are familiar with your agency's policy on selling items to clients.

Accepting tips and gifts may make the client feel obligated to give them in the future. This may also be seen as taking advantage. Again, you must obey your agency's policy on accepting gifts and tips. Even if they are permitted, you must be particularly careful not to take advantage of a client.

You don't have to be selling something or accepting something to take advantage of a client. It can happen whenever your client feels obligated to do something you suggest.

For example, suppose you visit a particular client each Thursday. This Thursday, your sister is coming to visit for two days on her way to Mexico. You haven't seen her in two years and want to spend the day with her. However, you don't want to lose the work. You tell your client about your sister's visit. You also say how much it would mean for you to be able to spend the day with your sister, but that you can't afford to lose the work. You let the client know that you hope the client will agree to have you come on Wednesday this week, even though you know that Wednesday is not a good day for the client. In this instance, the client may feel obligated to change the day.

6. The Obligation to Use Best Efforts

Support workers must always use their best efforts to assist the client. This principle means many things: doing your best at all times, using your skills to the best of your ability, and learning any skills you need to learn (within the bounds of your role) to assist your client.

Keeping your skills and knowledge up to date is one important way of meeting this obligation. Taking a personal support training program will prepare you to work in the field. You will also find that you will want to take additional training to enhance your skills and knowledge. Make sure to take part in the inservice training your agency provides. Find out what training is offered by other organizations. For example, you may learn a great deal about assisting a person who is dying by taking a course offered by your local palliative care or hospice service.

Once skills are learned, you must then keep them up to date. Wherever possible, you must use the skills you've learned. If you cannot, you must make sure that you can perform the skills properly. You can do this by taking a refresher course or workshop, or by having your supervisor review your skills and observe you performing them.

Your supervisor can be of great help in identifying and meeting your learning needs. In addition, skilled and experienced coworkers as well as other team members can also be tremendous resources.

Questions for Review

1. What do we mean by the term ethics?

2. Name four personal ethics. For each, give one example of how it would apply to everyday life.

3. Name and describe six important ethical principles which apply to support work.

4. How could the obligation to do no harm be applied to assisting a client to bathe and dress?

5. Why should you keep your skills and knowledge up to date?

Questions for Discussion

1. Discuss what you would do in the following situation:

   Suppose that you are visiting Mrs. Smith, a client who has had severe diabetes for many years. You have been cautioned not to add sugar to anything you cook for her.

   Today, when you're going shopping, you notice that chocolate bars are on the shopping list. When you ask Mrs. Green what kind, she looks embarrassed and says, "Any kind will do. They're for my grandchildren, you see."

   You get a sense that this is not the case. For one thing, Mrs. Green's grandchildren live out of town and are not coming to visit for at least three weeks.

   What would you do in this situation? What principles would guide you?

2. Speak with an experienced support worker who has faced an ethical problem. How did the support worker solve it?

You, the Support Worker

Code of Conduct   A statement that is intended to guide support worker practice. It is often made up of ethical principles, support worker qualities, and skills. It is sometimes called a *code of ethics*.

Distress   Stress that prevents us from functioning in the way we would like.

Stress   A psychological and physiological condition that arises when we respond to stimulation or adjust to changes and demands.

Stressor   A particular source of stress.

The Value of Support Work

Stop and Reflect 4-1

Imagine that you have been asked to speak to a community group about what you do. The group would like you to focus on the benefits that support work provides to clients.

What would you say?

_____

In what way do you think clients benefit from support services?

_____

_____

_____

In what way do you benefit from providing support?

_____

_____

_____

Support work is more than housekeeping and physical care. It involves a relationship between you and the client. That relationship provides support and comfort to the client. It usually benefits both the client and the worker.

The value you place on providing support will directly affect the benefit you get from providing it. If you do not see the role as rewarding, you will not put much effort into performing your duties and will probably not get much benefit from them.

How you provide support is also affected by other beliefs you may have. For example, if you feel very strongly that families should care for a person who needs support, you may find it difficult to work for a client whose family cannot or chooses not to provide that support. Similarly, if you feel very strongly that a person is responsible for what happens to her or him, you might find it difficult to provide support to a person who feels that her or his situation is beyond their own control.

This does not mean that holding such beliefs is a reason not to become a support worker. It is important to know what beliefs you hold so that you can guard against letting them affect your work. You may find that your beliefs change over time as you work.

Personal Qualities and Attitudes

Many personal qualities and attitudes are essential in providing effective personal support. If you are working in the field, you likely are familiar with some of these. We'll identify thirteen qualities here.

1. Interest in People

It is very difficult to work in such a people-oriented career unless you have a genuine interest in people. All of your working time will be spent in direct contact with others, including your client, coworkers, other members of the team, the client's family and friends, and your supervisor (Photo 4-1). Your day will be very long indeed if you do not have an interest in people.

Photo 4-1
Support work requires you to work with many people. Here members of the team gather to discuss a client concern.

Source: Leisureworld Preferred Institute/ Leisureworld, Inc.

Photo 4-2 *Is the glass half full or half empty?*

2. Positive Outlook

Look at Photo 4-2. Is the glass half empty or half full? Having a positive outlook will help you see the best in situations. You will have hope and you will be better able to provide encouragement.

3. Sensitivity

The nature of many support tasks and the closeness of your relationship with clients requires you to be sensitive to your client and your client's needs. This includes becoming sensitive to each client's nonverbal communication and preferred ways of doing things.

4. Sense of Personal Responsibility

Many people will rely upon you to do your job and to do it well. You must take responsibility for your own actions. You must also honour your commitments. Unless there is an emergency that prevents you from fulfilling your duties, you must complete any assignment you accept, arrive at work on time, and do the tasks assigned to the best of your ability.

If you have made a commitment to an employer or agency, you must make sure that you are able and available to fulfill it. If you tell your employer that you are available for certain shifts, you must accept them when asked. When you accept a shift, you must work the entire shift.

Personal responsibility also means making sure that you are mentally and physically prepared to complete any assignment you have accepted.

Personal responsibility also includes handling mistakes properly. You should admit any mistake you make. You should also take action to correct the mistake and use your best efforts not to repeat it.

5. Maturity

The ability to see the other person's perspective, make thoughtful decisions, and take responsibility are part of maturity. Mature people constantly grow and develop. They know that no one is perfect. They have the ability to accept constructive criticism, listen to the wisdom of others, and learn from their mistakes.

6. Patience

You may have heard the phrase "Patience is a virtue." In support work, patience is essential. Patience is the ability to slow your pace, repeat instructions, and respond to repetitive questions without frustration. Many people with disabilities and many older adults take longer to do things. So do people adjusting to a new condition who must adapt old techniques or learn new ways of doing things. Support workers must constantly demonstrate patience.

7. Skill

To be skilled means to be competent, current, and comfortable. These are called the *Three C's*. You must know the right technique (be competent). You must practise the technique so as to keep your skills up to date (be current). You must feel confident performing the technique (be comfortable). Only if you meet the Three C's will you perform your tasks safely, efficiently, and properly.

8. Accuracy

Have you ever tried to make a recipe without measuring the ingredients? Chances are that your recipe didn't turn out properly. Your work must be accurate and complete. You must complete all tasks assigned to you if possible. If you cannot complete all the tasks assigned, you must advise your supervisor of those tasks which remain and the reason you could not complete them.

9. Attention To Detail

It's the little things that mean a lot. Paying attention to details is essential, whether that means completing all the elements of a task or paying close attention to how you do the task. The extra step it may take to put a client's water glass just where they like it, fold the towels the way the client likes them, or make sure that the dishes are fully dry before you put them into the cupboard will please your client and make you feel good about what you do.

10. Personal Cleanliness and Appearance

As a support worker, you will be in close physical contact with clients. Personal cleanliness is a must (Photo 4-3). You should shower or bathe daily and use an effective *unscented* deodorant or anti-perspirant. You should not wear strong colognes or fragrances at any time. Bear in mind that, because of their condition, some clients may not be able to tolerate any scents at all. Keep your fingernails short and smooth.

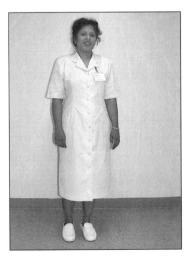

Photo 4-3
A well-groomed and well-dressed support worker conveys a professional appearance.

Source: Leisureworld Preferred Institute/ Leisureworld, Inc.

Employer dress codes vary. Over the past few years, many agencies have relaxed their dress codes. Some employers may allow you to select a uniform from several options. Other employers may no longer require uniforms at all.

What you wear may also vary because of the setting in which you will be working. You would probably not wear a uniform if you were assisting a client who is attending a business meeting. You may dress professionally but casually if your duties require you to assist residents on an outing.

Whether or not your employer has a dress code, you must dress appropriately for the work you are to do and the setting in which you are to do it. Your clothing should always be clean, neat, and in good repair. Do not wear stained clothing, even if it is freshly washed.

Keep your jewellery to a minimum. Rings with sharp edges or raised stones can catch and tear the client's skin or clothing. Do not wear them. Refrain from wearing long, dangling necklaces or bracelets as they can catch, scrape, or tear. Hoop earrings can easily be caught on many things and may tear your ear lobe. Wear small studs or post-style earrings if you must wear any at all.

11. Flexibility

You will work with many different clients with different personalities and ways of doing things. Flexibility is essential. You must be able to adapt your style to how the client does things or would like them done. This is harder than it sounds. We all have preferred ways of doing things. We often resist changing our ways because we are comfortable, not because an alternative is wrong or unsafe.

CASE EXAMPLE 4-1

Susan works for Mrs. Kyle. Each week, Susan does the laundry. She notices that Mrs. Kyle does not seem to be really pleased with how she does this task. Susan asks Mrs. Kyle if there is something she should do differently. After a bit of hesitation, Mrs. Kyle explains that she would like her towels folded in a different way and that she would prefer her blouses to be hung on hangers to dry. She shows Susan how to fold the towels and tells her where the plastic hangers can be found. Mrs. Kyle is happy that her laundry is done the way she prefers. Susan feels appreciated and pleased that she has met her client's needs.

Sometimes illness, pain, or stress will affect a client's interest or participation in the tasks planned for a particular visit. You will have to be flexible. For example, a client who usually helps you perform certain tasks may not feel like doing so if they have a cold. A client who is having a particularly good day may want to do tasks they don't usually do. You must be able to reorganize your visit to adapt to these changes.

12. Creativity

Creativity is the ability to look at things in different ways. Support workers must be creative. They help clients decide priorities for support. They adapt their approach to their clients, and figure out how best to help each client do what the client needs to do.

13. Organizational Skills

Support workers must be extremely well organized. You often will have a great number of tasks to do for a client within a short period of time. You must be able to plan your tasks so as to accomplish priorities and get as much done as possible in the time available. If you work for more than one employer, you must also carefully organize your schedule to avoid conflicts and to make sure that you don't miss appointments.

Codes of Conduct

Many agencies combine ethical principles, support worker qualities, and skills into a *Code of Conduct* or a *Code of Ethics*. A **Code of Conduct** is intended to guide support worker practice in the agency. An example is given in Exhibit 4-1.

Interface Personnel
Code of Ethical Practice

It is the responsibility of all staff members to practise in a manner based on respect for the client, his or her caregivers, and other involved in providing care.

All staff members are expected to

1. Work in a manner which supports client well-being.
2. Respect and support client choice.
3. Respect client privacy and the right to confidentiality of their information.
4. Respect the client's views on the sanctity of life, within the bounds of legislation, and professional standards of practice.
5. Respect the role of the substitute decision maker (if any) with regard to client support and care.
6. Maintain commitments to clients:
   a. Assume responsibility for their own actions, admit mistakes, take corrective action, and take steps to prevent repetition of a mistake.
   b. Be reliable and consistent, arrive at work on time, at the right location and complete the full assignment.
   c. Dress appropriately for the assignment.
   d. Remain available to the client at all times during the assignment.
   e. Give reasonable notice if changes need to be made in the work schedule.
   f. Comply with the policies (if any) of the setting in which they are working.
   g. Treat the client with respect at all times.
   h. Treat the belongings of the client with respect and care.
   i. Refrain from requesting tips, loans, or other gifts. Seek guidance from supervisor before accepting tips or gifts.
   j. Ensure that personal activities and needs do not interfere with judgment and performance of the job.
   k. Refrain from involving the client in their personal problems.
   l. Refrain from acting as a witness to the signing of any legal document.
7. Maintain commitment to their designated profession:
   a. To practise in accordance with the standards established by their training.
   b. Maintain commitment to Interface Personnel.
   c. To accept the job requested by Interface Personnel and to advise Interface Personnel if unable for any reason to complete the assignment.
8. To raise issues with regard to employment and client service and to actively participate in the resolving of those issues.
   a. Actively take part in furthering the quality of Interface Personnel's client service.
   b. Ensure that personal activities and needs do not interfere with judgment and performance of the job.
9. Maintain commitment to personal professional development:
   a. Identify areas for professional development and to actively seek opportunities to meet those needs.
   b. Practise in an honest, equitable and fair manner.

I have reviewed this Code and commit to practise in accordance with its tenets.

Date _____   Signature _____

Exhibit 4-1 *A Sample Code of Conduct*

Source: Interface Personnel.

How many of the personal qualities described in this chapter did you find in this code? Can you see where the ethics we discussed in Chapter 3 are included?

Note that this code is signed by the support worker. When you are first hired, many agencies require you to read and agree to work in accordance with their code.

Balancing Your Commitments

In the previous section, we discussed the need for organization. As a support worker, you will have many different demands placed on your time. You will have to identify priorities, organize your time, and manage the positive and negative stress that you will experience.

Stop and Reflect 4-2

What are your current commitments?

To your family:

_____

_____

To your job:

_____

_____

To yourself:

_____

_____

You likely found that you have a number of commitments. You may have family obligations such as making sure that you are there when your children or spouse need you, doing household chores, getting your children to school, and making sure that lunches are made.

If you are currently working, you will have a number of work commitments such as arriving at work on time and doing your job properly. We often say that a full-time job is a 40-hour week. In reality, you probably spend closer to 55 hours per week, if we count getting ready for, going to, and coming from a full-time job.

You should also be sure you fulfill your commitments to yourself. Training for a new career, getting enough rest, or taking time to relax for a bit are common examples. You need to do these things in order to feel good about yourself and to have the energy to meet your other commitments. In Chapter 10, we will discuss time management in detail.

Stress

When we hear the word *stress*, we often think of negative things. This is a misconception: everything we do causes stress. **Stress** is a psychological and physical condition that arises when we respond to stimulation or when we adjust to changes and demands.

Stress can be both good and bad. In fact, we all need some stress to live. However, each of us functions best at a different level of stress. You might be able to handle more demands and changes than a friend. In turn, another friend may be able to handle more changes and demands than you can and still do quite well.

All of us experience *distress*. We can define **distress** as stress that prevents us from functioning the way in which we would like. We'll discuss how to cope with distress later in this chapter.

Where Does Stress Come From?

Anything can cause stress. A particular source of stress is known as a **stressor**. In support work, it's helpful to think of stress as coming from four main sources: our expectations of ourselves, the meaning we give to the work that we do, the value we place on caring for or supporting others, and the changing expectations of support work. Let's examine each of these sources.

Our expectations of ourselves.   On one hand, setting realistic goals or expectations can be very motivating. Attaining a realistic goal can give us a sense of accomplishment.

On the other hand, setting unrealistic goals or expectations for ourselves can create distress. These goals may be related to what we feel others expect of us but, in fact, we are the ones setting these expectations.

The meaning we give to the demands we feel are made of us.   It's fine to attach importance to other's needs. You wouldn't be very caring if you didn't. However, you must keep other's demands in perspective.

The value we place on caring for or supporting others.   You always must balance caring for others with caring for yourself. If you do not, you run the risk of expending all of your energy caring for others without taking the time to restore your own resources. In extreme cases, you can become bitter or burned out. Consider the following situation.

CASE EXAMPLE 4-2

Karen is a support worker in assisted living. She works with clients who are on a fixed income. Because three of her clients have physical problems, Karen does grocery shopping for them.

Over time, Karen has gotten to know her clients' favourite foods. Occasionally, she has even picked up a favourite item, using her own money. This has stretched Karen's budget at times.

Her clients are always grateful for these "treats". Although they have never indicated that they expect these things, Karen has begun to feel that she should *make these purchases. She has begun to see it as a way of showing how much she cares.*

Karen realizes that she must rethink the value she puts on caring when she finds herself putting back a treat for her own child so that she can afford to buy a treat for a client. She decides to change her behaviour. Now, she sets aside a small amount of money for client favourites and tries to get one client one small item every other month. Karen feels comfortable with this, as it allows her to do something she enjoys without taking anything away from her family.

Karen was able to see the signs of always putting others' needs ahead of her own and her family's. She was able to stop and change her behaviour before she became angry about feeling expected to do something—even when she created that expectation herself.

Changing expectations of support work.   Like many health and human services, support work is changing. Client needs are becoming more complex, and client expectations are increasing. Support workers, like all other workers, are expected to do more and to do what they do more efficiently. In this type of environment, the support worker must be especially careful to monitor and cope with stress.

When Is Stress Distress?

As we mentioned earlier in this chapter, stress becomes distress when it prevents us from functioning in the way we would like. The same demand or change may not create distress in every person. Much depends upon the following six factors:

1. You.
2. Where the stress is coming from (who or what is causing it).
3. How you see the stress and what meaning you attach to it.
4. How much control you have over the stress.
5. Your coping mechanisms.
6. What other changes and demands you must deal with at the same time.

Consider the following situation.

 Stop and Reflect 4-3

Imagine that you are a support worker in a long-term care facility. You are a new employee and want to do everything perfectly. Tonight, several residents are coming down with the flu and the staff are very busy trying to keep up. Because you are new, you are slower than the other support workers. Just as you are getting towels to wash a resident who vomited, one of the most experienced support workers says to you: "You're going to have to be a lot more organized if you're going to keep working here."

How do you feel? Are you experiencing distress? Look at the stress you are feeling in this situation in light of the six factors listed above. Would your level of stress have changed if:

- You had been more experienced?
- You had worked at that facility before?
- The residents weren't coming down with the flu and needing more care than usual?
- So many things hadn't happened at the same time?

We can change the meaning of stress we experience by looking at the stress in a different way and changing what it means to us.

Responding to Your Own Distress Signals

There are many distress signals. These signals are your body's way of telling you it is having trouble coping with the level of stress you are having. The signs may vary from person to person. Some physical and emotional signs are given in Table 4-1.

TABLE 4-1	Some Common Signs of Distress
Physical Symptoms	**Feeling or Thinking Symptoms**
shallow breathing	panicky
headache	uncertain
backache	agitated
diarrhea	irritable
pounding pulse	sad
red face	unfocussed
breathlessness	forgetful

It's important to be aware of the stresses that cause these symptoms. When you notice them, try to identify the cause.

Burnout

Burnout occurs when stress becomes so great that the person is unable to cope. Burnout can be emotionally, physically, and mentally draining.

Some of the common signs and symptoms of burnout are listed in Table 4-2.

TABLE 4-2	Some Common Signs of Burnout

Feeling irritable
Distrusting others' intentions
Lacking creativity
Lacking physical or emotional energy
Attempting to feel good about yourself by focussing on how much you do
Feeling overly emotional or not emotional at all
Feeling pessimistic
Sweating at night
Grinding your teeth when asleep

Burnout is a serious condition. Some health studies link burnout to illness. If you start to experience some of the signs listed in Table 4-2, you should seek help. You may want to talk with your supervisor, your doctor, or another trusted and knowledgeable person about how to manage the distress you are experiencing.

Managing Stress

Don't sweat the small stuff.

You should learn to manage stress before it becomes distress and leads to burnout. You will find it easier to manage stress if you first separate the stresses you can change from those you cannot. Take a good look at each stressor and ask yourself three questions.

1. Is the stressor really a threat to me? In other words, will I be harmed if I just ignore it?
2. If the stressor is a real threat, is it worth the stress I'm feeling?
3. If the stressor is a threat and is worth the stress I'm feeling, could I change the stressor if I wanted to?

If the answer to any of these questions is no, it's either not important or out of your control. Either way, you will be better off changing the meaning you have given to this stressor. See it differently–reduce its effect upon you. If necessary, accept that you cannot change the stressor.

If you've answered yes to any of the questions, you can change the effect the stressor has on you. You can do this by using the following techniques:

- Change your routine so that the stressor no longer affects you.
- Change how you react to the stressor.
- Strengthen your stress management skills so that you can better respond to the stressor.

Sometimes it's easy to change your routine so that the stressor no longer affects you. For example, if driving to work through heavy city traffic is stressful, you might try taking public transit.

At other times it's not easy, or even possible, to change your routine to eliminate the stressor. Then, you'll need to focus on how you react to the stressor. Have you ever said to yourself "I'm not going to let this get to me"? Were you able to change how you responded? If so, you've changed how you react to a stressor. Changing your response may be all you need to do to reduce the stress to a manageable level. Sometimes changing your response is difficult. You may have to work on a particular response for a while, each time getting closer to how you want to respond.

Finally, you may want to strengthen your stress management skills so as to be better able to handle stress. Many stress management skills also help you to balance your need for work, rest, and recreation. Stress management skills include relaxation techniques, exercise, recreation, and creative hobbies.

Some people attempt to manage stress through things which are harmful such as drinking, taking drugs, and smoking. These activities, which do harm you, provide only temporary relief from your stress. Focus on stress management techniques which give you good value—that do not harm you or take more energy to use than they give back.

Stop and Reflect 4-4

What are the major stressors in your life?

when I got no job

when someone is sick in my family

What do you do to manage them?

do breathing exercise

Traveling, like going to some places you did see during holidays

What stress management techniques give you good value?

Talking to someone

Visiting places

Which stress management techniques do not give you good value?

isolating myself

What new stress management technique do you think you would like to try?

Questions for Review

1. How can your beliefs about the value of support work affect how you provide support? Using your own beliefs, give two examples.

2. Describe thirteen personal qualities and attitudes that are important in providing effective personal support.

3. What are the *Three C's*? Why is each important?

4. What is a Code of Conduct? Why is it useful to you as a support worker?

5. What is stress? Where does it come from? Is it always bad?

6. What are some common signs of distress?

7. What are some common signs of burnout?

8. What three questions should you ask about any stressor?

9. Describe three effective ways of managing stress.

Questions for Discussion

1. With five other colleagues, develop a Code of Conduct for personal support workers.

2. Share with your classmates the stress management techniques that work for you. Do you use some of the same techniques as others in your group? Do you use techniques that others don't? Did you learn about any new techniques?

3. If you felt that you were experiencing some of the signs of distress or burnout, with whom would you talk?

4. Imagine that you are a support worker working for two community agencies. Although you were hired on a part-time basis, you often are scheduled for 30 hours per week or more by *each* agency. You also work for a local facility on a casual basis (they call you when they are short of staff for a shift). You want to work as much as possible so that you can earn enough money to provide well for your family.

   Over the last two months, you have averaged 66 hours of work each week. This week, you have agreed to work 70 hours for the community agencies. You will be working six days this week. You are not scheduled to work Friday and are really looking forward to having this one day off, as you are tired and want to spend some time with your children. In fact, you have planned to take your two children to a movie Friday night.

   On the Thursday, you receive a call from the facility, asking you to work the Friday evening shift. The rate of pay the facility offers is very good and you really enjoy working with the facility's residents.

   You are tempted to work this shift as you will earn much needed money. However, it would mean giving up your only day off and cancelling your plans with your children. You find yourself feeling resentful that the agency called you. You are also beginning to feel that none of your employers appreciates you.

   What stressors can you identify? What signs of distress or burnout can you identify? What actions would you take to respond to the stressors and reduce the distress you are experiencing?

The Support Team and Its Members

Care Plan   A written document that outlines the support a client is to receive. This document often describes client needs and support goals and includes names and contact information for family members and other services involved in the client's support. There are many forms of care plans. These plans are also called support plans or service plans.

Service Agreement   A document that spells out the services to be provided, but does not usually include goals or client needs. Service agreements may be called service contracts.

Team   The term used to describe the group of people who work together (and depend upon one another) to provide support to a client.

Therapists   Professionals who help the client regain ability or adjust to changes.

What Is a Team?

A **team** is a group of people who work together toward a common interest or a common goal. In a team, members rely upon one another to get tasks done (Photo 5-1). This is called *interdependence*.

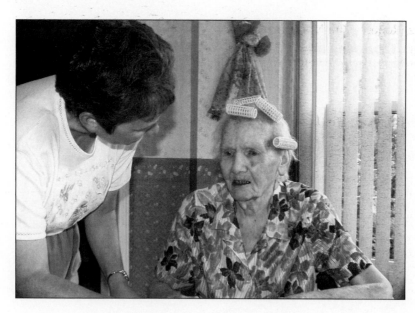

Photo 5-1
The team works together to meet the client's needs. Here, the client and her daughter discuss an issue.
Source: CHATS.

All of us are members of teams. In a sense we, along with our families, form a team. We might even say that a group of friends are a team. We don't often think of these groups as teams, but they are. Each is a group of people who share common interests or goals and who rely upon one another to do tasks related to those interests or goals. Let's take a look at the life of Robert, a support worker.

CASE EXAMPLE 5-1

Robert is a support worker. He is also a husband and father of two young girls. He lives in Vancouver, near his brother, sister, and parents. He is a member of many 'teams'.

As a member of his family team, Robert is responsible for sharing the care of his children with his wife. He is also responsible for contributing to the family's income and for helping keep the family's home clean and in good repair. In turn, Robert relies upon the other members of the team (his wife and daughters) to perform certain tasks. For example, his wife also contributes to the family's income and shares in household duties. Robert's children have been assigned chores that help contribute to a clean, safe, and comfortable home. All members are affected if one member does not do his or her part. If Robert is ill, his wife must take on some of his responsibilities. Likewise, if Robert's wife is away, Robert must

take on some of the tasks she would usually do.

Along with his brother, sister, and parents, Robert is also a member of another family 'team' focussed on caring for Robert's parents. Robert's father is 86 and has some problems getting around after his stroke. As he is a support worker, Robert helps his father with some personal care. His sister assists their mother with shopping. Robert's brother helps out with the upkeep of their parents' home. In this team, each person contributes what they can do best. They rely upon each other to do their respective parts.

Robert is a support worker for a home support agency. He also works in a local facility. Each of Robert's clients has a support team, and Robert is a member of each. Robert has specific responsibilities as a member of each team, as we'll see later.

As you can see, Robert's family teams are essential to the health and well-being of the team's members. They share goals and interests and work together to get tasks done.

Stop and Reflect 5-1

To what teams do you belong?

_____

_____

Who else is a member of each team?

_____

_____

_____

What are your responsibilities as a member of each team?

_____

_____

_____

Have you ever been unable to fulfill your responsibilities to the team? If so, what happened? Did other members take on some of your responsibilities? Did some tasks remain undone?

_____

_____

_____

How did the other members feel about this?

_____

_____

_____

How did you feel when you were unable to complete your responsibilities?

_____

_____

The Benefit of Teams

Have you heard the expression "Two heads are better than one"? There are five major ways that teams make working together easier and more effective. Teams provide their members with the opportunity to see situations in many different ways, to solve problems, to share information, and to share responsibilities. Teams can also bring together people with different strengths and abilities. Each of these benefits is described below.

Different Views.   Each team member brings a unique perspective to the team. The team provides the opportunity to see a situation from many different points of view. This can help all team members understand a client's situation, or better understand an issue. Have you ever shared an issue with other people and found that they saw the issue differently than you saw it? It's likely that looking at the issue in a different way made it easier to understand.

Varied Strengths and Abilities.   The team brings together people who have different training, experience, and skills. This variety means that the team can apply a great deal of expertise to resolving issues and problems.

Information Sharing.   Through team meetings and established ways of communicating, members of the team can easily share information. This means that information is less likely to be lost.

Problem Solving.   By sharing information with each other, the team can examine a problem in many different ways, and identify many approaches to solving it.

Responsibility Sharing.   As you saw in Case Example 5-1, members of the team share the responsibility for any tasks. Because the team brings together people with different strengths and abilities, it's often easy to find the right person to perform a task.

Purpose of the Support Team

Client-Focussed

The general purpose of a support team is to provide the best support possible to the client. Each team will have specific goals that relate to the needs of the client for whom the team is formed. The team develops a plans to help address the needs of the client. A **service agreement** is a document that spells out the services to be provided but does not usually include goals or client needs. They may also be called service contracts. **Care plans** are written documents that outline the support a client is to receive and often describe client needs and support goals. The contact information for family members is included and other services involved in the client's support are listed. Care plans come in many forms and are also called support plans or service plans.

Despite the level of participation the client has in the team's activities, the client is the focus of the team's activities. The client should always feel a part of the team, and feel free to speak openly to members of the team.

Types of Support Teams

We'll define two general types of teams: those common to community settings and those common to facility settings. We'll discuss each team's characteristics in terms of membership, leadership, and communication.

Remember that each support team is unique. A specific client's team will be made up of the people involved in that client's care.

Community Support Teams

Membership and Leadership

The community team usually includes the client, support workers, a support worker supervisor, the client's case manager, *therapists* (if involved in the client's care), as well as family members and other caregivers. **Therapists** are professionals who help the client regain ability or adjust to changes. A specific client's team may include many other people such as a pharmacist, clergy, clergy member, friends, or volunteers.

The case manager is often the person responsible for organizing and leading the activities of the community support team. Other team members may perform this role. A client may also take on the leadership of a support team.

Communication

Community teams usually communicate *indirectly* that is, they do not necessarily meet on a regular basis. In fact, the team may only meet when there is an issue that requires all the members to be present. Day-to-day communication is often done through telephone calls between members of the support team, through progress notes written by team members, or through entries in communication logs. Most agencies have specific policies and procedures and forms for communication. You are responsible for using the method approved by your agency.

CASE EXAMPLE 5-2

As we mentioned earlier, Robert's position as a home support worker requires him to take part in a different support team for each of his clients. For example, when Robert provides respite care to his client Mr. Ross, Robert is a member of a support team that includes Mr. Ross, Mr. Ross' wife and daughter, as well as the nurse who visits , and Robert's supervisor.

Robert doesn't often see all the other members of the team. In fact, Robert's visits are scheduled so that he is not at the Ross' home when the nurse is there. As well, Robert's visits enable Mrs. Ross to get out to do some shopping and to relax. She usually doesn't stay in the home when Robert is there.

Robert does communicate regularly with members of the team. Robert usually speaks briefly with Mrs. Ross when he arrives to get an update on Mr. Ross' status. In turn, Robert reviews his visit with Mrs. Ross when he is getting ready to leave.

Robert keeps in regular contact with his supervisor. He immediately reports any significant change in Mr. Ross' status, any needs beyond the scope of his role, or any problems which cannot be resolved. In addition, he submits to his agency monthly support worker reports which provide an overview of Mr. Ross' situation and support.

Occasionally, Robert is asked to attend a meeting of Mr. Ross' support team. These meetings are scheduled to discuss significant changes in Mr. Ross' care or to deal with specific problems that have arisen.

Facility Support Teams

Membership and Leadership

The facility support team members may include many people: registered nurses and support workers, the client's physician, therapists (if the client receives therapy), as well as the facility's pharmacist, activity director, and other staff members. The team may include the client and the client's family, as well as professionals from other agencies involved in the client's care.

Often, a registered nurse is responsible for organizing and leading the team. Sometimes, other members may take on this role. It is less common (although not impossible) for a client to lead the facility team. This is because many clients living in facilities have conditions which make support team leadership difficult for them.

CASE EXAMPLE 5-3

Robert's work as a care aide in a local facility requires that he be a member of a different type of support team. The facility support team differs from the community support team in two ways. First, almost all members of the support team work in the same location. As a result, it is easier for Robert to meet with members of this support team. Second, the same support team assists all of Robert's residents. (Only the client and family members are different.) This means that the team has many opportunities to work together.

Because it is so easy for facility support team members to speak with one another, information sharing is often verbal. Each team member must be particularly careful to make sure that necessary information is communicated to all team members who need it and, where appropriate, that the information is written on the appropriate form.

When Robert arrives, he checks in with the charge nurse to receive his schedule and up-to-date information about his clients. At 11 a.m., Robert advises the activity director that a client, Mrs. Reager, asked about attending a program. This is the first time that Mrs. Reager has expressed any interest in activities and Robert wants to make sure the activity director knows about her interest.

Just after lunch, another client asks Robert for help changing clothes, as the client is going out with her daughter. Robert checks with the charge nurse to make sure that the appropriate arrangements have been made. While at the nursing station, Robert makes a note in Mrs. Reager's chart about her interest in activity programs and his discussion with the activity director.

At 2:30 p.m., Robert attends a team meeting to discuss Mrs. Crane, one of Robert's clients. The team meets monthly to discuss each client. At this meeting, Mrs. Crane's support plan will be reviewed and updated.

Contributing to the Support Team

As you've learned so far, communication is essential to the work of support team (Photo 5-2). If members do not share information and work together, the team will not attain its purpose of providing the best support possible to the client.

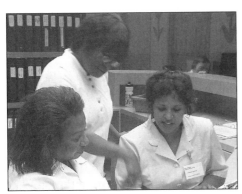

Photo 5-2
Support workers discussing the support provided to a facility resident.

Source: Leisureworld Preferred Institute/ Leisureworld, Inc.

Each member has the responsibility to share information with the other members of the support team. Because each team member has a different role with the client, each member sees the client in a different way. If members do not freely share their views and observations, the support team will not have a complete picture of the client, and the support provided to the client may suffer as a result. It's a bit like putting together a puzzle when you don't have all the pieces. The picture will be incomplete, and you will likely end up a bit frustrated.

Each support team member's information is equally important. You should never feel that your information is less important than that of another member. In fact, you may be the team member who spends the greatest amount of time with the client and thus you may have a great deal of useful information to share.

When you share your observations with the team, it is important to gather your thoughts and present them clearly. It is equally important to listen carefully to the reports of other team members. In Chapter 11, we will discuss team communication.

Members of the Support Team

As we discussed earlier in this chapter, some types of professionals and other caregivers are more likely to be members of a support team. Table 5-1 identifies the most common members of the support team. Be aware that the descriptions provided here include the *general* tasks of the profession. Provincial and agency regulations will determine each professional's scope of practice in a specific setting. Also, remember that the client, the client's family, as well as volunteers are members of the team. Finally, an individual client' support team is made up of the people who work together to assist that client and may well include people not listed.

TABLE 5-1	Common Members of the Support Team			
Profession	**Regulated by**	**Training**	**Common Duties**	**Common Relationship to Support Worker**
Activity Director	No mandatory regulation	Provincial requirements vary. Common preparation includes gerontology programs, social service rehabilitation diplomas and/or degrees. Some provinces have developed specific training programs.	Coordinates social programs and conduct groups in long-term care facilities. Some Activity Directors work in day programs, day hospital, and seniors centres.	Support Workers may assist with programs, transport residents to programs, coordinate assistance to residents so that they can attend programs.

TABLE 5-1	Common Members of the Support Team *(continued)*			
Profession	**Regulated by**	**Training**	**Common Duties**	**Common Relationship to Support Worker**
Adjuvant Activity Aide	No mandatory regulation	Provincial requirements vary. Common preparation includes health care aide training, personal support training, rehabilitation aide training, as well as gerontology.	Usually works in facility settings. Assists Activity Director with small groups, with therapy follow-up, etc.	Support Workers may assist with programs, transport residents to programs, coordinate assistance to residents so that they can attend programs.
Clergy	Determined by religious organization	Determined by religious order	Religious/spiritual guidance, counselling	Support Workers may be asked to assist with specific practices (for example, assist a person to kneel to pray) or to observe specific food preparation guidelines.
Dietitian	Professional College R.P. Dt. (Registered Professional Dietitian) designation is given to graduates of specific training who join the College.	University training	Assess nutritional needs; devise special diets; provide public education.	Support Workers may implement a diet prescribed by a R.P.Dt.
Doctor (M.D.)	Provincial Professional College	University and Medical School	Diagnosis, treatment, able to perform all 13 controlled acts defined by the RHPA.	Support Workers may receive direction from M.D.
Homemaker Supervisor	No one	No specific program. Training may include nursing, social services, or other health/human service training. Some supervisors are former Support Workers.	Supervise, guide (and sometimes schedule) Support Workers.	Supervisory.

TABLE 5-1	Common Members of the Support Team *(continued)*			
Profession	Regulated by	Training	Common Duties	Common Relationship to Support Worker
Occupational Therapist	Provincial Professional College	University	Assistance with meaningful movement (e.g., regaining of life skills, etc.) vocational rehabilitation.	May treat client Support Worker sees; may give some guidance to Support Worker as per specific needs of clients (for tasks within Support Worker's role).
Physical Therapist	Provincial Professional College	University	Assistance with adaptation and/or regaining movement, including range of motion, walking, positioning, as well as breathing assistance (postural draininge, chest clapping, etc.)	May treat client Support Worker sees; may give some guidance to Support Worker as per specific needs of clients (for tasks within Support Worker's role).
Registered Nurse	Provincial Professional College	Diploma program from provincial college, or University program. A *Registered Nurse* may hold either a degree or a diploma – the title refers only to membership in the provincial professional college.	Assists the client to solve actual or potential health problems. The scope of practice is controlled by the regulating college.	May treat client Personal Support Worker (PSW) sees; may give some guidance to PSW as per specific needs of clients (for tasks within PSW's role).
Registered Practical Nurse Licensed Practical Nurse Registered Nursing Assistant	Provincial Professional College	Community College diploma	Subset of Registered Nursing duties. Actual scope of practice varies among provinces.	May treat client PSW sees; may give some guidance to PSW as per specific needs of clients (for tasks within PSW's role).

TABLE 5-1	Common Members of the Support Team *(continued)*			
Profession	Regulated by	Training	Common Duties	Common Relationship to Support Worker
Respiratory Therapist	Provincial Professional College	University degree	Assist clients who have respiratory problems, implement respiratory therapy and treatment.	May treat client PSW sees; may give some guidance to PSW as per specific needs of clients (for tasks within PSW's role).
Social Worker	Varies from province to province	University degree	Counselling, group work, related to psychosocial and emotional issues.	May treat client PSW sees; may give some guidance to PSW as per specific needs of clients (for tasks within PSW's role).

Questions for Review

1. What is a team? To what kinds of teams do you belong?

2. What are the five major benefits of teams? Using one of the teams you listed in your answer to Question 1, give an example of each benefit.

3. What are the two major types of support teams? What is one major difference between these two types?

4. What is the one purpose common to all support teams?

5. Are support teams organized for community services and for facilities different? If so, how?

6. What is the support worker's role as a team member?

7. Who are the 11 most common members of the support team? What is each member's key responsibilities?

Questions for Discussion

1. How do you resolve disagreements in the team?

2. Is there ever a time when a team approach is *not* the best way to assist a client? If so, under what circumstances is another approach better?

3. Are support workers always equal members of the client's support team? What specific contributions do support workers make to the team? Do other team members always listen to the support worker's views? What can you, as a support worker, do to make sure your contributions to the team are heard by the other members of the team?

PART TWO

THE
CLIENT

CHAPTER SIX

The Client

Learning Objectives

Through reading this chapter, you'll be able to:

1. Describe individuality.

2. List the five major aspects that make each person's life unique.

3. Discuss the five needs most people have and, for each, describe common ways that people might meet these needs.

4. Describe the relationship between common roles people have and life satisfaction.

5. Tell what personal culture is and apply the concept to your life.

6. Identify *support system* and the components of a support system.

7. Describe the usual responsibility a support worker has in helping to meet a client's needs.

Chapter At A Glance

Individuality

Needs of the Individual

Social Roles

Culture

Family and Other Members of the Client's Support System

Applying What You've Learned About Yourself to Your Work with Clients

Terms You'll Use

Ethnicity   A person's ethnic origin.

Life Satisfaction   Being content with our lives.

Life Span   The length of time a person is alive.

Need   Something we must meet in order to survive or feel satisfied with our lives.

Personal Culture   The mix of many factors including ethnicity, religion, race, and experience, that make a person unique.

Personality   The psychological traits that each person has.

Personhood   The characteristics, attributes, and strengths of an individual.

Social Role   Activities that are grouped together because of the expectations of a group or society.

Individuality

In order to be irreplaceable, one must always be different.
– Coco Chanel

Stop and Reflect 6-1

Who are you?

_____

_____

How would you describe yourself as a person?

_____

_____

How would a friend describe you?

_____

_____

This chapter will examine what makes us individuals. We'll talk about what shapes our sense of **personhood**—the characteristics, attributes, and strengths that make us a unique individual (*Personhood: A Teaching Package*, Educational Centre for Aging and Health, McMaster University, 1993). Personhood includes five aspects of a person: the physical, psychological, spiritual, social, and functional (Figure 6-1).

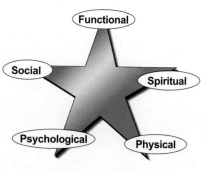

Figure 6-1 *The Personhood Star*

The Physical Aspect

Take a look at your answers to *Stop and Reflect 6-1*. Did you first describe yourself in terms of your being male or female, how old you are, your health or fitness, the colour of your hair, or other physical characteristics? Our physical characteristics play a significant role in how we define ourselves (Photo 6-1). Changes in health and body image can affect our sense of personhood. Some people's sense of personhood is affected by age.

The Psychological Aspect

The psychological aspect includes many things, including our personality, our patterns of behaviour, and our sexuality. You probably described some of these things when you described yourself earlier in this chapter. We'll discuss each below.

Stop and Reflect 6-2

Have you ever experienced a change in your body image? Perhaps you broke a leg or arm and had to wear a cast, or had to wear an obvious bandage due to an injury or surgery.

_____

_____

Did you feel that this change affected how you saw yourself? Did this change affect how others saw you?

_____

_____

Were there differences in these views? If there were differences, what were they?

_____

_____

_____

Sexuality

Sexuality refers to our sense of ourselves as sexual beings. It is an important part of our sense of personhood.

Part of our sexuality is rooted in biology—we are born with it. Other aspects of our sexuality are learned from others. From the time we are born, people treat us as *boys* or *girls*. As a society, we still often identify roles or activities as masculine or feminine. For example, you may still hear people refer to a nurse who is a man as a "male nurse".

Stereotypes about age and disability can affect one's sexuality. For example, some people may assume that a person using a wheelchair is not attractive or even that the person does not have sexual feelings. Similarly, an older person may be seen as sexless. Neither of these assumptions is valid.

Personality

Personality refers to the psychological traits we have. For example, you might describe yourself as shy and quiet or outgoing and bubbly. You might say that another person is sweet or pleasant. These terms describe the traits that help to make us unique.

Like the other factors, personality is determined by our biology and how we have developed in relation to other people. Researchers have identified two general types of theories of personality development: stage theory and life span theory. Each is discussed below.

Stage Theories

This group of theories looks at personality and psychological development as a series of stages. At each stage, the person is faced with a challenge. If the person successfully meets the challenge, he or she grows as a result. If the person does not meet the challenge, the person's growth is altered and future growth may be changed and more difficult. Some stage theorists feel that a person cannot "skip" a stage and continue to develop in a positive way. Table 6-1 lists some common elements among stage theories.

There are many stage theorists. Most stage theorists focus on child and young adult development. They usually do not deal with middle age or later life. This has been seen as a weakness in these theories.

Erik Erickson is the author of the most well-known stage theory. If you have taken any child care courses (or have had children of your own) you may have read about Erickson's Eight Stages of Ego Development. Unlike most theories, Erickson's does discuss middle and later life.

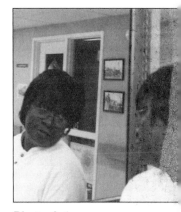

Photo 6-1
Our physical images form a part of our sense of personhood.
Source: Leisureworld Preferred Institute/ Leisureworld, Inc.

TABLE 6-1	Common Elements of Stage Theories
Ages	**Common Tasks**
Birth - 18 months	Developing a sense of oneself as a lovable and desirable person Developing an awareness of other people Learning to trust others

TABLE 6-1	Common Elements of Stage Theories (continued)
Ages	**Common Tasks**
18 months - 3 years	Developing a sense of onself as an individual, with his or her own thoughts and needs Developing a sense of the world around him or her Learning about the world in a concrete way — fun activities, limits, dangers Testing limits
3-7 years	Defining what is real from what is imaginary. Learning about the world — interest in how babies are born, why the sky is blue, etc. Understanding the relationship between things (for example, the need to go to bed early because he or she must get up early the next day) Using creative methods to solve problems
7 - pre-adolescence	Developing a sense of values Developing relationships with peers Developing abstract ways of thinking Developing a sense of mastery of activities: developing skills, tasks and other psychomotor and intellectual activities
Adolescence	Developing a personal identity in relation to others Developing a sense of a plan for the future Establishing independence, testing limits, reconciling different values
Young adulthood	Developing a sense of oneself as a productive person Balancing many demands Forming an intimate relationship with another
Middle Age	Developing a sense of social awareness Generating ideas, activities Acceptance of limitations and the need to choose among opportunities (accepting that one can't "have it all")
Late Life	Reviewing one's life, putting events into perspective Attaching meaning to activities Developing a sense of acceptance

Life Span Development Theories

The life span development approach sees the person as continually changing from the time they are born until the time they die. **Life span** refers to the length of time a person is alive. Unlike stage theories, life span development views aging as a lifelong endeavour—one that starts at birth and ends at death (Nowak, *Aging & Society: A Canadian Perspective*, 1997). Thus, who we are is the result of how we have responded to a number of life events. These events are grouped into three types: events expected to happen by virtue of a person's age; events that are unexpected, cannot be planned for, and do not generally happen to everyone; and historical or social events that affect a community, nation, or society as a whole. Figure 6-2 provides some examples of life events.

Each of us has our own combination of these three types of events. The combination we have faced and our responses to the events shape our personality. For example, you may know someone who lived through the *Great Depression* in the 1930s. Chances are that person's experience (what happened to them and how they coped with it) has had an effect on who that person is today. Similarly, a person who expected to retire from work at age 65, but could not, is shaped by that experience.

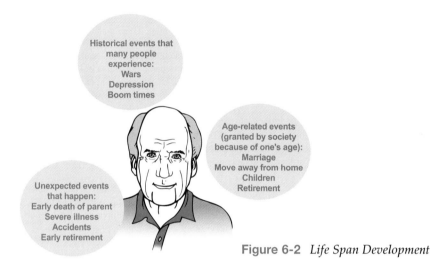

Figure 6-2 *Life Span Development*

Stop and Reflect 6-3

Consider your own life in light of the three types of events described by the life span development model. In what way has each type of event affected you? For each type, identify the event and how it has helped shape who you are.

Age-Related Events (Such as marrying at an older or younger age than was expected of you)

_____

_____

Historical Events (Such as having a family member in Bosnia, or having lived through a flood or forest fire)

_____

_____

Unexpected Events (Such as an accident or untimely death of a family member or close friend)

_____

_____

If you like, compare your answers with those of your colleagues.

We do not see the whole person if we separate them from their past. Consider the following essay in Exhibit 6-1.

This essay is taken from Are You Listening? *It was written by Gladys C. Atkins, an older adult.*

I am a senior citizen, but, as well, I am a person—the product of heredity, environment and of all the events of my life. The happiness, sorrows, achievements and disappointments have given me the ability to see life with a clarity of perception and appreciation not possible 50 years ago.

The beauty of a sunset, the flash of a hummingbird poised over a flower or the smile of a child can move me to tears. But, on the other hand, the slights or hurts, real or imagined, can wound more deeply than ever. I resent being ignored or merely tolerated, left out of a conversation or disregarded by a waitress. It doesn't happen often.

I love this beautiful world and have compassion (not pity) for its under-privileged, perhaps because I remember the years of Depression. The social benefits which seniors now enjoy compensate somewhat for the hard years and we should be grateful. We are able to live in a dignified manner with a sense of independence.

I am, though widowed, fortunate to be in my own home, to drive my car and be able to travel. My life might be compared to a river flowing along smoothly but with undercurrents below the surface. Under the serenity of small-town life, family and volunteer work, lies concern for personal, social, political and international problems. The media keep me informed. I avoid self-pity and I do not worry for "to worry is to pay interest on a loan before it is due." I strive "to have the serenity to accept the things I cannot change, the courage to change the things I can, and the wisdom to know the difference."

The future, in my view, holds great promise. Everywhere I see goodness and kindness, especially in time of need. This far outweighs the adverse aspects of crime, greed and so on. Our young people are enterprising, imaginative and innovative far beyond my generation. Of course, their education and opportunities exceed ours in the same proportion. Or so we like to think.

As the eddies surface on the river, so, in the silence of the night or in the darkest hours before the dawn, a thought emerges in my mind. "I love this world but I must leave it—perhaps soon." But I have lived and loved. I have children and grandchildren of whom I am very proud. Somewhere along the way I must have done some good or left a pleasant memory. If so, I have not lived in vain. The future holds no fear.

Exhibit 6-1   *Life Span Development In the First Person*

Patterns of Behaviour

Have you ever travelled with another person? If so, did you find that the other person had very different ways of doing things? Perhaps you were a morning person and your travelling companion was a night owl. Perhaps you liked to plan events in advance and your companion preferred doing things on the spur of the moment. Our patterns of behaviour are how we go about doing things. These patterns are influenced by our personality. Because they are behaviours and are more readily seen by others, it's often easier to describe them than it is to describe personality traits. Think back to how you described yourself. You likely included some of your patterns of behaviour.

The Spiritual Aspect

The spiritual aspect (*spirituality*) includes the need for meaning or a purpose in life—hope. It can be defined as a part of oneself that is separate from the material world (Denton, 1999). Spirituality often includes, but is not limited to, religious beliefs. Keep in mind that holding religious beliefs or belonging to a particular religion is not essential to having a sense of spirituality. A person can be spiritual without being religious.

The Social Aspect

The social aspect is concerned with the way we are shaped by our relationships with others, such as family, colleagues, or other members of our community. The social aspect includes the roles we have (as a parent or a sibling, for example), as well as the concept of culture. These concepts will be discussed later in this chapter.

The Functional Aspect

The functional aspect includes *how* we do the things we need to do. Our sense of self is affected by our ability to perform as we prefer. If you have ever had to change your activities because of an injury, you might have felt frustrated that your normal activities were impaired.

This aspect includes the ability to do things as a result of physical ability, cognitive ability, psychological readiness, or opportunity. A person's function may be affected just as significantly by a person's anxiety or fear (psychological preparedness) as it might by a physical barrier. Similarly, a person may be affected by a loss of opportunity which does not allow the person to do what he or she wants. For example, an older person may be able to and be interested in having a romantic relationship with another person, but not have the opportunity because of a lack of suitable persons, or because the person is told that a romantic relationship is "inappropriate" at the person's age.

The functional aspect may be very significant to your clients. Your clients will likely have experienced losses and changes that affect how they function. The emotions that arise from not being able to do what the client wants to do can be very frustrating. Your role as a support worker will require you to work with the client to help him or her cope with challenges to their functional aspect.

Needs of the Individual

A **need** is something we must meet in order to survive or to feel satisfied with our life. We all have the same range of needs, but the priority (that is, how important a particular need is) may vary over time and from situation to situation.

Abraham Maslow is a well-recognized researcher on needs. His *Hierarchy of Needs* provides a useful way of examining common needs. It categorizes needs into five groups: physical needs, safety and security needs, social needs, esteem needs, and self-fulfillment needs (Figure 6-3). Here, we have adapted Maslow's hierarchy to include some examples of the needs in each of his categories.

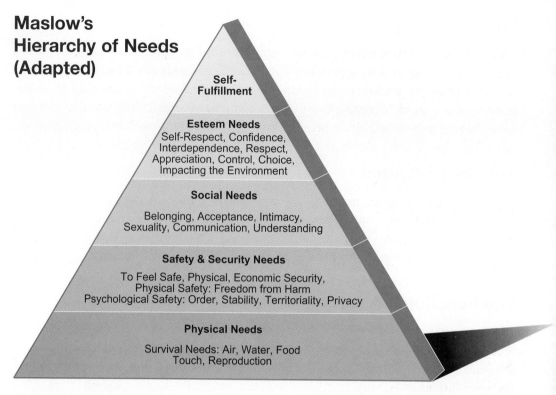

Maslow's Hierarchy of Needs (Adapted)

Self-Fulfillment

Esteem Needs
Self-Respect, Confidence,
Interdependence, Respect,
Appreciation, Control, Choice,
Impacting the Environment

Social Needs
Belonging, Acceptance, Intimacy,
Sexuality, Communication, Understanding

Safety & Security Needs
To Feel Safe, Physical, Economic Security,
Physical Safety: Freedom from Harm
Psychological Safety: Order, Stability, Territoriality, Privacy

Physical Needs
Survival Needs: Air, Water, Food
Touch, Reproduction

Figure 6-3 *Human Needs*

Photo 6-2 *Touch is an important need. Still you must be careful to respect a person's wishes for how he or she prefers to be touched.*
Source: CHATS.

Physical needs are those needs essential to our survival. Air, food, and water are clearly linked to our survival. At first glance, the link between touch and reproduction and survival may seem less clear. Let's examine these needs more closely.

The need for *touch* has been well documented in research. In fact, studies have shown that infant primates (high-functioning mammals who share many characteristics with humans) who are not touched often die before they reach the age of one year.

How, where, and by whom a person prefers to be touched is highly individual. (Photo 6-2). You should not assume that all clients prefer to be touched in the same way, or that they appreciate touch from you. Preferences for touch differ from one person to another and are heavily influenced by our *personal culture*.

Biologists have identified that the need to *reproduce* is essential to ensure that the species does not become extinct. This does not mean that every person is equally driven to reproduce. Rather, the intensity of this need, like that of touch, differs from person to person. It is, however, essential if the human race is to survive.

Security and Safety Needs

Security and safety may seem to mean the same things. They do not. Safety refers to the need to *be* safe. Security refers to the need to *feel* safe. For example, if you are riding on a roller coaster, you might not feel secure, even though you are safe.

Included in this group are needs which contribute to feeling secure: stability, territoriality, and privacy. Stability refers to the need for things to be predictable and known. Territoriality refers to the need to have one's own space. The need for privacy refers to the need to keep personal business private.

Social Needs

Social needs are those needs that are met through communicating with, and being accepted by, others. Meeting social needs makes us feel less alone and more a part of a community. The need to be recognized by others as a sexual being is a part of the need to be accepted. The need for intimacy refers to a particular kind of closeness that requires acceptance, communication, and a sense of belonging. The concept of inter-dependence—the reliance we all have upon others for some things—is a social need.

Esteem Needs

Esteem needs are needs which are met through one's activities with others. These needs are met in two ways: through the response of others to how we perform activities and through the personal satisfaction we get from doing them. One example of this is the need to make choices in one's life. We can meet esteem needs when we have the opportunity to make choices and have the satisfaction of making choices in a way that satisfies us (e.g., making the "right" choice).

Self-Fulfillment

Self-fulfillment means attaining a goal one sets for oneself. Unlike social and esteem needs, self-fulfillment is met primarily through the person's own measure of his or her own activities. For example, only you know whether you have tried your *best* at a task.

Attaining one's potential is very much a personal thing. Only you can set your personal goals and know when you have put your best efforts toward achieving them.

Stop and Reflect 6-4

Imagine that you are on holidays with friends. Look at Figure 6-3. What needs would be most important to you?

Now, imagine that you have been robbed while on this holiday. While you are physically unhurt, your car has been broken into and all of your possessions have been ransacked. Some items of sentimental as well as monetary value have been taken. Look again at Figure 6-3. What needs are most important to you now? Are these needs the same as those you identified above?

_____

_____

_____

_____

_____

In the first instance, you probably identified needs like belonging, acceptance, or perhaps self-fulfillment. In the second instance, you might have identified safety or security.

Social Roles

Social roles are activities that are grouped together because of the expectations of a group or of society. For example, the role of *mother* includes the things that society expects of mothers such as caring for their children, providing guidance, and providing a stable home environment. In turn, these expectations help us to know what we need to do in order to fulfill the role—to be a "mom".

We hold many roles throughout life (Photo 6-3). Recall your answer to *Stop and Reflect 6-1*. You likely included such roles as parent, worker, friend, or spouse. Table 6-2 describes some of the roles we may have over our lifetime.

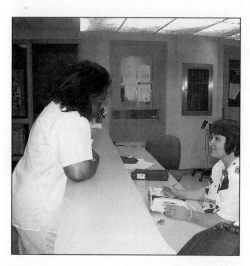

Photo 6-3
We all have many roles: worker, consumer, family member.

Source: Leisureworld
Preferred Institute/
Leisureworld, Inc.

TABLE 6-2	Common Social Roles	
Worker	Handy Person	Comic/Jokester
Grandparent	Attractive Dresser	Leader
Consumer/Buyer	Cook	Organizer
Religious Person	Student	Decision Maker
Friend	Gourmet	Singer
Sister/brother	Gift Giver	Sports Fan/Spectator
Citizen	Boss	Musician
Lover	Supporter	Breadwinner
Voter	Helper	Hunter
Spouse	Traveller	Head of Household
Homemaker	Advice Giver	Child
Significant Other	Athlete	Stimulator/Idea Generator
Mother/Father	Expert	Problem-Solver
Attractive Person	Game Player	Master of My Own Destiny
Hostess/Host	Reader	
Dancer	Group Member	

As we age, we discard some roles and take on others. Sometimes, the activities associated with a role change as we grow older. For example, your role as a child changes as you grow up. You might discard a role because you can no longer do it. For example, your role of child will end when your parents die. Similarly, you may take on new roles, such as that of grandparent or of your family's breadwinner.

Some roles change because society changes its expectations of the role. For example, the role of mother is different today than it was 50 years ago.

SR *Stop and Reflect 6-5*

Look over the roles listed in Figure 6-4. What roles do you have now?

_____

_____

_____

Which roles are most important to you?

_____

_____

_____

Roles and Life Satisfaction

Roles provide us a way of meeting our needs. Fulfilling roles can cause us to be accepted and respected by others and to have a sense of self-fulfillment through accomplishing a personal goal. Through this process, we can attain **life satisfaction**, or being content with our lives.

Culture

What Is Culture?

Culture refers to the patterns of learned behaviours that are shared among members of a group. Many people assume that culture is the same as *ethnicity*. It is not. Culture includes many things: ethnicity, language, religion/spiritual beliefs, race, gender, age, sexual orientation, geographic origin, education, upbringing, life experiences, and rites of passage. **Ethnicity** refers to a person's nation of origin. Figure 6-4 illustrates a number of aspects which may make up a particular individual's culture.

Personal culture refers to the way in which culture affects the individual, given the individual's personality. Personal culture is the result of the way in which the individual relates to and balances the demands of his or her culture (Figure 6-4). For example, second-generation Canadians may have to balance the demands of their ancestral cultures with their current cultures.

Significant Relationships • Age • Values and Beliefs
Geographic Origin   Rites of Passage
Life Experiences   Language
Education   Gender
Religion   Family
Ethnicity   Race

Figure 6-4 *Many Aspects Can Make Up One's Personal Culture*

Stop and Reflect 6-6

What is your personal culture?

Examine the aspects of personal culture identified in this section.

Which of these have most influenced you?

_____

_____

In what way were you influenced by these aspects?

_____

_____

Have you had any "cross-cultural" interactions—for example, marrying into another religious or ethnic group, or working with people who have different backgrounds? If so, how did you learn about the other culture? How did you share your culture with the others?

_____

_____

_____

The Dangers of Stereotyping

A *stereotype* is a fixed set of ideas or assumptions about a group of people. For example, many people have stereotypes about older adults, or about people from an ethnic group, religion, or race. We often stereotype by sex, calling certain jobs "women's work" or "men's work". Stereotypes are dangerous because they can cause a person to forget that everyone is a product of their own personal culture.

Stereotypes can often make it harder to get to know an individual. They can lead to misunderstandings that may make both people uncomfortable. As a support worker, you must be careful to examine the beliefs you have about people to make sure that you do not hold stereotypes. When working with clients, you must always focus on the client's personal culture.

Stop and Reflect 6-7

What stereotypes have you encountered? Has anyone made assumptions about you because you were a man or a woman, or because of your age or how you looked?

It's about me mistaken as a chinese or Filipino sometimes about my age.

If so, how did you feel?

I felt good if they say that I'm young in fact I'm older of what they think about me

Share your answers with your colleagues. In what ways were your experiences and feelings similar?

Some experience I have is always about my age. compared to my friend and coleague.

Working with People from Different Cultures

We are all different from other people as each of us has a unique personal culture. In many cases, these differences do not significantly affect how we work together with other people. In some cases, the differences are significant and make working together a challenge. This can be because there are a number of differences or because a single aspect (for example, language) is very different.

As a support worker, you must work with clients to make sure that you develop the best working relationship possible. In order to do this, you must have the knowledge, skills, and attitudes necessary to address cultural differences. We'll examine each in this section.

Attitudes

In order to work effectively with people whose culture differs from yours, you will need to be aware of your own values, cultural biases, and stereotypes and how these may effect your work with clients. For example, if you were raised to believe that an older adult should be cared for by family members, you may find it difficult to work with a client whose family does not share in the client's support. If you are not aware of the effect your belief might have on the support you provide, you might unknowingly behave in a manner that indicates you disapprove of the family's decision.

Several other attitudes are useful. As you saw above, you must be *open* to examining (and possibly changing) your own views. You must be *sensitive* to any differences and *respect* your client's preferences and practices, no matter how different they may be. Finally, you must be *flexible* so that you may adapt your approach to best support the client.

Knowledge

You'll need to learn about your client's significant cultural practices and beliefs. If your client speaks a different language, you should learn words and phrases in the client's language. (If you have ever been in a country where no one spoke your language, you'll have a sense of how wonderful it is when you hear words in your own language.)

As you learn about your client's practices, remember that he or she has a personal culture. Your client's practices may not be the same as other members of his or her religion or ethnic group. Learn from your client and your client's family.

Some specific techniques you might use include the following:
1. Showing interest in the client's foods, dress, and other habits. For example, you might ask the client for favourite recipes and then prepare them.
2. Respecting the client's values, beliefs, attitudes, traditions, and rituals.
3. Encouraging the client to tell you about their culture. You may share information about your culture if it helps the client to tell you about theirs.
4. Asking family members for information, if appropriate.

It is sometimes helpful to read about the client's culture. If you do, keep in mind that the person may not hold all the beliefs or values, or take part in all the rituals and traditions that are considered to be a part of the overall culture. Always verify this information with your client.

Family and Other Members of the Client's Support System

What Is a Support System?

A support system is the network of people upon whom we rely to help us meet our needs. Have you ever heard the saying, "No man is an island"? We all have support systems to help us. Most of us are part of one or more support systems that help others.

Stop and Reflect 6-8

Various types of support are listed below. Read over each type, thinking carefully about the sources you have for each. Sources can include: your family, friends, or people you know through your work or your participation in organizations, community services, or agencies.

Type of Support	Source(s)
Admiration Who praises me, gives attention to me, or shows an interest in me?	
Satisfaction Who expresses pleasure at what I give to or do for them?	
Love Who cares for me, gives me affection?	
Physical intimacy	
Companionship With whom do I share activities or have a sense of belonging or togetherness?	
Encouragement Who gives me emotional support, reinforcement, expresses confidence in me?	
Acceptance Who gives me respect, has empathy for me, trusts me, understands me, is a good listener for me?	
Comfort Who reassures me, is someone I can rely upon?	
Example Who is my role model or mentor?	
Guidance Who gives me advice, direction, or spiritual help?	
Help Who gives me material assistance, does things for me?	
Knowledge Who shares their expertise with me, gives me information, or teaches me things?	
Honesty Upon whom can I rely for honest feedback, to be a sounding board for my thoughts?	

Take a look at your answers. Who does your support system include? Does one person provide more support to you than the others? You likely listed family and friends in your support system. You may have listed some people many times and other people only once. If you compare your answers to those of your colleagues, you will probably find that their support systems are different from yours.

Each of your clients has a unique support system. Like yours, it may be made up of a combination of family members, friends, and others. Who provides each type of support may differ, as may the total number of people involved in the system.

We often think of the client's family as the client's support system. While family members commonly make up an individual client's support system, there may be other people to whom the client is close and who provide support. Some clients have no living family or no family who live nearby. Their support systems may be made up of friends or neighbours. You must remember that one client may be just as close to a friend or neighbour as another client may be to a spouse or child.

CASE EXAMPLE 6-1

Mrs. Anderson is an 80-year-old widow and retired farmer. Since 1960, she has lived on a farm outside Regina. She has two daughters, both of whom live in Ontario. Mrs. Anderson has four very close friends who live in her community.

Mrs. Anderson's support system is made up of her family, her friends, and other people from her community. For example, she relies upon her friends for social support and emotional support. However, when Mrs. Anderson was approached to sell her farm, she sought the advice of her daughters.

When Mrs. Anderson broke her arm last year, her friends brought meals and helped with her housekeeping. A member of Mrs. Anderson's church cut her lawn. Her daughters were not able to visit, but kept in contact in order to provide emotional support.

Mrs. Anderson provides support to her friends and family. She provided advice when her grandson was thinking of buying a farm. Now that her broken arm has mended, she volunteers to bring meals to members of her church who cannot cook for themselves.

Who makes up Mrs. Anderson's support system? What kinds of help does each member provide? Did you notice that Mrs. Anderson is part of other support systems?

 Stop and Reflect 6-9

Who do you support? Pick three people (other than clients) to whom you provide some kind of support. Then, complete the table below.

	Person #1	Person #2	Person #3
I provide this kind of support			

	Person #1	Person #2	Person #3
My relationship to the person			
How emotionally close to this person am I?			
How geographically close to this person am I?			

What did you learn about the support you provide? Do you always have to live near the person to be emotionally close to them? Are you related to all three people you listed? Are you closer to some friends than to some relatives? Do you provide support to people who also provide support to you?

Working with a Client's Support System

The support team we discussed in Chapter 5 usually becomes part of the client's overall support system. It's important to remember that the support team does not replace the client's support system. It simply makes the system a bit larger and adds more resources to assist the client. Consider the following situation.

CASE EXAMPLE 6-2

Mr. Bowen is 95 years old. He is a widower who lives in the town in which he grew up. He has four children and 12 grandchildren, all of whom live in the same town.

Mr. Bowen has arthritis, which makes it difficult for him to do many routine activities. Over the years, his family has taken on more responsibility for preparing meals and making sure Mr. Bowen's home is clean and in good repair.

Last month, Mr. Bowen fell on his way to the bathroom in the middle of the night. He was not able to get up and lay on the floor until his youngest daughter happened to drop by the next morning. As a result, Mr. Bowen became afraid to stay alone. After speaking with his children, he sold his home and moved into a retirement home.

When he first moved to the home, the retirement home's support team met with Mr. Bowen and members of his support system to determine what support each person would now provide. In this way, Mr. Bowen receives support from the most appropriate person.

Now, many of Mr. Bowen's needs (such as meals, some laundry, and some opportunities for social activities) are met by the retirement home's support team. Mr. Bowen's family continues to provide affection and many other types of emotional support. Mr. Bowen's eldest daughter washes Mr. Bowen's clothes at her home, just as she did when he lived in his own home. Mr. Bowen regularly has dinner at one of his children's homes, although he no longer needs a family member to bring meals to him.

Each client's support system has a unique way of working. This pattern is usually established over a number of years. It may be handed down from generation to generation. For example, some support systems are traditionally led by the eldest male of the family. Others are led by the eldest female. The members of one system may discuss things openly. The members of another support system may not.

Remember, your client's support system may not work the way your own support system works. You must always respect the way the client's system works, even if it is not the way you would like it. Because the client's support system becomes part of the overall support team, it is important to find a way of working together that allows everyone to provide the best support possible to the client.

CASE EXAMPLE 6-3

Mrs. Ball uses home support services. Susan is her support worker. Susan comes from a family where members openly stated their opinions and ideas.

Susan's client is very different. Mrs. Ball has always been uncomfortable stating her own opinions and ideas. She has always relied upon her eldest daughter to speak for her.

When Susan was first assigned to Mrs. Ball, Susan found it difficult to adapt to Mrs. Ball's way of communicating her preferences. She felt a bit hurt that Mrs. Ball was not comfortable enough with her to speak openly.

Susan mentioned her concern to Mrs. Ball's daughter. Mrs. Ball's daughter explained to Susan that Mrs. Ball has always communicated in this way. Susan then recognized that she must adapt to Mrs. Ball's communication style, even though it is not the way Susan would communicate.

Applying What You've Learned About Yourself to Your Work with Clients

In many ways, your client is affected by the same types of things that affect you. Each person will respond differently to the same situation. Take a moment to complete Stop and Reflect 6-10.

 Stop and Reflect 6-10

Talk to a person whom you know well who is at least 20 years older than you are.

1. Are there events (such as wars, deaths, successful careers) in the person's life that have shaped them? If so, how?

_____

_____

_____

2. Were there events in the person's personal life that were unusual (such as the loss of parent at an early age, an early or late marriage, or the loss of a child)? How did these shape the person?

_____

_____

_____

3. What sorts of roles has the person had over time? What roles have been most satisfying to the person? What meaning did the person attach to changes in roles? What roles do they see themselves as having now?

_____

_____

_____

4. How does the person describe him or herself?

_____

_____

_____

5. What sorts of things make up the client's personal culture? How has that culture shaped the person?

_____

_____

_____

6. If the person had the opportunity, would they be 18 years old again? Why would they want or not want to do so?

_____

_____

_____

Pay attention to your responses to the person's comments. How do the person's comments change your perception of him or her?

Questions for Review

1. How would you describe yourself in terms of the five aspects of the person discussed in the chapter?

2. Review the *Hierarchy of Needs*. What needs are most important to you? How do you meet these needs?

3. Speak with a colleague. What roles give him or her satisfaction in life? What makes these roles so satisfying?

Questions for Discussion

1. How would you define yourself in terms of your culture? Compare your responses with those of your colleagues. Look for similarities and differences in your responses. Are you and your colleagues more or less alike than you thought?

2. Most families have traditions around major life events. What are the traditions that your family has when a family member gets married? Compare your traditions with those of your colleagues. In what ways are your traditions similar? In what ways are they different?

3. Read over the following case study. Respond to the questions at the end.

Sarah Wieldon is a new client. She is 39 years of age. She was seriously injured in a car accident three months ago that killed her husband and injured her two children. Mrs. Wieldon has just returned home from a rehabilitation hospital. Her leg is in a cast and has several pins holding it secure. She can move around the house in a wheelchair, but cannot get up and down the stairs. As a result, her bedroom has been moved to the first floor. Mrs. Wieldon's children are being cared for by her husband's parents. The children have largely recovered from their injuries, but are still dealing with the loss of their father.

Mrs. Wieldon is currently on leave from her job as a bank manager. You are aware that she was well-respected in her job and that she took pride in getting things done for her customers. She is a detail person, always the one who makes sure that all loose ends are tied up and that everything required is done perfectly. She has been active in her children's school and in a recreation local committee. You are also aware that she has had to stop all activities in order to recover.

Mrs. Wieldon has a devoted family (one sister and one brother) in addition to her husband's parents. She also has a small circle of close friends, many of whom have offered help.

You, along with four other support workers, have been assigned to provide 24-hour support for Mrs. Wieldon. You know that she wants to recover as quickly as possible, so that her children may return home. She has also stated that she is anxious to get back to work.

What do you think Mrs. Wieldon's needs are at this time? Upon whom might she rely to help her meet these needs? What needs might she rely upon you to meet?

CHAPTER SEVEN

The Client-Worker Relationship

Learning Objectives

Through reading this chapter, you'll be able to:

1. Explain what the importance of the client-worker relationship.
2. List five fundamental abilities that characterize a positive personal relationship.
3. Portray interdependence as it applies to you and to your work with clients.
4. Identify the three stages of a client-worker relationship.
5. Outline the rights that clients enjoy.
6. Outline the rights that support workers enjoy.

Chapter At A Glance

The Client-Worker Relationship

Fundamentals of Positive Relationships

The Power Balance

Interdependence and the Client-Worker Relationship

The Three Stages of the Client-Worker Relationship

Client and Worker Rights

Terms You'll Use

Communication   The ability to share your ideas, explore others' ideas, and resolve conflicts. The aim of communication is to understand and to be understood.

Empathy   The ability to sense what others are feeling while respecting that you will never fully understand their emotions.

Flexibility   The ability to adapt to changes in a relationship, setting, or situation.

Independence   The ability to do things for oneself.

Interdependence   The reliance we all have on others to help us do things.

Mutuality   The ability to see how both people in a relationship benefit from it.

Respect   The ability to recognize and accommodate others' thoughts, opinions, behaviour, needs, preferences, and decisions.

Right   Something we have the authority to do.

The Client-Worker Relationship

> *The quality of our human existence is grounded in our relationships.*
> – John Powell, *The Secret of Staying in Love.*

A relationship can be described as the feelings which exist between two people. It is made up of a series of expectations, ways of doing things (behaviours), psychological and emotional distance. Your personality and the other person's personality will also help determine the quality of the relationship you have with each other.

Relationships—even brand-new ones—give meaning to our lives. Consider the following situation.

 Stop and Reflect 7-1

You are shopping with your best friend. You enter a store that boasts about its wonderful selection, reasonable prices, and good service. The store is clean, well organized, and attractive.

After some time, you select an outfit and take it to the sales counter. As the clerk starts to ring up your purchase, you ask her if the store carries luggage. The clerk looks at you, rolls her eyes, and says to you, "What do I look like, the answer lady?"

How do you feel about the store? What has influenced your feelings?

_____

_____

_____

_____

It's likely that your feelings about the store were most influenced by the exchange you had with the clerk, not how clean or attractive the store appeared, or even the attractive prices. Our need to communicate and to make connections with other people leads us to place importance on human interactions.

Each Relationship Is Unique

Each relationship is the product of the two people who are involved in it. As a result, each relationship is unique. Relationships can be close or distant, good or bad, healthy or unhealthy. It is even possible for each person in the same relationship to have a somewhat different view of it.

A relationship requires some commitment from both people involved. Sometimes this commitment is voluntary, such as when you want to make friends with someone.

The relationship exists as long as the two parties want it to or as long as they are brought together by circumstances, whether or not the people are in daily contact.

Relationships can be personal or professional. Occasionally, some relationships start out as one type and become another. This can pose problems for both people involved, as the personal relationship may make harder what you need to do in the professional relationship. The nature of the work you do will often cause you to work with clients over a long period of time. You and your client will likely get to know each other well, making this personal-professional distinction hard to define. Consider the following client-viewpoint.

CASE EXAMPLE 7-1

When asked, a consumer of attendant services defined the relationship she has with her support staff (attendants) in this way.

The relationship between me and my attendants is almost impossible to define. It isn't a parent-child relationship, as we need each other. I need services and my attendants need work meaningful to them. It's more of an adult-adult relationship. The relation- *ship is sometimes that of employer and employee but at other times, perhaps surprisingly, the relationship is one of friendship. I don't want someone who adopts a paternal stance toward me, or assumes I am "sick" rather than a well person with a disabling condition. My attendants and I must be able to 'get along' on a personal level for the overall relationship to work.*

Fundamentals of Positive Relationships

Stop and Reflect 7-2

Think about a really positive working relationship you have with another person. Perhaps this relationship is between you and a coworker. It might be between you and a supervisor or between you and a client.

What makes the relationship such a positive one for you?

_____

_____

_____

_____

Would the other person involved see this as a positive relationship? If so, what makes it that way?

_____

_____

_____

_____

What makes your relationship so positive? It's likely that you listed such things as: *we like the same things, we see things the same way, I can really talk to her,* or *I can count on her.*

Five abilities are fundamental to your ability to form and maintain a positive relationship with another person: communication, respect, mutuality, flexibility, and empathy. We'll discuss each in this section. These abilities are necessary for *any* positive relationship, not just one you would have with your client.

Communication is essential to sharing your ideas and exploring the other person's ideas, as well as to resolving any conflicts which might arise. In Chapter 8 we will discuss communication skills further.

Respect means several things: recognizing and accommodating a person's opinions, patterns of behaviour, and preferences. It includes respecting the other person's needs and behaving in a way that does not intentionally hurt the other person.

Respect also means that you respect the person's *boundaries,* the limits we all set on the information we share and the things we will do. Boundaries change with each relationship. For example, your client might not wish you to know very much about his or her relationship with a family member, even though the client may freely share this information with another person.

Mutuality is the ability to see how you both benefit from the relationship. Despite the fact that your client benefits from the support you provide, it's quite likely that you also benefit from the relationship. Give some thought to the following questions.

Stop and Reflect 7-3

Think of a situation where you have provided support or assisted another person. This can be a work situation, a volunteer situation, or any other where the reason for the relationship was your helping the other person.

How did you benefit from this relationship? For example, did you learn from the other person or attain a sense of satisfaction?

_____

_____

_____

_____

Flexibility includes the ability to adapt to changes in a relationship. Most of us have good days and bad days. We may be tired one day and energetic the next. Clients are no different. As you'll learn in the next section, relationships change over time. You must be flexible in your approach in order to appropriately respond to your client.

Empathy is the ability to sense of what the other person is feeling, while respecting that you will never fully *understand* the person's emotions. Empathy includes respect for the person's boundaries as to what they will share with you. It also includes the person's right to have feelings to which you cannot relate, or with which you do not agree.

The Power Balance

In every relationship, there is a sense of equity (an equal balance of power) or of an imbalance in the power one person has relative to another. Consider the following situation.

Stop and Reflect 7-4

Recall a time that you needed help from another person for help with everyday activities. (For example, when you were recovering from surgery, or recovering from a broken leg or arm.) If you cannot recall such a time, try to imagine yourself in one of these situations.

How did you feel when you had to rely upon this person?

_____

_____

_____

_____

Did you find that your feelings affected how you related to this person?

_____

_____

_____

_____

Did you feel as though you were dependent upon the person? Even if you had a good relationship with the person who helped you, you may have felt that you were not quite equals.

The balance of power is affected by the degree of *interdependence* between the parties involved.

Interdependence and the Client-Worker Relationship

As you read in Chapter 6, **interdependence** can be defined as the reliance we all have on other people for some things. You will often hear colleagues talk about **independence** (the ability to do things for oneself). Remember that no one is completely independent. The ability to do certain things for oneself is a goal for many clients. However, many clients have a preferred mix of activities they would prefer to do independently and activities with which they would prefer help. Consider the following situation.

CASE EXAMPLE 7-2

Erin Young is 35 years old and a senior manager in an insurance company. Five years ago, Erin was diagnosed with multiple sclerosis and has lost strength in her arms. As a result, she finds that her ability to do certain tasks (such as those that require her to open and close jars or to grip items firmly) is diminished. Additionally, her energy level has diminished to the extent that performing many routine activities, such as making a meal, leaves her exhausted.

For the past eight months, Erin has received frozen Meals on Wheels. Seven meals are dropped off at Erin's home each Monday night. Erin takes one to work with her each day, heating it in the staffroom of her office.

Erin's use of the frozen meals means that she is able to save her energy for more important things in her life. If she had to make meals each day, she would not have the energy to bathe, dress, and get herself to work. If she were to use 'fast foods', she would not be able to eat the balanced diet she needs.

Ironically, by being more physically independent by making her own meals at home, Erin might, in fact, become financially dependent through the loss of her ability to work because of the resultant exhaustion.

Can you understand why Erin has made the choices she has? Like all of us, she has made decisions as to when she will rely upon others and when she will do things for herself. This is much the same as a decision you might make to hire someone to paint a room for you or to mow your lawn. It is not to say that you cannot do those tasks, you may be perfectly able to do them. You simply have chosen to do other things.

Some caregivers find it difficult to accept a client's decisions as to what tasks they prefer to rely upon others to do particularly when the caregiver feels that the client *could* do the task. Did you find yourself thinking about Erin, "*She could make herself meals if she wanted to*"? If so, you can understand the caregiver's view. Many of us are raised to believe that a person must be as independent as possible. This can make it difficult for us to understand a person's decision not to do something of which he or she is capable. We all make these choices and you must respect your client's right to do so (Photo 7-1).

Photo 7-1
Mutual respect is essential to good client-worker relationship.
Source: CHATS.

The Three Stages of the Client-Worker Relationship

Your relationship with the client can be described in three phases: the introductory phase, the productive phase, and the parting phase. Each phase is described in this section.

The introductory phase.   This is the phase during which you and your client get to know each other. Your tasks in this phase include identifying your client's preferences as to what needs to be done, how it will be done, learning your client's ways of communicating, problem-solving, and learning what the nature of the client-worker relationship will be. It is natural for both you and your client to be a bit anxious during this phase.

The productive phase.   This is the phase during which you and your client should feel comfortable. You appreciate each other's preferences and habits and you have worked out ways to resolve any conflicts which arise. Your working relationship is a good one and there is enough consistency in the routine that it is predictable without becoming tiresome. Your tasks in this phase include making sure that you remain responsive to your client's preferences and needs, even if the routine does not change for a long period of time.

The parting phase.   This is the phase in which you wind down your relationship, usually because you will no longer be visiting the client. The task here is to acknowledge the change and to recognize that you both have benefited from the relationship. It is not unusual for both you and your client to feel a sense of loss when you are leaving a relationship.

Client and Worker Rights

We can define a **right** as something that we have the authority to do. People speak about rights in many ways, such as legal rights, moral rights, and human rights. Sometimes, a person has certain rights because he or she is in a particular situation. For example, a person has certain rights as a worker, as a client of an agency, or as the purchaser of some property.

Legislated Rights

Many rights are legislated or regulated, that is, they are written into law or into the regulations that governments establish to implement the law. Sometimes, the rights are combined together into a *bill of rights*. Other times, the rights are simply stated in the law. These rights do not usually change quickly.

Rights Established by Associations and Agencies

Some rights are established by voluntary associations, such as a long-term care associations. These rights do not have the force of law, but the association that establishes them usually requires its members to agree to respect them as a requirement of membership.

Some rights, like those accorded to someone who uses the services of a particular agency, are determined by the agency and may be changed whenever the agency decides to do so, provided that they do not conflict with any rights also guaranteed by legislation or other means.

Client Rights

Most provinces have several types of legislation that provide for client rights: a human rights code, long-term care services acts, and acts that protect the confidentiality of client records. Some provinces provide for client rights in landlord and tenant legislation (if the client lives in a retirement home). Each province has different titles for these pieces of legislation. Table 7-1 highlights the rights that each type of legislation typically includes. Table 7-2 describes Ontario's long-term care facility residents' *Bill of Rights*.

TABLE 7-1	Typical Client Rights
Legislation Type	**Rights**
Human Rights Code	Prohibits discrimination on the basis of: race, ancestry, place of origin, colour, ethnic origin, citizenship, creed, sex, sexual orientation, disability, age, marital status, family status, record of offences.
Long-Term Care Act	Provides a *Bill of Rights* for persons receiving long-term care services in the community and in a facility. Some provinces use separate legislation to guarantee rights in each setting.
Health Records or Privacy Act	Usually protects patient health information. Provides guidelines as to how it can be accessed by clients as well as shared among providers.
Guardianship, Power of of Attorney Act	Usually allows you to appoint someone to look after your affairs. Different provinces may have very different provisions with regard to people's rights under this legislation.

The client does not lose rights simply because he or she is a client. For example, the client is still protected by tenant legislation (if the client is a tenant) or by consumer legislation (if the client enters into a purchase contract).

TABLE 7-2	Ontario's Long-Term Care Facility Residents' Bill of Rights

Residents' Bill of Rights

Every licensee shall ensure that the following rights of residents are fully respected and promoted:

1. Every resident has the right to be treated with courtesy and respect and in a way that fully recognizes the resident's dignity and individuality and to be free from mental and physical abuse.

2. Every resident has the right to be properly sheltered, fed, clothed, groomed, and cared for in a manner consistent with his or her needs.

3. Every resident has the right to be told who is responsible for and who is providing the resident's direct care.

4. Every resident has the right to be afforded privacy in treatment and in caring for his or her personal needs.

5. Every resident has the right to keep in his or her room and display personal possessions, pictures and furnishings in keeping with safety requirements and other residents' rights.

6. Every resident has the right,
   1. to be informed of his or her medical condition, treatment, and proposed course of treatment,
   2. to give or refuse consent to treatment, including medication, in accordance with the law and to be informed of the consequences of giving or refusing consent,
   3. to have the opportunity to participate fully in making any decision and obtaining an independent medical opinion concerning any aspect of his or her care, including any decision concerning his or her admission, discharge, or transfer to or from a nursing home, and
   4. to have his or her medical records kept confidential in accordance with the law.

7. Every resident has the right to receive reactivation and assistance towards independence consistent with his or her requirements.

8. Every resident who is being considered for restraints has the right to be fully informed about the procedures and the consequences of receiving or refusing them.

9. Every resident has the right to communicate in confidence, to receive visitors of his or her choice, and to consult in private with any person without interference.

10. Every resident whose death is likely to be imminent has the right to have members of the resident's family present twenty-four hours per day.

TABLE 7-2	Ontario's Long-Term Care Facility Residents' Bill of Rights *(continued)*

11. Every resident has the right to designate a person to receive information concerning any transfer or emergency hospitalization of the resident and where a person is so designated to have that person so informed forthwith.

12. Every resident has the right to exercise the rights of a citizen and to raise concerns or recommend changes in policies and services on behalf of himself or herself or others to the residents' council, nursing home staff, government officials, or any other person inside or outside the nursing home, without fear of restraint, interference, coercion, discrimination, or reprisal.

13. Every resident has the right to form friendships, to enjoy relationships, and to participate in the residents' council.

14. Every resident has the right to meet privately with his or her spouse in a room that assures privacy and, where both spouses are residents in the same nursing home, they have a right to share a room according to their wishes, if an appropriate room is available.

15. Every resident has a right to pursue social, cultural, religious, and other interests, to develop his or her potential, and to be given reasonable provisions by the nursing home to accommodate these pursuits.

16. Every resident has the right to be informed in writing of any law, rule, or policy affecting the operation of the nursing home and of the procedures for initiating complaints.

17. Every resident has the right to manage his or her own financial affairs where the resident is able to do so and, where the resident's financial affairs are managed by the nursing home, to receive a quarterly accounting of any transactions undertaken on his or her behalf, and to be assured that the resident's property is managed solely on the resident's behalf.

18. Every resident has the right to live in a safe and clean environment.

19. Every resident has the right to be given access to protected areas outside the nursing home in order to enjoy outdoor activity, unless the physical setting makes this impossible. R.S.O. 1990, c. N.7, s. 2 (2).

Worker Rights

Each province has legislation that protects workers. Most provinces have legislation that sets out responsibilities for workers in certain settings. Each province has a different name for this legislation. However, each province guides the work of support workers through six common types of legislation: human rights legislation, workplace safety legislation, employment legislation, labour relations legislation, and legislation specific to long-term care services and client records. Additionally, Ontario has established the *Regulated Health Professions Act*, legislation which indirectly affects a support worker's scope of practice.

Unlike legislation which provides for client rights, legislation which affects the worker includes legislation that provides for worker rights *and* legislation which makes specific requirements of the worker (such as to practise in a certain way or to report certain types of events). Table 7-3 highlights common rights and obligations found in various types of legislation.

TABLE 7-3	Common Rights and Obligations
Legislation	**Usually Includes**
Employment Standards Act	Basic rules about worker entitlement (minimum wage, vacation pay, public holidays, hours of work, etc.)
Labour Relations Act	Right to form and/or join a union, take part in lawful union activities, allow your union to negotiate wages and other working conditions with your employer on your behalf, to strike (and the employer's right to lockout), and identify the criteria for unfair labour practices.
Workplace Safety Act	Issues of workplace injury and compensation, worker and employer rights when an injury occurs.
Human Rights Code	Prohibits discrimination on the basis of: race, ancestry, place of origin, colour, ethnic origin, citizenship, creed, sex, sexual orientation, disability, age, marital status, family status, record of offences. There are limitations to the extent of prohibition in many cases.
Community Long-Term Care Act	What services are covered, a definition of personal support services, how services through are to be provided, what records to be kept. Sometimes includes criteria for providers.
Long-Term Care Facilities Act	Sets out requirements for the operation of long-term care facilities. Includes regulations specifying records to be kept, documentation, the level of training required to administer medications, etc.
Health Records or Privacy Act	Rights and rules about access, disclosure, and retention of client health records (including community support agency records).

Questions for Review

1. Why is the client-worker relationship important?

2. Select a positive personal relationship you have now or have had. How did that relationship reflect the five fundamental abilities discussed in this chapter?

3. What legislation protects clients in your province? What branch of the government administers this legislation?

4. What legislation protects workers in your province? What branch of the government administers this legislation?

Questions for Discussion

1. Select a *professional* relationship you currently have. This could be a relationship between you and a client, or a relationship between you and another person. How does the concept of interdependence apply to this relationship? How many examples of interdependence can you define?

2. Read the following case study and then discuss the questions that follow.

   You work with Mrs. Brown, a 55-year-old client who has lung cancer. She has been receiving chemotherapy that has eased her symptoms. She is aware that the treatment will not cure the cancer, but that it will reduce the effects of the disease and prolong her life. Mrs. Brown is a lifelong smoker. She has continued to smoke, despite the link between cigarette smoking and lung cancer. You have grown fond of Mrs. Brown and worry that her continued smoking will offset the benefits of the chemotherapy.

   How do you feel about this situation. What are Mrs. Brown's rights in this situation? How might you demonstrate respect for Mrs. Brown's rights?

3. Assume that you and three or four of your colleagues are in the following situation. Discuss the questions at the end of the situation.

   You and your colleagues are residents of a long-term care facility. You have been asked to develop a resident's bill of rights. Instead of using the bill of rights presented earlier in this chapter, you want to write your own. What rights do you think you—and the other residents—should have? List at least ten rights.

PART THREE

FUNDAMENTAL SKILLS

Source: CHATS.

CHAPTER EIGHT

Basic Communication Skills

Learning Objectives

Through reading this chapter, you'll be able to:

1. Describe how we communicate.
2. Tell why good communication skills are important in support work.
3. Explain what good communication is.
4. Express the three principles of communication.
5. List the two common types of communication.
6. Tell what the process of communication is.
7. Outline common barriers to communication with clients and, for each, list one thing a support worker can do to try to overcome the barrier.
8. Use the ten principles of client teaching to assist a client to learn and practise a new skill or relearn an old one.

Chapter At A Glance

What Is Communication?

Communication and Support Work

What Is Good Communication?

The Process of Communication

Filters and Barriers

Culture and Communication

Understanding and Being Understood

Client Teaching

Adult Learning   Changes in behaviour that result from new information.

Barriers   Things that prevent the message from getting across when communicating, such as language or hearing impairment.

Body Language   Communication through posture, facial expressions, and movements. This is often called non-verbal communication.

Client Teaching   The instruction given to a client by a support worker.

Content   Information communicated through words.

Feelings   Emotions communicated through words and body language.

Filters   Things that affect how we communicate including body language, mood, and stress.

What Is Communication?

Communication is depositing part of yourself in another person.
– Anonymous

Communication is essential to our everyday life. Researchers have linked communication to physical well-being, to our ability to define who we are, and to our ability to form relationships. We also must communicate in order to make our needs known.

Despite the time we spend doing it, we generally spend very little time thinking about communication and how we communicate. We often take it for granted—until something goes wrong!

Stop and Reflect 8-1

Try this test. When you are with a group of friends or family, try *not* to communicate for five minutes. Pay particular attention to what happens when you do this.

How easy was it to not communicate? Did you find that you were tempted to talk? Did you try to use gestures and facial expressions to communicate your needs?

_____

_____

_____

_____

▶▶

How did the people you were with react to you? Did they attempt to communicate with you? If they did, how did they try to communicate?

_____

_____

_____

_____

Did the other people *think* you were communicating? If so, what message did they think you were sending?

_____

_____

_____

You probably found it very difficult to do this exercise. Even if you did not try to communicate, chances are that you did. You likely *received* communication from the others (perhaps through their reactions and their comments). It's also likely that the other people felt that you *sent* a message. In this exercise, you have proved several principles. This section discusses three principles of communication.

You cannot *not* communicate. Your "**body language**", your posture, facial expressions, and movements all send messages, even if you don't say a word. Recall the way the other people reacted to your attempt to not communicate. They likely thought you were communicating some message.

You communicate, whether or not you mean to communicate. When you tried the exercise at the beginning of this chapter, did you find that the other people around you thought you were sending a message, even though you were attempting not to communicate? We often communicate without meaning to, through how we look. Some of us are better at filtering our body language. For example, you may know someone who is said to have a "poker face", because it's hard to read their emotions from their body language. Nonetheless, everyone communicates.

You cannot undo communication. You've probably watched a television show where a jury was listening to testimony. A witness says something to which the defendant's lawyer objects. The judge tells the jury to "disregard the witness' statement". Do you think that the jury really could pretend as though they never heard the statement? Probably not.

Communication and Support Work

As a support worker, you will constantly communicate with clients. How you communicate can make the difference between a positive experience for you both, or one that you both dread. Many clients will have difficulty communicating and you will have to adapt your methods to make the communication as positive as possible.

What Is Good Communication?

Stop and Reflect 8-2

If you had to tell someone what 'good' communication is, what would you say?

_____

_____

_____

_____

Good communication can be described as "understanding and being understood". If your definition is close to this, you have the right idea.

You may have described communication as involving listening and asking questions. If you did, you've included some of what we can call the *process* of communication. These are the techniques that help us to understand and be understood. The more we know about the process and the techniques, the better able we are to make sure that good communication takes place—or to figure out what went wrong when it doesn't.

The Process of Communication

The process of communication is presented in Figure 8-1. It involves a *sender* and a *receiver*. In most communication, each person is alternately a sender and a receiver, depending upon whether or not the person is giving or getting a message.

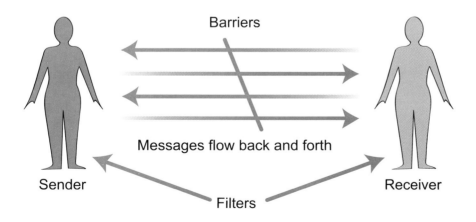

Figure 8-1 *The Process of Communication*

Getting the Message

Messages generally come in two parts: *feelings* and *content*. **Feelings** are emotions communicated through words and **content** is factual information communicated through words. Not all messages have both: some messages have content only. For example, giving someone directions to the mall might not involve much feeling, but the message contains a lot of content. Table 8-1 describes some characteristics of feelings and content.

TABLE 8-1	Characteristics of Feelings and Content
Feelings	**Content**
▪ Expressed in both words and body language	▪ Usually expressed in words
▪ Are neither good nor bad	▪ Often are based in facts, describing events, desires, issues, acts, etc.
▪ Can conflict with one another (e.g., be happy and sad at the same time)	▪ Can conflict with other parts of the message
▪ Always make sense to the person	▪ Always make sense to the person
▪ Denial will not make them go away	▪ Denial will not make them go away

Filters and Barriers

If all we had to do is speak and hear in order to have good communication it would be easy. Alas, there are many things which can affect the transmission of the message.

Filters

Filters affect how we say or hear things. They may even make us not say or hear things. Filters include the following:

Body Language
Past Experiences with the Person or Situation
Whether or Not the Person Is in a Position of Authority
Attitudes and Stereotypes
Mood, Personality
Words, Tone of the Other Person
Stress, Physical Health

Nonverbal Behaviour (Body Language)

It's important to remember that we get a great deal of information from another's *nonverbal* behaviour (body language). Some studies suggest that most of the message we get comes from the nonverbal communication. Likewise, *our* body language tells others a great deal about us. Many of the filters listed above will show up in your body language. Some people naturally show more body language than others.

Body language includes a number of things: facial expression, how we sit or stand, the gestures we use, how we move about, whether we sigh or yawn, as well as the tone and pace of any words we use.

It's sometimes difficult to describe these things. You might have been tempted to say that the person "looks angry". That's what you asked them to do! But, what is it about how the other person looks that makes you say that they look angry? The physical appearance is what conveys the feeling.

Stop and Reflect 8-3

Try this exercise with a friend or colleague. Ask the other person to pretend that they are mad at you for some reason. Look at their nonverbal behaviour and answer the following questions.

How does the person's face (eyes, mouth, brow) look?

_____

How does the person stand or sit?

_____

Where does the person put his or her hands?

_____

Does the person cross his or her arms?

_____

Does the person clench his or her fists?

_____

If the person spoke to you, how did they sound?

_____

Did the person speak rapidly or slowly?

_____

What tone of voice did the person use?

_____

Stop and Reflect 8-4

Take a look at the following situations. Describe how you would show your feelings in each situation. Be sure to describe how you would look. For example, what would your face look like? What would your posture be?

Situation	How you'd **show** it
You're taking a walk with someone. You're walking in an area in which you feel uncomfortable. You're becoming frightened.	
You've planned an evening out with a friend who is visiting your city. Your husband was supposed to look after your three children. He comes home three hours late, saying that he forgot. You are angry that you have had to cancel your plans.	
You've just started visiting a new client. She is a bit forgetful and, although you've been taught how to respond, you haven't practised very much. You really don't feel too sure of yourself or your skills.	
You are going out with a good friend. She wants to do something that you really don't want to do. You don't want to hurt her feelings, but you really don't want to do what she wants.	

Share your responses with your colleagues. Would you all show the same feelings in the same way? Were there feelings you showed differently? Which ones?

It's just as important to learn to read the other person's body language (Photo 8-1). Along with their tone of voice, it can tell you much about the other person's message, and possibly about how your message might be filtered. Keep in mind that this is a two-way street—your body language and tone of voice will tell the other person about you. If your body language does not match your words, you'll likely confuse the other person.

Photo 8-1
Who would you rather see?

Source: Leisureworld Preferred Institute.

How we see the person can also affect not only what we say and how we say it, but how we interpret the message that person sends to us. Our attitude toward another person, whether or not we've had any past experiences with them, can affect the current communication. For example, we often speak and listen differently to children than we do adults or to a coworker differently than a supervisor. Likewise, if we've shared good experiences when we last spoke with that person, we are more likely to see the current communication as positive.

Appearance also affects how we interpret the other person's message. Looking too old or too young, too dressed up or too casually dressed, unclean or unshaven, can greatly affect the way communication happens. In Chapter 4, we discussed the need for a professional appearance. Dressing appropriately and professionally will affect how others see you and your role.

Culture directly affects how we interpret other people's messages. For example, people of British descent place great value on making eye contact when communicating. You might ask someone to look you in the eye when they are speaking to you or you may refer to "seeing eye to eye" with another person. People from other cultures may see direct eye contact as offensive or disrespectful. You must always make sure to appreciate how other people's culture affects their interpretation of messages.

Finally, our mood and whether or not we're stressed or not feeling well can affect how we give a message and how we interpret what we hear. If you've spoken sharply to someone because you weren't feeling well, you know what this can be like.

Because filters can dramatically alter the message you send and receive, pay particular attention to them. You should examine your responses to filters to make sure that you are not making communication more difficult.

Barriers

Barriers are things that actually prevent the message from getting to the other person. Many barriers have to do with the environment, but some have to do with the receiver.

Stop and Reflect 8-5

What things do you think might be barriers to communication? List your ideas below.

_____

_____

_____

_____

_____

_____

_____

A number of things can become barriers, including the following:

- Sensory Loss
- Environmental Causes
- Background noise
- Distractions
- Environment too hot or cold
- Offensive smells
- Furniture or decor
- No Common Language
- Nonverbal Communication that Is Misinterpreted or Not Understood
- Jargon
- Poorly Worded or Disorganized Messages
- Interruptions
- Lack of Attention

Sensory Loss

Losses in vision, hearing, and touch affect a person's ability to communicate. Communication can't take place if the words and gestures can't be heard, seen, or felt. Additionally, because so much of communication is nonverbal, vision problems can directly affect the message a person gets. In Chapter 9, we will discuss some of ways you can adapt your communication to meet the needs of the person with changes in vision, hearing, or touch sensation.

Culture and Communication

Culture affects communication in many ways. People from different cultures may not use the same words to describe things. Gestures and other nonverbal communication may mean different things to people of different cultures. Common sayings (phrases) may not have the same meaning—or any meaning at all to a person from a different culture. Sometimes, the differences are funny. Have you ever heard a person from England talk about being "knocked up"? In England, this means to be awakened, while in Canada, it means to become pregnant.

Many times, the differences result in a misunderstanding or lack of communication. Differences in nonverbal communication can lead to a lack of trust between the sender and the receiver (Figure 8-2). As discussed earlier in this chapter, many people of British descent want a person to look at them when the person is speaking. However, many Canadians from other cultures feel that making eye contact with another person in this way is a sign of disrespect. Understanding each other is very difficult when one person needs to make eye contact and the other person does not.

Figure 8-2 *Cultural differences can have a significant effect on communication.*

Understanding and Being Understood

In most situations, good communication is reasonably automatic. We send and receive messages with little difficulty. Table 8-2 lists the qualities of messages. Yet, there are times when even the best communicator has problems understanding and being understood.

If any of the following are present, you need to be particularly careful to make sure that your message gets across.

- Barriers
- Filters that will hamper communication (yours or the other person's)
- A complex or difficult message
- An emotionally charged message

Asking yourself the following five questions will help make you more easily understood by others.

Is your message clear?   Are you saying what you want to say? Have you put your message in simple language? Are you using words you know that the other person will understand?

TABLE 8-2	Qualities of the Message
	Is Your Message...
✔	Clear?
✔	Complete?
✔	Congruent?
✔	Sent in the Right Climate?
✔	Caring?

Is your message complete? Have you left any gaps? Will the person have to "fill in any blanks"?

Is your message congruent? In this instance, congruent means that your body language matches your words. For example, if you're concerned, do you look concerned? If you're happy, do you look happy?

Is your message sent in the right climate? Have you picked the right setting to say what you have to say?

Is your message caring? Have you picked words that will not needlessly hurt the person? Even when you are upset with something that a person has done, you can let the person know without being mean to the person. Table 8-3 gives some examples of caring and uncaring communication.

TABLE 8-3	Which Would You Rather Hear?	
"You're so lazy."	or	"I'm angry because you didn't do the chores I asked you to do."
"Why can't you do anything right?"	or	"I'm upset about the mess that you left in the kitchen."
"Can't you see that I'm busy?"	or	"Could we talk about this later, after I finish this phone call?"

Client Teaching

What Is Learning?

Learning is a change in behaviour that results from new information. This information can be in the form of knowledge, such as knowing the signs of shock. It can also be in the form of skill, such as the ability to safely assist a client to transfer from a bed to a chair. Finally, it can be in the form of information that causes you to re-examine your attitudes, such as information that causes you to examine a stereotype.

We often think of learning as a formal process that occurs in school. In fact, we learn every day of our lives. Many things that we learn, we learn informally from other people, from things that we read, even from television.

Photo 8-2
Learning is a life-long activity. Here two day centre participants discuss the centre's "Thought for the Day".
Source: CHATS.

Adult Learning

Have you ever heard the statement, "I'm just too old to learn"? It's not true! We can and do learn well into our eighties and nineties. *How* we learn does change, though. As adults, we learn differently than we did when we were children. There are several major differences, as we'll see in this section.

Purpose in Learning   Adults generally want their learning to meet a need or to have a direct link to some benefit. There are three types of purposes: achievement, social, or self-fulfillment. Sometimes this purpose is *achievement*, to learn a task (such as to operate a new appliance). At other times, the purpose is self-fulfillment, by meeting a challenge one sets for oneself or overcoming a barrier (such as learning a new way of getting dressed), so that the client is no longer dependent on others. Sometimes, the need is social, such as when a client learns ways of communicating that allow him or her to connect with other people.

Learning Style   Adults are usually practical learners. We tend to learn best by doing the task being taught, or by applying information to "real world" case studies. We also tend to be social learners, learning best when we can discuss things and ask questions as well as when we have the support of others as we learn.

Learning Ability   In general, adults take longer to learn new things. Adults are also more susceptible to interference—things that distract us or make it harder for us to concentrate. For example, fatigue, anxiety, and illness can all make learning more difficult. Trying to take in too much information at one time can be overwhelming and make it harder for the client to learn.

We all have the opportunity to be teachers. Most of us have shown someone how to put together a child's toy. We often tell someone how to cook something. Many of us have taught a child how to tie a shoelace. When you teach someone, you probably find out that there are certain ways to teach things that make it easier for the person to learn.

Stop and Reflect 8-6

Recall a few people who have taught you something. They could have been formal teachers, or simply someone from whom you learned something.

What did they do than made it easier for you to learn?

_____

_____

_____

_____

How did they help you to learn?

_____

_____

_____

Was your "teacher" supportive? Did he or she give you time to practise? Did they find a way to make the information interesting and easy to learn? These approaches make the information easier to learn. They are often called *teaching strategies* or teaching techniques.

Strategies Useful in Client Teaching

The teaching that you do as a support worker is similar to the teaching you have done all your life. Some strategies are the same, such as providing support and encouragement. Others are different. In this section, we'll discuss the 10 strategies useful in **client teaching**, the instruction that you give to clients.

1. **Find out what the client is interested in learning.**   The client may be more interested in learning one task than another. Adults are more motivated to learn when the task interests them.

2. **Break the task into smaller activities.**   Even a simple task, such as making a cup of tea, actually has several steps. Take a moment to identify the activities that make up the task. Teach one activity at a time.

3. **Organize the information.**   Group information for the client to make it easier for him or her to remember. Use verbal clues, or help the client develop a mental image of the task. For example, you might remind a client that his or her water glasses (something that holds water) are in the cupboard nearest the sink (where the client would get water). Similarly, you might help a client who is relearning to grocery shop to organize the list by food type.

4. **Put the client at ease.**   Reassure the client. Try to have some fun.

5. **Let the client set his or her own pace.**   People learn at different rates. Some tasks will naturally be easier for the client to learn. Illness and fatigue will also affect the pace. Give the client time to rest when he or she needs to. Realize when it is best to leave the task for the day.

6. **Start at the easiest.**   How did you learn to ride a bicycle? You likely started with a tricycle, then moved to a two-wheeler bike with training wheels before attempting a 10-speed. Use the same approach with the client. Start with the easy steps. The client will more easily master the task. The satisfaction at completing the easy task builds a sense of accomplishment, making it psychologically easier to attempt the next more difficult task.

7. **Practise the "tell-show-do-review" model.**   1. Tell the client the steps of the task. 2. Show the client the steps. 3. Let the client attempt the task. 4. Review the client's success.

8. **Appreciate "almost right".**   Don't be unrealistic in your expectations. Encourage your client to be realistic in his or her expectations. Few of us perform a task perfectly the first time. Be sure to recognize the parts of the task done well, even when other parts need more work.

9. **Provide support and encouragement to the client.**   Learning takes time and effort.

10. **Let the client practise what he or she learns.**   Give the client ample opportunity to practise. This helps the client retain the information and gives you an opportunity to offer praise and encouragement.

Questions for Review

1. Recall a recent conversation where you felt that communication really went well. What made the communication so good?

2. Recall a time that communication went wrong. What happened? Looking back, what could you do to correct the process?

3. How would you attempt to communicate with a new client?

4. Recall a communication situation in which you felt that the other person was not saying what they really felt because the person's body language did not match the words the person used. Describe the body language and define why you felt that it did not match the words.

5. Look at each of these drawings. What does the person's body language tell you?

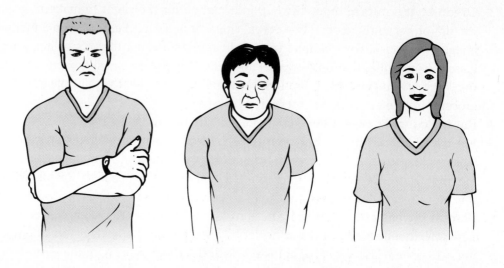

Questions for Discussion

1. What techniques can you use to improve communication with a client whose cultural background is not the same as yours? Share your ideas with your colleagues.

2. You are assigned to a new client. You know that this client had a worker she really liked, but that worker has moved and can no longer visit. You also know that this client takes a long time to "warm up" to anyone. She is Ukranian and has spoken Russian most of her life. She learned English in her sixties and still has some difficulty finding the words she wants to use. She is also a bit hard of hearing. When you first meet her, she says, "You look awfully young".

   What things filter your communication with her?

   What things do you think filter the client's communication?

   Are there any potential barriers you can identify? What are they?

3. Read the situation below. Then discuss the questions with your colleagues.

   You have been assigned to assist Mr. James. He is recovering from a stroke and you have been assigned to assist him as he relearns how to cook and do laundry. These are tasks that Mr. James only started to do six years ago when his wife died.

   What factors would you consider when you work with Mr. James? How might you help him to learn more easily?

CHAPTER NINE

Adaptive and Augmentative Communication

Learning Objectives

Through reading this chapter, you'll be able to:

1. Describe adaptive communication.
2. Define augmentative communication and list common communication aids.
3. Explain aphasia and 15 techniques you can use to assist the person with aphasia to communicate.
4. Define apraxia and dysarthria and identify two techniques you can use to assist a person with either condition to communicate.
5. Relate the communication barriers posed by sensory loss. For each type of sensory loss, identify three techniques you can use to help overcome the barrier.

Chapter At A Glance

What Is Adaptive Communication?

Augmentative Communication

Common Conditions Requiring Adaptive or Augmentative Techniques

Aphasia

Tips for Communicating with the Person with Aphasia

Dysarthria and Apraxia of Speech

Tips for Communicating with the Person with Dysarthria or Apraxia of Speech

Communication Aids for Language or Speech Production Conditions

Sensory Loss

Assisting the Person with Sensory Loss

Communication Aids to Compensate for Sensory Loss

Terms You'll Use

Adaptive Communication   A form of communicating in which a group of techniques is used to adapt communication to the specific needs of the sender or receiver.

Aphasia   The complete or partial loss of language skills because of an injury to the brain.

Apraxia   A condition that results from an injury to the brain, making voluntary, physical control of purposeful movement difficult.

Augmentative Communication   A form of communicating in which physical aids are used in communication.

Dysarthria   A condition that results from a weakness or lack of coordination in some of the muscles involved in speaking.

Presbyopia   A condition in which vision changes due to increasing age. Also called far-sightedness.

Sensory Loss   Changes in the senses that result in a loss of hearing, smell, touch, taste, and sight.

What Is Adaptive Communication?

Adaptive communication refers to the group of techniques to adapt communication to the specific needs of the sender or receiver. Most often, adaptive techniques are used to help people overcome a language problem (such as *aphasia*) or a *sensory loss* (such as hearing loss).

CASE EXAMPLE 9-1

Maggie James has hearing loss that resulted from an infection she had as a 50-year-old. Her type of hearing loss cannot be helped by a hearing aid. As a result, Maggie has learned to lip-read and has become quite good at picking up conversation. In fact, many people do not know she has a hearing problem and don't realize that she needs to see the person speak in order to "hear." Maggie then has to remind the person to face her directly.

As you can see in Case Example 9-1, the client's condition makes the adaptation necessary. As a result, the adaptations are often put in place by the person speaking to the client (such as facing the client when speaking). Some clients use various techniques themselves. For example, a visually impaired client may write memos to himself in large block letters on a white board (Photo 9-1).

Photo 9-1
A whiteboard can be a useful communication aid.

CASE EXAMPLE 9-2

Mrs. Fried has macular degeneration. She cannot easily discriminate among dark colours such as navy, black, dark green, or brown. As a result, Mrs. Fried has worn clothing that does not match. Occasionally, she has worn dirty clothing as she cannot easily see the soil. This has embarrassed Mrs. Fried.

As a result, Mrs. Fried has devised a system that helps her to wear matching and clean clothes. After each wash, she asks her daughter to colour-code her outfits. Mrs. Fried's daughter puts a fluorescent paper sticky dot on the label of each item. Each navy item receives a fluorescent green dot, each dark green item receives a fluorescent pink dot, and each brown item receives a flourescent yellow dot.

Mrs. Fried can easily distinguish the fluorescent colours and thus knows what articles of clothing match. She removes the dot as she puts on each item. This way she knows that the item will be worn and may be soiled.

Adaptive approaches are *techniques*, such as using large type, changing the pace of the communication, or using short sentences. These approaches require little other than the use of a marker and paper. Most techniques have been developed through trial and error.

It's quite likely that you will encounter clients who use adaptive techniques. Remember that each person who uses adaptive approaches has usually tried a number of techniques before selecting those that best fit his or her needs. Remember also that necessity is the mother of invention. Many clients will have developed very creative techniques that work for them. Always take the time to learn the specific techniques your client prefers. If a client has a technique you've never seen before, take the time to find out how it works.

If you have learned of a technique that seems particularly useful, you may choose to tell other clients about it. This is fine, as long as you do not force the idea upon the client or breach confidentiality in describing the technique (by divulging the first client's name or other identifying information).

Augmentative Communication

Augmentative communication techniques include all approaches that use some form of communication aid. For example, the person who cannot speak but communicates by pointing to various words on a page is using an *augmentative* device—the paper with the words written on it. A hearing aid is another augmentative device, as are the FM devices provided by some theatres to their hearing-impaired patrons.

A computer that synthesizes voice (such as the one used by theoretical physicist Stephen Hawking) is a high-tech augmentative device. However, many of these devices are much less technologically sophisticated (Photo 9-2). Strictly speaking, eyeglasses are augmentative devices!

Photo 9-2 *Augmentative devices need not be expensive or complex.*

Most people with communication problems use a communication aid. Low-tech aids are more common, in part due to their affordability and simplicity. Some clients, particularly younger ones, may use more technologically advanced aids.

Common Conditions Requiring Adaptive or Augmentative Techniques

Many conditions can create the need for some change in communication techniques. Some conditions are the result of aging, others result from disease or injury. In this section, we will discuss four common types of conditions: *aphasia*, *dysarthria* or *apraxia*, sensory loss, and cognitive loss. There are many other conditions which may affect communication. As well, a particular condition will probably affect different people differently. The need to determine what works best for your client is essential.

It is extremely important to remember that a person who has problems communicating does not necessarily have a dementia (a condition discussed in Chapter 22). The person may be able to problem-solve, understand, and remember very well. He or she simply has a problem communicating.

Overcoming a communication problem takes time, patience, and creativity. It also can take a great deal of energy. The ongoing difficulty in getting one's message across can be extremely frustrating. Recall how difficult it was for you when you were not able to communicate.

Aphasia

Mrs. Retman had a stroke two years ago. As a result, she lost most of her ability to use language. Through speech therapy, Mrs. Retman has regained some of this ability. She can now use approximately one hundred words easily.

She has also learned to alter the way in which she says key words so that she can make the best use of the vocabulary she has. Support workers assisting Mrs. Retman have learned what the variations of these words mean, making it easier for Mrs. Retman to have her wishes understood. Support workers also assist Mrs. Retman to practise tasks assigned by her speech-language pathologist.

Aphasia is the complete or partial loss of language skills because of some injury to the brain. There are four general causes: physical assault to the brain, dementia, progressive primary aphasia, and transient aphasia. Each is described in this section.

One of the most common causes of aphasia is a stroke (cerebral vascular accident), but aphasia can also be caused by a head injury or brain tumour. Aphasia that results from these causes often improves over time with speech therapy. Approximately one-third of all persons who experience a severe head injury develop aphasia (National Aphasia Association, 1999).

One type of aphasia, called primary progressive aphasia, results in the progressive loss of language *without* any loss of other cognitive functions. Usually, people with primary progressive aphasia gradually lose the ability to speak. They often retain their ability to understand.

Transient aphasia is a temporary aphasia. It might last only a few hours or days. Most people with transient aphasia recover fully.

Dementia and Language Loss

Some dementias such as Alzheimer Disease, Pick's Disease, or Creutzfeldt-Jakob Disease can cause language loss. Language loss resulting from dementia is one of many symptoms of cognitive loss. This type of language loss becomes worse over time. Some researchers call this type of language loss aphasia. Others feel that this language loss is not aphasia. Chapter 22 discusses dementia and its effects on communication in greater detail.

The Extent of Aphasia

The extent of aphasia is determined by the location of the brain that is affected and its size. Aphasia can range from minor word-find problems to the total inability to understand what is said to the person or to create meaningful sentences. Sometimes, only one aspect of language is lost (such as the ability to spell). Usually, more than one aspect of language is impaired.

Types of Aphasia

There are five major types of aphasia: global, Broca's, mixed non-fluent, Wernicke's, and anomic. Although most people with aphasia have one of these five types, some people may have other, less common forms, such as *alexia* (a disorder of reading). Each type of aphasia has specific characteristics, as we'll discuss in this section.

It's important to have some idea of the various types of aphasia that exist, so that you can understand that there are many ways this condition can impair a person's ability to communicate. A particular client may have symptoms of more than one type. You always must use communication techniques that work for your client, according to the type of aphasia he or she has.

Global Aphasia   The most severe form of aphasia. People with global aphasia cannot read or write, nor can they understand language or produce meaningful language. Global aphasia may occur right after a trauma or stroke. It may improve very quickly after the incident.

Broca's Aphasia   Broca's aphasia usually affects the person's ability to express language. The person may speak only in short phrases and may have great difficulty speaking them. Usually, people with Broca's aphasia have difficulty writing, although the person may be able to read and to understand written and verbal communication.

Mixed Non-fluent Aphasia   Mixed non-fluent aphasia is similar to Broca's aphasia, except that the person's ability to understand language and to read are also impaired.

Wernicke's Aphasia   Wernicke's aphasia is often called *fluent aphasia*, because the person's ability to string words together is not impaired. However, the words the person says often have no meaning or don't make sense in the sentence. Sometimes the words are not words at all—they are made up by the person. People with Wernicke's aphasia usually have difficulty understanding spoken language, as well as difficulty reading and writing.

Anomic Aphasia   Anomic aphasia is the inability of a person to find and use significant words (usually nouns or verbs). The person's spoken language may be very difficult to follow, as it often lacks many of the key words.

Tips for Communicating with the Person with Aphasia

1. **Do not exclude the person from social contact.**   Remember, the person may well be able to understand you even if he or she cannot speak. The opportunity to interact is important. Even if the person's ability to understand is impaired, he or she will benefit from the sense of being included.
2. **Speak to the person naturally.**   If the person appreciates being cued to respond, you can ask questions. If the person becomes frustrated in attempts to respond and prefers not to be asked questions, then form your communication in state-

ments or use questions that can be answered by a no or yes (by a nod or shake of the head).

3. **Speak to the person as an adult.**   Loss of language does not mean that the person is confused. Speak with the person as you would like someone to speak to you.

4. **Minimize background noise and other distractions.**   Doing so makes it easier for you both to concentrate on the communication.

5. **Make sure your nonverbal communication shows that you are listening.** Make eye contact, do not do other tasks when the person is speaking to you, and listen actively (Photo 9-3).

Photo 9-3
Facing a person when speaking to him or her makes communication easier.
Source: CHATS.

6. **Be sensitive to the person's nonverbal communication.**   Learn what the facial expressions and gestures mean.

7. **Find out what communication is reliable and use it.**   For example, the person may be able to reliably tell you yes by a nod of the head. You can then phrase your communication to the person in a way that allows him or her to respond with the gesture.

8. **Encourage social communication.**   The language associated with greetings and other frequently used social behaviours may be more easily picked up by the person.

9. **Use short sentences that highlight the key words.**   This allows the person to focus on a few words at a time.

10. **Speak slowly and pause between sentences.**   Experiment to find the right pace for each person.

11. **Give the person time to respond to statements.**   Resist the temptation to answer on his or her behalf. Only respond for the person if he or she signals to you that the inability to respond is quite distressing and the person prefers you to respond for them.

12. **If the person has difficulty understanding, rephrase your sentences or use other words that mean the same thing.**   Some words are more easily understood than others.

13. **Be creative in your attempts to understand the person's language.**   Look for clues. Does the person use words that describe the use of an item, even though he or she cannot name it? Does he or she use gestures or point to something? Does a particular phrase usually mean a particular thing? Try to look at all the ways you might be able to make sense of the person's statements. Be sure to test out your assumption by asking the person to show you (by whatever means is reliable for the person) that you have the right idea.

14. **If you cannot figure out what the person means, try changing the subject for a bit.**   The person's ability to use language may vary from hour to hour. Come back to the issue at a later time.

15. **Don't show concern about the person's speech.**   The person is doing the best that they can.

16. **Do not force the person to speak in front of others.**   This can be embarrassing to the person and actually make speaking more difficult.

17. **Support the person's efforts to speak.**   If, after repeated tries, the person says something that is still not clear, rephrase the person's statement and ask for confirmation. Remember that the person needs to practise their language skills.

Dysarthria and Apraxia of Speech

Dysarthria and *apraxia* of speech are conditions which arise from the brain's inability to properly and consistently control the physical aspect of speaking. Although these conditions seem to result in the same type of impairment, dysarthria and apraxia of speech are different. **Dysarthria** is the result of some weakness or lack of coordination in some of the muscles involved in speaking. **Apraxia** results from an injury to the brain that makes the voluntary control of speaking difficult.

People with either condition can have difficulty forming words, pacing their speech, and breathing at the right point in communication or rhythm. As a result, their words may be poorly formed. They may rush through a sentence or take a long time to say a few words. People with apraxia may also have inconsistent sound substitutions. For example, a person with apraxia may say the word "fence" as "pence", "tense", "shentz", or "fesce".

These conditions are often confused with aphasia. People with dysarthria or apraxia of speech do not necessarily have aphasia, although many people with apraxia of speech have some level of aphasia. A person with severe apraxia of speech may only have a mild form of aphasia.

Dysarthria and Apraxia of Speech Are Not Dementia

The speech of a person with either dysarthria or apraxia of speech may sound very different. It may be very difficult to understand. However, this has nothing to do with the person's ability to understand or to think. The person with dysarthria or apraxia of speech simply has a problem performing the mechanics of speech.

CASE EXAMPLE 9-4

Gerry is a 26-year-old man with cerebral palsy. His ability to produce speech has been impaired by his condition. As a result, Gerry's speech is slower than that of most other people and some words sound different than when others say them.

Because of this, Gerry has found it difficult to use a telephone. He is often hung up on by people who assume that the call is a prank because of Gerry's speech. He also finds that people often assume that he has difficulty understanding and thinking as a result of his speech.

Gerry has taken the time to work with the people around him so that they can more easily understand his speech. He is well able to communicate with his staff to fulfill the responsibilities of his job and with his support workers to ensure that his requests are understood.

Tips for Communicating with the Person with Dysarthria or Apraxia of Speech

Many people with apraxia also have aphasia. If this is true for your client, you may want to try the tips listed earlier in this chapter. Some of the tips listed below are similar to those we listed for working with people with aphasia. However, you must remember that the person with dysarthria or apraxia of speech *can* likely use language.

1. **Do not exclude the person from social contact.**   Remember, the person understands you even if he or she cannot speak well. The opportunity to interact is important.
2. **Speak to the person naturally.**
3. **Speak to the person as an adult.**   Speak with the person as you would like someone to speak to you.
4. **Minimize background noise and other distractions.**   Doing so makes it easier for you both to concentrate on the communication.
5. **Make sure your nonverbal communication shows that you are listening.** Make eye contact, do not do other tasks when the person is speaking to you, and listen actively.
6. **Learn the person's way of saying common words and phrases.** A person with dysarthria may be consistent in how he or she says something, even if the word or phrase does not sound the same as when you say it.
7. **Ask the person to speak more slowly.**   This may make it easier for you to determine breaks between words.
8. **Ask the person to rephrase the sentence.**   Sometimes using different words makes the communication more clear.
9. **Ask the person to repeat the statement if you cannot understand.**   The repeated phrase may be clearer. If you got part of the message, repeat it and ask the person to start from there.
10. **Have patience.**   The person may speak slowly, or may have to repeat words or phrases a number of times before you can understand. Time spent learning a pattern (if the person's speech is consistent) will make future communication much easier.
11. **Pay particular attention to the person's gestures and nonverbal communication.**   These signals may provide valuable clues as to the message the person wants to convey.
12. **Consider writing or the use of a letter or word board when verbal communication does not work.**   Some people with dysarthria may be able to write down the message for you to read. Other people may benefit from a word list as described in the section on communication aids.

Photo 9-4
Some people find word lists helpful. Pointing to words on a list helps the person to more easily communicate.

Photo 9-5
A person uses a letter/word board to communicate.

Communication Aids for Language or Speech Production Conditions

Augmentative devices range from the simple (paper and pen) to the complex. This section focusses on items that are common or easy to create. Always be observant of the techniques your client uses. Another client may also find them useful as well.

1. **Word boards and word lists.**   If the person has some language, he or she can point to words to communicate. Some boards have many items printed on them. Others are made up of one list, usually containing words that are similar in use (Photo 9-4). Lists can be purchased or made up at home. Some people place word list cards in a photo book or binder. The person flips to the page containing the words he or she wants to use.

2. **Letter cards or letter lists.**   Letter cards or lists are similar to the word lists described above. In this instance, the alphabet is printed out. The person points to the letters he or she wants, composing words (Photo 9-5).

3. **Photo or picture albums.**   These aids can assist the person who cannot use word lists. Photos or drawings illustrating things the person usually wishes to communicate are put into an album. The person can then point to the appropriate photo or drawing to convey a message. The books may also include information the person likes to share, such as photos of memorable family or social events, or photos of favourite places. It can include items the person needs or wants (such as a photo of a hairbrush) or of desired activities (such as a photo of a few compact discs to indicate a desire to listen to music).

4. **Yes/no or smile/frown cards.**   These cards can be used when the person can reliably indicate yes or no by pointing to the correct word, or to the appropriate 'face' (smile means yes, frown means no).

5. **Cards with pictures of commonly used items or tasks.**   The person simply selects the appropriate card. Some people use flash cards for this, but care must be taken to make sure the drawings are simple but not childlike.

6. **An object basket.**   Some people relate best to the actual item in need. A basket, box, or plastic carry-all is filled with items that the person might use. For example, the basket might contain a cup, toothbrush, hairbrush, empty shampoo bottle, and a razor (with blade removed). The person simply selects the specific item to indicate what they want or what they want to do.

Sensory Loss

Sensory losses refer to changes in hearing, vision, touch, taste, and smell. It's important to remember that sensory loss can't easily be seen. While you might be able to notice that a person has a vision or hearing problem by how he or she does certain tasks, you'd likely have to watch the person for a while. You wouldn't be able to tell by just looking at him or her (Figure 9-1).

Figure 9-1 *Can you tell if this woman has impaired hearing?*

Many of the communication problems you will encounter are the result of *age-related* sensory changes that happen to everyone if they live long enough). Age-related changes usually develop gradually, over a long period of time. The change is so gradual, that we often don't realize that changes are taking place. For example, most of us don't even notice that our vision is changing until we can't easily read the print in the telephone directory.

Age-related changes usually add to the sensory problems a person may have had all his or her life. Many of us have worn eyeglasses since we were children; some of us have used hearing aids. The conditions that made the glasses or the aid necessary don't get better as we age, and sometimes the age-related changes make them harder to cope with.

Changes in Vision

Vision makes communication easier. We use our sight to recognize body language, to know when someone is speaking to us, as well as to communicate nonverbally with others. Changes in vision can certainly hamper communication.

Vision changes can happen to people at any age. In fact, some babies are *born* with vision problems such as blindness, cataracts, or the inability to focus. Many children have vision problems that require them to wear glasses.

Age-related changes in vision are called **presbyopia**. The lens of the eye, the liquid which fills the eye, and the pupil all change with age, as do the *rods* and *cones* (parts of the inner eye that translate images to impulses that can be understood by the brain). The most common problems are described below.

Changes in colour perception.   The lens of the eye yellows, making it difficult to distinguish between greens and blues or pink and melon colours.

A need for more light to see well.   This is due to a decrease in the size of the pupil as well as changes in the rods' ability to react. It is estimated that the average 80-year-old needs three times the light a 20-year-old needs to see as well.

A slowing of the pupil's ability to react to changes in levels of light.   This slowing can make it difficult for a person to see well indoors after coming in from outside on a sunny day (Photo 9-6).

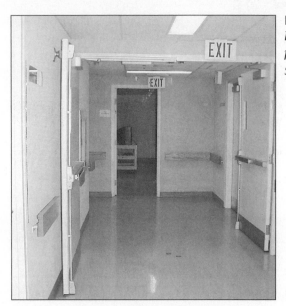

Photo 9-6   *Rapid changes in levels of light may make it difficult for an older person to see.*
Source: Leisureworld, Inc.

Difficulty focussing on things close up.   Reading a prescription label may become very difficult or even impossible.

Problems with glare or the ability to see things near a source of bright light.   For example, written material printed on high-contrast paper (such as black print on fluorescent pink paper) is very difficult for older people to read. It's also very difficult for many older people to see the facial expression of a person who is standing in front of a source of bright light (such as standing in front of a window on a very bright day). This is similar to a photograph of people taken when the photographer was facing the sun. You probably cannot see any detail in the subjects' faces.

There are some vision diseases which are more common in older people. These are not age-related changes, though, and do not affect everyone who is older. Some researchers estimate that 40 percent of residents living in nursing homes have significant vision loss. Some of these conditions are macular degeneration, glaucoma, diabetic retinopathy, and detached retina.

Changes in Hearing

It is estimated that over 50 percent of the population over age 60 has some level of hearing loss, and that the percentage of those experiencing hearing loss increases with age. Yet, many people do not want to admit to hearing loss and tend to be uncomfortable about wearing a hearing aid.

Age-related hearing loss starts at age 20, and develops gradually. It is largely the result of changes in the middle ear, and usually affects a person's ability to hear high-pitched sounds first, like the sounds made by many consonants. (Consonants are the letters of the alphabet other than a, e, i, o, u.) In particular, s, c, sh, ch, th, st, and words starting with g, b, or d can be difficult. The person's ability to hear low- and mid-pitched sounds is usually not affected. Often, this can cause other people to assume that the person chooses not to hear things when, in fact, they cannot.

Most of us experience some hearing loss over our lifetimes (Table 9-1). Much of this loss likely comes from everyday "injuries" to our ears, such as those that come from exposure to loud noise. Infections and injuries to the ear can also diminish hearing. This type of hearing loss can make all sounds more difficult to hear.

TABLE 9-1	Do You Have Hearing Loss?

Check off the number of statements that apply to you.

1. People tell me I raise the volume of the radio or television up too high.

2. I frequently have to ask people to repeat their message because they mumble.

3. I cannot tolerate loud sounds or voices.

4. I sometimes don't hear the telephone or the doorbell.

5. I have more trouble hearing female voices than hearing male voices.

6. I find it difficult to understand others' speech when there is background noise, such as difficulty in carrying on a conversation while the television is playing, or difficulty following conversation in group situations.

7. I find it hard to tell the direction from which sound is coming.

8. I find myself turning one ear or tilting my head toward the person who is speaking.

9. I have ringing or buzzing in one or both of my ears.

10. When I use the telephone, I find it hard to hear the other person.

More than three checkmarks may mean that you have difficulty hearing. Hearing loss should be thoroughly investigated by the appropriate health care professional.

Changes in Sensitivity to Touch

Touch is considered to be a basic human need. Physical contact with other people and objects is considered to be a necessary part of life satisfaction. The decrease in sensitivity to the sensation of touch is of great importance because it makes it more difficult for us to meet our need to touch and to communicate.

Sensitivity to touch actually refers to four things: texture, temperature, pressure, and pain. Not all researchers agree that a person's sensitivity to touch changes with age. However, illness, injury, and some medications can change a person's sensitivity to touch.

Your use of touch with a client must always be guided by the client's preferences for touch. The client may have preferences for who, where, and when he or she is touched by others. Always ask if the client appreciates a hug or gentle squeeze of the shoulder before you do these things.

Assisting the Person with Sensory Loss

Be aware that the person with the sensory loss has a great deal of experience coping with the loss. Always take the time to find out how the person copes with the loss and what techniques the person finds successful.

Compensating for Vision Changes

1. **Don't stand in front of a bright source of light when speaking to a person.** The person will find it very difficult to see your face (Photo 9-7).
2. **Stand so that the person can see you.**   Experiment with the distance and position that works best for your client.
3. **Tell the person where you are and what you are doing.**   If you are walking or riding with a person, describe the surroundings.
4. **Be specific in your communication.**   Saying to the person, "It's over there" is of little help. Say something like "The chair is about two steps away, on your right."
5. **Let the person know if you leave the room.**
6. **Use large type (or write in large letters) when writing information.**
7. **Avoid decorative fonts, all capital letters, or underlining information.**   In fact, all of these things make printed information *harder* to read.

Photo 9-7
What do you see?
Source: CHATS.

Compensating for Hearing Changes

1. **If the person uses a hearing aid, make sure that it is in place and working properly.**
2. **Make sure the person is wearing his or her glasses, if needed.**   This is particularly important if the person reads lips.
3. **Use notes or sign language.**
4. **Avoid shouting.**   It can be painful and make understanding more difficult.
5. **Speak using your face, your hands, and your eyes.**   Use gestures, point to objects that will help you get your message across.
6. **Stand or sit where your face can be easily seen.**   Make sure that the person is able to read your lips.
7. **Be sure that you have the listener's attention.**   Does he or she know you are talking to him or her? Always try to communicate at eye level and establish eye contact.
8. **When you speak, don't chew gum, smoke, or put your hand over your mouth.** 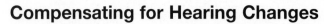 These things distort normal lip movement and make lip reading impossible.
9. **Move away from background noise (such as an air conditioner, television, or a crowded room).**

10. **If you are not understood, rephrase your statement using different words.** For example, substituting a phrase like "false teeth" for the word "dentures" may make it easier for the person to understand.

11. **Be positive.** Have patience.

12. **Bear in mind that an ill or tired person will not hear as well as he or she might when rested or well.**

13. **Lower the pitch of your voice, but keep the volume up.** Experiment with different volumes and different tones.

14. **Vary your position relative to the person.** Some people hear better when the sound comes from a particular direction.

15. **Decrease your rate of speech.** We all speak much faster than we think we do!

16. **Avoid words with consonants if you can.** Double consonants like ss, ch, st, and ch are particularly difficult to hear. If possible, substitute a word without these combinations.

17. **Learn and use sign language.**

Compensating for Changes in Touch Sensitivity

1. **Make use of opportunities for touch.** A handshake, hug, walking arm in arm, gentle rubbing of arms or shoulders are ways of communicating by touch. Be careful, though, not to force touch on a person who does not want it. We all vary in the amount of touch that we need.

2. **Use touch to get the person's attention.** A brief touch on the arm will let the person know where you are.

3. **Let your touch linger for a moment.** A quick, gentle pat on the hand may be fine for a teen, but an older person may not realize you have even touched him or her.

Photo 9-9
Magnifying sheets are also available.

Communication Aids to Compensate for Sensory Loss

Many of the following items can be purchased at variety stores or made by you.

Photo 9-8
A magnifying glass can enable a visually impaired person to read directions or other small print.

Aids to Compensate for Vision Loss

1. A magnifying glass can enable a visually impaired person to read directions or other small print (Photo 9-8). Magnifying bars and sheets are also available (Photo 9-9).

2. A clamp-on lamp with a magnifying lens in its centre provides illumination as well as magnification (Photo 9-10).

3. Increasing the lighting in frequently used rooms (without creating glare) can make it easier for a person to see faces and gestures.

Photo 9-10
A clamp-on lamp with a magnifying lens in its centre provides illumination as well as magnification.

Aids to Compensate for Hearing Loss

1. **Flashing lights for doorbells and telephones.** These items flash when the door bell is rung or when the phone rings.
2. **Pen and paper.** Some people find it easier to lip-read if the topic of the conversation is written down. Others prefer to jot notes to communicate.
3. **A hearing aid.** Encourage the person to contact the appropriate health professional if the person feels the aid is broken or not suitable. Many problems can be eliminated through adjustments to the aid or to its settings.
4. **Systems to assist a hearing-impaired person with the phone.** One kind uses typewriter-style machines to allow the person to type messages which are sent to teletype terminals. Another, more sophisticated kind is a computer-based system which allows the person to select predetermined phrases which are then converted to speech and subsequently transmitted to another person.

Questions for Review

1. Describe the difference between adaptive and augmentative communication.

2. Identify at least six approaches you can use to assist a client with aphasia to communicate.

3. Describe two augmentative communication aids.

4. You are working with a client with hearing loss. What are three things that you can do to make communication easier with your client?

5. What guideline should you follow when learning about the level of touch your client prefers?

6. List two ways of helping a client meet his or her needs for touch.

7. How might you better communicate with a person who has apraxia of speech? List at least five methods.

Questions for Discussion

1. Imagine that you could not express yourself verbally. How would you feel? How would you make your needs and wants known?

2. Review Case Example 9-4. How would you feel if you were Gerry? Share your answers with those of your colleagues.

3. Develop your own personal word list (as described in the section on communication aids). What words would be important to include? Share your list with those of your colleagues. How do their lists differ from yours? Does this reflect the differences in your hobbies and other activities?

CHAPTER TEN

Setting Priorities and Working Effectively

Learning Objectives

Through reading this chapter, you'll be able to:

1. Describe the three elements of effective time management.
2. Discuss the importance of setting goals.
3. Generate SMART goals.
4. Tell what equity in time management is.
5. Depict overlapping tasks and apply the technique to manage multiple tasks.
6. Define assertiveness and describe behaviours that indicate assertiveness.
7. List the four skills involved in problem solving.
8. Apply the problem-solving process to address a problem.

Chapter At A Glance

The Elements of Time Management

Time Management in Support Work

Assertiveness

What Is Assertiveness Training?

Problem Solving

Terms You'll Use

Assertiveness   A technique that helps you respect others' views, concerns, and needs while not compromising your own.

Clarifying   Describing things clearly so that others understand or asking questions so that you understand..

Negotiating   The give-and-take used in problem solving.

Overlapping Tasks   Tasks that are started and allowed to continue while another task is finished or begun.

Priorities   Goals that you want to attain before others.

SMART Goals   Criteria for describing the effectiveness of goals.

Time Management   Making the most of the time you have, in light of your priorities.

The Elements of Time Management

> *The secret of life is enjoying the passage of time.*
> – James Taylor

Do you have enough time? You probably said no. The truth is, you have all the time there is to have. **Time management** means making the best of the time you have. This means developing skills in three things: knowing what your goals are, disciplining yourself to stay focussed on those goals, and using techniques that make the best use of your time.

In this chapter we'll make a distinction between managing your personal goals and time and managing work goals and working efficiently. Each is different, but still essential to effective personal support work.

What's Important? Setting Personal Goals

Personal goals are the things you as a person want to attain. At least some of them are probably linked to your decision to become a support worker. Knowing what your goals are helps you to attain them (Figure 10-1). In fact, some research suggests that a person becomes more effective at managing time *simply* by defining his or her goals.

We have many types of personal goals. We have goals related to our work and goals related to our own personal life. Remember, the work goals we talk about here are *your* goals for *your* professional development. These are different from the work goals you set with an individual client in order to work effectively.

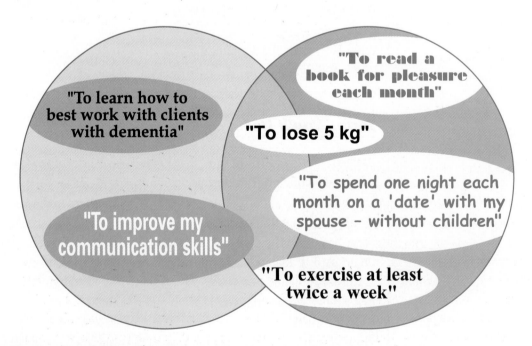

Figure 10-1 *Spheres of Goals*

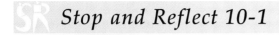

Stop and Reflect 10-1

What is most important to you? For each of the headings below, write down three goals you want to attain.

Personal Goals

_____

_____

_____

_____

Work Goals

_____

_____

_____

_____

SMART Goals

To be effective, goals must also be SMART.

Specific
Measurable
Attainable
Require resources that are available
Timely

Have you ever started a fitness plan? If so, chances are you had a goal in mind, such as to be able to do 50 sit-ups at a time or to be able to run two kilometres. These goals are specific and measurable. Whether they are attainable depends upon your overall health status. Similarly, the amount of time you could devote to the goal is an indication of whether you have the resources.

A timely goal is one that is measured in a reasonable time period. There is no set definition of a reasonable time period, it depends upon the other factors. For example, allowing enough time to attain the goal is a function of how much work you must do to be able to complete the 50 sit-ups or run the two kilometres and how many resources you can devote to it. For example, if you have never even walked two kilometres, it would likely be unrealistic to expect that you could learn to run two kilometres in, say, two weeks.

You always must be realistic when you set time frames. Setting your goals too high—expecting to attain too much—can discourage you. Similarly, setting your goals too low often results in little satisfaction because the goal was too easy.

You should plan in blocks of three months. If you have ultimate goals such as to complete a course or to have children in the next five years, give some thought to what you have to do in the shorter run to make the ultimate attainable. These short-run goals are the ones to focus on now.

Stop and Reflect 10-2

Take another look at the goals you set for yourself in the previous *Stop and Reflect* box. Rate each goal against the SMART criteria, using a time period of not more than three months. For example, if you had listed the goal "eat better", you might rewrite it as "by the end of three months, I will eat balanced meals at least 4 days per week". Rewrite your goals here.

Personal Goals

_____

_____

_____

Work Goals

_____

_____

_____

It's important to keep your goals in mind. You might want to write them on a card that you keep in your billfold. You might find that writing them in your appointment book helps you to keep your goals in mind.

Getting There

Knowing your goals is important. However, you'll still need a plan to get there. There are often many steps involved in attaining the goal. Consider the following situation.

CASE EXAMPLE 10-1

Erin is a support worker at a seniors' day program. For some time now, she has wanted to lose 10 kilograms and to become more fit. However, she has not been able to do so.

Erin mentions her frustration to a friend. As they discuss the issue, Erin identifies two actions she could take to attain her goal. First, Erin can start walking to and from work. This will require her to *leave for work 15 minutes earlier than she currently does and she will get home 15 minutes later. Second, Erin can replace the convenience foods she currently brings for lunch with healthier choices.*

Through these two actions, Erin is able to lose 10 kilograms in 14 weeks. She feels better and has the satisfaction of having attained a much-desired goal.

Managing Your Time

Setting SMART goals and identifying approaches to attain those goals are necessary components of time management. As singer Willie Nelson said, "If you don't know where you're going, you're liable to end up somewhere else." The third step requires you to evaluate what you do against your *priorities*, making changes so that most of your time is spent attaining your goals. **Priorities** are those things that you want to do first. Consider the following case example.

CASE EXAMPLE 10-2

Eric is a support worker. He is also taking a course to upgrade his skills. He plans to attain his certificate in the spring. With a certificate, Eric will receive a raise that will allow him to better provide for his family.

He attends class one night each week. This week, a classmate asks Eric to join him for a coffee after class. Even though Eric has to work the next morning at 7 a.m., he agrees.

The classmate tells Eric about a personal problem. He is very upset over a breakup with a girlfriend. By the time Eric leaves his classmate it is 3 a.m. Eric heads home.

Eric is awakened by his wife at 6:30 a.m. He rushes to get ready, but knows that he will be late for work. As he is leaving, the custodian of Eric's apartment building stops him. "I need your door keys," the super tells Eric. "We're changing the locks and I may as well give you your new keys now." Although Eric's wife will be home to let him in when he returns from work, Eric follows the custodian. Fifteen minutes later, he has his new keys.

By the time Eric gets to work, he is 45 minutes late. He apologizes to his coworker (who has had to work extra hard because Eric was not there) and does his best to catch up. He also has to explain his lateness to his supervisor.

What are Eric's goals? Did Eric's actions support his goals? If you were Eric, what would you have done differently?

Making sure that your activities support your goals doesn't mean that you are self-ish. It is still important to help others. You must learn to balance your needs with those of others. For example, you may well have done what Eric did—helped a classmate. You might not have stayed out until 3 a.m. with that friend, though.

Time Management in Support Work

Managing your time at work is a bit different than managing your personal time. At work, your priority is to provide the best service possible to your client. In a very real sense, your goal is to help your client attain his or her goals.

In Case Example 10-3, Karen illustrates three principles of time management with clients: she knows her clients' preferences and goals; she has planned her work with the clients; and she makes best use of her time by *overlapping tasks*. We'll discuss each of these principles in this section.

CASE EXAMPLE 10-3

It's 7:05 a.m. Karen has just started her shift. She is responsible for 12 residents, all of whom need some help getting up and dressed before breakfast at 8:10 a.m.

Three residents take a great deal of time to get started in the morning. Four need assistance with toileting as well as complete help with dressing. Three need someone to lay out their clothes in order. Two need reminders to dress and someone to do up shoelaces, buttons, and zippers.

Karen knows her residents well. She knows who likes to rise early and who wants to stay in bed until the last minute. She knows who needs 30 minutes to adjust to waking up and who does not. In the first room on her assigned unit, Karen begins with the residents who like to rise early and need time to adjust. She wakes Mrs. Baker, leaving her to rouse as she wakes and assists Mrs. Morse into the washroom. When Karen returns to the room, she lays out Mrs. Baker's clothes in the order Mrs. Baker will put them on. (Mrs. Baker prefers to dress herself, even though her arthritis makes this very difficult.) Karen then helps Mrs. Morse dress. The room's third resident, Mrs. James, likes to sleep in so Karen leaves her and proceeds to the next assigned resident room. She'll return to wake Mrs. James after all her other residents are cared for.

■

Learning Your Client's Goals and Priorities

One of your first tasks when assigned a new client should be to talk with the client to find out his or her goals and priorities as they relate to your work with him or her. This includes two things: what the client wants to attain, and *how* the client would like you to assist them.

If you work in the community, you may receive a referral form for each client prior to your first visit that describes the client's general goals and tasks you are to do. If you work in a facility, you will likely learn this information through a care conference or from the charge nurse when you report for work. The information you get before you meet the client can help you plan your work. Still, you should talk with your client to determine his or her priorities for your visit and how the client would like you to do what you are assigned to do.

Keep in mind that priorities may change from day to day. A client whose family member is coming to visit may prefer that you spend more time helping him or her get washed and dressed. A client who normally has a bath during your Wednesday visit may ask that you assist her on another day.

A client's goals may also change over time, just as your goals do. Sometimes, a goal is attained and replaced by a new one. For example, a client who is recovering from a stroke may have set a goal of being able to get dressed without help. You may have helped the client practise techniques that made it easier to accomplish this goal. However, once the goal was attained, the client may have set another. You would then assist the client with attaining that new goal.

Planning Tasks Together

If at all possible, plan your tasks with the client. This gives you three benefits. First, you let the client know that his or her priorities are important to you. Second, you learn from the client what is important to him or her. You can ask questions so that you actually understand the client's needs. Third, you learn how the client would like you to assist, including the parts of any tasks assigned that the client would like to do.

Organizing Overlapping Tasks

Like Karen's job, most of your work will require you to perform a number of tasks in a short period of time. You must develop skill in scheduling **overlapping tasks**—those you start and then can leave for a bit while you do something else.

Most of us have some experience in organizing overlapping tasks. For example, you likely do other things while your laundry is in the wash. Chances are, you start the washer and then do other things while the cycle runs. You come back to the washer when the cycle is finished. Especially if you take your laundry to the laundromat, you bring along something to do as you wash and dry your clothes.

Stop and Reflect 10-3

How do you make best use of your time by organizing overlapping tasks? List at least five tasks you do while waiting for something else to finish.

_____

_____

_____

_____

_____

Share your answers with your colleagues. Do they use different techniques? Are there any techniques they use that you might try?

_____

_____

_____

_____

Assertiveness

What would you do in the following situation?

You are the health care aide assigned to Mrs. Smith. Today, just as you're about to leave Mrs. Smith's room, she begins to tell you about her sister's visit. While you would like to hear about the visit, you have other clients to care for. Yet, you know Mrs. Smith has very few family or friends who visit.

What do you say to Mrs. Smith?

_____

_____

_____

_____

Have you ever been in a situation where you gave in to another person's requests, even though you didn't want to? Perhaps you did this in order to avoid conflict. Did you feel angry about this afterward? Perhaps you got angry after another person continually put their needs before yours and 'dug your heels in' about an issue you didn't really care about. You might have felt guilty afterward. Assertiveness training can help you to avoid these situations.

Assertiveness is a behaviour that can be learned and practised. It has been described as a technique which helps you to:

- Respect each person in the communication.
- Consider your needs and express them clearly.
- Consider the other person's need and respect it.

It can also help you to more easily resolve issues and problems.

Assertiveness *doesn't* mean always getting your own way. It helps you to balance your needs with those of the other person. Table 10-1 describes the relationships among assertiveness, passivity, and aggression.

As we said earlier, assertiveness is a behaviour. Table 10-2 describes some of the characteristics associated with passive, assertive, and aggressive behaviours.

TABLE 10-1	Are You a Pansy, a Partner, or a Porcupine?	
Pansy	Partner	Porcupine
Passive "Whatever you want"	Assertive "What do we both want?"	Aggressive "My way or the highway!"

TABLE 10-2	Characteristics of Passive, Assertive, and Aggressive Behaviours		
	Passive	**Assertive**	**Aggressive**
Behaviour	Lets others make decisions; Doesn't express feelings, ideas, wants; Gives in; Hedges; Apologizes; Hopes someone will guess what he/she wants	Appropriately honest; Expresses wants and feelings directly; Chooses for him/herself; Exercises his/her rights; Respects rights of others; Listens, uses direct language ("I" statements)	Inappropriately honest; Puts others down; Ignores others' rights; Chooses for others; Is sarcastic; Blames; Overreacts
Reasons for the behaviour	Wants to avoid conflict, upset to other people.	To get a win-win situation if possible, to know he/she has done his/her best to meet needs.	To get what he/she wants at all costs; may only see things in terms of "I win only if you lose".
Feels this way about his or her behaviour	Guilty, helpless, hurt, powerless. Can feel angry or resentful afterward.	Confident, relaxed, good.	Hostile, defensive, righteous.
How others feel	Guilty, angry, disrespectful, frustrated.	Respected, respectful, sometimes threatened.	Hurt, humiliated, defensive, angry.

What Is Assertiveness Training?

Assertiveness requires two things:
- That you know your soft spots—the people or situations in which you find it difficult to be assertive.
- That you develop a sense of comfort in your right to express your needs and what you want.

It's not uncommon to be more assertive with certain people or in certain settings. You might be very assertive with your coworkers, but not at all with your clients. You could be a real partner to your sisters, but a real pansy when it comes to your brothers.

Take a few minutes to think about how assertive you are in the following settings.

SR *Stop and Reflect 10-5*

Where/with whom are you:

A Pansy?

_____

_____

_____

_____

A Partner?

_____

_____

_____

_____

_____

A Porcupine?

_____

_____

_____

_____

Developing a sense of comfort in your right to express your needs and what you want is often difficult. As caregivers, we're taught to put others' needs first. The key word here is practise. Start by stating your wants with something simple, perhaps in a discussion of what movie to see or where to go for dinner. When you've become comfortable with that, go on to something more difficult. Don't worry, it will take time. Be sure to savour the good feeling that comes with having expressed yourself.

Remember, it is not disrespectful to state your own needs and desires, so long as you state them in a way that does not deny others their right to do the same thing. Rights always come with responsibilities. Table 10-3 lists some common rights and their respective responsibilities.

TABLE 10-3	Rights and Responsibilities
If you have this right...	**You also have this responsibility...**
■ To Speak Up	■ To Listen
■ To Take	■ To Give
■ To Have Problems	■ To Find Solutions
■ To Be Respected	■ To Respect

Assertiveness becomes easier with practice. It sometimes helps to "think through" how you might respond assertively in a situation. Use the Stop and Reflect box 10-6 to plan your communication.

Stop and Reflect 10-6

Answer the following questions. Your answers will help you plan to become a more assertive person.

One situation in which I'd like to become more assertive is:

_____

_____

_____

_____

I can become more assertive in that situation by doing/saying:

_____

_____

_____

_____

I need to practise becoming more assertive in that situation by:

_____

_____

_____

_____

You may also want to practise a difficult situation with a friend. Have your friend take on the role of the person with whom you find it difficult to be assertive. You can then practise responding assertively.

Problem Solving

Sometimes, despite our best efforts, we encounter a situation that must be worked through. Perhaps the communication wasn't as clear as we thought it would be. Perhaps the interests of the people concerned just don't seem to match up.

Problem solving involves four skills: information sharing, *clarifying* of each person's views, identifying priorities, and *negotiating*. **Clarifying** involves describing things clearly so that others understand. **Negotiating** refers to the give and take used to solve a problem. Problem solving is made easier by the ability to express one's views and feelings openly (while respecting those of the other person involved).

There are three types of problems: those that aren't worth bothering with; those that are minor and require only a quick answer; and those that require work. In this section, we'll call these molehills, foothills, and mountains.

 ## Stop and Reflect 10-7

Recall a situation in which you spent a lot of effort (perhaps worrying or deciding what to do) on a problem that you realized later simply wasn't worth it.

How did you feel?

_____

_____

_____

Molehills

In Chapter 3, you learned not to "sweat the small stuff" when you manage stress. This saying applies equally well to problem solving. When you commit time and effort to a problem that is not worth it, you're really wasting it. Before you decide to spend a great deal of effort on an issue, ask yourself the following questions.

1. **Is it really a threat?**
2. **Is it worth the worry?**
3. **Even if I want to, can I change the outcome?**

Is the problem really a threat?   Is the problem really affecting you, or is it just that you're reacting to the change it might bring? Ask yourself what the problem really threatens. If it's simply that it's different, go no farther. It's not worth the effort. If it does threaten something you hold dear, ask yourself Question 2.

Is the problem worth the effort?   How important is it? Is the problem worth the effort it takes to solve it?

If your answer to this question is no, and the problem is not a major one for any of the parties, spend a few minutes generating ideas about what to do. Then, make a quick decision (or let others make it) and get on with things.

If your answer to Question 2 is yes, proceed to Question 3.

Even if I want to, can I change the outcome of the problem?   Have you ever complained about the GST? Even if it's a threat and worth the effort, can you change it? Not likely. If your answer to this question is no, put your efforts toward adapting to the decision that you'll have to live with.

If the answer is yes, then you haven't got a molehill, you have a problem. Proceed to the next section.

If your questions have led you to believe that you've got something other than a molehill on your hands, you'll need to look deeper. In particular, you'll need to get answers to the following questions:

1. What is the real problem?
2. What information do you need to deal with it?
3. Who else (if anyone) needs to deal with it?
4. What does a solution look like?

Once you have this information, you can follow the four steps of problem solving: generate ideas, rank ideas, select the most likely, and implement the best option.

Unlike molehills, it's very important here to resist the temptation to act too quickly. We often feel the pressure to fix things but, with a serious problem, acting too quickly may only address the symptoms, leaving the underlying cause undisturbed. If so, the problem will return. If at all possible, take the time (and make the time) to get the answers to the above questions.

> *When I'm getting ready to reason with a man I spend one-third of my time thinking about myself and what I am going to say—and two-thirds thinking about him and what he is going to say.*   –Abraham Lincoln

Communication skills are essential to problem solving. At each step in the process, you need to take the time to explore how the other person sees things as well as explain your view. Only if you know how the other person sees things will you know how much you have in common.

Table 10-4 outlines an effective procedure to use when you want to find out how the other person sees things (Adapted from Tom Rusk, *The Power of Ethical Persuasion*).

TABLE 10-4	Exploring the Other Person's Opinion

1. Agree that your first task is to understand each other's opinion, not to immediately solve the problem.

2. Ask the person how he or she sees the issue and how she or he would like to see it change.

3. Ask the person to help you understand their view. DO NOT argue with the person or defend your position.

4. Once the person shares their view, repeat it in your own words to show that you understand.

5. Ask the person to correct what you said so that you can fully understand.

6. Repeat the process until the person agrees without hesitation that you understand his or her view. Responses like "I guess so" or "sort of" do not indicate agreement.

Always listen to the other person's viewpoint first. When you express your opinion, follow the steps in Table 10-5.

TABLE 10-5	Explaining Your Own Opinion

1. Ask the person to hear you out.

2. Carefully explain your thoughts and opinions as *your opinion*, not the "way things really are".

3. Ask the person to repeat what you have said. Correct any errors until you can truthfully say that the other person understands.

Once you have explored each other's opinions, look for the similarities. Chances are that you can agree on some things. Look for the common ground—the things you see the same way. Repeat this technique at each step in the problem-solving process.

It's the Real Thing

Stop and Reflect 10-8

Consider the following situation.

You have a 17-year-old child. You have set a curfew of midnight on weekends, 9 p.m. on week nights. Your child constantly breaks curfew, coming in 1/2 to 3/4 hour later than required.

What is the issue?

_____

_____

_____

_____

If you said something like "She doesn't respect me," you're not alone. But, is that *the issue*? Or, is it more likely a symptom or a cause?

A *problem* refers to a situation which is not planned and not desired. To resolve it, you've got to know what *is* the desired state of things—the real thing, before you can figure out what's gone wrong.

Focus on the behaviours. If your response to the curfew problem was something like "He doesn't listen to me," or "She wants to do her own thing," you're going down the wrong path. What is it that the person is doing that makes you say these things? That's likely the behaviour (or part of it) you need to get at.

Flesh out the issue. When does it happen? Does it always happen that way? Who is involved? Are there causes you can identify?

Whose Issue Is It, Anyway?

Once you've got the issue/problem described, it's time to consider ownership. Ownership refers to who should be involved in dealing with the issue, *not whose fault the issue or problem is.*

Many systems have been developed for identifying who should be involved in re-solving a problem. A simple test is to ask yourself the following three questions:

Do I need the cooperation and support of others to make this solution work?   If so, involve those people in the decision. Some challenging situations will require you and your client to work together to problem solve.

Do I need expertise I don't have?   If so, get it. You may need to contact your super-visor for information and guidance. With your supervisor's permission, you may ask others for help.

Do I need both cooperation and expertise?   If so, get the parties together.

What Do We Want? Setting Criteria

CASE EXAMPLE 10-4

The story is told of the two hard bargainers. These two, who are sisters, are staying at a cottage miles from the nearest town. They have supplies but, between them, have just one orange. One sister needs the juice of an entire orange for juice; the other needs the rind of the entire orange for a cake. Both want the entire orange. They argue. As neither will give in, they split the orange in half. Neither gets what she wants and neither is happy.

The moral of this story? *The best solutions are those which address your "must haves" not those which give a specific answer.* There may be many ways to satisfactorily address an issue. You help to ensure success by identifying the criteria a good solution must meet, rather than identifying just one right answer.

What Do You Want? What Does the Other Person Want?

When you figure out what the real problem is, you should have developed some idea of what the desired solution might look like. This will give you an idea of the criteria any solution must meet. You may also have criteria set for you, such as: any solution must not cost more than a specific sum. These ideas are a start toward developing cri-teria any solutions must meet.

You may also find that you have two types of criteria: "must haves" and "like to haves". This is fine.

If you're working with others, you may find that your criteria differs from others in the group. If the differences are complementary (e.g., they can coexist), include both. If one or more contradicts another, you'll need to negotiate. Use a similar process in the event that one of your 'musts' is another's 'like'. Generally, if one person sees a criteria as a 'must have', it's best to simply include it.

CASE EXAMPLE 10-5

Instead of insisting on having the entire orange, the sisters decide to take a moment to decide what each really wants. The first sister determines that she needs only the juice. The other sister decides that she needs only the peel. The sisters quickly determine that their needs are complementary. Both can get what they want from the single orange. They squeeze the orange for the juice, then grate the rind for the cake.

Do We Have Everything?

At some time in this process, you may find that you need additional information. Information on how others have approached a similar issue, an expert opinion, and success stories, are all useful, if you know what you want from them.

Before you search for information, know what kind of information you want to find. Be specific about your needs, and collect only that which is useful in making the decision.

How Can We Get It? Creating the Options

Sometimes setting the criteria will suggest the best option. For example, when the sisters described their needs, the best option to solving their problem was clear.

Sometimes, the answer is not so obvious. The problem may be complex or one of the parties may feel very strongly that a single answer is the only answer. The most desirable option may not be possible for reasons beyond any of the parties' control.

Consider the situation below.

Stop and Reflect 10-9

You have just been assigned a new client. One of your assigned tasks is to wash the client's kitchen floor.

When you arrive at the client's home, she shows you where her cleaning supplies are kept. When you ask for the mop to wash the kitchen floor, the client tells you, "Oh no, you don't use a mop. That would hardly clean at all. You must use the brush instead. That's the only way you'll get the grout clean." The client points to a toothbrush in the bucket.

The client's kitchen floor measures three metres by two and one-half metres. It's covered with ceramic tile. It would take hours to scrub tiles and grout with the brush. You are only assigned to the client for two two-hour visits each week and you have other tasks to do.

You contact your supervisor for advice. She tells you that your agency frowns upon staff scrubbing floors, preferring you to mop instead. Your supervisor also tells you that she cannot authorize any additional hours of service. However, it's up to you to work it out with the client, as long as all the tasks assigned (a bath, laundry, and meal preparation) are also done.

You speak with the client. She tells you that it is very important to her to have a floor that is clean and the only way to make sure it's clean is to scrub it with the brush.

What are your criteria here?

_____

_____

_____

_____

What do you think your client's criteria are?

_____

_____

_____

_____

What options can you generate that might solve this problem?

_____

_____

_____

_____

Share your answers with your colleagues. Did they generate other options?

_____

_____

_____

_____

There is no obvious solution here. The client's needs seem to differ from yours. Furthermore, some options (such as having additional time at the client's) are impossible. You would have to work with the client to determine her criteria, figure out yours, and then generate options to address the issue.

When you discussed the above situation with your colleagues, did you find that you came up with even more options? Chances are that you did. Each person sees the situation a little differently. This difference in perspective allows us to see other options. The discussion of these different points of view often spawns creativity.

Creativity is at its peak when we are young. Remember when you were a child? Do you remember making up stories about imaginary friends, animals, almost anything? Anything was possible: stories knew no rational bounds. Until you grew up.

As we grow, we learn rules. Research suggests that our creativity at age 40 is 5 percent of what it was at age five. Luckily, regaining the creativity of youth is not like regaining the energy of youth. We can do it, with a little practice.

Brainstorming is perhaps the oldest and best known of all the creative idea generating methods. It is done by having a group contribute ideas in a free-flowing session, without any initial evaluation of the ideas. The function of brainstorming is to generate a wide variety and number of ideas quickly, without censorship, judgment, or premature evaluation. Remember these ground rules:

1. No comments or judgments on the ideas until it is time for discussion.
2. Write down all the ideas you generate.
3. Share all ideas that come to mind, without prejudging.
4. The idea-generating time period can be either specific or open-ended, although a specific time period seems to work best, as it helps to keep the group on task.

Brainstorming can generate an amazing number of ideas in a very short time, if you stick to the rules. This can be difficult, as we all tend to examine each idea as it comes along. You may have found this happened when you discussed your responses to the floor-washing situation. If you heard a lot of things like, "if you do that, you'll never be..." or "that won't work", you know how difficult it can be to not prejudge an option.

Getting the Best Fit—Evaluating the Options

Once the options have been generated, they need to be ranked against the criteria you generated earlier. Ideally, one or more options will meet all criteria but, if not, you have two choices.

1. Select options which meet as many of your criteria as possible.
2. Go back and generate other options.

It's important to work with your client to attain agreement on the options you'll try first. Consider again the floor-washing situation. What options do you feel would meet your criteria? What options would meet your client's? Which option seems most likely to meet both your needs?

Then, Do It

Once you've determined the first option to try, put it in place. If it doesn't work out, go to the next option.

Questions for Review

1. Review the personal goals you set in Stop and Reflect 10-1. For two of your goals, write down the steps you must take in order to attain each goal.

2. What is an overlapping task? Give an example of a set of overlapping tasks.

3. What three benefits can you attain by planning tasks with your client?

4. Describe assertiveness. What are the three things that assertiveness help you to do?

5. What is the problem-solving process?

6. What are the four skills involved in problem solving?

Questions for Discussion

1. Review the following case study. How would you use problem-solving, assertiveness, and negotiation skills to help resolve this issue?

   You are the client attendant in a seniors' day program. Your agency has planned a bus trip for clients and their spouses. Your supervisor has already left on the first bus, after telling you to take care of everything while she is gone—including solving any problems that might arise.

   Mr. Gray, the husband of a client, approaches you. He is holding his wife's torn coat. He appears very angry as he holds the coat out to you and says, "This should never have happened. The bus driver didn't even look when he closed the door. I told him the coat was caught, but he didn't stop. What are you going to do?" You speak with the bus driver, but he says that he neither saw the coat nor heard Mr. Gray. Furthermore, he says that the bus company isn't responsible for these things, and points to a sign on the bus that says just that.

2. What do you do to make better use of your time? Share your ideas with your colleagues.

3. With a group of your colleagues, review the list of rights and responsibilities listed in Table 10-3. Are there other rights and responsibilities you might add?

Contributing to the Client's Support Plan

Terms You'll Use

Appearance   Observations about body language, dress, and cleanliness.

Assessment   The phase of support planning that determines the type of support needed.

Behaviour   Observations about actions, awareness and interest in surroundings, and awareness and interest in others.

Communication   In reporting, this means observations about messages including what is said and how it is said.

Confidentialilty   A term that describes privacy of a person's information.

Documentation   Written reports such as notes, reports, and checklists.

Evaluation   The phase of support planning that reviews the client's situation, needs, and preferences.

Goal Setting   The phase of support planning in which client goals are identified along with the methods that will be used to attain the goals.

Implementation   The phase of support planning in which the methods identified in the goal setting phase are put into practice.

Status   Observations about a client's condition, function, and any change that was seen.

Support Plan   The foundation for all services that a client receives. Also called a *care plan*.

Support Planning Process   The process used to identify the goals and preferences of the client.

What Is the Support Plan?

The **support plan** is the foundation for all the services the client receives. The plan provides a central point of reference for information about the client, the client's goals, and the services the client receives. Many different terms are used to describe the support plan, such as: care plan, service agreement, bookings, or support agreement.

Most of your clients will have had a support plan developed with them. However, some persons who direct their own care do not develop a support plan. When there is no support plan in place, you must be certain to get clear direction from the client as to the needs and tasks to be done.

The support plan is one of several documents that provides up-to-date information about the client and the client's needs. These other documents can include client assessments, referral forms, progress notes, and reports of any therapy the client receives. Other documents may be included. Each agency develops its own set of documents, although some agencies in the same area may share certain forms.

The support plan is a *dynamic document*. It changes as the client's needs, condition, or goals change. It is intended to be developed, then reviewed and revised as required.

The Support Planning Process

The *support planning process* is often a function of the support team we discussed in Chapter 5. The client or the client's representative should *always* be involved in the support planning process, where the goals and preferences are identified.

The **support planning process** is much like the nursing process. It contains four phases: *assessment*, *goal setting*, *implementation*, and *evaluation* (Figure 11-1). Each of these phases is described in this section.

Assessment Phase   A client's initial assessment is often done by the person who will be responsible for organizing the support provided. The **assessment** involves determining what types of support are needed. This person may complete the entire assessment or take the responsibility for organizing assessments from other care providers. In community settings, a case manager is often responsible for the assessment. In a facility setting, a charge nurse often takes the responsibility for coordinating the assessment for a resident of a long-term care facility.

Client situation, needs, and preferences are reassessed on a regular basis. Most provinces have regulations as to how often this assessment must happen. A significant change in a client's situation should always trigger a reassessment.

Goal-Setting Phase   Goal setting is usually done at the time of the assessment. **Goal setting** is essential to the success of the support plan and ensures that the client's goals are identified, and that the methods to be used to help the client attain the goals are in line with the client's preferences.

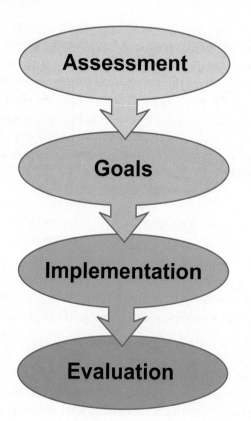

Implementation Phase   The **implementation** phase occurs when the methods identified in the goal-setting phase are put into practice. The actual provision of direct service begins with this phase. Many times, methods are tried and then refined so as to get the best effect. Occasionally, new goals are identified in this phase.

Evaluation Phase   **Evaluation** is not necessarily a distinct phase that occurs after implementation and it involves the evaluation of needs, goals, and methods is ongoing. Nonetheless, a review of the client's overall situation, needs, and preferences is usually done on a predetermined basis.

Figure 11-1 *The Phases of Support Planning*

The Role of the Support Worker in the Support Planning Process

The support worker is often the person who spends the most time with the client. As a result, the support worker is often the first person to identify changes in the client's situation, needs, or preferences. It's also likely that the support worker is the person who is responsible for implementing many of the methods identified in the client's support plan. Thus, the support worker may learn valuable information about the effectiveness of the methods.

The information the support worker obtains must be shared with the other members of the support team. The support worker's role is to make accurate observations and to communicate those observations clearly to the team.

CASE EXAMPLE 11-1

Sheryl is a support worker for an Alzheimer Day program. The support team includes the program's director and social worker, each client and client's family. When a new client comes to the program, the support team meets to establish the support plan. Sheryl attends the meeting, making note of any information that she may need in her work with the client. She also helps identify the methods to be used to assist the client to attain his or her goals.

Sheryl is often the person responsible for carrying out many of the methods. As she works with each client, Sheryl makes note of any changes to the methods used, as well as any other pertinent information.

Sheryl documents in the client's progress notes any new information she learns and any changes in method she has made. If appropriate, Sheryl discusses the changes with other members of the support team.

Each client's support plan is reviewed monthly. At this meeting, Sheryl informs the team of the information she's learned and of any modifications she has made to the methods identified. In turn, Sheryl makes note of the other team members' observations and changes in approach, including changes in client goals, needs, and preferences. She joins the team in updating the support plan.

Observation Skills

Because support workers tend to have more contact with the client, other members of the support team often rely upon the support worker to be their "eyes and ears". This places a special responsibility upon the support worker to meet three aims when making observations: to be complete, to be sensitive to detail, and to include only significant information.

You will want to pay particular attention to any unexpected condition as well as to any changes in the client's *appearance, behaviour, communication*, or *status*. You must also be careful to provide the *significant information*: the information that other members of the team will need. Do not "pad" your observations with great details about insignificant items. To do so only makes it more difficult for the other members of the team to find the information they need.

Observations should follow the ABCS: appearance, behaviour, communication, and status. We'll discuss each of these in this section.

Appearance   **Appearance** includes facial expression, posture, and stance (recall the discussion on body language in Chapter 8). It also includes the client's dress and cleanliness.

Behaviour   **Behaviour** includes any action the client takes, the level of awareness of his or her surroundings, his or her interest in the surroundings, and interest in others.

Communication   **Communication** includes what the client says and how he or she says it. This includes any feelings or emotional "message" the client sends.

Status   **Status** includes the client's current condition and how well the client functions.

Table 11-1 lists common types of observations under each ABCS. Be aware that you may be asked to observe for specific things with a particular client.

TABLE 11-1	Common Client Observations

Appearance

Client's dress, cleanliness.
Client's skin condition, presence of swellings, colour of lips, fingers, and toes.
Clarity of client's eyes, presence of any discharge from the client's nose or ears.
Client's environment: such as too hot, too cold, messy, or odours present.
Weight gain or loss.

Behaviour

Client's mood.
Client's ability to respond appropriately to stimulation (such as picking up the phone when it rings, ability to follow communication, and remember what has been said to him or her).

Communication

Client's ability to hear, see, and sense touch in communication.
Client's ability to start a conversation, to understand what is said to him or her, to appropriately respond to questions, to ask questions, ability to respond to non-verbal communication.
Quality of client's communication: use of complete sentences, ability to form words, use of nonverbal communication.

▶▶|

TABLE 11-1	Common Client Observations *(continued)*

Status

Client's sensory status: ability to see, hear, touch, smell, and taste.

Client's cognitive status: orientation, to pay attention to stimulus, to organize information, to remember, and to problem-solve.

Client's physical status: respiration, heart rate including pain, sleeping habits, movements, appetite, thirst.

Client's functional status: ability to bathe, dress, groom, feed him or her self, to move about, to grasp things.

Describing What You Observe

You must be particularly careful to describe the ABCS, not to make an assumption. *Describing* the event means just that: giving a description of what happened or what something looked, sounded, or smelled like. An assumption is a guess that may or may not be correct. Documenting an assumption does not give the reader the facts and may give the reader false information. Table 11-2 describes some common "Do's and Don'ts" of describing.

TABLE 11-2	Describing Do's and Don'ts	
DO Describe	**DON'T** Assume	
Mrs. Jones ate all of her lunch: a sandwich, coffee, and small salad.	Mrs. Jones had a good meal.	
Mrs. Jones was crying when she talked about her husband's illness.	Mrs. Jones is depressed over her husband's illness.	
Mrs. Jones was angry when the taxi came late to take her for her appointment.	Mrs. Jones was aggressive.	
Mrs. Jones' skin colour is an unusually pale shade of pink.	Mrs. Jones is ill.	

Reporting Opinions

At times, you may be asked to give an opinion about what you have observed. Opinions are drawn from the observations you have made and usually include possible "cause and effect" relationships. For example, you might observe that every time a client eats peanut butter, the client has trouble swallowing. Your observation as to the possible cause of the client's problem could be most useful in resolving the problem.

Opinions are *not* the same as assumptions. An opinion asks you to draw a conclusion from what you have observed. An assumption is a *guess*. While opinions can be useful, assumptions can be dangerous. Always make sure your opinion is based on a valid observation.

For example, if your client tells you she always feels better after speaking with her sister, she is telling you the cause and effect relationship. If you report this, it is a report of your observation. If you notice that the client seems happier after each call from her sister, you may report this as your opinion. You have seen two things happen (a call and a change in the client's behaviour) and drawn a conclusion.

 Stop and Reflect 11-1

Recall the last visit you had with a client. (If you do not yet work in the field, recall your last interaction with a friend or family member.) Describe the person, following the ABCS of observation. Write down your description.

_____

_____

_____

_____

Tell your observations to a colleague. When you are finished, ask the colleague to tell you what they heard you say. Did you find that you made some assessments? Were your observations complete? Did you miss any essential details?

_____

_____

_____

_____

Reporting Your Observations and Actions

Your observations are of little use unless you report them to the appropriate person. No one will know if the client is receiving proper care unless you report on your actions. These written reports and transcripts of verbal reports are part of the client's record. A client's record is a legal document, and may be subpoenaed for an inquest or other legal proceedings. It is important that any documentation be complete and give an accurate picture of the client's situation and the service provided.

Each agency has policies for reporting information. These policies cover the ways that information must be reported, to whom it must be reported, and when it must be reported.

Observations and Actions

When you report, you must include your actions, as well as your observations. You should also include any questions you have about the client's service. Table 11-3 discusses a simple method for organizing your information into a concise format.

TABLE 11-3	One Method of Organizing Your Information

This method of organizing information is easy to use. It organizes information into four categories: the event, the action, the result, and the client response.

Event

Can be an observation:

- Client is flushed, crying
- Client is not dressed

Can call attention to more detailed instructions found elsewhere:

- Client has new diet—details in progress notes

Can be a change in schedule:

- Client must change visit date, as has conflicting medical appointment

Can be an issue or problem

Action/Plan

The action you:

- take as a result of the event
- record that someone else took as a result of the event (based upon the report made to you)
- record to advise another to follow up on the situation

Result

What you expect (or hope) will come of the actions you take

Response

The client's response to the actions taken

Verbal and Written Reporting

There are two types of reporting: verbal and written. Within each type, there are many variations. Each agency develops their own forms. Make sure you are familiar with the forms your agency uses and with the procedure for completing each form.

Verbal reporting can take the form of a face-to-face communication, a telephone conversation, or a message left on voice mail or relayed through a third party (such as an answering service or a ward clerk).

Written reporting can take the form of a progress note, a completed checklist, a note written in a communication log, or a telephone message transcription.

No matter what type of reporting you use, you must be objective, accurate, complete, and clear when you report observations or your actions to others. Your reporting should also be organized so that the most important observation or action is presented first. You must also make sure that the person receiving your report knows the name of the client about whom your report is made, as well as the time of your observations or actions and the time of your report.

Organizing Your Report

No matter what type of report you are making, always take the time to organize the information you will be reporting *before* you report. This ensures that all your information is in order and will be presented clearly. This is particularly important if you are reporting your observations for more than one client at the same time.

Organize your observations by client. For each client, use the following procedure.

1. State the client's name.
2. State the date and time of your visit.
3. State the *most important* information first.
4. State the next most important information.
5. Repeat step four until all information has been recorded.

Making a Verbal Report

Each agency has its own policies and procedures for making verbal reports. If you are working in a long-term care facility, you will most often give a verbal report directly to another staff member. If you are working in the community, you may find that you make most of your verbal reports by telephone. The information in this section provides general guidelines for making a verbal report.

1. **Be sure you have the correct telephone number and (if applicable) extension.** Always keep the correct telephone numbers handy. You must also keep handy any extensions (voice mail numbers) you require to report information. Remember that many agencies do not have a live receptionist to forward after-hours calls. You may not be able to leave a message if you do not have the proper extension number.
2. **Let the person you are speaking to know who you are.**   If you are reporting by telephone or voice mail, make sure to state your name.
3. **State the day, date, and time of your call.**   Make sure to state this information *before* you report your observations.

4. **If you need a return call, be sure to leave the telephone number at which you can be reached.**   Make sure that the number you leave is the one at which you can be reached *when the person you are calling is likely to return your call.*

5. **Report the information about each client as described in** *Organizing Your Report.*   Verbal reports are much harder than written reports to follow. Make sure your information is well-organized.

6. **Know what kinds of information your agency requires you to report to a live person.** Certain types of information (for example, client emergencies) cannot be left on voice mail or on an answering machine. Always follow your agency's policies and know how to contact the on-call supervisor.

SR *Stop and Reflect 11-2*

Review this transcript of a report left on a supervisor's voice mail. What information is missing? What information should not be in the message at all? How could you restate this message to make it more clear, concise, and easily understood?

Hi, it's me. I saw Mrs. Rose today. Boy, is she fussy! Nothing I could do would please her! Did you know that her whole house is filled with antiques? I could hardly get the sweeper through the living room. I did notice that you've scheduled me to go back next week. I can't, because I have a doctor's appointment and won't be finished in time to get there. Oh, while I think of it, Mrs. O'Neill has to reschedule her visit for Friday because she has a doctor's appointment. Anyway, Mrs. Rose finally settled down, although she wouldn't let me do half of the things I was scheduled to do. Let me know if I should reschedule next week's visit with Mrs. Rose, OK?

_____

_____

_____

_____

_____

Written Reporting

Written reporting is called **documentation**. There are several types of documentation: such as checklists, progress notes, summary reports, and incident reports.

Checklists   Checklists require you to place a check mark in a box. Checklists provide little space for writing any information. These forms are commonly used to record outine events, such as whether a bath was given, or if vacuuming was done. Many agencies refer to these forms as "tick sheets". A sample form is shown in Figure 11- 2.

When recording on a checklist, you must be particularly careful to make sure you have the right client's form and that you are placing a check mark in the proper box. It is easy to accidentally place a check mark on the wrong row or column. This may change the information dramatically and result in improper client care.

Task \ Day	M	T	W	T	F	S	S
Activity Log							
Assist with bath							
Mouth/Skin Care							
Intake/Output							
Client Safety							
Ambulate/Mobilize							
Meal Prep							
Next Day Meal Prep							
Special Diet							
Shopping							
Feeding							
Light Cleaning							
Laundry							
Clean Fridge/Stove							
Cupboards							
ADL							
Children ADL							
Socialization							
Take to Drs. Office							
Pick Up From Hospital							
Caregiver Relief							
Other							

Client Name _____

Dates: _____ to _____

Figure 11-2 *Sample Tick Sheet*

Progress Notes   Progress notes usually contain information about the client's status and changes over time. Some agencies have separate notes for each discipline. Others use a common note: a form on which all members of the team record.

Summary Reports   Summary reports are reports which summarize a client's service over a period of time. Some agencies require support workers to complete monthly reports for each client to which they are assigned. In other agencies, support workers join the other members of the team to complete a summary report when the support plan is reviewed.

Incident Reports   Incident reports are completed when an accident or unexpected event involving a client occurs. In some cases, incident reports must be sent to the government agency that regulates the agency.

Guidelines for Recording

How you write your progress notes is also important. An illegible, messy note will not convey the information you want to share. In fact, it could mislead others who read the note incorrectly, or who have problems deciphering your handwriting.

Observing the following 10 rules will help to ensure that your notes are clear and accurate.

1. **Write legibly.**
2. **Write accurately.**   Use specific words that mean what you intend to say.
3. **Record concisely.**   Do not add information that is not useful. This can sometimes cause the person who reads your note to miss essential information.
4. **Record events chronologically.**   Make sure that you record Monday's activities before Tuesday's activities, for example. This way, the reader can follow the events as they happened.
5. **Leave no spaces between notes.**
6. **Record information as soon as practical.**   Information is always best recorded when it is fresh in your mind.
7. **Sign or initial your notes.**   Initial your note or sign your name according to your agency policy.
8. **Write in ink—do not change inks in the same note.**   Changing inks gives the impression that the note was written at two different times.
9. **Use terminology and short forms of words according to your agency policy.**
10. **Correct errors openly and honestly.**   Draw a line through the error and write the word "error" above it.

Common Terminology and Abbreviations Used in Documentation

Each agency has its own list of approved terms and abbreviations for common words and phrases. Make sure that you know the terminology and short forms your agency has approved. Table 11-4 lists some common terms and abbreviations.

TABLE 11-4	Common Terms and Abbreviations Used in Documentation
Word or Phrase	**Term or Abbreviation**
Words describing people	
client	cl
resident	res
case manager	cm
homemaker	hm
ambulates	amb

TABLE 11-4	Common Terms and Abbreviations Used in Documentation *(continued)*
Word or Phrase	**Term or Abbreviation**
Verbs	
complains of	c/o
increase	↑
decrease	↓
leading to	→
Descriptive words	
full-time	ft
part-time	pt
with	c̄ or w/
plus	+
without	w/o or s̄
Service	
morning care	am care
evening care	hs care
Frequency	
once a day	q1d or 1xd or od
twice a day	2xd or bid
three times a day	tid
every two days	q2d
every 2 hours	q2h
every 4 hours	q4h
as required, as needed, as the client prefers	prn
Equipment	
wheelchair	w/c
oxygen	O2 or O_2

Maintaining Confidentiality

In Chapter 3, we discussed confidentiality. Maintaining **confidentiality** or privacy of information you report or document is particularly important. There are three areas to which you must pay particular attention: when you receive client information (such as an assignment or a referral), when you report information (such as when you leave information on your supervisor's voice mail or complete a summary report), and when you must keep client information in your possession.

Keeping Assignment and Referral Information Confidential

You must be cautious when you receive client information or updates. Many community support workers receive client assignments and information through messages left on their voice mail. If you receive information in this manner, make sure that you retrieve those messages in a private spot so that the message cannot be overheard and any notes you make are not seen by people who are not authorized to see them.

Many facility support workers receive client updates and information through a report at the beginning of each shift. Always take care to receive this information in a secure area so that other residents, family, and other visitors to the facility do not overhear confidential information.

Keeping Information You Report Confidential

When you report client information by telephone, make sure that you are in an area that is secure (e.g., where you cannot be overheard by persons who should not hear the information). You must also make certain that you keep confidential any notes you have used to organize your thoughts.

In a facility, it can be very tempting to share client information when you see another member of the health care team. Always make sure that your communication cannot be overheard by others.

Figure 11-3   *Sharing Too Much?*

Written reports must be completed and handled so as to be kept out of the view of unauthorized persons. When you write a note or report, make sure that your work is not left where others can see it. For example, facility support workers should not leave written reports on the ledge of the nursing station. Community support workers who must complete reports at home should not leave reports on the kitchen table or in other places where unauthorized persons can see them.

If you have difficulty completing a report, speak with your supervisor. Never ask a family member, a friend, or even a colleague to help you.

Keeping Information in Your Possession Confidential

Many community support workers are required to carry client information with them. If you must keep client information in your possession, you must be extremely careful to keep it secure. Do not leave the information where it can be seen by others. Most community agencies have policies about how this information is to be kept.

Facility support workers often handle client information. In some facilities, duty rosters are printed out and given to support workers. Support workers often make notes about specific requests or changes in routine. As many people who are not staff members may be in the facility, you must also take care to keep confidential any information in your possession.

In most cases, there is no need for facility workers to keep client information with them when they are not on duty. Never take client information out of the facility without your supervisor's approval. Follow your agency's procedures for handling any confidential information accidentally taken out of the facility.

Questions for Review

1. You have been assigned to a new client. What information would you expect to find in the client's support plan?

2. What is your role in the support planning process?

3. What four types of observations should you make?

4. What is the difference between a description and an assumption? Why should you avoid documenting an assumption?

5. What is the difference between an opinion and an assumption? When should you document an opinion?

6. Why is it important to organize your information prior to making a verbal or written report?

7. Review the note to the right. Identify the errors in it. What information is unclear? What information is missing? What information is unnecessary? How would you rewrite the note?

8. What are four common types of written reports? What kinds of reports does your agency use?

Tuesday, 9:25:

Mrs. Jones was really agitated. She just wouldn't settle. Says something is wrong with her leg. Checked and looked OK to me.

Says dtr is coming to take her to store. I wonder if she'll be here for tomorrow's visit. Told her to call the office.

Harriet

Questions for Discussion

1. A resident, Mrs. Grant, asks you if you can keep a secret. She then tells you that she has been incontinent four times in the last week and is very frightened. What do you do? Should you keep the information to yourself? Why or why not? What are the possible consequences of sharing this information? What are the possible consequences of keeping it to yourself? Are there people with whom you feel you *should* share this information?

2. You are one of three support workers assigned to work with Mr. Harris, a particularly challenging client. He requires a great deal of help and reassurance. You sometimes feel that you aren't sure just how to best provide the emotional support he needs. Today, in the grocery store, you see one of the other support workers assigned to Mr. Harris. You very much want to talk to her about his support. Is this an appropriate setting to share information? Why or why not? What are the possible consequences? What might you do to share information and maintain confidentiality?

3. You work in a long-term care facility in a small town. Everyone seems to know everyone else. Today, one of your neighbours asks you about a resident, Mrs. Claire. "I know that she's been ill," the neighbour tells you, "How is she feeling now?". What do you say to the neighbour?

CHAPTER TWELVE

Safety

Learning Objectives

Through reading this chapter, you'll be able to:

1. Define safety.

2. Identify common risks related to clients, where support is provided, and the type of support.

3. Explain the chain of infection and infection control.

4. Demonstrate the appropriate handwashing technique.

5. Express the application of universal precautions.

6. Tell what the Workplace Hazardous Materials Information System is and how it applies to work in a client's home and in a long-term care facility.

7. Describe fire prevention and the steps to take in the event of a fire emergency.

8. List the general procedures to follow in the event of a client emergency.

9. Discuss the use of physical restraints as a safety measure.

Terms You'll Use

Antibacterial   An agent that destroys bacteria and/or prevents bacterial growth.

Antibiotics   Drugs that treat bacterial infections.

Bacteria   Microscopic plant life that we commonly call germs.

Chain of Infection   The process of transmission of an infection.

Clean Technique   A method of destroying many pathogens to prevent transmission of infection; also called medical asepsis.

Disinfection   The process of destroying pathogens.

Fire Hazards   Things in the environment that pose a risk of fire or could make a fire spread.

Fungi   Bacteria that use spores to reproduce. *[handwritten: Pathogen]*

Infectious Agent   Microorganism capable of causing disease. These are also called pathogens.

Isolation Precautions   Techniques used to prevent transmission of serious and highly contagious diseases.

Means of Transmission   The method of transfer of a causative agent from a reservoir to a susceptible host.

Medical Asepsis   The destruction of many pathogens to prevent transmission of infection; also called clean technique.

Microorganisms   Organisms that are microscopic, including bacteria, viruses, protozoa, rickettsia, fungi, and parasitic worms.

Nosocomial Infections   Infections acquired after admission to a facility.

Parasitic Worms   Multi-celled organisms that live within the human body and obtain nourishment from this host.

Pathogens   Microorganisms that cause infection.

Polypharmacy   The use of more than one medication.

Portal of Entry   The path into the body through which the infectious agent enters the host.

Portal of Exit   The path by which the infectious agent leaves the reservoir.

Protozoa   Parasitic, single-celled organisms that thrive in areas of poor sanitation.

Reservoir   The place where the infectious agent survives.

Rickettsia   Microscopic organisms that can only live inside cells and are almost always transmitted by insects

Susceptible Host   A person lacking resistance to a particular infectious agent.

Universal Precautions   A set of procedures used to prevent the spread of a communicable or contagious disease.

Viruses   Microscopic organisms that grow in living cells and use the cells to sustain themselves.

WHMIS   The Workplace Hazardous Materials Information System used to provide information about the proper use, handling, and storage of hazardous materials.

Safety

As we discussed in Chapter 6, safety is a basic need and is closely linked to our need for security. We all need to feel safe and secure, whether we are at home, at work, or elsewhere.

We usually think of our homes as safe. We usually consider long-term care facilities to be safe. In fact, accidents can—and do—occur in both settings. According to Statistics Canada, 60 percent of the injuries older adults sustain happen at or near their homes. Twenty percent of injuries to people aged 20 and under happen at home (Statistics Canada, *National Population Health Survey*).

Safety encompasses many factors: the client, the environment, equipment, supplies, and procedures.

We cannot eliminate all risk of harm. However, no one wants to experience a needless injury. Most injuries can be prevented. Taking proper precautions can save your client—or you—pain and frustration. Your clients entrust their safety to you when you are providing support. You must always look out for both your and your client's safety. Remember that a safe environment promotes a sense of security.

Risks Related to Your Client

Many clients are at increased risk for injury. This can be due to the client's age, health status, or medications he or she is taking. Let's take a look each factor.

Types of Risks

One of the most common risks is the risk of tripping or falling. Children can be seriously injured in a fall (for example, falling from a counter). A fall can result in significant injury or even death to an older person. Burns and injuries from fires claim over 500 victims in Canada each year (Statistics Canada, *National Population Health Survey*). Food poisoning (usually due to improper food handling or storage) also poses a hazard.

Age

Infants, children, and older adults are at greater risk for injury than are adults. Infants and children are not aware of many risks. They are naturally curious and want to touch, taste, and manipulate the things around them. A child may want to touch what's on top of the stove and may not know that the stove is hot and will burn the skin. Furthermore, an infant or young child may not be physically able to avoid a risk. For example, an infant or toddler left in a car seat in the hot sun is not able to move to avoid sunburn or heat stroke.

Older adults are also at increased risk for injury. An older client may well know that the stove is hot, but due to a diminished sensitivity to temperature and pain, may not know that he or she can be burned by accidentally touching the stove. Similarly, an older client may not see a fold in a scatter rug, catch his or her leg on the fold, and fall. Any of these changes can make a person more susceptible to injury.

Additionally, older adults are often very aware that they do not see, hear, or feel things as accurately as they once did. This can cause the older adult to become very anxious or even fearful about doing things. Sometimes this loss of security can become disabling, for example, preventing a person from going out of the house.

Health Conditions

A health condition can put a person of any age at greater risk for injury, particularly if the condition is new and the person is still adjusting to any changes it has caused. Health conditions may alter a person's balance, affect the person's ability to walk, or make the person tire more easily and be less aware of what is around him or her.

Some health conditions affect a person's cognitive ability. The person may become less aware of his or her surroundings, may not be able to perceive things properly, may not be able to make sound judgments or to problem-solve. A person whose cognitive ability has been affected may pose a danger to the person and others around him or her.

Medications

Medications may affect a person in many ways. They may alter vision or balance, make a person drowsy, or even affect how a person thinks. Some medications can make a person fearful or suspicious. A medication does not have to be a prescription medication in order to produce these types of side effects. For example, many over-the-counter cold and allergy medications can make a person drowsy.

Additionally, **polypharmacy** (the use of more than one medication) may pose particular problems. Some medications produce different side effects when combined with other medications. Sometimes, an effect becomes much more pronounced. For example, a medication that causes mild drowsiness may cause extreme drowsiness when mixed with another medication.

Risks Related to Where You Provide Support

Your client's physical surroundings may pose risks that must be addressed. Some of these risks may be related to the actual structure. Others may be related to where the building is located or to the number of other people who use the building.

Risks Related to a Client's Private Home

Many private homes you will visit will be older. Some may not be in good repair. Staircases may be very steep or not well lit, making it easy to fall. Bannister spindles may be placed too far apart, making it possible for a young child to slip between them and fall into the staircase opening. There may be loose stair treads or missing railings. A client may draw water from an unsanitary well, or may not have the space to properly store food. Clients may have old electrical equipment that has frayed or damaged cords.

Risks Related to a Long-Term Care Facility

Long-term care facilities may have equipment or supplies that could be harmful if used improperly. They may have elevator and stairway access that could allow a person to leave unescorted. Hallways may have shiny floors and be too brightly (or unevenly) lit, making it difficult for the client to see where he or she is going. Noise from other activities in the facility may distract the client, making it difficult to pay attention to the risks around him or her.

Risks Related to Location

Workers providing support in the community must be aware of any risks related to the location of their clients' homes. Some clients may live in neighbourhoods that were once residential, but are now commercial. There may be fewer people around, particularly in evening hours. The worker must be cautious of personal and client safety if travel after dark is required.

Caution must also be taken when travelling to and from the client's home, particularly late at night or early in the morning, when you are not familiar with the location of the client's home, or during months when weather is severe.

Most agencies have policies governing these issues. Always follow your agency's procedure. Discuss the issue with your supervisor if you feel that your or your client's safety is at risk.

Risks Related to the Type of Support Provided

There are two significant types of support activities that pose a risk to clients and support workers alike: the risk of physical injury and the risk of infection.

The risk of physical injury.   Support workers frequently provide physical assistance to clients who may not be able to support their own weight or move independently. Good body mechanics and proper technique are essential for both your and your client's safety. Chapter 13 discusses the fundamentals of safe physical assistance.

The risk of transmitting infection.   Infection poses a significant health risk, particularly to a client who is frail or whose immune system is compromised. Remember that an infection that produces a brief illness in a strong and healthy adult may produce a life-threatening illness in a person who is frail. Some infections are perilous to all.

The nature of personal support will require you to be in very close physical contact with clients. You must be certain to reduce the opportunity to transmit infections to a client, to transmit infections from one client to another, or to pick up an infection from a client. The risk of transmission is present in both individual homes and in long-term care facilities. We call infections obtained in facilities **nosocomial infections**. This term is not used to describe infections obtained in a client's home. We'll discuss infection control in the next section.

Health and Safety Legislation

Each province has its own health and safety legislation. This legislation usually covers employer responsibilities for safe procedures and equipment, employee responsibilities to work safely, as well as what to do if an emergency or an unsafe condition arises. This legislation usually applies to work done in a long-term care facility, but only some portions of the legislation may apply to work done in a client's home.

Infection Control

Three groups of people are at risk of infection: clients, staff, and, through exposure to staff and clients, the community at large. Support workers play a significant role in controlling the spread of infection through preventing the spread of **pathogens** (*microorganisms* that cause infection).

Types of Microorganisms

Microorganisms are microscopic organisms and are divided into six major types: *bacteria, viruses, protozoa, rickettsia, fungi,* and *parasitic worms.* Among these, bacteria and viruses are the most common. However, any of the six types can cause a serious infection.

Most disease-producing microorganisms produce toxins as a waste product of their activity. The body's immune system tries to fight off these toxins. This results in the common symptoms of an infection: inflamed, reddened, or hot areas; pain; aches; swelling; fever; chills; or discharge (runny eyes, nose, ears, or pus from a wound).

Bacteria.   **Bacteria** are microscopic plant life. They can multiply quickly. One common name for bacteria is *germs.* Bacteria thrive in an environment that is warm, moist, dark with plenty of oxygen, and some form of nourishment. Bacteria can survive on living or dead material, as long as oxygen and nourishment are available. Not all bacteria are harmful. In fact, some are necessary for our bodies to break down food.

Some bacteria are harmful only if they enter certain areas of the body. For example, the bacteria *Escherichia coli* is found in the intestinal tract, where it helps break down food particles. When *E. coli* enters other areas of the body, such as the urinary tract, it can cause an infection.

A healthy person is usually able to fight off many mild bacterial infections. Many drugs called **antibiotics** have been developed to treat more severe bacterial infections. Antibiotics work in one of two ways: killing the bacteria directly or by stopping bacterial growth so that the body's own immune system can effectively fight the infection. You've likely taken an antibiotic for a sore throat or to treat another type of infection.

Remember that antibiotics are developed to treat specific bacteria. An antibiotic effective against one type of bacteria may not be effective against another type. Additionally, bacteria can adapt so as not to be affected by antibiotics developed for the initial strain. Many researchers have linked antibiotic use to the development of antibiotic-resistant bacteria.

Viruses.   **Viruses** grow in living cells and use the components of the cell to sustain themselves. They are extremely small and are harder to treat because any drug must kill the infection *without* killing the cell in which the infection lives. Antibiotics are not effective against viruses. However, some viruses (e.g., measles, polio, and many strains of influenza) can be prevented by vaccines.

As with bacteria, a healthy person may be able to fight off weak viruses. However, some viruses may actually make it easier for the person to catch other infections (viral or bacterial).

Protozoa.   **Protozoa** are parasitic, single-celled organisms that thrive in areas with poor sanitation. Malaria is the most common disease caused by a protozoan. Toxoplasmosis is another protozoa-borne infection that is carried by cats and can be contracted by humans through the improper handling of cat feces. Some strains of protozoa-borne infections are resistant to drug treatment.

Rickettsia.   **Rickettsia** are similar to viruses in that they can live only inside cells. Rickettsia are almost always transmitted by insects. Many rickettsia are not harmful to humans. Some common rickettsia-caused human infections are Rocky Mountain Spotted Fever and typhus. Most rickettsia-transmitted infections can be treated effectively with antibiotics.

Fungus. Fungi are bacteria that use spores to reproduce. Fungi can be found in air, soil, and water. Fungi are not a major cause of infection. One of the most common fungal infections is athlete's foot. Many fungal infections respond well to antibiotics.

Parasitic worms.   **Parasitic worms** are multi-celled organisms that live within the human body and obtain their nourishment from this host. One of the most common of the parasitic diseases is *trichinosis* which can occur when raw or undercooked pork is eaten. *Beef tapeworm* can be contracted by eating insufficiently cooked beef from a cow that was infected by the tapeworm. Another common, but lesser known parasitic infection, is *hookworm* which can be transmitted from dogs and cats to humans through poor pet care and poor hygiene. There are a number of drugs that can treat parasitic infections.

How Infection Is Transmitted

Six things must be present for an infection to be transmitted. These six items are often called the *chain of infection*. The chain represents the process as well as the cyclical nature of infection transmission.

The Chain of Infection

The **chain of infection** has six components: the infectious agent, the reservoir, the portal of exit, the means of transmission, the portal of entry, and a susceptible host (Figure 12-1). Each component is defined in this section.

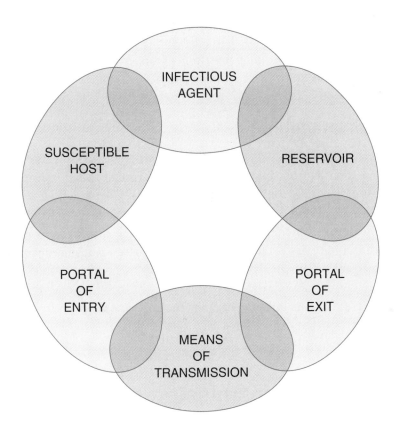

Figure 12-1 *The Chain of Infection*

Infectious agent.   **Infectious agents** are one of the microorganisms capable of causing disease. These are also called pathogens.

Reservoir.   The **reservoir** is a place where the agent survives, such as on or in a client, support workers, other caregivers, equipment, and the environment. Remember that the reservoir need not be a living thing. It simply must have access to the nutrients required to survive. For example, an agent can live on moisture and deposits left by a handprint on a doorhandle.

Portal of exit.   The **portal of exit** is the path by which the infectious agent leaves the reservoir. This is usually through blood, wound drainage, respiratory secretions, feces, or other body substances.

Means of transmission.   The **means of transmission** is the method of transfer of a causative agent from a reservoir to a susceptible host. This includes physical contact, breathing in of airborne pathogens, or ingesting pathogens. Unclean hands are among the most common means of transmission.

Portal of entry.   The **portal of entry** is the path into the body, such as a break in the skin (a cut or other wound) or through a mucous membrane (such as the eye, mouth, vagina, rectum). For example, a person who contracts an agent on his or her hand may transmit the agent to a mucous membrane by touching his or her mouth, eye, or other membrane.

Susceptible host.   A **susceptible host** is a person lacking resistance to a particular pathogenic agent. Host factors which influence susceptibility include: underlying disease, immune status, medications, nutrition status, as well as certain types of treatments (such as chemotherapy or immunosuppressive drugs).

Nosocomial Infections

Clients who are receiving support come in contact with many people. They may receive treatments and services from many people (formal caregivers and family members). They may have more visits from friends or neighbours. Clients who live in long-term care facilities are often in very close contact with other clients who have illnesses.

We use the term nosocomial infections to describe an infection acquired after admission to a facility. Clients receiving services at home are also at increased risk for infection as a result of this increased contact. In fact, clients at home may come in contact with many people who are not aware of the need to take the proper precautions. As a result, clients in home settings may be exposed to more infections than one might expect.

Photo 12-1
Handwashing is the simplest and most effective method of infection control a support worker can use.

Reducing the Transmission of Infection

In order to reduce the transmission of infection, you must break the chain of infection. The primary method by which a support worker can break the chain is by destroying pathogens before they can be transmitted to other people. We use the term **disinfection** to describe the process of destroying pathogens.

One of the most effective ways the support worker can destroy pathogens is by practising **clean technique** (also called **medical asepsis**). Clean technique does not remove all pathogens, but it does reduce the number of pathogens.

Handwashing is the most important component of clean technique (Photo 12-1). Proper handwashing helps eliminate microorganisms that can cause disease.

Microorganisms on human skin are grouped into two types: resident microorganisms that live within the skin and transient microorganisms that are acquired through routine activities. Handwashing is very effective in eliminating transient microorganisms and (with *antibacterial* soap) can be effective against resident microorganisms. Antibacterial soap contains an **antibacterial** agent that destroys bacteria and prevents bacterial growth.

In order for handwashing to be effective, it must be done correctly and as often as practical. The best handwashing technique is of no use if it is not performed when necessary. You should wash your hands:

- before and after giving care to a person
- before putting on gloves
- after removing gloves
- when you have been in contact with any body fluid or substance, whether it is your own or that of another person

- after you have coughed, blown your nose, or sneezed
- before you handle, prepare, or eat food
- after you handle money
- after you have touched any surface that is unclean
- after using the washroom

Studies indicate that people think that they wash their hands more consistently than they do. Other studies link the lack of proper handwashing to the potential for illness, many of which are serious and potentially deadly.

Table 12-1 describes three types of handwashing and when each is most appropriate and Procedure 12-1 describes the method of proper handwashing.

TABLE 12-1	Handwashing Types
Type	**Best to use:**
Plain soap and running water	after most activities requiring handwashing. Properly done, this process will remove dirt and transient microorganisms. This remains the best method of preventing the transmission of microorganisms.
Antibacterial soap and running water	in situations where risk of transmission is high (such as caring for a client whose immune system is depressed or who is very frail). In addition to removing dirt and transient micro-organisms, this process inhibits the growth of resident microorganisms. Remember that these soaps are not required in most instances and their overuse may contribute to antibiotic-resistant bacteria.
Alcohol hand-rub products	when handwashing is not possible, but **only** when hands are not soiled with dirt, blood, or other matter. These products kill or inhibit the growth of transient and resident micro-organisms, but do not remove them. Alcohol hand rubs do not remove dirt. Alcohol hand-rub products are relatively new items. As they are alcohol-based, excessive use may cause excessive skin dryness and increase the risk of skin cracking. Care must be taken in their use.

EQUIPMENT

Soap

Clean paper towels

Orange stick or
nail brush

Wastebasket

Procedure 12-1: Proper Handwashing

Liquid soap is preferable to bar soap, as bar soap often harbours microorganisms. If you must use bar soap, rinse it off under the running water before you use it. Be aware that liquid soap dispensers (particularly those found in many homes) can also be dirty. Take the time to wash off the plunger of the dispenser if necessary.

1. Make sure that your arms are bare at least 10-12 centimetres above your wrists. Push up your sleeves and your watch.
2. Remove rings.
3. Turn on the tap and adjust the water to a comfortable, warm temperature.
4. Wet your hands and wrists thoroughly under the running water. Be sure to keep your hands lower than your elbows, so that dirty water does not run up your arm.
5. Apply soap. Work up a lather by weaving your fingers together and moving them back and forth.
6. Continue this motion for 10-15 seconds, longer if your hands are very dirty or if obvious signs of dirt remain.
7. Wash sides and backs of each hand.
8. Wash under fingernails by rubbing the fingertips of each hand against the palm of the other. Use a nail brush or orange stick if necessary. You will find it easier to keep this area clean if your nails are kept short.
9. Wash your wrists.
10. If you are using bar soap, *drop* the soap back onto its dish. Avoid touching the dish or any soap residue in it.
11. Rinse your hands thoroughly.
12. Using a clean paper towel, dry your hands.
13. Using another paper towel, turn off the taps. Avoid touching the taps with your hands.
14. Dispose of the paper towels.

Universal Precautions

Universal precautions are a set of procedures used to prevent the spread of a communicable or contagious disease. There are many such diseases. Some of the more common ones are measles, chicken pox, and mumps. Human immunodeficiency virus (HIV), hepatitis B, and tuberculosis are communicable diseases that can have serious consequences.

Universal precautions are focussed on establishing barriers to prevent contact with bodily fluids. They were first established by the Centers for Disease Control and Prevention (CDC) in the United States. The CDC suggests that universal precautions be used with all clients. Many agencies have policies on the use of universal precautions. Make sure that you are aware of your agency's policy.

Most Canadian agencies follow the CDC's universal precautions. Table 12-2 describes these precautions.

TABLE 12-2	Universal Precautions

1. Protective, disposable gloves should be worn:

   - when touching any client's blood, body fluids, mucous membranes, or non-intact skin;
   - when you have broken skin;
   - when you come in contact with surfaces soiled with blood or body fluids (such as a bathroom floor, soiled linens, or incontinence briefs);
   - when changing diapers if visible blood or diarrhea is present; or
   - when handling clothes, bed linen, or equipment that has been soiled by body fluids.

2. Gloves should be disposed of after each contact. Never wash disposable gloves for reuse.

3. Hands should be washed with warm, soapy water before gloves are put on, immediately after gloves are removed, and any time hands are soiled.

4. Gowns, aprons and, if needed, eye protection, should be worn during procedures that are likely to generate splashes of blood or other body fluids (such as vomit or urine).

5. Masks may be worn when working with a client who is coughing excessively.

6. Precautions should be taken when disposing of sharps, including needles. To prevent needlestick injuries, needles should not be recapped, purposely bent or broken by hand, removed from disposable syringes or otherwise manipulated by hand. After they are used, dispose of syringes and needles in an empty coffee can. Cover the can with a lid. When the can is full, place it in a plastic garbage bag. Dispose of this bag as directed by your agency. Similar procedures should be followed when disposing of razor blades.

7. Wear gloves when collecting specimens of body fluids (such as urine, feces, or sputum). Tightly close the container so it will not leak and place it in another, larger container for transportation.

8. If you accidentally get contaminated bodily fluids on a mucous membrane or broken skin, or are stuck by a contaminated needle, you should:

   - immediately wash the contaminated area thoroughly with soap or antiseptic cleanser and warm water. It is not necessary to use a hard brush, as this may irritate skin and result in an open sore;
   - contact your supervisor to report the exposure; and
   - be prepared to consider having your blood tested and periodically retested during the following year.

9. If you have a skin lesion or weeping dermatitis, you should not provide direct client care or handle client-care equipment until the skin condition is cleared up.

The Use of Gloves

Using gloves is an important part of the universal precautions. Gloves help to reduce transmission of infectious agents. Procedure 12-2 outlines the way to apply, use, and remove gloves.

Procedure 12-2: Applying, Using and Removing Gloves

Applying and Using Gloves

1. Use a new pair of gloves for each client. Replace the gloves if you touch unclean surfaces.

2. Wash your hands before applying gloves.

3. Pull your gloves over your wrists. If you are wearing a gown, pull the glove over the cuff of the gown.

4. Remove gloves before touching surfaces not part of the client's care (such as answering the phone or door). Put on a fresh pair of gloves when you return to the client's care.

5. If your glove develops a hole, rip, or tear, remove both gloves immediately, wash your hands, and put on a fresh pair. Remember that jewellery and long or ragged fingernails can easily puncture a disposable glove. Trim nails and remove jewellery before applying gloves.

6. If your gloves become contaminated, remove and replace them before completing your client's care.

Removing Gloves (See Figure 12-2)

1. Remove one glove by grasping it just below the cuff. (Figure a)

2. Pull the glove down over your hand, making sure that the glove is inside out. (Figure b)

3. Hold the glove you have removed in your gloved hand.

4. Slide two fingers of your *ungloved* hand between your skin and the glove on your other hand. Do not touch the outside of your gloved hand.

5. Pull the glove down over your hand and over the other glove.

6. Holding the gloves by the *inside*, dispose of the gloves.

7. Wash your hands.

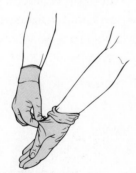   

Figure 12-2a   **Figure 12-2b**   *Removing Gloves*

Isolation Precautions

Isolation precautions are frequently used when a client has a disease that is serious and highly contagious. Isolation precautions can also be used when a client is so frail that the risk of infection must be minimized. Table 12-3 describes the major components of isolation technique.

TABLE 12-3	Isolation Technique

1. Isolation procedures may require you to wear gloves, a gown, a mask, or eye protection. You may have to use special procedures (such as double-bagging contaminated items). Make sure you know what specific precautions are to be followed.

2. Collect all necessary equipment before you enter the room. This reduces the number of trips in and out and reduces the potential for drafts and other irritants. It also means that you can spend more time with the client.

3. Remember that anything that falls to the floor is considered to be contaminated.

4. Use paper towels to handle contaminated items. If your gloves or hands become contaminated, do not handle clean items.

5. Do not touch your eyes, nose, mouth, hair, or other body parts when caring for your client.

6. Remove and dispose of gloves, gowns, and other protective garments properly.

7. Wash your hands after removing any protective garments.

Isolation can have devastating effects on the person. A person with a serious and highly communicable disease may worry that he or she will infect others. The person may feel unclean, untouchable, and unwanted. The person can become very lonely as visits are often limited and the ability to receive real, caring touch is severely restricted.

Remember that it is the disease the person has that is undesirable, not the person. Make sure to treat the person with respect and to preserve his or her dignity. If possible, provide things in the person's room that interest him or her and help occupy the person's time, such as a telephone, radio, television, magazines, or books. Whenever possible, spend a few minutes visiting with the person. Make sure that your body language as well as your words show the person that you care for him or her.

Cleaning Equipment

Equipment must be kept clean to reduce the potential of transmitting harmful microorganisms. In most cases (particularly in a client's home), a thorough washing with soap and water is all that is needed. A thorough cleansing washes microorganisms away.

In some cases, there is a need to disinfect items to further reduce the risk of the transmission of microorganisms. Disinfection either kills microorganisms or inhibits their growth. Most commercial items sold as chemical disinfectants are not effective against all microorganisms.

Sterilization kills virtually all microorganisms. Boiling is the most common method of sterilization.

You must realize that disinfection and sterilization by themselves do not remove dirt. Dirt can harbour microorganisms. Thus, the best disinfection or sterilization procedure will not be effective if the area is dirty (Figure 12-3). A good rule of thumb is, "Clean first, then disinfect or sterilize when necessary."

Figure 12-3 *Remember that disinfection and sterilization do not remove dirt. You must clean first.*

You always must be careful when cleaning or disinfecting with chemicals. In the next section, we'll discuss a labelling system that helps you to identify the proper procedure for handling and storing chemicals.

Workplace Hazardous Materials Information System

The Workplace Hazardous Materials Information System (*WHMIS*) was created by the Government of Canada in 1987. The legislation governing WHMIS and how it is used is governed by both federal and provincial legislation.

WHMIS' purpose is to make sure that employers and workers have the information they need about hazardous materials so as to handle, use, and store these materials safely. There are three components to the WHMIS system: product labels, material safety data sheets (MSDS), and worker education. These three components apply to all long-term care facilities. Provincial regulations govern how WHMIS applies to work done in clients' homes but, in most cases, provincial legislation requires that workers be educated in the handling, use, and storage of hazardous materials they may be expected to use.

WHMIS groups hazardous materials under three general headings: flammability, reactivity, and health.

Flammability

Flammable substances are things that can ignite and burn easily. Many things other than open flame can ignite a flammable substance. Sparks from electrical equipment and heat from a source, such as a stove, toaster, or dryer, can ignite flammable substances.

Reactivity

Reactive substances are things that can react with another substance to form a hazardous material. It's important to note that substances that are relatively harmless alone can react with other substances to become very toxic. For example, vinegar is a common item in many homes and is often used for cleaning. Used alone, it is quite safe. When vinegar is mixed with bleach, it produces a toxic gas.

Health Risk

Many common substances can pose a health risk if used improperly or for too long a period of time. For example, many cleaners (including bleach) can irritate skin if the substance is left in direct contact with the skin. Even shampoos and other personal care substances can irritate mucous membranes. Some substances (such as household bleach) can irritate the airway if inhaled.

Labelling of Hazardous Products

WHMIS legislation does not require that household products be labelled. However, many of the six WHMIS Symbols are commonly used to label household products, as well as materials found in long-term care facilities. Each label and its meaning is presented in Figure 12-4.

Flammable   Corrosive   Explosive   Chronic Hazard   Biohazard   Reactive

Figure 12-4 *WHMIS Symbols*

Always read the label (and, if available, the Material Safety Data Sheet) when using cleaning and other household substances. Make particular note of any protective equipment you need to safely work with the substance, as well as the proper procedure for use. Ask your supervisor if you are unsure how to properly use a substance.

Fire Safety

When we speak about fire safety, we are actually describing two things: *fire prevention* and *safety in a fire emergency*.

Fire prevention refers to the steps that you take on a day-to-day basis to prevent a fire emergency from occurring. Many of these steps are much like those you would do to keep your own home safe such as: not smoking in bed, checking for frayed electrical cords, or not leaving items on the stove unattended. Some procedures are different, though. We'll discuss specific approaches in this section.

Safety in a fire emergency means the steps that you take to respond to a fire. These steps are broken down into two parts:

1. The actions that you take if you are the first person to discover the fire; and
2. The actions that you take if you hear a fire or smoke alarm.

In each case, the **main purpose is to ensure the safety of the clients, visitors, volunteers, and other staff.**

The material in this section is intended to introduce you to the basic ideas about fire safety. You'll find that your agency has a specific fire safety procedure which must be followed.

The Main Components of Fire Prevention

There are two main components of fire prevention: reducing or eliminating *fire hazards* and reducing or stopping *hazardous behaviour*.

Fire Hazards

When we speak about **fire hazards**, we mean the things in the environment that pose a risk of fire, or that could make a fire spread more quickly. Clients may not be able to easily identify these hazards due to poor vision or sense of touch or, possibly, confusion. Some of the more common hazards are discussed in this section.

Ashes from cigarettes, cigars, or pipes.   The most careful smoker can accidentally dump hot ashes in a wastepaper basket or onto furnishings. As well, some ashtrays are shallow and allow cigarettes and ashes to easily fall off their edge. A person with impaired vision may not realize that he or she has placed a lit cigarette on a combustible surface.

You should make sure that all ashes are dumped into a metal can after the smoker is through. Be sensitive to the smell and sight of smoke—if you see or smell something, check it out.

Damaged electrical cords.   Often, people unplug an item by pulling on the cord, instead of the plug. This can break the wiring, even if the covering is not broken. As well, items, including cords, wear out. If the cord or plug is frayed or broken, or feels warm to the touch, it is a fire hazard. The cord should be unplugged until it can be checked by a qualified person.

Overloaded extension cords.   Extension cords present two potential hazards: fire and falls. Many older homes do not have the number of electrical outlets required to power the quantity of electrical appliances we use. Sometimes, the location of the outlet is inconvenient. Your client may use extension cords without thinking about whether the circuit is overloaded, or whether the amperage rating for the cord has been exceeded (Photo 12-2). It's good practice to use only one appliance per cord, and to unplug the appliance when it is not in use.

Damaged electrical equipment.   As with cords, equipment itself wears out or breaks. Damage due to a drop on a floor or getting wet, for example, often can't be seen. Unplug any electrical equipment you observe not functioning properly, or from which you get a shock.

Flammable materials.   Many chemicals we use on a daily basis are *flammable,* meaning that they can easily burn. It is often confusing because, in the English language, both the words flammable and inflammable are used to refer to these items. Any chemical or material labelled as flammable, that carries the WHMIS symbol for flammable materials, or which you know to be flammable, should be properly handled and stored. You should read, understand, and follow the use and storage instructions for flammable chemicals. Properly dispose of cloths or papers soaked in the chemical. If in doubt about how to handle a particular chemical, ask your supervisor.

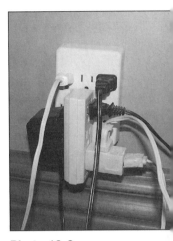

Photo 12-2
Overloaded electrical outlets can overload circuits, creating a fire hazard.

Hazardous Behaviour

Long-Term Care Facilities

One of the greatest hazardous behaviours in any facility is careless smoking. While the most careful smoker poses a risk, cognitively impaired or physically disabled smokers are at much greater risk, both to themselves and others. Cognitively impaired smokers may no longer understand why it is not safe to smoke in bed. They may drop ashes in wastebaskets. A physically disabled smoker may not be able to pick up a lit cigarette from his or her lap, a couch, or carpet.

Most nursing homes, homes for the aged and retirement homes have set policies about smoking: where (and possibly at what times) residents can smoke, whether some residents can smoke without supervision, or carry their own cigarettes, matches, etc. Make sure that you know the policies of your own facility about smoking. If you do encounter a hazardous situation, report it to your supervisor.

Community Settings

Clients living in their own home or apartment can unknowingly have unsafe behaviours. Sometimes, the client simply doesn't realize that something is a hazard. At other times, the client may not have realized that a situation has become unsafe (such as not noticing that an electrical cord is frayed). Occasionally, the client cannot see, hear, smell, or feel things accurately enough to know that there is a potential problem.

Clients should be provided information on fire hazards, including smoking, overloading electrical wiring, and improper use of the stove. Many fire departments provide brochures on fire safety free of charge. Remember that your client has a great deal of control over how he or she will use this information and whether he or she will follow the advice given.

Be the eyes, ears, hands, and nose for your client. Identify fire hazards you see and talk them over with the client. Most clients will want to change a situation that is hazardous.

Safety in a Fire Emergency

The other component of fire safety has to do with handling a fire emergency. This component has two parts:

1. What to do if you are the person discovering a fire; and
2. What to do when you hear the fire alarm.

If You Discover a Fire

No matter where you work, in a fire emergency there are two important points to remember:

1. **The sooner the fire department is called, the sooner they will arrive.** You are not trained to fight fires—the fire department is. Make sure that the fire department is called as quickly as possible. Once they arrive, they will give you instructions as to what to do.
2. **Fire itself is not often the killer—smoke is.** Make sure that you do what you can to prevent smoke from spreading, such as closing doors or windows of the room that has the smoke.

Long-Term Care Facilities

Each long-term care facility has its own procedure to handle fire emergencies. In general, though, the procedure requires you to:

1. Pull the fire alarm or call the fire department.
2. Remove anyone in immediate danger, if possible.
3. If the fire is in a room or contained area, close the door to contain the fire and smoke.
4. Move residents out of the fire area, usually to an area protected by fire doors.
5. Close all other corridor and room doors.
6. If the fire is small, and you feel you can safely do so, try to put the fire out.

It is of extreme importance that you know and follow your agency's procedure for a fire emergency. This ensures that you are working as a team in the most effective manner.

Please note that most long-term care facilities do not immediately evacuate the entire building when the fire alarm sounds. These homes generally do what is called a 4-stage evacuation.

Stage 1   Removal of anyone in immediate danger, if possible

Stage 2   Horizontal Evacuation (like step 4, page 188)

Stage 3   Vertical Evacuation (move residents to a lower floor)

Stage 4   Premises Evacuation (move residents out of the building)

You would perform a Stage 3 or 4 evacuation when the fire marshall (the person on staff who is in charge in a fire emergency) or the fire department tells you to do so.

Community Settings

A fire emergency procedure should be tailored to each client's home. A fire evacuation plan should be developed, identifying the emergency exit for each room. As many fires start at night, any fire plan should include escape routes from rooms in which people sleep.

Many people live in apartment buildings. Often, the local fire department has specific recommendations as to the steps to take if a fire erupts in a client's unit. These recommendations often include the seven steps listed here.

1. Remove anyone in immediate danger, if possible. Assist your client to leave the building if able, or to wait in a stairwell landing, **with the fire door closed**, if not able to leave.
2. Close room or apartment doors to contain the fire.
3. Pull the nearest fire alarm or call the fire department.
4. Close all other corridor and apartment doors, if possible.
5. If possible, return to apartment to fight fire. Do this only if the fire is small, is not fed by gas or flammable liquid, and is reasonably safe to attempt.
6. If necessary, move others out of the fire area, usually to a stairwell landing protected by fire doors.
7. **Never use elevators in a fire emergency**.

Remember that the procedures in some buildings may require you to assist clients to get out **as a first step**. Often, these are buildings where all apartments have wheelchair access to the outside (they are all on the first floor, for example). It is essential to read and follow the procedure established for the client's setting.

If You Hear the Fire Alarm

Long-Term Care Facilities

These procedures vary from facility to facility. In general, though, the procedure asks you to:
1. **Report to the fire location**, bringing, if possible, wheelchairs to assist in transporting residents.

2. **Follow the directions of the person in charge** (the fire marshall) with regard to evacuating residents, closing doors, and/or helping in other ways.
3. **Unless instructed to do so, don't use the telephone to call** other floors, the switchboard, etc. You may prevent important calls from the fire department from getting through.

Community Settings

Clients living in apartments should respond to a fire alarm, even though the fire is not in their units. If you are visiting a client when the fire alarm sounds, you must assist the client. As with long-term care facilities, each apartment building (particularly buildings catering to older adults or persons with physical disabilities) has specific guidelines. In general, the following steps are often included:

1. **Call the fire department.** Meet the fire department in or near the lobby with a list of clients. If you can't leave the apartment, let the fire department know, and provide the list by phone, if necessary.
2. **Reassure the client.**
3. **If a client cannot leave the building without using the elevator, instruct the client to remain in their apartment, unless told otherwise by the fire captain or other person in charge.**
4. **Close the apartment door, but leave it unlocked.** This allows the fire department to quickly enter, should they need to do so.
5. **Block door with wet towel if smoke begins to seep in.** If smoke begins to enter heating or other vents, block them off with wet towels pinned or taped to the vents.
6. **If smoke enters the apartment, keep low to the floor.** Move client to a balcony, if available.

Client Emergencies

You should be prepared to provide emergency assistance to a client. It is strongly recommended that you take a first aid and cardiopulmonary resuscitation (CPR) course offered by a recognized safety organization in your province. Life-saving techniques such as CPR or clearing the airway of an unconscious victim should be learned and practised under the guidance of a trained professional. Speak with your supervisor to find out which organizations offer courses in your area.

This section provides basic information on responding to client emergencies. Some clients may have specific instructions to follow in the event of an emergency. As well, your employer will have specific instructions to follow in an emergency. It is important to know what the specific instructions are and to follow them if the situation arises.

In the absence of specific instructions, use the following as a guide:

1. Remember that the two purposes of emergency care are to prevent death and prevent additional injury.
2. Remain calm. You are of no use to your client if you become so upset that you cannot assist.

3. Assess the situation. Is it safe for you to assist the client? Are there hazards, such as fire or live electricity which must be controlled before you can assist? Can you deal with the situation or do you need to call for help to do so?

4. If possible, remove any hazards. Avoid moving the client unless you have no other alternative.

5. Practise universal precautions. You may have to adapt your approach if proper supplies are not readily available. For example, if gloves are not readily available, you may cover your hand with a plastic bag in order to apply pressure to a bleeding wound.

6. Check for signs of life-threatening conditions: no breathing, no pulse, or profuse bleeding.

7. Call for help or have someone else in the room do this for you. Table 12-4 outlines the information to have ready to provide the emergency personnel answering the call.

8. Keep the client warm. Use blankets, towels, coats, or sweaters.

9. If the client is conscious, ask if he or she has pain or discomfort. Discourage the client from moving as it may make an injury worse.

10. Reassure the victim that help is on the way.

11. Do not give a victim any food or liquids.

12. Assist the person, if possible. Table 12-5 provides accepted methods of treating common emergencies. **Never attempt a procedure you have not been trained to perform, unless you are following the step-by-step instructions of trained emergency personnel.**

13. Stay with the person until help has arrived. You may be asked to accompany the person to hospital. If so, advise your agency.

TABLE 12-4	Emergency Information

Contacting emergency services is commonly called *activating emergency medical services* or activating EMS. In many areas of Canada, you activate EMS by dialling 9-1-1. Some areas do not yet have this service, so make certain that you know the number for your area.

When you call emergency services, make certain you have the following information:

1. Your location: street name and number, unit or apartment number, if applicable. In a rural area, it's often helpful to know the nearest main intersection or landmark.

2. The telephone number from which you are calling.

3. What has happened. Be sure to tell the emergency personnel if the person has a life-threatening condition: no pulse, no breathing, or profuse bleeding.

4. Description of injuries.

EMS personnel may ask you specific questions or give you instructions to carry out while help is on the way. Provide this information and follow any instructions to the best of your ability.

TABLE 12-5   What To Do If...

This table describes accepted methods for responding to common emergencies. Be certain to:

- activate EMS for any serious emergency unless specifically directed to do otherwise; and
- follow your agency's procedure for handling emergencies.

Problem	Solution
The person is not conscious	Lean close to the person's ear and loudly say, "Are you OK? Wake up!"
The person appears to not be breathing	1. Open the person's airway by placing two fingers under the person's chin and and pulling the chin forward. 2. Place your ear near the person's mouth. Listen and feel for breathing. 3. If the person is not breathing, pinch the person's nose, place your mouth over theirs and slowly blow air into the victim's mouth. 4. If the air does not cause the person's chest to rise, reposition the head and try again. 5. If the person's chest still does not rise, the airway may be obstructed. Attempt to clear the airway using the Heimlich maneuver if the person is conscious. Use the procedure below if the person is not conscious or becomes unconscious.
The person's airway is obstructed	1. Attempt to clear the airway using the Heimlich maneuver if the person is conscious. 2. If the person is unconscious, locate the proper spot for compressions by running your finger up the person's rib cage to the point where the ribs join. Position your two fingers below this point, with your fingers pointing toward the person's head. Deliver quick upward thrusts to clear the airway.

▶▶|

TABLE 12-5	What To Do If... *(continued)*
The person is bleeding profusely	1. Use universal precautions. Wear gloves if possible. 2. Use clean material (washcloth, clothing, etc.) to cover the site. 3. Apply pressure directly over the site with your hand. 4. Leave your hand in place until the bleeding is controlled.
The person appears to be having a seizure	1. Lower the person to the floor. 2. Cushion the head by placing a towel under the head or by cradling the head in your lap. 3. Loosen tight clothing. 4. Push furniture or other objects out of the way so that the person will not hit them and injure him- or herself. 5. Do not place any object in the person's mouth. 6. Do not restrain the person's movement.
The person is burned	1. Stop the burning process. Extinguish flames by wrapping the person in a heavy blanket or coat to smother flames. Cool heat burns by running cool water over the site. Disconnect or unplug (if possible) any electrical appliance that is causing a burn by using an object that does not conduct electricity (dry rope or wood, for example). 2. Cover the burn with a clean, wet covering. DO NOT apply ointments, oils, or fats to the burn.

Restraints

Restraints are devices that restrict a client's movement. There are two main types of restraints: chemical and physical.

Chemical restraints are medications given to clients to control behaviours. Chemical restraints usually include drugs like sedatives or antipsychotic drugs. It is generally agreed that it is not acceptable to use these drugs to control behaviour that is bothersome but not unsafe.

Physical restraints alter a client's ability to move. Examples of these restraints are wheelchair lap belts, vest restraints, bed rails, geriatric chairs with tables, or even recliner chairs that prohibit a person from getting up and out of the chair.

For many years, restraints were seen as a way of keeping a client safe. For example, clients were restrained so as to keep them from falling, or to keep clients from entering unsafe areas of a building.

We now know that restraints can be very harmful or even deadly if improperly used. The effects of restricted movement can result in decreased muscle and bone strength, pressure sores (decubitus ulcers), incontinence, and constipation. An improperly applied restraint can cause a resident to slip and possibly asphyxiate. Clients who are restrained may become agitated, depressed, or angry as a result of the restraint.

Restraint use has decreased since the 1980s, largely because of increased awareness of the risks of restraint use, increased awareness of other ways to prevent falls, and the development of safer alternatives and less restrictive restraints. Table 12-6 lists several alternatives to restraints.

TABLE 12-6	Alternatives to Restraints

Many clients and long-term care facilities have found that the following alternatives can reduce the use of restraints.

1. Using positioning devices to assist a client to keep his or her balance in a chair. (Instead of a lap belt or vest restraint.)

2. Using lower beds, or placing a bed directly on the floor. (Instead of using bed rails that a client tries to climb over.)

3. Removing rugs and other items that present a risk for falls. (Instead of restraining a client's freedom to walk.)

However, there are times when a specific client's condition can benefit from a properly applied restraint. An example of this is a client's use of a velcro leg strap to assist him or her in keeping his or her legs properly positioned in a wheelchair. The client can open or reposition the velcro belt to maintain comfort, yet make use of the benefits of the strap to maintain his or her legs in the position the client desires.

Each restraint has a proper method of application. You must know and follow the procedure for the restraint, as well as know where and how to attach the restraint. The client must be checked regularly (this is a legal requirement) to ensure that the restraint remains properly applied. The restraint must also be removed on a regular basis to allow the client to move and, if necessary, to attend to bodily needs.

Each facility should have a policy covering the use of restraints. For example, a doctor's order is required to use restraints in Long-Term Care Facilities. You must follow the policy set by your facility. The following list provides some general guidelines for the proper use of restraints. You must always remember that any restraint is used for specific purposes, not for the caregiver's convenience or comfort.

1. Restraints should be used only after a thorough assessment of all other options. Assessment of the client's need for the restraint should continue after the restraint is used. A client may not always need to use a restraint simply because one was once necessary.
2. The restraint applied should be the correct type and size and be in good repair. Do not use any restraint that is damaged or so worn that it is unsafe.
3. Apply the restraint according to the manufacturer's instructions.
4. Adjust the restraint so that it is comfortable for the client. If at all possible, the client should be able to adjust the restraint.
5. Document the use of the restraint according to your agency's guidelines.

Questions for Review

1. What are the three types of risk encountered in support work? Give two examples of each type.
2. Describe the chain of infection.
3. Describe two things you can do to reduce the risk of transmission of pathogens.
4. Describe the three methods of handcleaning. When is it appropriate to use each type?
5. When should you wash your hands?
6. What are the two purposes of emergency care?
7. What are the five general guidelines you should follow when a client in your care uses a restraint?

Questions for Discussion

1. Consider these two case studies. Discuss:
   a. whether or not each client should be restrained; and
   b. what other measures might be taken.

   Case 1
   Mr. Greave is a resident in a long-term care facility. He spends most of the day wandering through the halls on his floor. He usually stays in the hall, but recently he has been entering other residents' rooms. The residents whose rooms he enters have become a bit upset. As well, Mr. Greave has recently had the flu and, as a result, is a bit unsteady on his feet.

   Case 2
   Mr. Ross is a resident of a long-term care facility. He is recovering from a fractured hip and has just begun to bear weight. Mr. Ross often forgets that he is not supposed to walk and tries to get up. He has been receiving physiotherapy and the therapists feel that he will soon be able to walk with a walker. The therapists do not feel Mr. Ross is able to walk alone.

2. Your client, Mrs. Ross, has chicken pox. As a result, she must keep away from pregnant women and others who have not had the disease. Mrs. Ross' daughter is pregnant with twins. As a result, Mrs. Ross has had to move to her son's home. Even at her son's home, she must remain away from the family as only her son has had chicken pox before. What are some of the effects this type of isolation might have on Mrs. Ross? How might these effects be lessened?

3. As a support worker, you may be called upon to work with clients who have incurable and communicable diseases. How do you feel about working with clients in these situations?

4. You arrive at your client's home to find her unconscious on the floor. There is a small amount of blood on the floor behind her head. What do you do? What would you do if the client was living in a long-term care facility?

PART FOUR

ASSISTING WITH ROUTINE ACTIVITIES

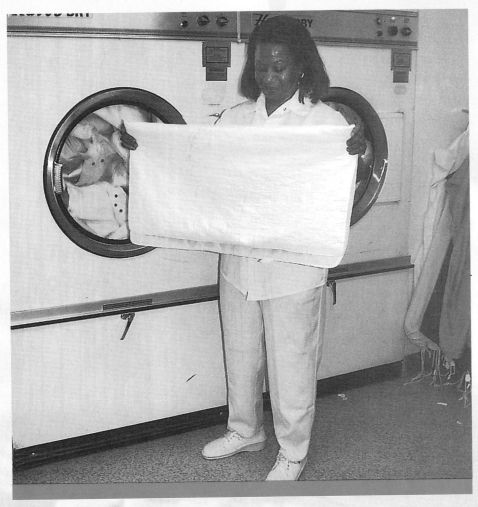

Source: Leisureworld, Inc.

CHAPTER THIRTEEN

Fundamental Terms and Concepts in Personal Support

Learning Objectives

Through reading this chapter, you'll be able to:

1. Define health, health condition, impairment, disability, participation, and handicap.
2. Describe prevention and how the concept applies to a client situation.
3. Describe habilitation and rehabilitation and how the concept applies to a client situation.
4. Define palliation and describe how the concept applies to a client situation.
5. Give two reasons why it is important to involve the client in his or her support.
6. List the nine levels of involvement a client may have in his or her support.
7. Outline six methods you might use to involve the client in his or her support.
8. Identify the actions a support worker should take when the support required is beyond the support worker's training or authority.

Chapter At A Glance

The Concept of Health

Health Conditions, Impairment, Disability, Participation, and Handicap

Fundamental Concepts of Support Work

Applying the Four Concepts in Your Work with Clients

Working with Your Client to Determine His or Her Involvement in the Support You Provide

When Your Client's Needs or Requests Exceed the Bounds of Your Role

Terms You'll Use

Disability   A limitation to a person's functioning, caused by an impairment, that affects things the person needs or wants to do.

Habilitation   A process by which a person chooses to gain or regain function, or to adapt to a change in function in order to attain self-fulfillment.

Handicap   Commonly used to refer to a disability or activity limitation; not as widely used as it once was.

Health   "A state of complete physical, social, and mental well-being, not merely the absence of disease or infirmity" (WHO, 1998).

Health Condition   Something that causes a change in a person's health status.

Impairment   A change in a person's functioning that differs from that expected of others of the same age or sex.

Palliation   Providing care, support, and comfort to a client whose condition cannot be cured.

Prevention   Avoiding the creation of unnecessary illness, impairment or disability.

Rehabilitation   A process that helps people regain desired activities and levels of participation when these things have been affected by an impairment.

The Concept of Health

We often assume that the term *health* refers to not being ill. While part of the concept of health refers to physical function, health is a much broader concept that takes into account many aspects of well-being. In this text, we'll use the definition developed by the World Health Organization (WHO). WHO defines **health** as *"A state of complete physical, social and mental well-being, not merely the absence of disease or infirmity."* (World Health Organization, *Health Promotion Glossary*, 1998).

WHO goes on to define health as a "resource for everyday life, not the object of living" that emphasizes an individual's social and personal resources as well as the person's physical capacities. In this sense, health is a means to an end in that it allows us to do what we need or want to do.

Stop and Reflect 13-1

Consider the WHO definition of health. Would you describe yourself as healthy? What factors did you consider when you consider your own health?

_____

_____

_____

_____

_____

Did you find that you tended to define your health in terms of how well you were able to do the things you need or want to do? If so, you are not alone. When asked if they are healthy, many older adults will respond that they are well enough to do what they want to do (Photo 13-1).

Photo 13-1
Health comprises many factors.
Source: CHATS.

Health Conditions, Impairment, Disability, Participation, and Handicap

Health Condition

Support workers frequently work with people who have some condition that affects their ability to do what they need or want to do. The World Health Organization defines a **health condition** as something that causes a change in a person's health status. Many things can cause this change: an injury, disease, distress, or a condition like pregnancy.

Impairment

An **impairment** occurs when the health condition results in a change in the person's functioning in relation to what is expected for people of the same age or sex. An impairment could be due to a loss of a body part, or an injury or abnormality of a body part, or a change in psychological functioning.

It's important to remember that although an impairment results in a change in functioning, it may not be a change that affects the person's everyday life. Even if it does, the person may be able to use a device that helps him or her to overcome the effects of the impairment. For example, nearsightedness is an impairment whose effects can usually be overcome by the use of eyeglasses or contact lenses.

Disability

Disability occurs when a person's functioning is limited by an impairment in a way that affects things the person needs or wants to do. Disability can be defined only in the context of the individual because the extent to which an impairment affects a person's activities will vary by the activities the person wants to do. As *Case Example 13-1*

CASE EXAMPLE 13-1

Erin Jones is 34 years old. She experienced significant hearing loss at age 7. She has no functional hearing. Erin can remember when she was able to hear. However, she has not been able to hear for many years and has grown quite accustomed to the impairment. As a statistical analyst, she finds that the absence of noise actually helps her in her work. "I can focus on what I'm doing without interruption," she says. Erin does not see her activities as being limited or herself as a "disabled person".

Carrie Weatherall is 38 years old. She experienced significant hearing loss at age 24. Like Erin, Carrie has no functional hearing. Unlike Erin, Carrie's activities are dramatically affected by the impairment. Carrie has had to leave her job as a recording technician (a person who mixes the sounds you hear on a compact disc) as the result of her impairment. She underwent a period of retraining and now works as a researcher for a university. Carrie misses her career in music and feels that her activities have been significantly limited by her impairment.

illustrates, it is quite possible for the same impairment to cause great disability for one person and very little disability (if any at all) for another person.

The term disability is often replaced by the phrase *activity limitation*. Activity limitation is seen as being a more accurate description of the changes affecting a person.

Carrie's and Erin's level of disability are very much different, despite the similarity in their impairments. Their experience is not unusual.

Remember that experiencing disability is not something that the person can completely control. Three things, the degree of impairment, societal attitudes, and physical barriers, affect the experience of disability.

Significant impairments may result in changes in ability which are impossible for a person to completely overcome. As with Carrie, the nature of the impairment may result in dramatic changes.

Secondly, societal perceptions and stereotypes can also create disability. For example, a person may be disabled by an employer's perception that a person who uses a wheelchair cannot possibly perform a specific job, or by a family that believes that a person in a wheelchair could not make a suitable spouse for its son or daughter.

Thirdly, physical barriers may impose disability upon a person. For example, a person's ability to obtain a job may be restricted by how accessible the building is to a person with a particular impairment. While many physical barriers can be removed, some cannot be easily resolved and may impose a disability upon a person.

As a support worker, you must take particular care to not impose disability upon your client through your attitude or the way you provide support. You must always take particular care to ensure that your attitude does not convey assumptions about what your client can or cannot do based upon his or her impairment.

Don't forget that small things can pose a real barrier for a person with an impairment. A glass of water left just outside the client's reach, or a load of laundry left in the washer when the client cannot lift it out and place the laundry in the dryer can be just as disabling as an inaccessible building. Make sure that all your activities *reduce* or eliminate barriers and don't create them.

Participation

Participation in the context of health refers to the ability to participate in all activities: social, occupational, and interpersonal, as well as physical and psychological. Ability to take part in life (e.g., to participate) is affected by the degree of disability experienced by the person.

Participation is closely linked to life satisfaction, in the sense that satisfaction with one's level of participation is a key component of satisfaction with one's life. Remember that more participation does not always equal more satisfaction. One person may be very satisfied with a lesser degree of participation than might satisfy another person.

Take the time to learn how your client prefers to participate in activities. Support the level of participation he or she desires. Avoid encouraging your client to participate in ways the client does not prefer simply because you feel that it might be good for him or her. This does not mean that you should not provide encouragement to a client who needs a bit of support to take part in an activity, but do not impose your preferences on your client.

Handicap

The term *handicap* has been used in several different ways. The term is considered by many people to have a negative meaning. It is less often used now than in years past. In the 1950s and 1960s, **handicap** was often used to describe what we would now call a disability or activity limitation. We still see some use of this meaning of the term in legislation.

Also, you might still see the phrase "handicapped parking" to designate parking spaces for use by persons with physical impairments. Handicap is also used to describe a disability created by society, either through physical barriers or attitudes.

Fundamental Concepts of Support Work

As we discussed in Chapter 1, the purpose of support work is to assist clients to accomplish the tasks of everyday living so that they can get on with their lives. This chapter is concerned with four concepts that guide *how* you work with your client to provide that assistance.

These four concepts: *prevention, rehabilitation, habilitation,* and *palliation* are based upon the ethical principles of autonomy, beneficence, and nomalificience we discussed in Chapter 3. All four principles are based on respect for the client's right to take risks and make decisions, to not cause harm, and to promote that which is good.

Prevention

Prevention refers to avoiding the creation of unnecessary impairment or disability. Support workers practise prevention in many ways, such as by encouraging a client to maintain activities he or she enjoys, by assisting a client with exercises to maintain muscle tone and movement, or by providing personal care in a way that minimizes the risk of skin breakdown. Case example 13-2 illustrates one type of prevention.

CASE EXAMPLE 13-2

Mrs. Hopkins has several serious health conditions. She has lung cancer and chronic bronchitis. She also has a chronic liver condition. As a result of these conditions, she is too weak to walk or even to sit in a chair. She spends all her time in bed.

It's important for Mrs. Hopkins to be able to sit up in bed a few times each day. Not only does the change in

position help prevent skin breakdown by changing the pressure points on her buttocks and legs, it provides Mrs. Hopkins with a sense of accomplishment and a way to feel "more like her old self" again. Mrs. Hopkins relies upon her support workers to assist her to sit up in bed, using a procedure laid out by an occupational therapist.

Rehabilitation

Rehabilitation refers to a process that helps people to regain desired activities and levels of participation when these things have been affected by an impairment. Rehabilitation includes two general aims: the regaining of function that has been lost and the learning of new skills or abilities to provide a more effective way of attaining desired activities and participation. Many people take part in rehabilitation as part of their recovery from a stroke or to regain function after having broken an arm or a leg.

Some professionals feel that rehabilitation includes assisting a client to *retain* function. The phrase, "If you don't use it, you'll lose it" is an example of this view. In this sense, many of the activities we do to keep fit can be seen as rehabilitative, as well as preventative. On the other hand, many professionals feel that the use of the term rehabilitation in this manner places too much emphasis on everyday activities as therapy.

Stop and Reflect 13-2

What sorts of things do you do to maintain your abilities? For example, do you do crossword puzzles to help keep up your mental skills and your vocabulary? Do you exercise to maintain muscle tone and range of motion?

_____

_____

_____

_____

_____

It's likely that you do many activities that could be seen as rehabilitative. It's also likely that you don't think of these things in this way. Most of us think of these activities as helping us attain a desired goal, such as feeling better or taking some time to relax with an activity we enjoy.

This is probably the way that your client thinks about the things that he or she does—in light of what he or she wants to accomplish, not as a specific activity he or she wants to be able to perform. As we discussed earlier in this chapter, health is a means to an end, not an end in itself. Keep this in mind when you assist your client: activity must have a purpose that is meaningful to the client and that purpose is more likely centred around what a particular ability lets the client do, as opposed to having the ability to perform the activity.

Habilitation

Habilitation can be defined in two ways. The most common definition describes **habilitation** as the process by which a person attains his or her optimal function, when the person has had a lifelong impairment or acquired an impairment at an early age. Habilitation differs from rehabilitation in that it is concerned with *acquiring* ability—not regaining ability lost to an impairment.

Another, newer definition of habilitation describes it as a process by which a person chooses to gain or regain function, or to adapt to a change in function in order to attain a sense of self-fulfillment. This concept of habilitation includes the adaptation of the person's surroundings (both the people and the setting) if necessary to assist the person to attain his or her optimal level of functioning. This concept can be particularly useful when the client cannot or chooses not to gain or regain function. Case Example13-3 describes one such situation.

CASE EXAMPLE 13-3

Anna Reese has Alzheimer Disease. She lives with her son and his family. Mrs. Reese has always enjoyed being a homemaker and hostess. In years past, she enjoyed preparing and serving meals to her family and guests.

Now, Mrs. Reese's condition makes it impossible for her to safely use a stove without help. Her condition

makes it impossible for her to regain this ability. So, Mrs. Reese's daughter-in-law and grandson adapt. They assist Mrs. Reese in preparing some dishes while taking on the aspects of the meal that are now too difficult for Mrs. Reese to perform. Her family's adaptations assist Mrs. Reese to participate in activities that are meaningful for her.

Palliation

Palliation refers to providing care, support, and comfort to a client whose condition cannot be cured. Palliation is often referred to in the context of terminal (or life-threatening) illness. In fact, palliation can be appropriately provided at any time that a condition cannot be cured, whether or not the condition is terminal. For example, osteoporosis cannot be cured, yet measures can—and should—be taken to prevent excess disability, maintain client comfort, and preserve function.

Applying the Four Concepts in Your Work with Clients

As a support worker, you will regularly apply the concepts of prevention, rehabilitation, habilitation, and palliation in your work with clients. You may even apply all four concepts to your work with a single client. Consider the following example.

CASE EXAMPLE 13-4

Cassie works with Mrs. Jamieson. Mrs. Jamieson has diabetes and arthritis and has recently undergone a knee joint replacement. Cassie applies the concepts of prevention, rehabilitation, habilitation, and palliation to her work with Mrs. Jamieson in the following ways.

Because Mrs. Jamieson's diabetes requires her to follow a strict diet, Cassie makes sure to adhere to any dietary guidelines when she prepares meals for Mrs. Jamieson, so as not to introduce foods that will affect her client's condition. (Prevention)

Cassie regularly assists Mrs. Jamieson with knee and leg exercises set out by Mrs. Jamieson's physiotherapist. These exercises are designed to help Mrs.

Jamieson regain the ability she had before her knee deteriorated. (Rehabilitation)

Although Mrs. Jamieson's knee is progressing well, and she is physically able, she has decided that climbing the stairs to the second floor is simply too much effort. As a result, Cassie is now helping her client to reorganize the main floor of her home so that Mrs. Jamieson will not need to climb stairs. (Habilitation)

Finally, Cassie assists Mrs. Jamieson with specific activities designed to minimize the pain of her arthritis. Although these activities will not cure Mrs. Jamieson's arthritis, they do provide relief from pain and discomfort. (Palliation)

Although Cassie applies all four concepts to her work with her client, she does not organize her thoughts and activities into four distinct categories. She provides the support the client requires in response to her client's goals and preferences. She is able to change her focus from rehabilitation to palliation to habilitation to prevention as her client's needs require.

Always attempt to apply these concepts as appropriate to your client, even if you do not feel that you would make the same decision as your client has made. For example, your client may make a decision to cease playing cards at the seniors' centre as it requires too much effort for the benefit he or she receives. You may feel that the activity is worthwhile and, if you were the client, you would maintain the activity. You may feel that the client *should* maintain the activity because it is good for her to get out. Despite your feelings, you must support the client's decision. For example, if your client decides to cease participating in the seniors' centre, you might work with him or her to find and make use of alternate ways to interact with others.

In some specific cases, you may not be able to support your client's decisions. This may be because the client no longer has the ability to make sound decisions (for example, as the result of a dementia) or when the client's decision requires you to do something that is prohibited by law or by your employer's policies (for example, the client asks you to drive his or her car, or to witness a legal document). Often, the client's support plan provides information on how to respond to these situations. In other cases, you may need to speak with your supervisor or other members of the support team to determine the best response.

Working with Your Client to Determine His or Her Involvement in the Support You Provide

As you learned in the previous section, the activities you perform with a client must be placed in the context of the client's goals. Two clients may have very different desires and goals in response to the same health condition. By discussing your client's goals, needs, and preferences with your client, you will be able to put your activities in the proper context (Photo 13-2). You will also understand each activity's significance to your client.

In addition, working with your client involves your client in the process. Most of us respond more fully and are more satisfied when we are involved in the decisions that affect us. Your client is likely no different.

Although most clients want to have some level of participation in planning or helping to provide the support they receive, the exact type and extent of participation each person wants is unique. One client may want to assist with as many activities as possible. Another client may simply want you to know what is important to him or her. Moreover, your client's level of participation may increase or decrease, depending upon the activity. For example, your client may be very interested in participating in grocery shopping, but have no interest in how you do the laundry.

Photo 13-2
Worker and client discussing an issue.
Source: CHATS.

Levels of Client Participation

As Figure 13-1 illustrates, there are nine general levels of participation (adapted from Mace, *Doing Things*, 1987). Remember that an individual client's level of participation may be a combination of one or more levels, and that any client's level of participation may vary over time.

Techniques to Involve Clients in Their Support

It's often the support worker's responsibility to discuss preferences and client participation with the client. If you are working with a client for the first time, you will need to take a few minutes to go over this information.

When you do, bear in mind that the client has the right *not* to participate at all in his or her support (unless the client has agreed to participate as part of the support plan). You should never attempt to coerce a client into participating in a manner or to an extent with which he or she is uncomfortable. On the other hand, you should always try to make use of a client's willingness to participate. Try the following ideas to involve your client.

1. **Ask the client what he or she would like to do.** For example, you might say "I'm happy to do the laundry, Mrs. Green, but are there parts of this task you would like to do, or that you would like us to do together?"

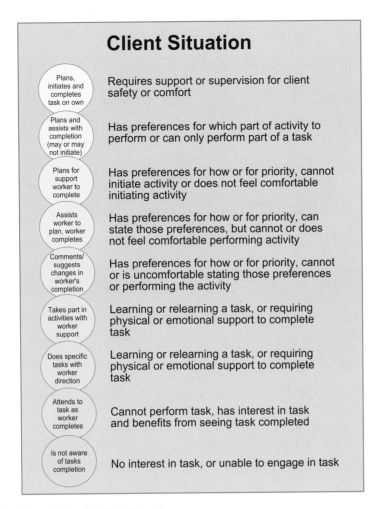

Figure 13-1 *General Levels of Participation*

2. **Accept and encourage client interest in taking part.** If necessary, break the task into manageable components that the client can perform. If the client requires a great deal of time to complete a component of an activity, consider starting that part earlier. Your client can then work on that component as you do other things. For example, a client may be able to (and interested in) dressing him or herself if you lay the clothing out in the order it will be put on.

3. **Recognize that a client "complaint" about how something is done may simply indicate the client's interest in being involved.** If your client says something like, "That's not how I would do it," or "Why would you do it that way?", don't become defensive. Take a few minutes to ask the client how he or she would do it. You may be able to use your client's technique. You may also find that the client's approach is easier and quicker. At the very least, your client will feel that you have taken his or her needs into account.

4. **Recognize that for some clients observation is participation.** Your client may benefit greatly from watching you do a particular activity. Encourage the client to talk with you (if possible) as you complete the activity.

5. **Modify your approach to take into account your client's "good" and "bad" days.** Your client's level of participation may change in light of many factors: stress, health conditions, the number of other things going on at once. If your client is not

up to a task he or she customarily enjoys, be prepared to adapt your approach to accommodate the tasks.

6. **Support and encourage your client's efforts.** Your client may not perform a task perfectly, but you must support and encourage his or her efforts. Be aware that the performance of the task may be more important to the client than the actual degree of perfection.

When Your Client's Needs or Requests Exceed the Bounds of Your Role

Occasionally, a client will have needs or requests for support that you cannot fulfill. This may be because the request exceeds the bounds of your role or you are not trained to perform the specific task. Your agency may not allow you to perform tasks that you have not been trained to do.

If your client does make such a request, explain the situation to the client. Many times, clients are not aware of the boundaries of your work. They will understand if you tell them why you cannot fulfill their request.

If you cannot resolve the situation with the client, speak to your supervisor. Your supervisor will work with the client to resolve the issue.

Questions for Review

1. How does the World Health Organization define health? According to this definition, would you describe yourself as healthy?

2. What is an impairment? How does it differ from a disability or a handicap?

3. How are habilitation and rehabilitation different?

4. What is excess disability? How might you prevent it?

5. Why should you attempt to involve the client in his or her support?

6. What are the levels of involvement the client may have in his or her support?

Questions for Discussion

1. Consider the definitions of impairment and disability. Do you have an impairment? If so, in what ways (if at all) does it limit your ability? Do you consider yourself to be a disabled person? Why or why not?

2. Mrs. Smith asks you to take her to the grocery store in her car. Your agency does not allow you to do this. What do you do?

3. When might it be a good idea to do something for a client that the client is able to do for him or herself? When might it be a bad idea?

CHAPTER FOURTEEN

Working in the Client's Home

(**Terms You'll Use**)

Biodegradable   A material that is easily broken down into chemicals that do not harm the environment.

Home Management   The process of taking care of the client's home.

Laundry Symbols   Symbols that indicate the type of care a garment should receive.

Sense of Home   The feeling that a person has about where they live.

The Client's Home

SR Stop and Reflect 14-1

How would you describe your home? How does your home provide you with a comfortable place to live?

_____

_____

_____

_____

Are there things about your home (such as what it looks like, specific possessions, where it is located) that provide you specific comfort?

_____

_____

_____

_____

Have you ever heard the phrase, "A man's home is his castle"? We all need a place where we can feel safe, at ease, and in our own domain. We look forward to having a place where we can relax and get away from the pressures that face us.

Stop and Reflect 14-2

Recall a particularly hectic day you have had. Did you look forward to going home?

_____

_____

If you did look forward to going home, why did you?

_____

_____

_____

If you did not look forward to going home, why not?

_____

_____

_____

Did you find that your home took on a special significance when you had a hectic day? If so, you may have some idea of how important home can be. In Chapter 6, we discussed the needs for territoriality, privacy, and control. We often look to our home as a setting in which we can meet these needs.

In a very real sense, a home is more than the building itself. Whether the home is a house, an apartment, or a room in a long-term care facility, it has special significance to the client.

The Purposes of Home Management: Safety, Comfort, and Well-Being

The purpose of _home management_ is determined with the client when the service is planned. For clients receiving community services, this information may be listed in the referral information you receive. This information may not always be identified when a client moves into a long-term care facility. In these cases, you may be able to identify some things that are important by talking with the client or with the client's family.

In general, **home management** meets three purposes: client safety, comfort, and well-being.

- _Client safety_ is attained through the management of pathogens and pests, by proper cleaning and storage of foodstuffs.

■ *Client comfort* is attained through many tasks: such as through clean and wrinkle-free clothing, towels and linen, through a dust-free environment, or by having clean floors.
■ *Client well-being* is attained through the satisfaction of having a clean and neat environment.

Be aware that there may be other purposes, as well. For example, a client who is recovering from a stroke may want you to assist in relearning certain household tasks, such as making a bed.

As a support worker, you must always remember that the household tasks you perform for a client may be as important to the client as any personal care you provide. In fact, these tasks can contribute greatly to your client's well-being.

How a support worker might assist the client in meeting these purposes and maintaining a sense of home will vary according to where the client lives. In the next section, we'll discuss the support worker's role when the client lives in the community. The following section will discuss the role of the support worker when the client lives in a long-term care facility.

Stop and Reflect 14-3

Have you ever had someone visit you for a long period of time? If so, did you find that you began to crave a bit of privacy, even though you enjoyed the person's visit?

_____

_____

If that person tried to help out with the household chores, did you find that they did things differently than you would do them? Did you have mixed feelings about the help—for example, grateful but a little frustrated that he or she did things differently?

_____

_____

_____

_____

When Support Services Are Provided in the Client's Home

If you found yourself answering the preceding questions with something like, "I really like her, but we just do things differently", you have experienced some interference with your control over your domain. If you have had the help of support workers (perhaps when you were recovering from an illness) you probably experienced loss of your privacy as well.

A client who receives the help of support workers experiences many significant changes in how he or she lives in her home. Support workers may perform tasks the client once enjoyed and took pride in doing "just so". Support workers may be handling items that have particular significance to the client, yet the client may not feel that he or she can tell the worker about the item's importance (Photo 14-1). The client who receives help frequently may feel a loss of privacy and control.

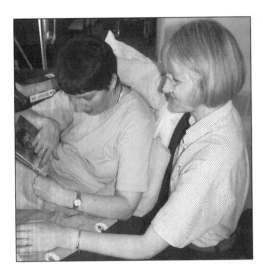

Photo 14-1
A client's possessions are important and must be respected. Handle them gently to prevent damage.
Source: CHATS.

Helping the Client to Maintain a Sense of Home

As a support worker, you will often be the person who is with the client most frequently. You can do a great deal to help the client maintain a *sense of home*, no matter where that home may be. A **sense of home** is the feeling that a person has about where they live. Make use of these six techniques when assisting your client.

1. **Always work in a manner that shows that you know you are a guest in the client's home.** Keep to the tasks you are assigned to do. Do not assume that you should be involved in any of your client's affairs beyond those tasks.
2. **Be aware that people differ in their standards for cleanliness.** One client may thrive in a somewhat disorganized or cluttered environment. Another may require a very organized and clean environment in order to attain a sense of comfort and well-being. You will have to adapt your approach to take into account the client's standards. Speak with your supervisor if you are concerned that a client's safety is at risk due to severe clutter.
3. **Learn your client's preferences and keep them in mind as you assist the client.** Remember that the client may well have done the tasks you are now doing. Ask how your client prefers you to do these tasks. As far as possible, try to follow the client's preferences.
4. **Support your client's control over things that happen in his or her home.** A client may not be able to perform all of a certain task, but may want to and be able to perform some of it. Work with the client to find out what the client prefers to do. For example, a client who is very particular about how precious figurines are displayed may be able to return them to their proper spot after you dust.
5. **Realize that items need not be of obvious value to be significant to the client.**

Many items have sentimental value. Treat all client items as though they are significant.

6. **Always respect the client's territory.** We all need personal space. (For example, you probably have a favourite room or space in your home that is "your" space.) Respect the client's preferences about what areas of the home you may enter and what you may do in those areas.

The Tasks of Home Management

 Stop and Reflect 14-4

Put yourself in this situation.

You have just returned home after a particularly hectic day. You walk in to your home to find that your children have left your living room in a mess. Pop cans, potato chip bags, and magazines are all over. A note in the hall table tells you that your children have gone to the recreation complex.

You decide to go to the kitchen to make yourself dinner. When you get to the kitchen, you find that there are no clean dishes. The dishwasher is full, yet no one turned it on. You find a microwave meal in the freezer. You pop the package in the microwave, wash a mug, and put the kettle on for tea. You clear a spot at the breakfast table and sit down to have your meal. As you sip you tea, you notice that the floor hasn't been cleaned in some time. There's a spill on the floor under the table and dirty footprints on the floor near the back door.

You decide to take a bath and relax. Once in the bathroom, you find that the tub has not been cleaned and there are no fresh towels.

How would you feel in this scenario? Defeated? Discouraged? Out of sorts? Angry? Most of us would not be happy. In general, all of us are happier when our surroundings are clean and neat.

As we said earlier, the tasks of home management may be as important to the client as any support that you may provide. Assigned tasks such as dusting, cleaning, and doing the laundry are not "add-ons" to the client's support: they form an essential *part* of the client's support (Photo 14-2).

Photo 14-2

Caring for a client's clothing, towels, and linens is often a part of support.

Source:
Leisureworld, Inc.

Performing Household Tasks Effectively and Safely

There are six principles to remember when cleaning any area.

- Work from top to bottom.
- Work from far to near.
- Work from cleanest to dirtiest.
- Put clean items in clean areas: put dirty items in dirty areas.
- Change cleaning solutions, rinse water, and cloths *before* they become dirty to avoid spreading dirt and microorganisms.
- Unless instructed to do otherwise, rinse all washed surfaces.

Working in this manner helps to avoid contaminating a clean area. For example, if you are wiping down a refrigerator door, starting at the top and working your way down allows the dirty water to run down over dirty areas.

Similarly, if you are mopping a floor, you would start from the corner farthest from the entrance to the room and work toward the entrance. This avoids having to track over the freshly-cleaned areas to clean the rest of the floor.

There are three major exceptions to the principle of working from cleanest to dirtiest. You should:

1. Blot or mop up large spills before cleaning any area.
2. Treat first any dirt that has the potential to stain.
3. Spot-clean an area first when you know the area will require a second cleaning.

The Supplies You'll Need

Most clients will have the necessary cleaning equipment and supplies for the cleaning they need to have done. At a minimum, the client should have a broom and dustpan, clean water, cleaners, clean rags, a mop, a pail, and a brush. Speak with the client or your supervisor if the client does not have the necessary equipment.

Most clients have preferences for the cleaning products they use. Many clients prefer to use environmentally-friendly cleaners when possible. Do not ask your client to use a cleaner you prefer. Speak with your supervisor if the client uses cleaners that you feel are unsafe.

Using Cleaning Products Safely

You may hear of environmentally-friendly cleaners. There are generally two types of these cleaners: those that are formulated by a manufacturer to be **biodegradable** (easily broken down into chemicals that do not harm the environment) and those that are made from common household chemicals. Remember that some common household chemicals can form deadly gasses when combined. Always use caution when combining chemicals, even if the instructions come from a known and reputable source.

Even the safest chemical can be harmful if used improperly. Be sure to observe the following guidelines:

1. Always read the directions for use on the product label. Follow the instructions, paying particular attention to the amount to be used.
2. Do not mix chemicals unless you have been instructed to do so by someone who is knowledgeable. Improper mixing of chemicals can produce toxic gases or cause damage to surfaces.
3. Always check with a knowledgeable person before using a strong or abrasive cleaner on a surface to make sure that the chemical will not harm it.
4. Do not leave cleaners on any surface for a long period of time, as this can cause discolouration, etching, or other damage.
5. Use caution when scrubbing a surface. Excessive rubbing or pressure can mar the finish.

6. Do not use products in unlabelled containers. If you must use a container to store a cleaner, make sure to use a clean container and clearly mark the contents on the container with permanent marker.

7. Store all cleaning products according to the manufacturer's directions. Ensure all products are kept out of the reach of children and pets.

Care of Cleaning Equipment

You cannot clean properly if your equipment is not clean. Before you start any cleaning job, make sure that you have a clean mop, dustmop, broom, pail, sponge, and cloths. Keep your equipment clean by doing the following:

1. Shake your dustcloth and dustmop frequently to remove accumulated dust. To avoid spreading dust in the client's home, shake the cloth or mop outside. If you cannot get outside to shake the equipment, shake it out an open window.

2. Wash cleaning cloths and dustcloths after each use. Wash mop heads and dustmop heads as required. Do not put these items in the washer or dryer if you have used them with a flammable solvent because fire can result.

3. Change wash water before it becomes dirty. If necessary, wash out the pail.

4. Store equipment properly after use.

Operating Electrical Equipment Safely

It's likely that your client will have a vacuum cleaner or other electrical cleaning equipment. When you use electrical equipment, you must be careful to:

1. Ask for help if you are unsure how to use a particular piece of equipment. Read the instruction manual (if available) to learn how to use the equipment.

2. Check the equipment for frayed cords and loose parts. Do not use equipment that has a frayed cord or that works only when the cord is in a certain position. Unplug any equipment that gives you a shock when you operate it or that causes a fuse to blow (or a circuit breaker to trip) when it is operated.

3. Do not operate electrical equipment with wet or damp hands or when standing in a wet or damp spot.

4. Do not use a vacuum to pick up any liquids, unless the vacuum is a "wet-dry" vacuum. Even "wet-dry" vacuums must have special preparation to be used to pick up liquids.

5. Do not use objects such as a screwdriver or knife to attempt to clear a jam in any appliance.

6. Unplug any appliance before you disassemble any part of it, such as replacing the vacuum cleaner bag or opening the crumb door on the bottom of a toaster.

7. Unplug any appliance before you wipe it off. Use a damp cloth to wipe off the equipment. Never place electrical equipment in water or any other liquid.

General Cleaning Procedures

General cleaning includes dusting; spot-cleaning; washing dishes; washing counters, bathroom fixtures, and other surfaces; emptying garbage; and cleaning floors. Your specific assignment may include cleaning kitchen appliances or washing windows. In general, you should dust, empty garbage, spot-clean, wash surfaces, and then wash floors. Always observe the principles of infection control when cleaning.

Dusting

Use a clean, lint-free cloth or duster when dusting. If possible, spray the cloth with a commercial dusting spray or mist the cloth *lightly* with water to trap and hold dust. Turn the cloth frequently so that you are using a clean part of the cloth to dust. If you are using a duster, make sure not to move the duster too quickly, as it can spread the dust.

Some clients may have specially-treated cloths to use for dusting. Be sure to follow the instructions for caring for these cloths.

Dust can aggravate a client's allergies. You may have to dust more frequently or use a vacuum cleaner to pick up dust.

Spot-Cleaning

Blot up excess liquid and matter before attempting to clean the spot (Photo 14-3). Use a butter knife to scrape off excess sticky or dried material, if this will not damage the underlying surface. An ice cube can harden some sticky materials and make them easier to remove.

Once all excess material has been removed, apply the appropriate cleaning solution to the stain. Follow the directions for applying the solution. You may need to leave the solution on the spot for a few moments.

Avoid scrubbing the spot, as this may mar the surface or alter its colour. Gently blot the spot, or carefully rub the spot, working from the outside of the spot to its centre. Some spots will require a second application of cleaner. Once the spot is gone, allow the surface to dry. Use caution when using heat to dry an article with a stain. Heat can set stains, making them very hard to remove. If you cannot remove the stain, or are concerned that you will damage the surface, consult your client or your supervisor.

Photo 14-3
Blotting a spill helps to prevent the spread of the material and makes cleanup easier.

Washing Dishes and Other Small Washable Objects

Hand Washing

Use dish detergent to wash dishes and small washable objects. Wear rubber gloves to protect your hands. Use moderately hot soapy water to wash items and moderately hot clean water to rinse items. Wash the least dirty items first.

If possible, place the items on a dish rack to air-dry. Be sure to use a tray under the dish rack to collect the water running off the items. If it is not possible to air dry items, use a clean tea towel to dry them before storing. Damp or hot dishes can mar wooden shelves.

Using the Dishwasher

Load the dishwasher so that dishes do not touch one another. Make sure that all items placed in the dishwasher are dishwasher-safe. Scrape excess food off plates before placing in the dishwasher. Rinse the dishes off before placing in the dishwasher if your client prefers, or the dishwasher's operating guide advises you to do so.

If possible, run the dishwasher only when full to save water and energy. Use the recommended amount of dishwasher detergent. Never use *dishwashing* detergent, as it will foam excessively.

Unless you are instructed to do otherwise, never place anything but dishes, cutlery, and glasses in the dishwasher.

Washing Kitchen Counters and Other Surfaces

Remove all items from the counter or the surface before you wash it. Place these items in a safe area. If you must set them on an area that has been cleaned, make sure to wipe the items off first.

Wash the counter or surface, starting with the area furthest from you. Work from farthest to closest, until the counter is cleaned. Let the counter air-dry or wipe dry with a clean cloth before replacing the items. Clean and dry off all items before replacing.

Bathroom Fixtures and Surfaces

Many newer homes have bathroom fixtures made of acrylic. These fixtures can easily be scratched by the use of scouring powders or abrasive pads. Use a bathroom cleaner designed for use on acrylic surfaces, following the directions carefully. As an alternative, you can use laundry detergent on a cloth. No matter what cleaner you use, rinse the surfaces well.

Clean the toilet with a brush or cloth used *only* for that purpose. Wipe down the tank and outside of the bowl. Raise the seat and clean the rim of the bowl. Clean the bottom of the seat. Use a separate cloth to wipe down the top of the seat.

Use a toilet bowl cleaner to clean the bowl. Follow the directions carefully. Brush down the sides of the bowl with a brush. Be sure to brush under the rim. Flush the toilet to remove the solution. Rinse the brush in the flushing water. Hang the brush to dry.

Emptying Garbage

If possible, empty dry garbage (such as that found in bedrooms or living rooms) first. Empty wet or messy garbage last. Use plastic garbage bags for this purpose, if the client uses them. If the client uses garbage cans, empty the garbage into the can.

If possible, line garbage pails or wastebaskets with the appropriately sized plastic bag. Empty the garbage by removing the bag and placing it with the garbage.

Make sure that the garbage bag is tied or the can lid securely attached when you are done. Garbage can attract insects and animals. Some clients have containers to keep bags of garbage or garbage cans secured. If your client has one of these containers, make sure to use it. If animals getting into the garbage is a problem and the client does not have a container, try pouring a 125 ml (1/2 cup) of ammonia into the can or bag. This smell will discourage many rodents and animals from chewing through the garbage.

Cleaning Floors

High-traffic areas (halls, entrances, and frequently used rooms) must be swept or vacuumed regularly to keep dust, dirt, and other particles from accumulating. Some clients will have a vacuum that is suitable for use on noncarpeted floors. If so, be sure to use the correct nozzle. Always sweep a floor before you wash it.

Wash floors with the proper cleaner, prepared according to the instructions on the label. Some "no-wax" floors require a special cleaner. Wood floors usually require a special cleaner. Make sure you have the proper cleaner before you start. Wring out the mop each time you dip it into the pail so that you do not put too much water on the floor. Be aware that too much water can loosen tiles or ruin a wood finish.

Discuss with your supervisor before performing heavy cleaning tasks such as stripping wax from floors or cleaning carpets.

Cleaning Appliances

You should always wipe up spills in the refrigerator or on surface of the stove. This helps to keep the appliance free from microorganisms and helps to keep other items from becoming dirty.

Remember that your assigned duties may also include cleaning the client's refrigerator or stove. Speak with your supervisor if your client asks that you perform these tasks.

Refrigerator

Cleaning a refrigerator does not usually require special cleaners. Working from the top, remove items from the fridge, one shelf at a time. Remove the shelf (if possible), wash and dry. Be careful not to use very hot water to wash a glass shelf as it may cause it to crack. Wipe down the sides of the interior and replace the shelf.

Wipe off containers with a clean damp cloth and replace on the shelf. Take a moment to organize the items if possible. Ask your client about disposing of stale or old items. Repeat this procedure until all shelves are done. Clean the door bins in the same manner. When you have finished, wipe off the outside of the appliance.

Stove

There are many types of stoves and stove surfaces. Using a damp cloth to clean a surface (such as when you are wiping up a spill) is usually safe. It's usually safe to remove the drip pans (the removable metal plates below each burner) for cleaning. Do not line drip pans with aluminum foil as this may cause the burner to overheat. Some clients have a glass or ceramic cook top that has burners below the surface that cannot be removed. The glass or ceramic surface may easily scratch. Ask for direction as to how to properly clean this type of cook top.

Cleaning the oven may require cleaners specifically formulated for the client's stove. Do not attempt to clean an oven unless you are certain that you have the proper cleaner and know how to use it.

Caring for the Client's Clothing

Chances are that you are particular about your clothes. You might have specific outfits you wear only for certain occasions, or articles of clothing that are only worn with other articles. You might have specific ways of caring for your clothing. Most of us see our clothes as a way of expressing who we are. How our clothing looks (and thus makes us look) is important to us.

It's very likely that your client has preferences as to how his or her clothing is cared for. It's also very likely you will have to do your client's laundry. A few moments taken to properly care for your client's laundry will avoid damage to clothing and make the laundry tasks much easier.

Canada has implemented **laundry symbols** that indicate the type of care a garment should receive. These symbols cover washing, bleaching, drying, ironing, and dry-cleaning and use the colours of the traffic lights (red, amber, and green) to indicate how you should proceed. Figure 14-1 presents these symbols in black and white and gives their meaning.

General Laundry Procedures

Use the following guidelines to clean washable clothing safely.

Preparing Items for Washing

1. **Sort clothing by colour, fabric type, and washing requirements.** Group loads into similar colours, weights, and washing requirements. Avoid washing clothing

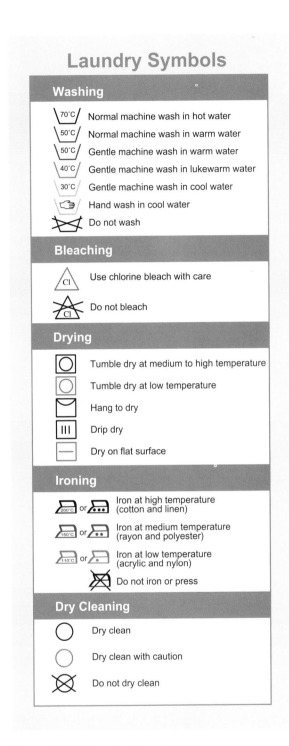

Laundry Symbols

Washing

70°C	Normal machine wash in hot water
50°C	Normal machine wash in warm water
50°C	Gentle machine wash in warm water
40°C	Gentle machine wash in lukewarm water
30°C	Gentle machine wash in cool water
	Hand wash in cool water
	Do not wash

Bleaching

Cl	Use chlorine bleach with care
Cl	Do not bleach

Drying

	Tumble dry at medium to high temperature
	Tumble dry at low temperature
	Hang to dry
III	Drip dry
—	Dry on flat surface

Ironing

200°C or	Iron at high temperature (cotton and linen)
150°C or	Iron at medium temperature (rayon and polyester)
110°C or	Iron at low temperature (acrylic and nylon)
	Do not iron or press

Dry Cleaning

	Dry clean
	Dry clean with caution
	Do not dry clean

Figure 14-1 *Laundry Care Symbols*

Source: Follow the Signs, Industry Canada. Reproduced with permission of the Minister of Public Works and Government Services Canada, 2000.

that is heavily soiled with clothing that is lightly soiled, even if they are the same colour, type, and have the same washing requirements.

2. **Close zippers, button buttons, and snap up snaps before washing.**
3. **Empty pockets and repair small splits in seams or tears.** If you cannot easily repair the garment, advise your client.

Washing Items

1. **Do not wash items that have been soaked in or spotted with gasoline or other flammable liquids.** Such items can ignite in the washer.
2. **Follow the manufacturer's instructions for loading the washer.** Load articles loosely. In general, top-loading washers may be filled to the top of the agitator. Make sure to place clothing evenly around the drum, so as to keep it balanced. Front-loading washers should be loaded so that the drum is no more than half-full.
3. **Adjust the water level to the amount of laundry to be washed.** Articles should have enough water to move about without rising above the water line.
4. **Adjust the water temperature appropriately to the clothing being washed.** Make sure that the detergent you use is appropriate for the water temperature.
5. **Use the appropriate washer cycle.** Special wash cycles (such as *permanent press*) have been developed to best care for specific types of items.
6. **Never pour detergent or fabric softener directly on clothing.** This can cause spotting and colour changes. If the washer has no detergent dispenser, fill the washer with water, add the proper amount of detergent and then load the clothing.
7. **Remove clothes from the washer as soon as possible after the cycle finishes.** Clothes left in the washer too long will develop a musty odour and wrinkles. If this happens, the items must be washed again.

Drying

1. **Avoid drying articles with fresh stains that have not been completely removed.** The heat from the dryer can set these stains and make them impossible to remove.
2. **Don't overload the dryer.** This can cause wrinkling and heat damage to clothing.
3. **Use the cycle most appropriate for the load.** Use the shortest time possible to dry the items to avoid possible damage and wrinkling.
4. **Remove items from the dryer as soon as they are dry.**
5. **Empty the lint trap after each load.** If you cannot find the lint trap, ask for help. Lint buildup can cause a fire.
6. **Never dry foam rubber, rubberized items, or any items that have been soaked in gasoline or other flammable liquids.** These can ignite and cause a fire.

Shopping and Banking

You may be asked to shop or do banking for a client. Most agencies have specific procedures to follow when these tasks are done. These procedures usually govern the amount of the client's money you may handle and how you must account for the purchases you are asked to make or the banking you are asked to do. Realize that these procedures are in place for the protection of both you and your client. Always follow the procedure established by your agency, no matter how well you know your client.

The Client in the Long-Term Care Facility

A client who lives in a long-term care facility often experiences a very strong sense of loss of control. The move to the facility usually means many changes; in surroundings, in the number and type of possessions, and in routine. If the client shares a room with another person, the client may experience a very real sense of loss of privacy.

It's likely that the facility's housekeeping department will be responsible for most cleaning of client rooms. However, you, as a support worker, can do much to ensure that your client's personal space is respected.

You must always be aware that the client's room is his or her home. It is the only personal space the client has in the setting. Treat the client's space as his or her home by adhering to the following guidelines.

1. **Help the client to have a sense of personal space by respecting the person's territory.** Knock before you enter a client's room, or ask before you approach the client's area in a shared room. Avoid walking through a client's personal area unnecessarily.
2. **Respect the client's possessions.** It's likely that the client has brought his or her most cherished items to the facility. Thus, each may have special significance. Be careful when you must move the client's items. Don't set extra laundry or other items down on a client's bed or furniture.
3. **Encourage the client to do what he or she can and wants to do to maintain personal space.** For example, a client might be able to make his or her bed or put away some of his or her clothes. Encourage the client to do tasks that give the client satisfaction, even though the result may not be perfect.
4. **Encourage the client (or the client's family, if the client is unable) to bring permissible items that help the client to feel at home.** Remember that some things, such as electrical appliances, must be approved before the client can use them.
5. **If you are assigned to tidy the client's bedside table or cabinet, remember to place items where the client can easily find them.**

Questions for Review

1. How might a client's need for privacy, territoriality, and control be affected by having support services in his or her home?

2. Why is home management important to a client's sense of well-being?

3. What are six ways that you can assist your client to maintain a sense of home?

4. You must clean your client's kitchen counter. On this counter, there is a coffee maker, a set of canisters, a blender, this morning's dirty breakfast dishes, and a plant. A large jar of grape jam has been spilled on the counter. Apply the six principles of cleaning an area to this task.

5. What seven guidelines should you follow when using cleaning products?

6. What seven guidelines should you follow when operating electrical equipment?

7. You have a sweater that can be washed in warm water (below 50°C), on a gentle cycle. What does the laundry symbol for this type of care look like?

8. Why shouldn't you pour detergent or fabric softener directly on clothes?

9. What five things can you do to show a long-term care facility resident that you respect his or her home?

Questions for Discussion

1. Some people don't feel that household tasks are as important as personal care tasks. They feel that support workers should not have to do these tasks. How do you feel? Why do you feel this way? If you were a client, how might you feel?

2. Your client, Mrs. Berg, has always been particular about how household tasks are done. You have been assigned to assist her with household tasks. As you plan your work with her, you find that Mrs. Berg's expectations of how you are to dust and do laundry are very high. For example, Mrs. Berg wants each figurine on her shelves washed and dried by hand each week. She also asks that you wash her clothing by hand. If you follow all of her requests, you will not have time to do all your assigned chores. When you discuss this with your supervisor, she asks that you try to work out something with the client. How do you attempt to resolve this situation with Mrs. Berg?

3. Imagine that you were moving into a long-term care facility. What possessions would you like to have with you? How do you think you would feel about sharing your room with other people? How would you feel about having staff members in your room?

CHAPTER FIFTEEN

Meal Planning, Preparation, and Assistance

Learning Objectives

Through reading this chapter, you'll be able to:

1. List the five reasons we need to eat a balanced diet.
2. Explain *Canada's Food Guide* and give examples of balanced meal plans.
3. Describe changes in nutritional needs across the life span.
4. Outline the components of common special diets.
5. Describe four ways of making meals more appealing to clients.
6. Identify the steps to take when planning a menu with a client.
7. Discuss the factors to consider when shopping for food for a client.
8. Describe safe food practices.
9. Explain the 12 principles and proper techniques you should follow when assisting a client to eat.

Chapter At A Glance

Food and Nutrition
Canada's Food Guide
Nutritional Needs Across the Life Span
Client Preferences
Special Diets
Planning Meals
Making Meals Appealing to Clients
Safe Food Practices
Assisting the Client with Eating
Choking

Food and Nutrition

Food provides the **nutrients** (vitamins, minerals, proteins, fats, carbohydrates, and water) your body needs to become and remain healthy. These nutrients give the body energy, help to maintain strong bones and build muscle, help the body to repair and grow new cells, and help to fight off infections and disease. Each nutrient has a unique purpose. Table 15-1 identifies the function and common sources of these nutrients.

Vitamins

Vitamins are organic compounds that provide elements that the body needs to function. Our bodies manufacture some vitamins, but usually cannot manufacture them in large enough amounts to meet our needs. The bulk of vitamins must come from food. It's important to note that many of the body's functions require several vitamins at the same time: the function is disrupted when not all of the necessary vitamins are present. There are two types of vitamins: fat-soluble and water-soluble.

Fat-Soluble Vitamins

Fat-soluble vitamins are vitamins A, D, E, and K. They are absorbed with help from fats found in the diet. Fat-soluble vitamins can remain in the body for long periods of time.

Water-Soluble Vitamins

Water-soluble vitamins are vitamin C and the many B vitamins. Water-soluble vitamins cannot be stored in the body for very long. Good sources of these vitamins should be consumed every day.

Minerals

Minerals are inorganic materials that the body requires. Iron and calcium are probably the best-known minerals. However, there are many others: phosphorus, potassium, sodium, iodine, magnesium, zinc, and copper. Some minerals work best in combination with other minerals. For example, calcium and phosphorus work together to form strong bones and teeth. As almost all foods provide some minerals, it is not difficult to obtain the needed amounts of minerals through a balanced diet.

Proteins

Proteins are the body's second most prevalent substance and are essential for growth and tissue repair. They are made up of amino acids. Some foods provide all the amino acids required to produce protein. Other foods do not possess all the amino acids required and must be combined with other foods to provide a complete protein. For example, bread and butter, when eaten separately, do not provide a complete protein. When eaten together, they do provide a complete protein.

Fats

Some **fat** is essential for a balanced diet because it allows fat-soluble vitamins to be used by the body. There are two major types of fats: saturated and unsaturated. Saturated fats can contribute to excess cholesterol in the body (a condition linked to cardiovascular disease).

Carbohydrates

Carbohydrates are formed of starches and sugars and provide energy. Carbohydrates make up most of the diets of people around the world. Be aware that starches and sugars do not provide the same benefit to the body. Starches provide nutrients and are often found in foods which also contain amino acids. Sugars provide no nutrients, only calories.

Water

Water is the most common element in the body. Over half of the human body is water. This water is required by the body to make use of water-soluble vitamins and for the body's chemical reactions to take place.

TABLE 15-1	Common Nutrients, Their Functions, and Common Sources	
Nutrient	**Function**	**Common Sources**
Water	Helps water-soluble vitamins to be absorbed by the body. Brings nutrients to cells and carries away waste products. Regulates body temperature.	Drinking water, beverages, and fruits are common sources. Almost all foods (except fats and sugars) contain some water.
Protein	Essential for growth and tissue repair.	Complete proteins (come from animal sources): meat, fish, eggs, cheese, poultry, and milk. Incomplete proteins (come from plant sources): soybeans, nuts, grains, beans, peas, and other legumes. ▶▶

TABLE 15-1	Common Nutrients, Their Functions, and Common Sources (continued)	
Nutrient	**Function**	**Common Sources**
Carbohydrates	Provide energy and fuel for the body to generate heat.	Cereal grains and products made from these items (pasta, bread), potatoes, vegetables, and nuts.
Fats	Provide fatty acids which are required for growth. Provide medium for body to use fat-soluble vitamins.	Many foods, even vegetables, contain some amount of fat. Some products are primarily fat: lard, butter, margarine, vegetable oils, many salad dressings.
Minerals		
Calcium	Essential for healthy bones and teeth. Helps to regulate certain body processes.	Milk, milk products (except butter), canned salmon and sardines, and most dark green vegetables.
Iodine	Essential for proper thyroid gland function.	Iodized salt, sea-caught fish, some foods grown in iodine-rich soil, and many canned or processed foods.
Iron	Essential in forming hemoglobin (the part of blood that carries oxygen to cells).	Meats, especially liver and kidney, eggs, potatoes, dark yellow and green vegetables, dried fruits, and whole-grain products.
Phosphorus	Essential to proper formation of nerve tissue. With calcium, helps to form strong bones and teeth.	Found in many foods: legumes, whole-wheat products, oat products, meat, fish, poultry, nuts, and cheese.
Vitamins		
A	Essential to eye function, especially night sight. Essential to healthy skin, hair, and mucous membranes. Contributes to some types of infection resistance.	Apricots, cantaloupe, milk, cheese, eggs, organ meats (liver, kidney), dark green and dark yellow vegetables.

TABLE 15-1	Common Nutrients, Their Functions, and Common Sources *(continued)*	
Nutrient	**Function**	**Common Sources**
Vitamins		
B Complex	The B complex vitamins include four common vitamins: Thiamine (B_1), Riboflavin (B_2), Niacin, and B_{12}. In general, the B complex is essential for the proper functioning of nerves, digestion, oxidization, and metabolism.	Organ meats (liver, kidney), whole grains, milk, cheese, leafy green vegetables.
C	Helps cells to work together. Essential for sound condition of bones, teeth, and gums.	Fresh, raw citrus fruits and vegetables.
D	Essential for the body to make proper use of calcium and phosphorus.	Vitamin D fortified milk, fish-liver oils, eggs, and one non-food source: sunshine.

Canada's Food Guide

Figure 15-1 *Canada's Food Guide to Healthy Eating*

Source: Health Canada. Reproduced with permission of the Minister of Public Works and Government Services Canada, 2000.

While it's possible to develop your own menu plan to include all essential nutrients, it would be time-consuming. For this reason, Health Canada has developed *Canada's Food Guide*. Based on nutritional needs, *Canada's Food Guide* provides an easy way to ensure that people obtain the nutrients they require to build and maintain a healthy body.

The *Guide* groups foods into four categories: grains; raw vegetables; milk and milk products; and meats and meat products. Figure 15-1 illustrates these four groups as forming a rainbow. Note that the size of each group's arc represents the proportion each group should form in a balanced diet. Specific recommendations for the number of servings are included in the *Guide* and are presented in Figure 15-2.

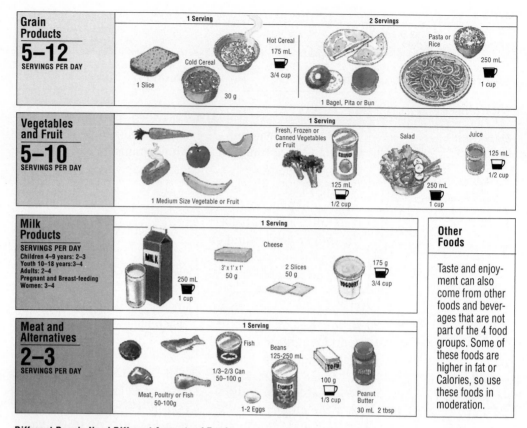

Different People Need Different Amounts of Food
The amount of food you need every day from the 4 food groups and other foods depends on your age, body size, activity level, whether you are male or female and if you are pregnant or breast feeding. That's why the Food Guide gives a lower and higher number of servings for each food group. For example, young children can choose the lower number of servings, while male teenagers can go to the higher number. Most other people can choose servings somewhere in between.

Figure 15-2 *Recommended Daily Servings*

Source: Health Canada. Reproduced with permission of the Minister of Public Works and Government Services Canada, 2000.

The guide also provides the following five principles to help people choose foods wisely:

Variety: Choose from each group, as recommended, each day. Select new items in each food group to introduce variety.

Lower-Fat: Choose lower-fat selections within each food group. Most Canadians eat much more fat than our bodies require for health. Use low-fat milk and dairy products and choose leaner cuts of meat.

Whole-Grain and Enriched Products: Whole-grain products are high in starch and fibre. Enriched foods have added vitamins and minerals .

Dark Green and Orange Vegetables: These vegetables contain more nutrients than do others.

Orange Fruits: These fruits contain more nutrients than do other fruits. Remember that orange fruits include cantaloupes as well as oranges.

Stop and Reflect 15-1

Record what you eat each day for a one-week period. Then, compare your daily portions to those recommended by *Canada's Food Guide*.

How well do you eat?

_____

_____

How easily could you change your habits?

_____

_____

_____

Did you find that your eating habits are in line with the *Guide's* prescriptions? If not, how easily could you change your eating habits?

Nutritional Needs Across the Life Span

While we generally need the same nutrients all our lives, the amounts we need may change with our age, condition, and size. For example:

- Older adults usually require fewer calories than they did when they were younger.
- A pregnant woman will require more calcium than a woman who is not pregnant.
- A pregnant woman needs more folic acid than one who is not pregnant.
- A person with severe burns may require two to three times the number of calories than does a healthy person of the same age.
- A tall and stocky male will usually require more nutrients and calories than would a petite woman.

Your client will have specific needs, based upon his or her age, size, condition, and any medications he or she is taking (Photo 15-1). Some lifestyle choices, such as smoking or use of carbonated beverages, affect how the body absorbs certain nutrients. Finally, peer pressure can affect the food choices some people (especially teenagers) make. You must be prepared to adapt your meal preparation to accommodate these differing needs.

Photo 15-1
If possible, you should plan menus with your client. Here a support worker and client review a grocery store ad before deciding on the menu and shopping list.
Source: CHATS.

Client Preferences

You likely will find that your client has specific food preferences. These preferences are the result of many things, including religious prescriptions, cultural practices, tradition, taste, appearance, smell preferences, and habit. These preferences are very hard to change, even if we are motivated to do so.

We often prefer certain types of foods in certain circumstances. For example, you might prefer a certain soup when you have a cold. The term *comfort foods* has been used to describe these foods that benefit us both emotionally and nutritionally.

You must respect your client's food preferences. You may have to learn how to make new dishes or to use ingredients with which you are unfamiliar. You may prepare familiar foods for the client to eat at times which seem unusual to you (for example, cereal and eggs as an evening meal). Do not force your client to eat meals that he or she does not prefer simply because you are more familiar with their preparation. You may find that your client does not eat a balanced diet. If so, you must not demand that the client change his or her diet. You might be able to talk with your client about other food choices and perhaps introduce a new food or two. You might find that your client does not eat a particular food because it was too difficult for him or her to prepare. The client may try this food if you are preparing it. With your client's agreement, you might be able to substitute healthier choices for some ingredients (for example, using low-fat milk instead of whole milk).

However, keep in mind that your client may not wish to change his or her habits. Discuss the issue with your supervisor if attaining a balanced diet is one of the reasons you have been assigned to assist a client and your client does not wish to alter his or her diet.

Stop and Reflect 15-2

How have your dietary needs and preferences changed over time?

_____

_____

Did you eat differently as a child? As a teen?

_____

_____

What factors influenced these needs and preferences?

_____

_____

Do you have certain foods you customarily eat at certain times?

_____

_____

Do you have certain foods that you prefer when you are ill?

_____

_____

Special Diets

Some clients will have a special diet that they follow. There are many types of special diets. Table 15-2 lists some common diets and their purpose. Be aware that your client's specific diet may not be identical to any of the diets listed in Table 15-2. Some clients have a diet that combines two or more of these diets, such as a diabetic and mechanically soft diet.

If your client has a special diet, you must take the time to learn about it and how it affects the food choices and cooking methods.

TABLE 15-2	Common Special Diets			
Diet Type	**Characteristics**	**Purpose**	**Foods Often Excluded**	**Foods Often Recommended**
Normal or Regular	Well-balanced diet	General-purpose (regular diet is often listed on support plans)	None	Full range of items included in *Canada's Food Guide*
Mechanical Soft or Dental Soft	Same range of foods as regular diet, chopped, diced, or otherwise tenderized to make them easier to eat	Clients with difficulty chewing or swallowing	None	As for regular diet
Low Salt Low Sodium No Added Salt	Limited amount of foods containing sodium; no added salt (e.g., no salt at the table)	Clients with water retention, heart, kidney, or circulatory problems	Canned vegetables, processed meats, dried meats, hot dogs, many "convenience foods"	Fresh vegetables, most meats bought raw and prepared, fruits
Diabetic Sugar-Free	Balance of proteins, fats, and carbohydrates as the client's needs dictate. Not just a sugar restriction	To match intake with bodily needs	Sugared foods or beverages	Fresh fruits and vegetables, low sugar or sugar-free products
High-Protein Diet	Regular diet supplemented with high-protein foods	To assist the body in recovery from illness or injury	None	High-protein foods

Planning Meals

Planning meals includes determining preferences, planning combinations for a period of time, determining supplies the client has on hand, and, possibly, shopping for food items. It is very important that you work with your client to determine dietary, cultural, or religious requirements, as well as the foods that he or she prefers to eat in a meal. You should use this information, the information in *Canada's Food Guide*, and the hints contained in this section and the section on presentation (later in this chapter) to develop a meal plan for a one- or two-week period.

It is vitally important that your client be involved (if possible) in the planning of the meals, even if only to state preferences. A lovely meal, prepared and served beautifully, is of no use if it contains foods the client will not eat.

Key Considerations in Menu Planning

In addition to requirements and preferences, there are four other items to be considered when planning meals: budget, volume, storage, and brand preferences.

Budget

You must consider a client's budget, even if you are not shopping for a client. You do not want to use up an item in a week, when the client cannot afford to replace it for two weeks. Make sure any menu planned is affordable.

Volume

Purchase amounts that can be used before they spoil. This may vary by the type of storage the client has. A client with ample freezer space may be able to purchase larger amounts of some items that can be frozen for a period of time.

Storage

If you shop for a client, make sure that you have sufficient appropriate storage for the items you purchase.

Brand Preferences

Many clients have specific brand preferences. Follow these preferences. Do not substitute another brand for the client's preferred brand unless the client has given you permission to do so.

Smart Shopping

Even though your client may have strong brand preferences, limited storage, and a limited budget, you can still shop "smart". The following things can help you get the most for your client's money.

Check Unit Pricing. If your client's budget, storage, and needs will allow the purchase of a larger package, compare the unit prices of the different sizes of the same brand (Figure 15-3). One size may be a better buy. Unit pricing can also help you compare the value of two similar products (if your client does not insist on a particular brand).

CARMIT SUGAR FREE WAFERS LEMON

$1.195/100GR

2.39 200GR

PK 12

01550502012

Figure 15-3
A unit pricing label provides information useful for comparison shopping. Comparing the price per unit of measure (shown at the right of the label, just below the item name) can help you to determine which brand or size is the best value.
Source: Aurora IGA.

Check Labels. There's a great deal of information on the package label. Although nutritional information (such as calories per serving and the amount of nutrients per serving) is not mandatory in Canada, manufacturers may voluntarily provide this information (Figure 15-4). You can use this information to compare different brands and varieties to select the best choice for your client's needs.

Ingredients

By law, ingredients must be listed in descending order of proportion. This means that the most plentiful ingredient must be listed first, followed by the next most plentiful, the third most, and so on. This allows you to compare the ingredients to see which brand has the amount your client prefers. For example, you may compare two brands of sweetened shredded wheat. Brand A may list wheat as the first ingredient, followed by a sugar. Brand B may list sugar first, then wheat. This tells you that Brand B has more sugar in it than any other ingredient.

Nutritional Claims

Canada regulates nutritional claims.

- Low—always associated with a very small amount.
- Less—must compare the product to an identified other product. For example, a product claiming "50% less fat" must identify the other product to which it is compared.
- Light or Lite—can refer to calories, nutrients, fats, or the taste of the product. You must look at the packaging to determine what's "light".

INGREDIENTS
WHOLE WHEAT, MALT EXTRACT, SUGAR, SALT, IRON, NIACIN, THIAMINE HYDROCHLORIDE.

NUTRITION INFORMATION

PER 35 g SERVING (2 biscuits)

ENERGY	133 CALORIES
	560 kJ
PROTEIN	3.7 g
FAT	0.7 g
CARBOHYDRATE	28.0 g
SUGARS	1.7 g
STARCH	22.0 g
DIETARY FIBRE	4.6 g
SODIUM	135 mg
POTASSIUM	190 mg

PERCENTAGE OF RECOMMENDED DAILY INTAKE

THIAMINE (VITAMINE B1)	53%
NIACIN	7.3%
IRON	33%

Canadian Diabetes Association Food Choice Value:
35 g serving (2 biscuits) = 1 1/2 ☐

Figure 15-4 *A Sample Nutrition Label*

- Low in Saturated Fat or Cholesterol—may not mean that the product is low in all fats, or low in calories. You must examine the packaging to determine the product's content.
- Milk and milk products must identify the percentage of milk fat contained in the product.

Expiry or "Best Before" Dates

These dates appear on many products. The product can safely be used before the date stated, if stored properly. Always check dates, and select the package with the latest date. As many stores put their oldest stock on the front of the shelf or cooler, you may have to look further back to get a package with a later date. Don't buy anything that your client will not use before the "best before" date.

Making Meals Appealing to Clients

Many things can affect how we eat. Busy schedules can cause us to rely on fast foods or to eat snack foods instead of more nutritious choices. Cooking only for ourselves may seem like a great deal of fuss for one person. We may get tired of the "same old thing" for lunch. Changes in vision, taste and smell, smoking, illness, and medications may make food less attractive to us. It's important to make meals as appealing as possible to your client.

Eating as a Social Event

Have you ever insisted (or wanted to insist) that your family be together for meals? For most of us, eating is a social event. We see meals as a time to share what has happened in our day, not just a time to eat.

It's quite likely that your client has lost many opportunities to enjoy the social aspect of meals. Your client may say to you things like "It's no fun just cooking for myself," or "I just eat in front of the TV for company." If your client misses the social aspect of meals, try to prepare a meal (or suggest that the client eat his or her meal) when you are there. You may still be able to complete other assigned tasks as your client eats, as well as provide company to him or her. Consider Case Example 15-1.

CASE EXAMPLE 15-1

Ginger is a support worker for Mr. Green. Mr. Green lost interest in eating when his wife died last year. Ginger makes a point of preparing a nutritious meal, much like the ones Mr. Green's wife prepared. While Mr. Green eats, Ginger folds laundry in the same room. This way, Ginger keeps Mr. Green company and completes her assigned tasks.

Remember that each person has his or her own preferences for the amount of conversation during a meal. Also, clients whose vision or hearing impairments make it difficult to eat and converse at the same time may prefer you to simply be around when they eat. Take the time to find out what level of social interaction your client prefers during a meal.

Attractive Presentation

Recall being in an elegant restaurant? How was the meal presented? Chances are, it was visually pretty as well as tasty. Meal presentation has a lot to do with how interested a person is in eating. Meal presentation has several factors such as portion size, variety of colour, tastes, textures, temperatures, placement on the plate, and the table setting.

Portion Size

Make sure that the size of the portion is appropriate to the client. Many clients are put off by portions that are too large. Ask your client how much of a food is enough. If you are asked to encourage the client to eat, offer second helpings rather than putting a large portion on the client's plate at one time.

Variety

Try to include foods of a variety of colours, textures, and temperatures in the meal you prepare. Place the items on the plate so that the colours are most appealing. For example, combining servings of fish, butternut squash, and a spinach salad provides variety and visual appeal.

Table Setting

Take a few minutes to set the table as the client likes it (Photo 15-2). Some clients prefer a tablecloth be used, others prefer a place mat. If possible, try to use colours that complement the meal.

Incorporate Food Preferences

Always prepare meals in accordance with your client's dietary, religious, or cultural requirements. If possible, incorporate your client's other food preferences into each meal. Ask your client about preferred foods and dishes, and the ways he or she prefers they be combined.

Don't Get into a Rut

Work with your client to keep the menu as varied as the client wishes. Be aware that some clients prefer the same breakfast each day, but may want much more variety in their lunch or supper. Try to combine enough preferences to result in the variety the client prefers.

Photo 15-2
An attractive place setting can make mealtime more enjoyable.

Safe Food Practices

Safe food practices include five things: shopping, storing, handling, preparing, and serving. You can keep food safe (and your client safe from food-borne illnesses) by practising a few techniques.

Shopping

Buy food that is in good condition.   Do not buy canned food in cans that are rusted, bulging, or otherwise damaged. Do not buy fresh meat, fish, or poultry that is not cold to the touch, or meats, fish, or poultry that are sold as frozen and yet are soft to the touch. Do not buy foods that appear spoiled or smell "off".

Try to buy frozen and fresh foods last.   Don't put them in your shopping cart first—they may sit at room temperature for 1/2 hour or more while you shop. Also, if you're running many errands for your client, do the shopping last. A car's trunk can reach unsafe temperatures for food storage even on a cold, sunny day.

Storing Food

Refrigerate ASAP

Make sure that you refrigerate fresh food as soon as you get to the client's home. A good rule of thumb is that the client's refrigerator should be as cold as possible *without* freezing the milk and other liquids. Put packages of fresh meat and other "juicy" items on plates so that the juices do not drip onto other items. In addition to ruining the taste of the foods the juices drip on, these juices often contain bacteria.

Freezing

Place any frozen item in the freezer, unless you are thawing it for immediate use. Do not refreeze any item that was frozen but thawed before you got it to the client's home. Check the labels of any non-frozen food products before you freeze them. Previously frozen products must not be refrozen.

It's always a good idea to write on the package the date you put the item in the freezer with a grease pen or a marker. This helps to keep food from being frozen too long and becoming unsafe.

Shelf Storage

Make sure that the item can be safely stored without refrigeration.   If your client has some of the same item that you have purchased (for example, a partial box of the cereal you have just bought) position the old box so that it is used first. It's always a good idea to write the date you bought the item on the box. Follow any special instructions for storage, such as storing in a dark or cool area.

Make sure that any opened packages are securely sealed when stored to keep out flying insects and rodents.   You may have to use a glass jar (with lid) or a plastic tub with lid. Be aware that some items must be refrigerated once opened.

Handling

No matter when the food was bought, check it before you use it. If you're not sure that it's OK, don't use it. Mould, a bad smell, or a "slimy" texture are all signs that the product has spoiled. Even food that is not obviously spoiled, but looks "funny" should be discarded. Remember: *"When in doubt, throw it out."*

Cutting out an obviously spoiled part and using the rest may expose your client to unseen microorganisms. Cooking will not fix food that has spoiled.

Always wash your hands before preparing food.   This helps to prevent the transmission of microorganisms to the food.

Wash your hands after handling any raw poultry, meat, or eggs.   When uncooked, these items can harbour harmful bacteria. Do not wipe your hands on a towel without washing them, as this simply transmits any bacteria to the towel where it can easily spread. Similarly, wash utensils and any cutting boards that have been used to prepare eggs, uncooked poultry, or meat before you use them for any other purpose.

Cooking

Thaw food in the refrigerator, oven, or microwave, never at room temperature. Marinate food in the refrigerator. Defrosting or marinating at room temperature allows the food to host harmful bacteria.

Cook foods thoroughly.   If possible, use a meat thermometer to determine when meat or poultry is done. Make sure to insert the thermometer carefully and properly, according to the manufacturer's instructions. An improperly inserted thermometer can give a false reading. If you don't use a thermometer, follow these guidelines:

- cook red meat until it is brown or grey inside,
- cook poultry until the juice is clear,
- cook fish until it flakes easily.

Remember that a microwave does not cook foods evenly.   Some parts of a dish may be well done while others are barely warm. Stir contents, and rotate the dish (if the microwave does not have a turntable) to make sure foods heat evenly. Also, microwaved food continues to cook during the "standing time" (the time after food is removed from the oven before serving). Serving food too soon may mean that it's not fully cooked.

Serving

Never leave food out at room temperature for more than two hours.   Bacteria multiply rapidly at room temperatures and can quickly render a dish harmful.

Use clean utensils to serve food. For example, never put cooked chicken on the plate that held the raw chicken unless you have washed the plate. Bacteria present on an unwashed utensil will contaminate the cooked food.

Divide leftovers into small dishes when storing. Small dishes allow the food to cool more evenly and quickly, minimizing the opportunity for bacteria to multiply. Separate warm dishes in the refrigerator to speed cooling. Containers should ideally be metal.

Make sure that you fully heat leftovers before serving. Cooked food can harbour harmful bacteria just as easily as uncooked food. Make sure the leftovers are heated thoroughly and completely to a minimum temperature of 77°C (170°F).

Assisting the Client with Eating

Some clients may require assistance with eating a meal. There are several reasons the client may require assistance: physical conditions (such as weakness, paralysis, or vision loss) as well as cognitive conditions (such as the loss of the ability to sequence events due to a dementia).

Principles of Assistance

The assistance you will provide each client is unique. Some clients will require only prompting. Others may require total assistance. All clients need the meal to be a pleasant experience that is not rushed. Keeping the following 12 principles in mind will help to ensure that the meal is as pleasant as possible.

1. **Take steps to avoid embarrassing the client.** If the client tends to spill foods, suggest that he or she wear a smock or apron that can be washed. Even men may not mind donning a chef's apron for the meal. Avoid using children's bibs or towels.
2. **If the client wears dentures, make sure that they are clean and in place.**
3. **Set a proper place setting, even if the client does not use all of the utensils.** Having the right cues may assist the client to be more independent. An attractive place setting simply may make the experience more pleasant.
4. **Make sure that foods are served at the proper temperature.** Cold peas or runny gelatin do not stimulate one's appetite!
5. **Cut, dice, or purée the food before taking the meal to the client.** It can be very embarrassing for the client to have his or her entrée cut while he or she watches.
6. **Use dishes that are appropriate to the consistency of the food being served.** One support worker found that her client was much more likely to eat puréed foods if they were served from a soup bowl.
7. **Season the food according to the client's preferences.** Be sure to avoid any forbidden seasonings.
8. **Follow the order the client prefers.** For example, some clients eat salad before their meal, others eat it with their meal. Additionally, some do not want a hot beverage until after the meal. Find out your client's preferences. If necessary, ask a family member.

9. **Do not mix foods on the fork or spoon.**   This can make the best food unpalatable. If you must moisten or thin a food, use broth, milk, or water.

10. **Assist the client to eat at a relaxed pace.**   Rushing the client will not allow time for him or her to be as independent as possible and may cause choking.

11. **Never force-feed a client.** If the client does not want to eat or closes his or her mouth when the food comes in contact with the lips, stop. A person who is not eating well may have ill-fitting dentures, sores, or abrasions in the mouth. Report the situation to your supervisor.

12. **Quietly clean up any spills.**   Do not call attention to any mess caused by the client.

Assisting the Client with a Tray or Table Meal

1. **Prepare your client for the meal.**   Many clients prefer to be toileted before a meal. Assist the client to wash his or her hands.

2. **Assist the client to the table, if appropriate.**   If the client is remaining in bed, position the client in an upright position. If the client is not able to sit up, place the client in a side-lying position.

3. **Be sure there are no unpleasant odours in the room as they can interfere with the client's desire to eat.**

4. **If the client receives a tray, ensure that the name on the food tray matches the client's.**

5. **If the client is served a tray, open cartons, remove covers, and cut food (if it cannot be done beforehand).**

6. **Add salt and pepper according to the client's preferences.**

7. **Assist the client as necessary.**

8. **Allow the client time to finish the meal before removing the tray or plates.**

Feeding the Client

1. **Prepare your client for the meal.**   Many clients prefer to be toileted before a meal. Assist the client to wash his or her hands.

2. **Assist the client to the table, if appropriate.** If the client is remaining in bed, position the client in an upright position. If the client is not able to sit up, place the client in a side-lying position.

3. **Be sure there are no unpleasant odours in the room as they can interfere with the client's desire to eat.**

4. **If the client receives a tray, ensure that the name on the food tray matches the client's.**

5. **If the client is served a tray, open cartons, remove covers, and cut food (if it cannot be done beforehand).**

6. **Add salt and pepper according to the client's preferences.**

7. **Position the client appropriately.**   A client who can sit up should be assisted to do so. A client who cannot sit up should be positioned with his or her head and shoulders at a 60° angle. Photo 15-3 shows proper positioning to assist a client.

8. **Wash your hands.**

9. **Use a fork or dessert spoon to feed the client.**   Do not use a soup spoon. Unless specifically prescribed, do not use a syringe or plastic utensils.

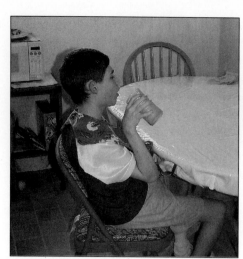

Photo 15-3

If possible, a client should be seated in a chair for meals. If this is not possible, make certain that the client is in as upright a position as is possible.

Source: CHATS.

10. **Sit close to the client so that he or she can see you and you can properly assist.** Do not stand, as this can cause you to scrape the roof of the client's mouth with the utensils. Figure 15-5 shows what can happen if you stand to assist the client.

11. **Tell the client what is on the tray.**

12. **Test the temperature of the food by testing a few drops on your wrist before giving to the client.**

13. **Serve the food in bite-sized pieces.**   Offer each piece slowly, so that the client has time to swallow each bite.

14. **Offer a sip of fluid after a few bites.**

15. **Stop when the client indicates he or she has had enough.**

16. **Note the amount of food and calculate the fluid intake if required.**

17. **Remove the tray or plates.**

18. **Assist the client to wash hands and face.**

19. **Assist the client to a comfortable position.**   It is wise to leave the client in the upright position or side-lying position for 15-20 minutes. (This helps to ensure that the food is out of the esophagus and prevents aspiration or the accidental intake of food into the respiratory tract.)

20. **Provide mouth care.**

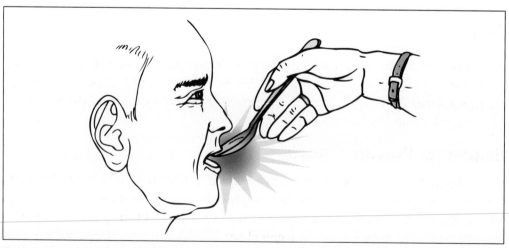

Figure 15-5 *Feeding a client from a standing position can scrape the roof of the client's mouth.*

Special Considerations When Assisting a Client to Eat

Paralysis

A client with paralysis affecting his or her ability to swallow should have an assessment by a qualified professional, such as a physician or speech pathologist. This assessment will indicate the foods the client can tolerate, how they must be prepared, as well as any special methods of assisting. In general, a client with hemiparesis (paralysis on one side of the body) can be assisted by putting small bites in the unaffected side of the mouth. You must be careful to allow sufficient time for the client to chew and swallow the bite before offering another. The client's mouth should be checked for food before you leave to ensure that no food is left for the client to choke on later. If the client begins to cough during feeding, he or she may be aspirating food into the lungs. If the client has difficulty breathing or cannot stop coughing, call for help.

Visual Impairment

Most visually impaired clients can eat independently if they are told what food is on the plate and where the food is located on the plate. Describe the location of each food item as if the plate was a clock. Take the client's hand and direct it to each item and then assist as necessary. Figure 15-6 illustrates a meal described by the clock method.

Location	Diagram
Your meatloaf is at 8 o'clock	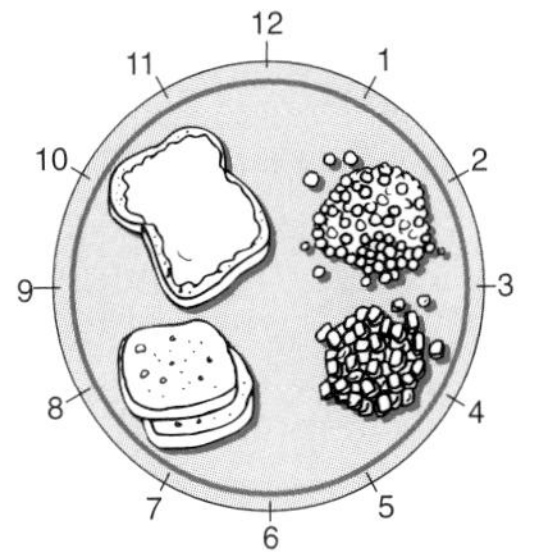
Canned baby peas are at 2 o'clock	
Steamed diced carrots are at 4 o'clock	
A buttered slice of whole-wheat bread is at 11 o'clock	

Figure 15-6 *Describing the Location of Food Using the Clock Method*

Choking

Have you ever taken too big a bite of something or had something "go down the wrong way" and began to choke? It's a frightening feeling, isn't it? Any client can be at risk for choking. A client who requires assistance eating is at additional risk.

Helping to Prevent Choking

Many clients with swallowing problems will show four common signs: drooling, chewing for a long time without swallowing, coughing when swallowing, or choking. You should always observe for these signs and report any difficulty swallowing that you suspect or observe. Following the guidelines for assisting a client presented in this chapter will also assist the person with swallowing problems and help avoid choking.

A client who has known swallowing problems may have specific techniques or routines which must be followed. Make sure that you are aware of any specific instructions for assisting your client. The following measures can also help prevent choking:

1. Arrange the client in an upright position. Place a pillow behind the client's shoulder blades to help keep the torso upright.
2. Encourage the client to keep his or her chin down when swallowing.
3. Avoid very sticky foods such as dry toast, peanut butter, or similar foods.
4. Consider using a thickening agent to thicken clear liquids such as tea, coffee, or water. Discuss this with your supervisor first, however.

If Choking Occurs

The actions you take in the event your client is choking depend upon whether or not the client can cough.

A client who can breathe, speak, cough, or make loud noises should be assisted to bend forward at the waist and lower his or her chin as close as possible to the chest. The client should be instructed to cough while in this position to clear the airway.

A client who cannot cough or who can only make high-pitched noises has an obstructed airway. In this case, the food has lodged in the larynx, blocking the passageway completely or almost completely. You must assist the client by performing the *Heimlich maneuver*. The procedure for this is as follows:

1. Reassure the client. Tell him or her that you will help.
2. Move behind the client, standing directly behind the client, facing the client's back.
3. Bring your arms around the client's waist, clasping your hands together just above the client's navel. (See Figure 15-7.)
4. Give thrusts in a quick upward motion until the obstruction is ejected.

Figure 15-7 *Proper Positioning of Hands for Heimlich Maneuver.*

Questions for Review

1. What are the benefits of a balanced diet?

2. What is a nutrient? What types of nutrients are there?

3. What are the four food groups defined in *Canada's Food Guide*?

4. What are five age- or condition-related changes in nutritional needs?

5. Why is it important for you to respect a client's food preferences?

6. What tasks are included in planning a week's meals?

7. Does the order in which ingredients are listed on a food item mean anything?

8. What principles should you keep in mind when you assist a client to eat?

9. What observations might mean that your client is prone to choking?

Questions for Discussion

1. If you had to rely on someone to plan meals, grocery-shop, and prepare meals for you, how would you react? What would you say your preferences are? How would you prefer to have your food prepared? How would you feel about someone using your kitchen?

2. Your client, Mrs. Rose, is a diabetic. Her diabetes is controlled by diet. You know that she has a sweet tooth. Despite knowing that she should not have sugar, Mrs. Rose sweetens fresh fruit with it. She also uses sugar in her tea. She tells you that sugar substitutes do not taste the same as the "real thing". How do you think you would react to this situation? What, if anything, would you do?

3. You are assisting Mrs. Mumm. One of your tasks is to prepare a meal for her to eat while you are there. When you serve her meal, she says, "Aren't you having any? I can't eat alone." You assure her that you'll just be working in the kitchen while she eats and that you can talk with her. She again asks you to join her and eat. What do you do in this situation? How do you feel?

CHAPTER SIXTEEN

Understanding the Elements of the Body

Learning Objectives

Through reading this chapter, you'll be able to:

1. Identify why a basic understanding of how the body works is helpful for support workers.
2. Explain how the body is organized.
3. Describe the structure and function of the 10 systems of the body.
4. Discuss in general terms growth and development of the person from birth to adulthood.

Chapter At A Glance

From Cell to System: How the Body Is Organized

The Systems of the Body

Age-Related Changes

Terms You'll Use

Age-Related Changes The changes that are part of the aging process that happen to everyone if they live long enough.

Alimentary Canal The structure that links the organs of the digestive system.

Anatomy The study of the body's structure.

Blood Assists in nutrition and elimination, regulation, protection, and oxygenation of the body.

Bones Hard, rigid, living structures that provide support for the body.

Cell The basic element of the human body and all living things.

Connective Tissue The tissue that forms bones, tendons, and cartilage.

Epithelial Tissue   The tissue that covers the internal and external body tissues.

Integument   Another term for skin.

Joints   The points where two or more bones meet and move.

Matrix   The substance found between cells and tissues from which a structure develops.

Muscle Tissue   The tissue that can contract and relax; may be smooth, striated, or cardiac.

Muscles   Part of the musculoskeletal system that helps maintain posture, movement, and body heat.

Nerve Tissue   The tissue made of nerve cells that transmits electrical signals from the central nervous system to various parts of the body.

Organs   Groups of tissues working together with a specific purpose.

Physiology   The study of the body's functions.

System   Groups of organs working together with a specific purpose.

Tissues   Groups of cells linked together by a matrix.

From Cell to System:
How the Body Is Organized

As a support worker, you will be called upon to provide assistance to your clients. As we have discussed many times in this text, you always must focus on the whole person, not just the person's disability or diagnosis. However, it is very likely that you will need to provide physical assistance to your clients. A basic understanding of *anatomy* and *physiology* will help you to understand why certain things happen and the reasons assistance is best provided in a particular way. **Anatomy** is the study of the body's structure. **Physiology** is the study of the body's functions.

The Cell

The **cell** is the basic element of the human body. There are over 75 *trillion* cells in the human body. Cells are too small to see with the naked eye, but we can easily see them under a microscope. There are over 100 types of cells in the human body. While all cells have the same basic structure, their size, shape, purpose, and life span differ with type. Some cells, like blood cells, replace themselves, while other cells, like nerve cells, cannot. This is why a person can give blood and make more, yet cannot recover from severe damage to nerve cells in the spinal cord.

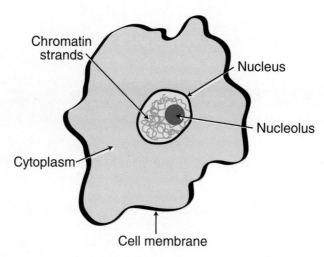

Figure 16-1 *The Basic Structure of the Cell*

Cells are made up of three main components: the membrane, the cytoplasm, and the nucleus. Figure 16-1 illustrates the basic structure of the cell.

The *nucleus* is the centre of the cell. It contains the cell's chromosomes (which, in turn, contain genes). Humans have 46 chromosomes and, within them, many hundreds of genes. Genes determine inherited characteristics like eye colour, hair colour, body type, and, in part, personality and susceptibility to certain kinds of disease.

The *cytoplasm* is the substance that fills the cell and surrounds the nucleus. Within the cytoplasm is protoplasm, a gel-like substance that contains structures that carry out the cell's function. *Metabolism* is the term that describes the work of the cells.

Each type of cell has its own life expectancy. Some cells (such as white blood cells) last only a few hours. Other cells, such as nerve cells, are expected to last a person's lifetime. Cells that do not last a lifetime generally divide into new cells in a process called *mitosis*. Mitosis results when one cell becomes two cells: the original cell and an exact copy.

The *membrane* is the outer covering of the cell. It gives the cell its shape and provides it with protection. Figure 16-2 shows different types of cells.

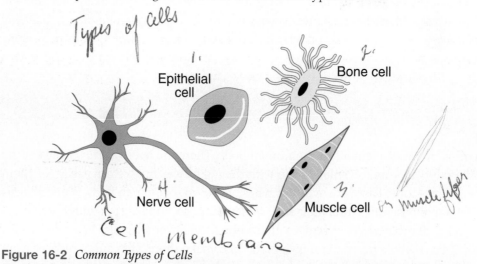

Figure 16-2 *Common Types of Cells*

Tissue

Most cells are grouped together, linked by a *matrix*, to form **tissues**. A **matrix** is the substance found between cells and tissues from which structures develop. There are four major types of tissue: muscle, nerve, epithelial, and connective. Each type of tissue has its own function with variants within the type. Let's examine them.

Muscle Tissue

1. **Muscle tissue** is the only type of tissue that can contract and relax. There are three types of muscle tissue: striated, smooth, and cardiac (Figure 16-3).

 1. Striated muscle tissue is the type of tissue found in the muscles that move your bones. Each striated muscle cell has many nuclei. These cells form tissue that can expand and contract to a much greater extent than can the other types of muscle tissue. Because the person controls when striated muscle tissue contracts and expands, the striated muscles are called *voluntary* muscles.

 2. Smooth muscle tissue is formed from cells that only have one nucleus in each. This tissue is able to contract and expand and to maintain a particular state for long periods of time. Smooth muscle tissue is found in the internal organs (except for the heart). Smooth muscle tissue cannot be controlled by the person and is called *involuntary*.

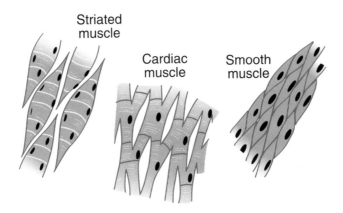

Figure 16-3   *Muscle Tissue Types*

 3. Cardiac muscle tissue is considered to be a very strong type of muscle tissue, as it controls the movement of the heart. Cardiac muscle looks a bit like striated muscle, but each cell in cardiac muscle tissue has only one nucleus. Like smooth muscle tissue, cardiac muscle tissue cannot be controlled by the person.

Nerve Tissue

2. **Nerve tissue** is tissue made of nerve cells and transmits electrical signals (also called impulses) from the central nervous system to various parts of the body. Nerve cells are also called neurons. Adults have between 10 billion and 100 billion neurons, most of them in the brain. Neuron development occurs before birth and stops at birth. Nerve cells do not replace themselves, although they can repair themselves to some extent. The neuron looks very different from other cells. It has a cell body, from which many

dendrites project. Dendrites are designed to receive electrical impulses and are shaped somewhat like branches. At the other end of the cell body is a long fibre called an axon. The axon ends in a number of finger-like structures. Figure 16- 4 illustrates a nerve cell. Some neurons are very small. Other neurons, such as those that travel from your spinal cord to your foot, can be over one metre long.

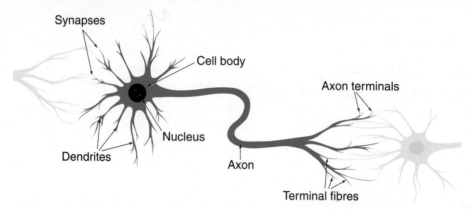

Figure 16-4 *A Nerve Cell*

Epithelial Tissue

Epithelial tissue covers the internal and external body tissues. The lining of your mouth, nose, and stomach, as well as your skin, hair, and nails are formed of epithelial tissue. There are several different types of epithelial cells which, in turn, form the various types of epithelial tissue. The epithelial tissue in the capillaries is only one cell thick, allowing for oxygen and nutrients from the blood to travel to other body tissues. Figure 16-5 illustrates some of the body's epithelial cells.

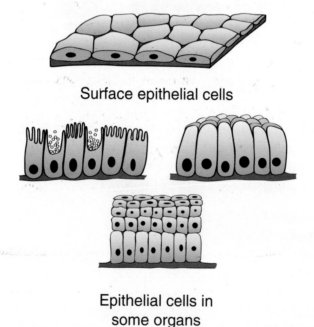

Surface epithelial cells

Epithelial cells in some organs

Figure 16-5 *Common Epithelial Cells*

Connective Tissue

Connective tissue is the kind of tissue that forms the bones, tendons, cartilage, and other types of connecting tissue. Unlike other tissue, connective tissue has cells *spaced* apart on a matrix. Often other material (such as fat or minerals) also attaches to this matrix. Some connective tissue is called *loose* connective tissue. Figure 16-6 illustrates this type of tissue. This tissue is found under the skin and around organs. Another type of connective tissue is densely packed and forms structures like the bones, tendons, cartilage, and ligaments.

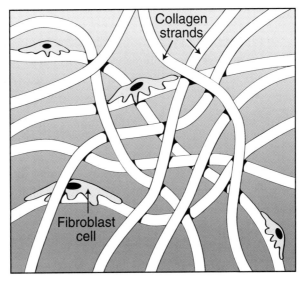

Figure 16-6   *Loose Connective Tissue*

Organs

Tissues group together to form **organs**. Each organ has a specific function. Some organs are very rigid, like the bones. Other organs, such as the skin, are very flexible. We'll discuss the various types of organs later in this chapter.

Systems

A group of organs with a similar purpose are grouped together into a **system**. For example, the digestive system groups together all the organs required to convert food into energy and eliminate solid wastes. This system includes the pancreas, liver, intestines, and other organs. There are 10 systems in the human body. The next section of this chapter provides an overview of the structure and purpose of each system.

The Systems of the Body

Within the body there are 10 systems, each with its own function. These systems are:

- The Integumentary System
- The Musculoskeletal System
- The Circulatory System (incorporating the lymphatic and immune systems)
- The Respiratory System
- The Digestive System
- The Urinary System
- The Nervous System
- The Sensory System

■ The Endocrine System
■ The Reproductive System

Although each system has a distinct function, each of these systems relies upon the function of the other systems in order to work. No system can function on its own. For example, you could not survive without your integumentary system—your skin—no matter how well your other systems could function. In fact, the loss of only one-third of a person's skin may cause death.

The inability of a system to function at peak ability may also affect the function of other systems. You likely will see this with your clients. For example, a respiratory system that does not work at peak capacity may well affect the ability of the cardiovascular system to work well. Thus, you may see changes in your client that are caused by a problem that doesn't seem to be related to the person's impairment.

The Integumentary System

The integumentary system is the largest system of the body. It is made up of the skin, or **integument**. The skin comprises epithelial, connective, and nerve tissue in addition to oil and sweat glands.

There are two layers in the skin, the epidermis and the dermis. Figure 16-7 illustrates these layers, as well as the other structures found in the skin. The epidermis contains both living and dead cells; the dermis contains only living cells. The living cells in the epidermis have pigment, and are what gives the skin its colour.

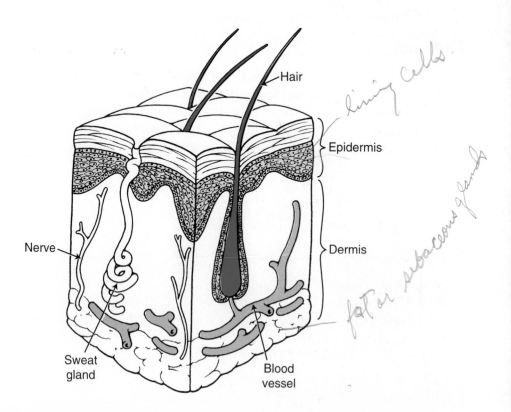

Figure 16-7 *The Skin*

Note that the epidermis has few nerve endings and no blood vessels. The dermis contains many nerve endings and blood vessels. This arrangement provides a barrier layer, preventing us from receiving so many sensations that it becomes overwhelming and reducing the potential for blood loss from the wear and tear of everyday activities.

The integumentary system performs may functions. First, it protects the body from bacteria and other potentially harmful substances and protects the organs from injury. Second, it prevents excessive water and fluid loss. Third, the system helps the body to regulate its temperature, through the evaporation of moisture through sweat glands. Fourth, it provides a way for the body to sense textures, temperatures, pressure, and pain, all of which can help to keep the person safe from harm.

Care of the skin is one of the most significant aspects of physical support. In Chapter 17, we'll look at common changes in the integumentary system and how these affect the care you provide.

The Musculoskeletal System

The musculoskeletal system provides the basic structure of the body and the mechanisms by which the body can move. This system contains *bones, muscles, joints,* ligaments, cartilage, and tendons.

Bones

Bones are hard and rigid structures. Despite this, bones are living structures made of cells. Bones have three main elements: the bone, the marrow, and the periosteum. Figure 16-8 illustrates these three components.

Marrow exists in the centre of the bone. Its purpose is to manufacture blood cells.

Periosteum is the outer covering of the bone. It contains blood vessels to nourish the bone.

There are 206 bones in the human body. These bones are grouped into four categories: long bones, short bones, flat bones, and irregular bones. Each has a particular purpose, as Table 16-1 illustrates.

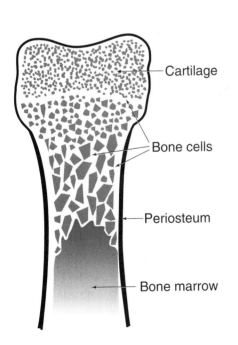

Figure 16-8 *Components of Bone*

| TABLE 16-1 | | |
Bone Type	Purpose	Example
Long Bones	These bones bear the weight of the body.	Leg bones (femur, fibula, tibia)
Short Bones	These bones allow for small, precise movement over a wide arc.	Wrist bones Hand bones (carpals and metacarpals) Foot bones (tarsals and metatarsals), fingers and toes (phalanges)
Flat Bones	These bones protect the organs of the body.	Skull (cranium) Shoulder blades (clavicle) Ribs Pelvis
Irregular Bones	These bones allow for specific degrees of movement.	Backbone (vertebrae)

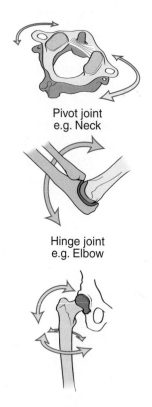

Pivot joint
e.g. Neck

Hinge joint
e.g. Elbow

Ball-and-socket joint
e.g. Hip

Joints

The **joint** is the point where two or more bones meet and move. Joints allow the body to move in specific ways. Bones are held together at the joint by ligaments. The point at which the bones meet is cushioned by cartilage (living, connective tissue). The synovial membrane lines the joint and produces synovial fluid (a lubricant that makes it easier to move the joint).

There are three types of joints: pivot, hinge, and ball-and-socket. Figure 16-9 illustrates these three types. *Pivot joints* allow side-to-side movement, such as the movement of the head on the neck. *Hinge joints* allow movement back and forth in a single direction. A knee joint is an example of a hinge joint. A *ball-and-socket joint* allows movement in all directions. This joint is made up of a hollowed end of one bone (the socket) into which fits the rounded end of another joint (the ball). Your hip joint is a ball and socket joint, as is your shoulder joint.

Figure 16-9 *Three Types of Joints*

Muscles

Muscles perform three essential functions: maintaining posture, moving the body, and maintaining body heat. As we discussed earlier in this chapter, muscles can be voluntary (i.e., moved by the person as they desire) or involuntary (i.e., moved in response to body process that cannot be consciously controlled by the person).

The human body contains over 500 muscles in various sizes. Figure 16-10 illustrates some of the major muscles. Muscles are attached to bones by *tendons*, a particularly tough form of connective tissue. As the muscle contracts, the tendon moves the bones.

The contracting and relaxing of muscles generates kinetic energy or heat. For example, you probably notice that you generate heat when you exert yourself. You may notice that your client may feel cold if he or she cannot move about a great deal. You probably shiver when you are very cold—these muscle contractions are your body's way of generating heat.

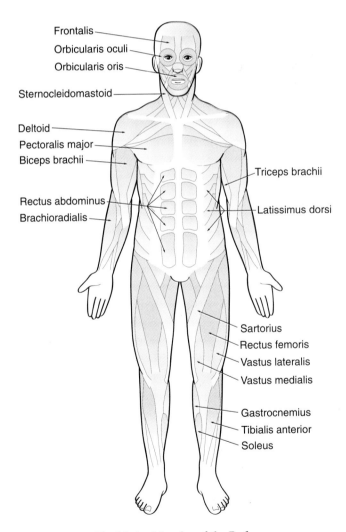

Figure 16-10 *The Major Muscles of the Body*

The Circulatory System

The *blood*, the heart, and the blood vessels make up the circulatory system (Figure 16-11). Blood is pumped through blood vessels by the heart. Figure 16-12 illustrates the path of circulation throughout the body The circulatory system performs four functions, as listed here.

- **Nutrition and Elimination.** Blood carries food and other substances to the cells and removes waste products from the cells.

- **Regulation.** Blood helps to regulate body temperature by carrying heat from muscles to other body parts. Blood vessels help to regulate temperature by constricting (to retain heat) and expanding to (to cool heat).

- **Protection.** Blood carries antibodies and other substances which help the body fight off disease.

- **Oxygenation.** Blood carries oxygen to the cells and removes carbon dioxide.

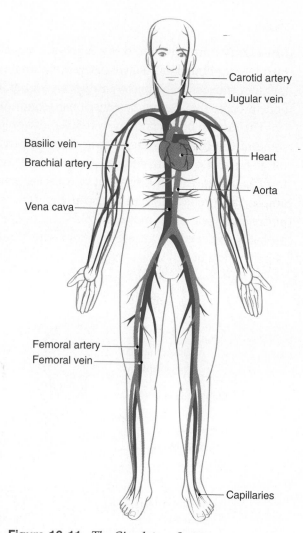

Figure 16-11 *The Circulatory System*

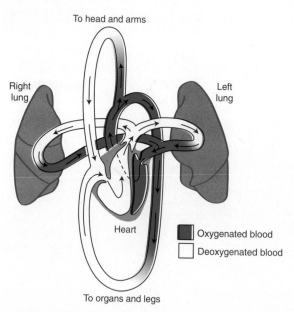

Figure 16-12 *Pathways of Circulation*

Blood

Blood assists in nutrition and elimination, regulation, protection, and oxygenation of the systems of the body. It is made up of two main components: blood cells and plasma. There are three types of blood cells: red blood cells, white blood cells, and platelets. Each has a specific function. Figure 16-13 illustrates the three types of cells.

Red blood cells are called *erythrocytes*. Red blood cells are created in bone marrow and live for approximately three to four months. There are over 25 trillion red blood cells in the body. These cells contain haemoglobin, a substance which picks up oxygen from the lungs and carries it to the cells, where it is exchanged for the cells' carbon dioxide. Figure 16-14 illustrates the functions of red blood cells. As red blood cells wear out, they are destroyed by the liver or spleen.

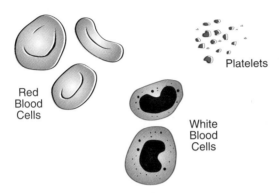

Figure 16-13   *Blood Cells*

White blood cells aren't really white. They are colourless. Known as leukocytes, the purpose of these cells is to assist the body in fighting infection and foreign substances. They are produced in bone marrow and in the lymphatic system (a subsystem of the cardiovascular system) and live about nine days. White blood cells make up a very small component of human blood: there is only one white blood cell for every 500-1000 red blood cells.

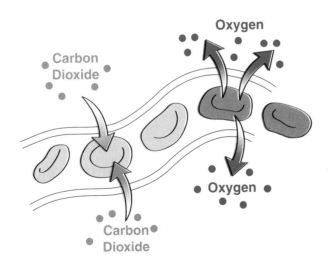

Figure 16-14   *Functions of the Red Blood Cells*

Anatomy of a Bruise

A bruise occurs when a force causes blood vessels under the skin to rupture and leak. The size of the rupture as well as the size of the vessel will determine the size of the bruise. As the vessel wall repairs, the flow of blood is stopped. Gradually the leaked blood is absorbed by the body and the bruise disappears.

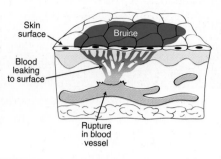

Platelets are substances in blood whose function is to assist blood to clot. This prevents excessive blood loss. Platelets are also created in bone marrow and live approximately four days.

Plasma comprises the fluid in blood. It is colourless, mostly water, and moves the blood cells and platelets.

Blood Vessels

There are two main types of blood vessels: veins and arteries. Veins lead blood to the heart. Arteries lead blood from the heart. Blood vessels can be so small that blood cells must travel through the vessel single file. Healthy blood vessels are smooth-walled and flexible (much like a new garden hose).

Sometimes due to disease, blood vessels become hard and their interior walls become rough with cholesterol or calcium deposits. This can make it difficult for blood to flow properly through the vessels. Additionally, pieces of these deposits can break off, causing a clot. When a clot occurs, the tissue served by the vessel can die. If the clot occurs in a vessel that nourishes the heart, that part (or all) of the heart muscle can die. If the clot occurs in an area of the brain, a cerebral vascular accident (a CVA or a stroke) occurs. This can cause the person to lose the ability to move, to see things properly, or even to speak.

The Heart

The heart is a very strong muscle that is approximately the size of your fist. The purpose of the heart is to pump the blood through the blood vessels. The heart pumps continuously, with enough force that blood circulates through all the vessels with each beat. The heart contains four chambers: two receive incoming blood and two receive blood to be pumped out. Figure 16-15 illustrates the chambers and major vessels in the heart.

The Lymphatic System and the Immune System

The lymphatic system and immune system are actually subsystems of the circulatory system. The lymphatic system is sometimes called the lymphatic network. It encompasses the lymph (a straw-coloured fluid), lymph nodes, lymph vessels, spleen, the thymus gland, tonsils, as well as some tissue in the intestinal tract. Figure 16-16 illustrates the lymphatic system.

The main purpose of the lymphatic system is to assist the body in fighting infection and disease through the production of special cells which bond to white blood cells. These special cells are called antibodies and can make a person resistant or immune to specific diseases. This action is often referred to as the immune system. Figure 16-17 illustrates how white blood cells destroy harmful viruses and create antibodies.

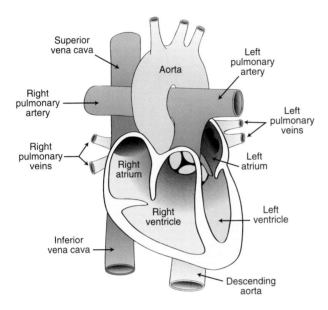

Figure 16-15 *The Heart*

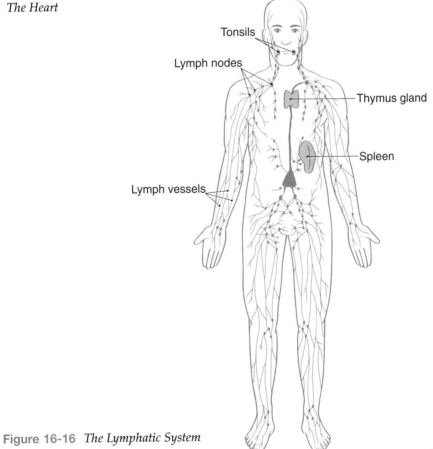

Figure 16-16 *The Lymphatic System*

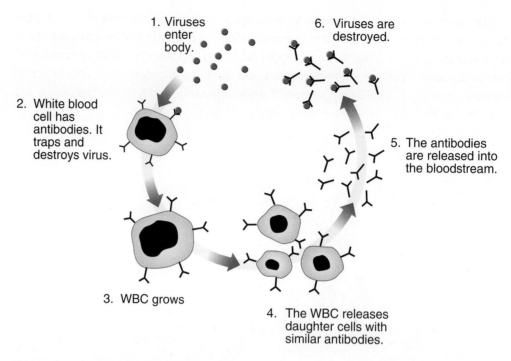

1. Viruses enter body.

2. White blood cell has antibodies. It traps and destroys virus.

3. WBC grows

4. The WBC releases daughter cells with similar antibodies.

5. The antibodies are released into the bloodstream.

6. Viruses are destroyed.

Figure 16-17 *How Your Body Fights Disease*

Sometimes, the lymphatic system attempts to defend the body against things that are not really harmful. We say that a person has an allergy when the person's body misidentifies a usually harmless substance and attempts to defend the body against it. The runny nose, watery eyes, and sneezes that some people get when they are near dogs or cats is a common example of an allergy. More severe forms of misidentification can cause a person's body to attack vital organs.

In addition to its role in the immune system, the lymphatic system helps the blood to transmit nutrients to the cells and to transmit toxins from the cells to the blood vessels.

Stop and Reflect 16-1

Have you ever had an infected cut? Perhaps you noticed that the area around the cut was swollen and reddened. You might even have had some whitish discharge from the cut. These things: the swelling, redness, heat, and discharge are signs that your white cells are fighting a foreign item.

The Digestive System

The purpose of the digestive system is to break down food (physically and chemically) so that the nutrients may be used by the body. This system is also called the gastrointestinal system and includes the organs which remove solid waste from the body. The digestive system of an average person will process between 29 000 and 60 000 kg of food over a lifetime. This process is called *digestion*.

The digestive system contains many organs such as the tongue, esophagus, stomach, small intestine, liver, and large intestine. The structure that links all these things together is called the **alimentary canal**. These organs are usually made up of layers of smooth muscle and are capable of manipulating the food in many ways. The alimentary canal is about 27 feet long, beginning at the mouth and ending at the anus. Figure 16-18 illustrates the alimentary canal.

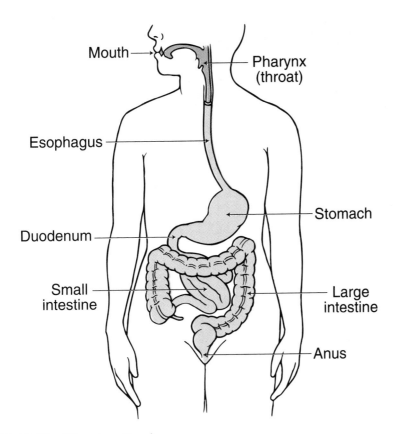

Figure 16-18 *The Alimentary Canal*

Digestion is a process that can actually begin before you start to eat. Has your mouth ever watered when you were thinking of your favourite food? Your digestive system is actually beginning to work, in *preparation* of eating. Digestive juices are flowing in anticipation of having food to break down.

At the first bite, food is broken into tiny bits by the teeth. The lining of the mouth helps to cool food to a temperature that makes it easy to swallow. Saliva moistens the food, making it easier to pass through the system.

Swallowing forces the food down the throat (pharynx). Figure 16-19 shows the major structures used in swallowing. A structure called the epiglottis automatically covers the windpipe so that the person does not inhale the food. Sometimes, when a person tries to swallow too fast, the epiglottis cannot close fast enough and some food enters the windpipe. You've probably had the experience of food "going down the wrong way". When this happens, you cough, forcing the food back up into the mouth where it can be properly swallowed.

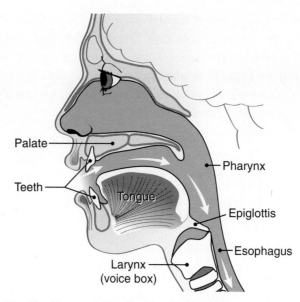

Figure 16-19 *The Structures Involved in Swallowing*

Food moves down the esophagus through a process called peristalsis. It takes only a few seconds to move food from your mouth to your stomach. Once in the stomach, the food is churned and tossed to mix with digestive juices. These juices help to kill off any harmful bacteria and to break down the food into nutrition that the body can use. Carbohydrates are the easiest substances to break down. They pass through the stomach first. Proteins and fats are harder to break down, so they remain in the stomach longer. This is one reason why most of us eat salad (comprised mostly of water and carbohydrates) *before* we eat other foods (which are usually higher in protein and fats) at a meal.

Material broken down in the stomach passes through the sphincter muscle into the top of the small intestine (*duodenum*). The sphincter opens and closes to let a small amount of matter pass into the small intestine.

The small intestine is the largest part of the alimentary canal. In the average adult, it is about 6.4 metres long. There are names for each part of the small intestine: the upper part is the duodenum, the middle part is the jejunum, the lower part is the ileum.

The small intestine uses secretions from the liver and pancreas to further break down the food into their basic elements. The lower sections of the small intestine allow nutrients to pass through to the bloodstream where they can then be carried to the cells.

Indigestible components of food are passed on through to the large intestine. The large intestine removes any needed water and chemicals that remain, passing the rest to the rectum for elimination.

The Respiratory System

The respiratory system consists of the lungs, the sinuses, and the windpipe (trachea). Figure 16-20 illustrates the major components of the respiratory system. The lungs bring in air to the body, absorb some of its oxygen into the bloodstream and release the carbon dioxide collected from the cells by the blood. They then release this air. This exchange of gases is a part of the process of respiration.

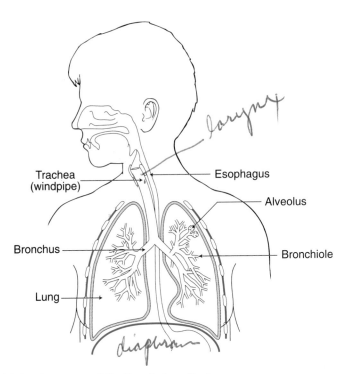

Figure 16-20 *Major Structures of the Respiratory System*

The lungs work closely with the heart. As oxygen infiltrates the blood in the lungs, it is sent to the heart to be pumped out to the rest of the body. The blood returns to the lungs via the heart with the cells' waste carbon dioxide. The carbon dioxide is removed from the blood and exhaled. Figure 16-21 illustrates this exchange.

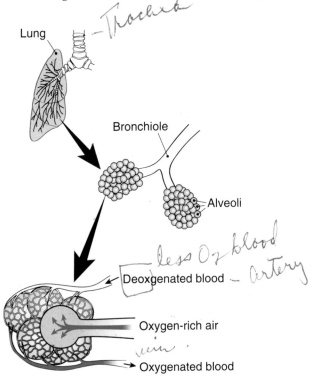

Figure 16-21 *Gas Exchange in the Lungs*

The lungs do not expand and contract on their own. They rely on the work of the diaphragm (sheet of muscle below the lungs) to move down and up, causing the lungs to expand and contract. This expansion pulls air into the lungs. Similarly, the contraction of the lungs forces air out. Figure 16-22 illustrates the mechanics of breathing.

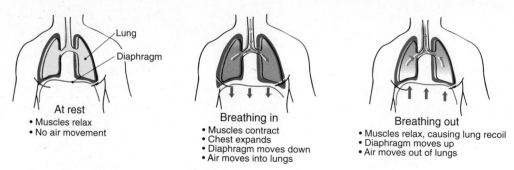

Figure 16-22 *The Mechanics of Breathing*

The Urinary System

The urinary system consists of the kidneys, the ureters and bladder, and the urethra. There are two main functions to the urinary system: to clean the blood and to regulate the amount of water in the body. Figure 16-23 illustrates the urinary system.

Kidneys

Each person has two kidneys, each approximately five inches long. The kidneys filter blood through special capillaries called *glomeruli*. Each day, these glomeruli extract approximately 170 litres of liquid (filtrate) per adult. The kidneys return most of the liquid to the body, retaining only a small amount that contains waste products from the organs. This fluid, amounting to a little over a litre each day, is urine.

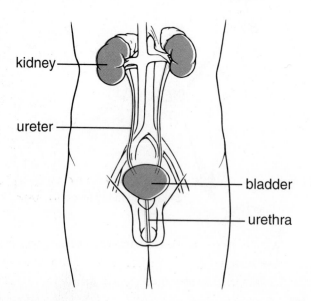

Figure 16-23 *The Urinary System*

Ureters and Bladder

Urine flows down the ureters into the bladder, an expandable sac at the base of the pelvis. The bladder collects urine. When full, the nerve endings in the bladder wall signal the need to urinate.

Urethra

The urethra is connected to the bladder by two sphincter muscles. The outer sphincter muscle is a voluntary muscle. Unless the need to urinate is overwhelming, a healthy person can control this muscle. For example, most of us have "waited" to get to a proper bathroom. When we relax this outer muscle, we allow the urine to pass down the urethra and out of the body. Many impairments and some medications can affect a person's ability to control this muscle. Chapter 20 will identify some conditions that can cause a lack of control.

The Nervous System

The nervous system has been described as the body's switchboard. The purpose of the nervous system is to transmit messages to and from the various parts of the body. It is composed of the *central nervous system*: the brain and the spinal cord. These structures are covered with three layers of protective membrane, called meninges. Cerebrospinal fluid flows between the innermost and middle layers of the meninges to cushion the brain against shock. Figure 16-24 illustrates the major components of the central nervous system. Figure 16-25 shows the position of the spinal cord in the bony spine.

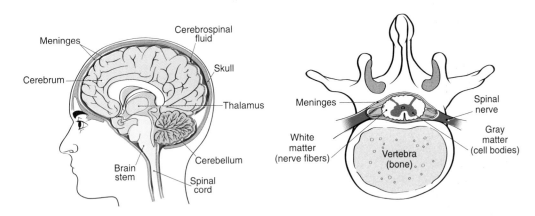

Figure 16-24 *The Brain*

Figure 16-25 *The Spinal Cord (cross-section)*

The peripheral nervous system comprises the nerves that emanate from the brain and spinal cord. These nerves have two types of fibres: motor fibres, which control movement, and sensory fibres, which transmit messages about various sensations. These two types of nerve fibres create the somatic nervous system. This system is responsible for controlling the body's relationship to the things around it.

Another part of the peripheral nervous system is the network of nerves connecting the internal organs. This network is called the autonomic nervous system, as it cannot be consciously controlled by the person. The brain operates this system through the *parasympathetic* and the *sympathetic nerves*. Figure 16-26 shows the peripheral nervous system.

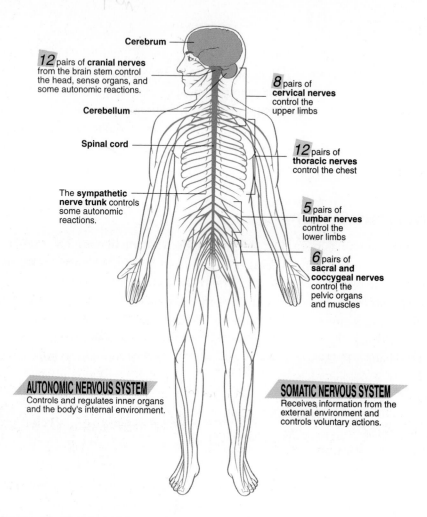

Cerebrum

12 pairs of **cranial nerves** from the brain stem control the head, sense organs, and some autonomic reactions.

Cerebellum

Spinal cord

The **sympathetic nerve trunk** controls some autonomic reactions.

8 pairs of **cervical nerves** control the upper limbs

12 pairs of **thoracic nerves** control the chest

5 pairs of **lumbar nerves** control the lower limbs

6 pairs of **sacral and coccygeal nerves** control the pelvic organs and muscles

AUTONOMIC NERVOUS SYSTEM
Controls and regulates inner organs and the body's internal environment.

SOMATIC NERVOUS SYSTEM
Receives information from the external environment and controls voluntary actions.

Figure 16-26 *The Peripheral Nervous System*

The Brain

The brain is the most complex part of the nervous system. It contains billions of neurons. When you see an image, remember something, or learn a new skill you are training your neurons to connect in new ways. Remember that neurons connect without making physical contact. Neurons connect when the axons of one neuron chemically connect with the dendrites of another. This chemical process is called a *synapse*.

As we discussed earlier, neurons cannot be replaced. Because of the number of neurons in the brain and the infinite ways that they can connect, researchers estimate that the capacity of the brain is limitless.

Specific functions are controlled by different areas of the brain. There are three main areas of the brain: the cerebrum, cerebellum, and the brain stem. Figure 16-27 illustrates the major structures of the brain.

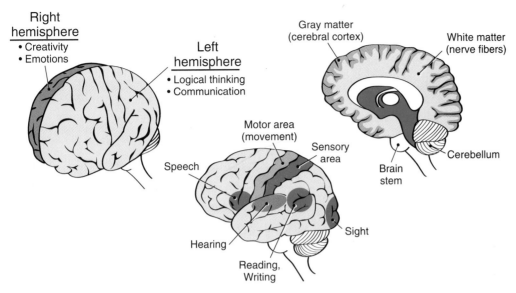

Figure 16-27 *The Major Structures of the Brain*

The cerebrum comprises two halves, called hemispheres. Nerve fibres connect these two halves. Each hemisphere is composed of a core of white matter (nerve fibres covered with a protective coating called myelin). This core is surrounded by a layer of grey matter called the cerebral cortex. The cerebral cortex receives all body sensations and controls all voluntary movements. It is also responsible for the things we call *cognitive function*, such as learning, judgment, and reasoning. Different functions are controlled by specific areas of the cerebrum. For example, the movements of the right side of the body are controlled by the left hemisphere of the brain. Similarly, the right hemisphere controls voluntary movements of the left side of the body. Sensory impulses are received by specific areas in each hemisphere.

Some categories of functions are controlled by a specific hemisphere. For example, the right hemisphere is responsible for spatial perception, creativity, emotions and impulse control, as well as artistic ability and creativity. The left hemisphere is responsible for logical thinking and, for most of us, the use of language in reading , writing, and speaking. (The language centre of some left-handed people may be in the right hemisphere.)

Some functions, like memory, are probably controlled deep in the brain and likely in more than one area of the brain. Chapter 22 will discuss memory and cognitive ability in greater detail.

The cerebellum sits at the back of the brain, near the base. It is responsible for the coordination of movement and plays a significant role in maintaining balance.

The brain stem is found at the top of the spinal column. Special nerve fibres here control such essential functions as heart rate, breathing, and blood pressure.

The Spinal Cord

The spinal cord begins at the base of your brain and extends about two-thirds of the way down your spinal column. Many nerves emanate from this column—some of them over one metre long. Nerves travel down the legs to the feet, allowing for movement and sensation. Similarly, nerves branch out all along the spinal column, controlling sensation and movement throughout the shoulders, arms, and torso.

The Sensory System

The sensory system brings information from the environment. A person's eyes see what is around him or her, the ears hear the sounds of the environment. The tongue responds to various tastes, the nose to various scents and odours. Your body's sensory nerves perceive temperature, texture, pain, and pressure. Without this ability to perceive what is around us, we would certainly fall victim to any number of perils.

The Eye

We are visual creatures. Most of us rely upon our sight to learn, to avoid danger, to help organize our activities (i.e., by colour-coding items), as well as to obtain information from others. Many researchers compare the eye to a camera. Yet, in many ways, the eye is an ultra-sophisticated camera—a natural creation that no technology can yet match.

The eye is a gel-filled organ, with an opening at the front (the *pupil*) and light-sensitive receptors at the back (the *retina* and the *macula*). Just in front of the pupil is the *cornea*, a transparent structure that protects the pupil. Behind the pupil is the *lens*. Figure 16-28 illustrates the structures of the eye.

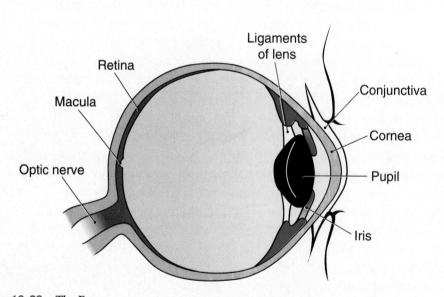

Figure 16-28   *The Eye*

In the simplest terms, the eye receives light through the pupil. This light is focussed on the back of the eye by the lens. When this image is reflected on the back of the eye, the image is reversed and upside down. The optic nerve receives the electrical impulses from the retina and macula and transmits them to the brain, where they are interpreted rightside up. Figure 16-29 illustrates this process.

If a person's retina is too close or far away from the lens, the image on the retina will be out of focus. In this case, a person would wear glasses or contact lenses to correct the problem.

The eye undergoes many changes over the life span. Babies are farsighted and are unable to focus on close objects until they are several months old. The eyesight of a middle-aged person also changes, often requiring the person to use reading glasses to see fine print.

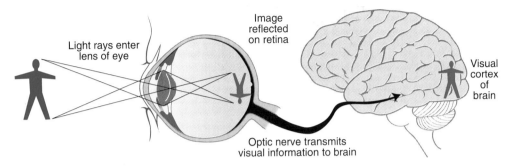

Figure 16-29   *How the Eye "Sees"*

The Ear

The ears perform two major functions. They provide a person's ability to hear and to assist the person in maintaining balance. There are three areas in the ear: the *inner ear,* the *middle ear,* and the *outer ear.* Figure 16-30 shows the major components of the ear. Each has specific functions.

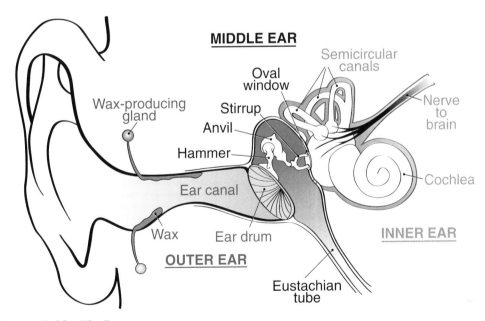

Figure 16-30   *The Ear*

The *outer ear* collects sound waves and channels them to the eardrum. The eardrum vibrates as these sound waves pound against it.

The shape of the external ear structure is designed specifically to collect sounds. Without it, a person would not hear well. You can test the effect of the shape of the external structure by cupping your hand behind one of your ears. Notice how sounds seem to sound different?

The outer ear also has a protective function. The ear produces ear wax, which along with thousands of tiny hairs in the canal, helps to trap dirt and other particles before they reach the eardrum.

The *middle ear* is responsible to concentrate the sound waves received from the outer ear. Within this structure are three bones: the hammer, the anvil, and the stirrup (these bones are named for their shapes). Each bone vibrates when sound waves vibrate the eardrum. These structures link to carry and concentrate that sound to the oval window. Also a part of the middle ear is the eustachian tube that leads to the throat. This tube opens when a person yawns or swallows and helps to equalize the pressure on both sides of the eardrum.

The inner ear contains the *cochlea*, a snail-shaped structure that contains the receptor cells for hearing. When sound vibrations reach the cochlea through the oval window, thousands of nerve cells (that look much like tiny hairs) vibrate, converting the physical movement into electrical impulses that are then transmitted to the brain by the acoustic nerve.

The inner ear also contains the semicircular canals, fluid-filled structures with receptor cells that report your position to the brain. Because these canals contain fluid, rapid movement (such as spinning or turning one's head suddenly) can cause a person to become dizzy, because the fluid stops moving *after* the body does.

The Nose

A human's sense of smell is useful in identifying objects (such as whether a paper bag contains cookies) as well as determining whether danger is present (as in sniffing for the scent of natural gas). Our sense of smell is closely linked to memories—the smell of a favourite food may bring a flood of memories of the meals associated with it.

The nose is the primary organ of scent. It contains receptor cells (called *olfactory rods*) which are surrounded by mucus. The mucus traps airborne chemical particles where these particles stimulate the olfactory rods. The rods then send an electrical message to the brain by way of the *olfactory bulb*, a structure containing nerve cells.

The Tongue

The tongue is the organ which transmits the sensation of taste. The tongue contains thousands of taste buds. These buds contain receptor cells that are sensitive to chemicals which are emitted from substances we swallow or chew. While there are four main categories of taste: salty, sour, sweet, and bitter, they can be combined in almost limitless ways to form unique taste blends. Specific areas on the tongue are more receptive to different tastes. Figure 16-31 shows these locations.

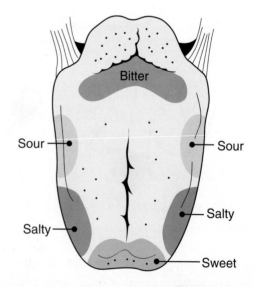

Figure 16-31   *Taste Sensitivity on the Tongue*

Many things can affect a person's ability to sense tastes. An illness or a medication may coat the tongue, making it harder for the taste chemicals to reach the receptor cells. The number and sensitivity of taste buds declines with age, a fact that may make it more difficult for older people to enjoy foods as they once did.

The senses of taste and smell work closely together. It's often hard to tell which is which. As you've probably realized when you've had a stuffy nose, food doesn't taste the same. This is because some of what your brain thinks is a *taste* sensation is actually a *scent* sensation.

The Endocrine System

The purpose of the endocrine system is to regulate many of your body's processes. This system comprises a number of glands, as Figure 16-32 illustrates. Each gland secretes hormones of varying types. These chemicals help to regulate your metabolism, your body temperature, as well as a female's menstrual cycle.

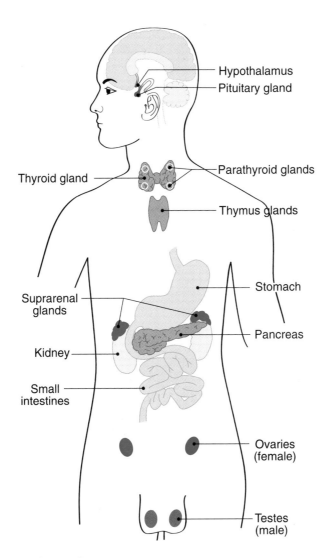

Figure 16-32 *The Endocrine System*

Two glands have tasks of particular importance. The *hypothalamus* controls the sensations of hunger, thirst, fatigue, and wakefullness, It also helps to regulate many involuntary functions, as well as the *pituitary gland*. The pituitary gland's purpose is to ensure that the body maintains the proper level of hormones.

The stomach, intestines, pancreas, and kidneys also secrete hormones for specific purposes. For example, the pancreas secretes insulin, which regulates the amount of sugar in the bloodstream. Insufficient amounts of insulin lead to *diabetes*, a condition where blood sugar rises to dangerous levels.

The Reproductive System

The purpose of the reproductive system is procreation. Unlike all other systems, the structures of this system are different in the male and female.

The Male Reproductive System

The male reproductive system contains two major organs: the testes and the penis. Figure 16-33 illustrates the organs of the male reproductive system.

The testes produce sperm, the cell that contains the male's chromosomes. They also contain other hormones and substances. The testes are contained in the *scrotum*, a sac at the base of the penis. The scrotum contains smooth muscle tissue and is capable of lengthening or shortening the distance between the testes and the body so as to maintain proper temperature in the testes.

The penis has two functions: to provide a vessel for sperm to leave the body and to provide a vessel for urine to leave the body. During sexual arousal, the penis becomes rigid with blood, and the opening from the bladder to the urethra closes, allowing only semen to travel down the canal. This also means that a male cannot urinate when sexually aroused.

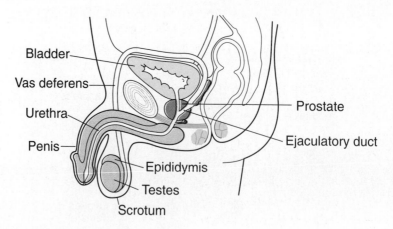

Figure 16-33   *The Male Reproductive System*

The Female Reproductive System

The female reproductive system includes the ovaries and the uterus. Figure 16-34 illustrates the major components of the female reproductive system.

The ovaries produce eggs, which contain the female's chromosomes. The uterus provides a host for a fertilized egg. Unlike males, who release sperm at various intervals, the female releases an egg approximately once every 28 days. This is called *ovulation*, a part of the *menstrual cycle*. The uterus develops a blood-rich lining in preparation for nourishing a fertilized egg. If the egg is fertilized by a male's sperm, the egg will implant itself into this lining and develop into a fetus.

If the egg is not fertilized, or for some reason does not implant in the lining, both the egg and the lining are "sloughed off" out of the uterus through the vagina. This is called the menstrual period.

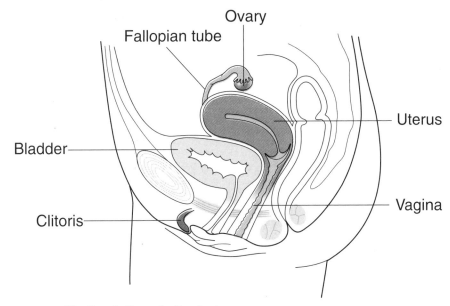

Figure 16-34   *The Female Reproductive System*

Age-Related Changes

Stop and Reflect 16-2

When you think of the phrase *old person*, what are some of the characteristics that come to mind?

_____

_____

_____

_____

_____

_____

_____

The body does change as we grow older. The changes that are part of the aging process and will happen to *everyone* if they live long enough are called **age-related changes**. However, many of the changes we think are age-related are more likely caused by a lack of proper care of one's body, disease, or other impairment. Look over your answers to Stop and Reflect 16-2. Compare your answers to those in Table 16-2 below.

Each person will experience age-related changes at different times. As well, the effect of any age-related change is often a function of their overall fitness level. The person who is extremely physically fit as an older person may be as physically able as a much younger person, even though the older person does not have the ability he or she once did.

TABLE 16-2	Age or Not?
Age-Related Changes	**Caused by Disease or Injury**
Grey or white hair	Hair loss (inherited or disease)
Decreased elasticity of skin	Excessive wrinkles (exposure to sun, inherited, smoking)
Decreased muscle mass	Arthritis (injury or disease)
Decreased cardiac output	Heart disease
Increased time required to react	Dementia
Decreased ability to hear high frequencies	Decreased ability to hear sound in general (disease, injury, abuse)

Questions for Review

1. What are the four types of tissue? Where is each found?

2. What four functions are performed by the circulatory system?

3. What is the purpose of bone marrow?

4. What organs make up the alimentary canal?

5. What organs make up the sensory system?

6. What are the four types of bones? For each, state its purpose and give an example of the type.

7. What is the function of the urinary system?

8. What do joints allow the body to do?

Question for Discussion

1. Select an older person you know well. How has aging affected his or her ability? Does the person assume that some things are caused by old age? If so, what?

CHAPTER SEVENTEEN

Mobility

Learning Objectives

Through reading this chapter, you'll be able to:

1. Identify three benefits of supporting a client's mobility.
2. Explain the differences between moving objects and assisting people to move.
3. Define and demonstrate good body mechanics and good posture.
4. List the four principles of good positioning.
5. Distinguish between a transfer and a lift.
6. Outline the twelve principles to be used when preparing to assist a client to move from one place to another.
7. Demonstrate the proper procedure for assisting a person to transfer and to pivot and transfer.
8. Identify the principles involved in safely using a mechanical lift to move a client.
9. List the five main purposes of mobility aids.
10. Describe the proper procedure for walking with a cane, crutches, walker, and rollator.

Chapter At A Glance

Mobility

Assisting People with Movement

Good Body Mechanics

Common Types of Assistance

Mobility Aids

Terms You'll Use

Alignment   The positioning of the body along a straight line.

Body Mechanics   Using your muscles correctly to move or lift objects properly.

Centre of Gravity   The point where mass is equally distributed.

Lateral   Side-lying. Also refers to body parts away from the midline.

Mobility Aids   Aids that are designed to improve a person's stability by expanding his or her base of support .

Posture   Position of the body.

Prone   Stomach-lying.

Supine   Back-lying.

Mobility

Stop and Reflect 17-1

Think back over this past hour. How many times have you physically moved? Perhaps you've gotten up to get a drink or to answer the phone. Maybe you've shifted in your chair to get more comfortable or decided to stretch out on the couch for a bit.

_____

_____

_____

Chances are that you moved frequently in that hour. Why? To meet a need, to become more comfortable, perhaps to take a few minutes to talk to someone. Now, imagine that you *could not* move independently. How do you think you might feel? Frustrated? Angry? Probably so. It's quite likely that your client, if faced with a reduction in his or her mobility, will have some of the same emotions.

There are physical, social, and psychological benefits to mobility.

■ **Physical.** Mobility promotes improved musculoskeletal strength, circulation, and breathing which are linked to increased resistance to illness and infection. It helps to maintain muscle mass and muscle tone, as well as overall fitness. Mobility can help to eliminate constipation. It can provide the person with the opportunity to "keep in practice" with walking and other movement, thereby reducing the risk of falls.

Improved mobility can also reduce *secondary effects*: the problems that arise because a person cannot easily get from one place to another, such as incontinence due to not being able to get to the bathroom in time.

- **Social.** Mobility helps us to get out, to see others, to have the opportunity to interact and maintain social skills. It broadens our range of activities.

- **Psychological.** The satisfaction that comes from being able to go where one wants to go, and to move about at will for comfort cannot be underestimated. Mobility supports the client's control over his or her activities and, in turn, promotes a sense of self-worth and confidence. There is evidence that mobility promotes improved cognition. Physical activity can help to reduce feelings of sadness and has been found to elevate the mood of clients with depression.

Assisting People with Movement

Assisting a person with movement differs from moving an inanimate object. While the principles of good posture and body mechanics are the same, helping a person to move adds two further dimensions to the assistance: the psychological and the physiological (Photo 17-1).

Photo 17-1
Assisting a client with movement has a psychological and a physiological dimension.
Source: CHATS.

The Psychological Dimension

Have you ever been afraid of falling or losing your balance? Perhaps you were up on a ladder or step stool. Maybe you were taking your first few steps after you'd been in bed with the flu. If you've been in one of these situations, you can appreciate the psychological dimension of movement. Uncertainty, fear, anxiety, as well as the effect of a previous experience all can affect how we approach movement.

The client who requires assistance with movement may experience many of the same emotions. There are a number of factors that contribute to the psychological dimension.

1. The client may experience emotions associated with having to rely upon another person for help, or associated with not knowing how the person helping him or her will assist.
2. The client's *desire* to move will also affect how he or she responds to assistance.
3. The client's culture may affect the level of comfort he or she has about being touched or having another person so physically close.
4. Changes in thinking and understanding (such as those associated with stress or with dementia) can heighten anxiety and fear.

CASE EXAMPLE 17-1

A personal experience of a client:

I had not been on my feet since the accident. I was finally allowed to get up (with help) to go to the bathroom. An attendant came to assist me.

My first sensation was of being swept off my feet. I had just begun to try to stand when I was almost lifted by the attendant. I had no time to right myself and became quite dizzy. I found myself leaning on her as she carted me to the bathroom.

The same attendant helped me back to bed. I was a bit stronger that time, yet I still had the sensation of having no control over my movement. I simply hoped that she wouldn't drop me.

The next time I needed to use the bathroom, I crawled there myself.

The Physiological Dimension

This dimension has to do with the client's actual degree of control over his or her movement, including strength and endurance, range of motion, ability to bear weight, and balance. There are many factors to be considered in assessing a person's physiological dimension. How much can the client do? What accommodation does the person have to make to address the impairment? Are there contributing physiological factors such as vision or hearing impairment that make it more difficult for the person to follow instruction or assist? Does the client have balance problems that may make it difficult for him or her to remain in one place?

Good Body Mechanics

Good **body mechanics** means using your body effectively and in a manner that preserves its physical health. Body mechanics includes proper **posture** or **alignment** and safe movement.

Good body mechanics are important for both you and your client. They keep you balanced, provide additional stability, and allow you to move about with minimum effort. You should use good body mechanics at all times: sitting, standing, or lying down.

Body Mechanics involves maintaining a *line of gravity*, a *base of support*, a *balanced centre of gravity*, as well as the proper use of *leverage*.

Line of Gravity

The line of gravity is the imaginary line that is exactly in the middle of your body mass, where each "side" is equally balanced. When you are standing upright, the line passes from your head to your feet. It runs vertically, midway between the front and back of your torso and midway between your shoulders. As the line progresses toward your feet, it passes in front of the centre of your hip bones, in front of your knees and ankles. Figure 17-1 illustrates the line of gravity in a person with good posture.

Do you remember your parents telling you to "sit up straight"? They did so for good reason: good posture is a part of good health. Proper posture maintains the natural curvature of the spine. A person whose mass is not distributed evenly may experience pain and fatigue, as well as risk joint or disc damage. Specifically, poor posture puts your back at risk for injury.

Many of us develop poor posture over a long period of time. The bad habits develop so slowly that our poor posture may feel comfortable. Muscles and ligaments that have stretched or shortened as a result of our body being out of alignment may ache when we correct our posture. It's important to work at attaining and maintaining good posture, even though it will take some time for the correct posture to feel right.

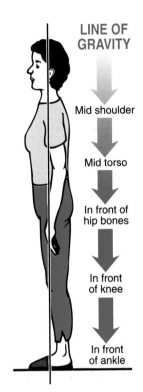

LINE OF GRAVITY

Mid shoulder

Mid torso

In front of hip bones

In front of knee

In front of ankle

Figure 17-1
The Line of Gravity

Stop and Reflect 17-2

Stand up, keeping your posture as you normally would. Is your body weight equally distributed along the line of gravity? If not, where is your weight unequally distributed?

_____

_____

_____

_____

Base of Support

Chances are that you felt more stable when your feet were flat and 30cm apart—when you had a wider base of support. A base of support is the area upon which an object rests. Generally, the larger the base of support, the more stable the object (Photo 17-2). Have you ever tried to balance a quarter on its edge? It's very difficult to do because the base of support (the part of the edge of the quarter that the coin is resting on) is very small. It's much easier for the quarter to rest on its face since the base of support is much wider.

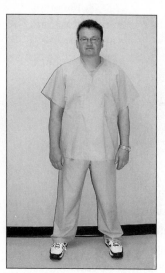

Photo 17-2
A good base of support increases stability and safety.

Stop and Reflect 17-3

1. Stand up, placing your feet approximately 30 cm apart (roughly the width of your hips).

2. Sway your body gently from side to side, noticing how stable you feel.

3. Move your feet closer together and sway gently. Do you feel more or less stable than you did when your feet were further apart?

4. Leaving your feet 30 cm apart, rise up on your toes. How stable do you feel?

5. Stand on one foot. How stable do you feel?

_____

_____

_____

_____

Centre of Gravity

The **centre of gravity** is the point where your mass (vertical and horizontal) is equally distributed. Both your physical mass and the mass of any person or object you are supporting must be included. For example, carrying a heavy backpack on your shoulders moves your centre of gravity toward your back and up to your shoulders.

No matter what you are carrying, your centre of gravity should be between your shoulders and your knees, as close to your line of gravity as is possible. Remember that the higher your centre of gravity (i.e., the closer it is to your shoulders), the harder it will be to maintain your balance. Figure 17-2 shows the centre of gravity for a person in various positions.

Figure 17-2 *Centre of Gravity*

Leverage

Leverage refers to making the most of the effort you expend. In the context of good body mechanics, leverage means two things. First, it means making the larger, stronger muscles (such as those found in the shoulders, upper arms, hips, and thighs) do the work. This allows you to expend less energy to perform a task and to ensure that you are not straining smaller and weaker muscles (such as those in your back or lower arms). Second, it also means keeping the weight closer to the body, reducing the resistance of the weight. When you hold a weight far away from the body, you increase the resistance, making your muscles work harder (Figure 17-3).

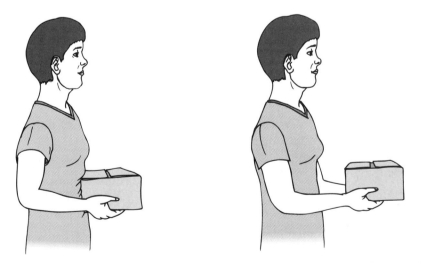

Figure 17-3 *Holding the object closer reduces resistance and the effort required to move it.*

Maintaining Good Body Mechanics

Maintaining good body mechanics is a matter of adopting a few simple work habits.

Arranging Your Work

1. **Avoid unnecessary bending and reaching.** If you can, move items that are frequently used from top or bottom shelves to middle shelves, use a good foot stool to reach higher items, and sit or crouch down to reach lower items. If you are assisting a person in bed, raise the bed height, if possible, as close as possible to your waist.
2. **Arrange your supplies to avoid excessive twisting and turning.** Put all the supplies in one location. Move your feet to turn your whole body in the direction of your movement.
3. **Position your body to face what you're doing.** This reduces the amount of twisting.

When Moving Objects

1. **Make sure that your body is well-aligned.** This minimizes excessive stress on a body part, maintains the natural curvature of the spine, and helps keep your centre of gravity close to your line of gravity.
2. **Keep your feet approximately 30 cm apart (hip-width).** This ensures a good base of support.

CASE EXAMPLE 17-2

Ellen is a support worker assigned to assist ten clients in a supportive housing unit. One of her many regular tasks is to prepare meals. In order to avoid unnecessary twisting and bending, Ellen assembles all the materials required for the meal and places the items on the counter where she is working. In addition to avoiding injury, this approach often saves Ellen time. She can then spend more time working with her clients.

3. **Bend your knees to bring your centre of gravity down.** This increases your stability and decreases the resistance of the load.
4. **Use the larger and stronger muscles to lift, carry, or move.** Bend from the knees, not the waist. If you are lifting heavy objects from the floor, bend your hips and knees. Maintain the natural curve of your back. As you raise the object, straighten your hips and knees. This allows you to use your leg and thigh muscles to bear the weight.
5. **Keep objects close to your body.** This keeps your centre of gravity closer to your line of gravity, enhancing your stability.
6. **Use both hands to carry a heavy object.**
7. **Push, pull, or slide a heavy object if possible.** These actions use less effort than lifting. A rug placed under an object may make it easier to slide and may protect the surface on which you're sliding the object.
8. **When pushing an item, move one leg forward.** When pulling, move one leg back.
9. **Use available aids.** Is there a dolly or trolly available for toting larger items? If so, consider using it to carry heavy or awkward items.
10. **Enlist the help of a coworker if the load is too heavy.**

When Helping A Person to Move

1. **Make sure that the person knows who you are.**   A startled person may move suddenly, throwing you and the person off balance.

2. **Make sure that you know the person's level of ability with regard to the movement.**   Can the person help? If so, how? Are there issues such as poor balance, poor muscle strength, lack of range of motion that have to be accommodated? Are there other impairments (such as vision or hearing loss) that affect the person's ability to follow instructions or assist?

3. **Make sure you have help if the person cannot assist.**   The client may have equipment (such as a mechanical lift) that enables you to assist him or her. Some clients may require the assistance of two persons. Make sure that you have the proper help.

4. **Explain what you are going to do.**   Does the person have a particular way of doing this activity? Can you use the person's technique safely?

5. **Identify the psychological dimension.**   Is the person motivated to help? Is he or she fearful or anxious?

6. **Enlist the person's help.**   The task will be much easier if you both work together. Plan the task with the client, if possible.

7. **Make sure that you assist the client, not perform the movement for the client.** Keep your focus on *assisting* the person, not performing the movement for them.

8. **Perform the transfer with smooth, even movements.**

9. **Ensure the person's privacy.**   Secure clothing so that it does not fall open during the transfer.

10. **Make sure that any catheters, drainage bags, or intravenous lines are moved *with* the client.**   Take care to ensure that any tubing does not get caught on furnishings and that the lines are not kinked.

11. **Ensure that the client has proper shoes.**   The best footwear provides a good firm sole that is neither too slippery nor sticky. Avoid flat slippers.

12. **Make sure you know how to safely use any assistive devices the client requires.**   Ask your supervisor for guidance if you are unsure of how to use a particular assistive device.

CASE EXAMPLE 17-3

Rebecca assists Mr. Green, an 80-year-old resident in a long-term care facility. A few years ago, he had a stroke. As a result, he is unable to walk or stand. In addition, he does not hear well and cannot see without his glasses.

When she first started to work with Mr. Green, Rebecca talked with him about how she could best help him to transfer. She learned what type of help Mr. Green needed and was able to adapt her approach to safely assist him. Even so, each time she assists him, Rebecca must make sure that Mr. Green has his glasses and is able to see her. She must also make sure that Mr. Green can hear her and understand what she is going to do so that the transfer goes smoothly.

Common Types of Assistance

There are three general types of assistance with body position and mobility: positioning, moving a person in bed, and transferring or lifting a person from one place to another. Let's take a look at each type in detail.

Positioning

Have you ever fallen asleep in a chair or couch in an awkward position? Chances are that some of your joints and muscles ached when you awoke. This is due to the poor position in which you slept.

Proper positioning (good alignment) is as important to the client as it is to you. There are three reasons that positioning is important. One, proper positioning is essential to body functions such as respiration and circulation. Two, it prevents excess discomfort in joints and muscles. Three, proper positioning can prevent injuries, such as pressure sores (decubitus ulcers) or contractures (shortening of muscle tissues).

There are five common types of positioning for the client who is in bed. These are: Fowler's position, Sims' position, *lateral* position, *prone* position, and *supine* position. Your client may prefer a particular position, or may alternate between two or more. A health professional may have prescribed a particular position or have advised the client to avoid a particular position. Make sure that you know of any preferences or restrictions before you assist the client. No matter what the position, be sure to ensure your client's comfort.

Proper positioning often requires the use of pillows, rolled towels, or positioning aids (such as foam wedges or bolsters). Some positioning devices have a distinct right or left orientation. Make sure you know how these items are used and where they are to be placed.

Fowler's Position

Fowler's position is a semisitting position. It is often used to make it easier for a person in bed to eat, watch television, or visit with other people. It is also used to make it easier for people with heart or respiratory disorders to breathe.

This position raises the back, neck, and head at a 45° to 60° angle. It's important to raise the head of the bed as much as the client can tolerate if they are eating in bed. A 75° angle may be preferable. If the client has an adjustable bed, this is usually done by raising the head of the bed. If the client's bed is not adjustable, a wedge bolster is often used.

No matter how the angle is attained, it is important to maintain the natural curvature of the client's spine. Many clients will also require a pillow to support their head and, possibly, pillows at each side to support their arms. Your client (or a family member or health professional) may give you instructions as to where any other pillows or supports must be placed. Figure 17-4 shows a person in Fowler's position.

Figure 17-4
A person in Fowler's position.

Clients in the Fowler's position will tend to slide down in the bed. As well, the client may experience *shearing*, a condition that occurs when the client's skin remains in place while the client's muscles and bones move in the direction of gravity. This can make the hips and buttocks very sore and can lead to skin breakdown. Figure 17-5 illustrates shearing. You must watch for this and assist the client to reposition as necessary.

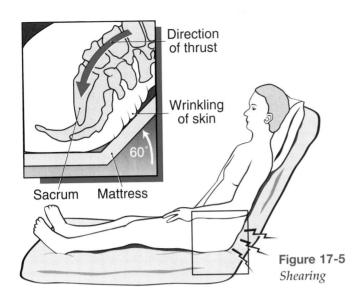

Direction of thrust

Wrinkling of skin

60°

Sacrum   Mattress

Figure 17-5
Shearing

Figure 17-6
A client in Sim's position.

Figure 17-7
A client in the lateral position.

Figure 17-8
A client in the prone position.

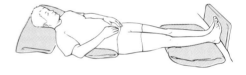

Figure 17-9
A client in the supine position.

Sims' Position

In Sims' position a client is lying on his or her side. The client's upper leg is flexed (bent) so that it is not lying on the lower leg. The leg is supported by a pillow. The upper arm is also flexed and is placed on a pillow. The lower arm and leg are slightly bent and not supported by a pillow. The client's head is to the side. Figure 17-6 illustrates a client in Sims' position.

Lateral Position

Many people prefer to rest on their sides (**laterally**). Proper support in the lateral position includes placing pillows under the client's head, under the forearm of the upper arm, and under the knee of the upper leg. A pillow is placed behind the client to assist him or her to remain in position. Figure 17-7 shows a client in the lateral position.

Prone Position

Prone means lying on one's stomach. A client in the prone position lies on his or her stomach with his or her head turned to one side. To ensure good alignment of the spine, pillows are placed under the client's head and shins. A pillow is sometimes placed under the abdomen, if this makes the client more comfortable. Some clients lie in the prone position with their legs over the end of the bed. If so, no pillow is placed under the shins. Figure 17-8 shows a client in the prone position.

Supine Position

The **supine** position is also called the *dorsal recumbent* position. In this position, the client is lying on his or her back. The client's arms are at his or her side. A pillow is placed under the client's head and each arm. A pillow may be placed under the client's knees. Figure 17-9 shows a client in the supine position.

Moving a Person in Bed

Some clients will require some help to move about in bed. Other clients will not be able to move about in bed at all. In addition to positioning, you may need to assist your client to move up in bed, to roll to one side, to move to one side of the bed, or to assist the person in sitting on the side of the bed.

As with any procedure, you must always observe the basic rules of assisting clients to move that we discussed earlier in this chapter.

Assisting a Person with Moving Up in Bed

Every client will slide down in bed if the head of the bed has been raised. This can happen even if the client bends his or her knees or uses a roll at the feet to minimize sliding. As well, some clients will move toward the foot of the bed, even if the head is not raised. A client who is too far down in the bed will be uncomfortable and unable to sit up properly. Furthermore, the client's feet may become pinched if they are pressed against the foot board.

If your client can assist, use Procedure 17-1.

Procedure 17-1: Assisting the Client with Moving Up in Bed

1. If the height of the client's bed is adjustable, raise the entire bed to waist height.
2. Lower the head of the bed so that it is as flat as the client can tolerate.
3. Lower the siderail (if any) on the side nearest you.
4. Stand next to the bed, facing the head of the bed. Maintain a good base of support, with your feet approximately 30 cm apart, with one foot ahead of the other.
5. Move the client's pillow to the headboard. This makes it easier for the person to help, as well as protecting the person's head from the headboard.
6. Ask the client to bend both knees and to place both feet flat on the bed.
7. Bending from the hips and knees, and maintaining the lumbar curve, slide one arm under the client's thighs and the other under the client's shoulders.
8. Explain to the client that, on the count of three, you will lift and move the client toward the head of the bed. Ask the client to assist by pushing up with his or her feet and pulling with his or her arms toward the headboard. Allow the client time to prepare to assist.
9. Move on the count of three, shifting your weight from your rear leg to your front leg.
10. Assist the person to become comfortable. Assist with positioning, smooth sheets, and replace the pillow behind the client's head.
11. Lower the entire bed and raise the head of the bed as the client wishes.
12. Place a pillow under the client's knees, if he or she wishes.
13. Raise the side rail (if present and required).
14. Move call bell (if present) to within easy reach.
15. Wash hands.

Procedure 17-2: Moving the Person Up In Bed with a Draw Sheet

EQUIPMENT

another person to help you

drawsheet or pad protector

Some clients will not be able to assist. In this instance, you will need to enlist the help of another person. You will also require a draw sheet or pad protector.

1. Follow the basic rules for moving a person.
2. If the height of the client's bed is adjustable, raise the entire bed to waist height.
3. Lower the head of the bed so that it is as flat as the client can tolerate.
4. Lower the side rail (if any) on the side nearest you. Have your partner do the same.
5. Move the client's pillow to the headboard. This makes it easier for the person to move, as well as protecting the person's head from the headboard.
6. Roll the side of the draw sheet or pad protector toward the client's side. (If the client does not have a draw sheet or protector on the bed, install one as per the procedure in Chapter 18.) Have your partner do the same.
7. Stand next to the bed, facing the head of the bed. Maintain a good base of support, with your feet approximately 30 cm apart, with one foot ahead of the other. Have your partner do the same on the opposite side of the bed.
8. Ask your client to cross his or her arms over her chest. Assist the client to do this if required.
9. Grasp the rolled sheet firmly near the client at shoulders and hips.
10. On the count of three, lift the draw sheet and create a sling. Move toward the head of the bed, shifting your weight from your rear leg to the front leg. Ensure your partner does the same.
11. Gently place the client in the new position.
12. Assist the person to become comfortable. Assist with positioning, smooth sheets, and replace the pillow behind the client's head.
13. Lower the entire bed and raise the head of the bed as the client wishes.
14. Raise the side rail (if present and required).
15. Move call bell (if present) to within easy reach.
16. Wash hands.

Moving a Person to the Side of the Bed

Sometimes, a client will need to move to one side of the bed. This could be because the client will be having a bed bath or other procedure. In some cases, the client will not be able to assist. When this is the case, use one of these two procedures.

Procedure 17-3: Moving a Person to the Side of the Bed, Single-Person Approach

1. Follow the basic rules for moving a person.
2. If the height of the client's bed is adjustable, raise the entire bed to waist height.
3. Lower the head of the bed so that it is as flat as the client can tolerate.
4. Lower the siderail (if any) on the side nearest you.

5. Stand next to the bed, facing the side of the bed. Maintain a good base of support, with your feet approximately 30 cm apart, with one foot ahead of the other. Bend your knees slightly.

6. Ask your client to cross his or her arms over his or her chest. Assist the client to do this if required.

7. Slide your arm under the person's neck and shoulders. Grasp the shoulder farthest from you with your hand.

8. Slide your other arm under the person's middle back.

9. Move the person's upper body toward you by shifting your weight from your front foot to the one in the back. Take care that the person does not move too close to the edge of the bed.

10. Repeat step nine with your arms under the client's waist and buttocks.

11. Repeat step nine with your arms under the clients thighs and legs.

12. Assist the person to become comfortable. Assist with positioning, smooth sheets, replace pillow behind head.

13. Lower the entire bed and raise the head of the bed as appropriate.

14. Raise the side rail (if present and required).

15. Move call bell (if present) to within easy reach.

16. Wash hands.

Procedure 17-4: Moving a Person to the Side of the Bed, Two-Person Approach

EQUIPMENT

another person to help you

drawsheet or pad protector

This approach is used when the client is too frail or heavy to be moved by the single-person approach, or when the client's spine must be kept straight. This approach requires a draw sheet and is very similar to the approach used to move a person up in bed.

1. Follow the basic rules for moving a person.

2. If the height of the client's bed is adjustable, raise the entire bed to waist height.

3. Lower the head of the bed so that it is as flat as the client can tolerate.

4. Lower the side rail (if any) on the side nearest you.

5. Stand next to the bed, facing the side of the bed. Maintain a good base of support, with your feet approximately 30 cm apart, with one foot ahead of the other. Bend your knees slightly. Have your partner do the same.

6. Roll the side of the draw sheet or pad protector toward the client's side. (If the client does not have a draw sheet or protector on the bed, place one as per the procedure in Chapter 18.) Have your partner do the same.

7. Ask your client to cross his or her arms over her chest. Assist the client to do this if required.

8. Grasp the rolled sheet firmly, near the client at shoulders and hips.

9. On the count of three, lift the draw sheet and create a sling. Move away from the side of the bed, shifting your weight from your front leg to the rear leg. Ensure your partner rocks forward, shifting weight from the rear to the front leg.

10. Gently place the client in the new position.

11. Assist the client to become comfortable. Assist with positioning, smooth sheets, replace pillow behind head.
12. Lower the entire bed and raise the head of the bed as the client wishes.
13. Raise the side rail (if present).
14. Move call bell (if present) to within easy reach.
15. Wash hands.

Assisting a Person with Sitting on the Side of the Bed

Assisting a person to sit on the side of the bed is also called *dangling*. A client might use this procedure when he or she is convalescing and before the client is able to weight bear. Some clients who cannot weight bear are assisted to sit up to vary their position. This procedure is also used when a client is preparing to transfer from a bed to a chair.

Procedure 17-5: Assisting a Person with Sitting on the Side of the Bed

1. Follow the basic rules for moving a person.
2. If the height of the client's bed is adjustable, raise the entire bed to waist height.
3. Raise the head of the bed so that the client is in a sitting position.
4. Lower the side rail (if any) on the side nearest you.
5. Stand next to the bed, facing the far corner of the foot of the bed. Maintain a good base of support, with your feet approximately 30 cm apart.
6. Slide one hand under the person's neck and shoulders and grasp the far shoulder.
7. Place your other hand over and behind the client's thighs, near the knees.
8. Pivot toward the foot of the bed as you bring your client's legs to the edge of the bed. DO NOT pull your client's buttocks too close to the edge of the bed. Your client's knees should be just at the edge of the mattress. Another way to gauge this is to position the client in bed approximately his or her thigh length away from the side.
9. Ask your client to straighten his or her arms and to make fists and press each of them into the mattress at the client's side. This helps to keep the client balanced.
10. If the client cannot maintain balance or is not used to sitting up, do not leave the client unattended.
11. If the client is not used to sitting up, observe for signs of distress (such as pallor or rapid breathing).
12. If the client is to transfer to a chair, lower the bed so that the client's feet are firmly on the floor but the knees are **not** higher than his or her hips.
13. Reverse the procedure to assist the client to lie down.

Transfers and Lifts

A *transfer* is a movement in which the support worker *assists* the client with the movement. A *lift* is a movement where the support worker takes the responsibility to move the client without the client's assistance or when the client can only minimally assist (due to extreme frailty or cognitive impairment).

The support team takes into account the physiological and the psychological dimensions when determining whether a transfer or a lift is the most appropriate procedure. Factors such as the client's stamina, ability to bear weight, degree of motivation, extent of any fear, and level of understanding are all taken into account.

Both transfers and lifts require cooperation between client and worker. Make sure to follow the basic rules of assisting a person with movement *each* time you assist a client.

Preparing to Assist

Before you begin the procedure, prepare! Make sure that you do the following:

1. **Review the process with the client.**   Even if you are certain that the client cannot understand, this step gives the client some time to adjust to your presence. It may prevent the client from being startled.

2. **Make sure that the area is clear of obstructions.**   Move furniture, sheets, and other items that may hinder movement.

3. **Make sure that the equipment you need is in proper position.**   Place the wheelchair in the proper spot, with brakes on and foot pedals clear of the client's path. Ensure you have any necessary assistive devices (such as a transfer board or a transfer belt).

4. **Ensure height of both surfaces are as equal as possible.**   For example, drop the height of the bed (if possible) to be level with the chair. The height of some power wheelchairs can also be adjusted.

5. **Make sure that the client has proper footwear.**   Make sure that the footwear provides the right amount of grip. Socks and many slippers can easily slide on hard floors. Crepe-soled shoes may be too sticky and cause the person to trip. Ensure that the footwear is the correct size to prevent the person from slipping.

6. **Maintain good posture and body mechanics.**

Transfers

There are two types of transfers: supervised and assisted.

Supervised Transfer

A *supervised* transfer occurs when the client is physically able to complete the transfer, but may require redirection or coaching to complete the task. For example, a client who has a dementia may require a supervised transfer.

Assisted Transfer

An assisted transfer is used when the client has difficulty getting started, but is able to bear weight and perform the remainder of the transfer appropriately. This is most often used to assist clients rising from a chair.

Procedure 17-6: Assisted Transfer

1. Follow the basic rules for moving a person.
2. Stand at the side of the seated client.
3. Ask the client to sit forward in the chair, bending at the hips.
4. Ask the client to ensure that his or her feet are in a side by side position, approximately 30 cm apart. Alternately, the client can place his or her feet in the step position (where one foot is slightly ahead of the other).
5. As the client bends forward, place the palm of your hand (the one nearest the back of the chair) at the middle of the client's upper back, about 6 cm below the neck. Apply pressure to assist the person to move forward.
6. As you are applying pressure, extend your other hand to the client. Allow the client to press down on your hand to assist the client to rise.

Pivot Transfer

One of the most common transfers is the *pivot transfer*. This transfer is used to assist a person to move from a bed to a chair, from chair to chair, or from chair to bed.

Procedure 17-7: Pivot Transfer

1. Follow the basic rules for moving a person. Make sure that the surface to which the client is transferring is at a right angle (90°) to the surface from which the client is transferring.
2. Ask the client to move forward to the edge of the seat. This can be done using a rocking motion, where each hip is brought slightly forward until the person is at the edge of the seat with his or her feet flat on the floor.
3. Position yourself in front of the client, with your body in a mirror image of the client's. Photo 17-3a illustrates this position.
4. Place your hands around the client's back. Place the palms of your hands on the area of the client's back that will require the greatest support. For example, if the client tends to fall back, place your hands on the client's upper back. If the client has difficulty moving his or her hips, place your hands on the lower back.
5. Ask the client to mirror your hand position and to hold firmly.
6. Ask the client to stand.
7. While holding the client, stand with the client.
8. If the client's feet tend to slip forward, place your foot slightly at an angle in front of the foot to block this movement. Photo 17-3b illustrates this position.
9. Make sure that the client can sense being on his or her feet.
10. Turn with the client toward the surface. Continue until the client can feel the edge of the surface behind his or her knees.
11. Maintain your hands in position as you mirror the client's position as he or she sits down.

Photo 17-3a
Position in front of the client, with body in a mirror image of the client's.

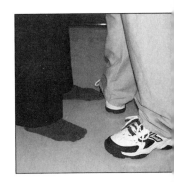

Photo 17-3b
Blocking client's foot.

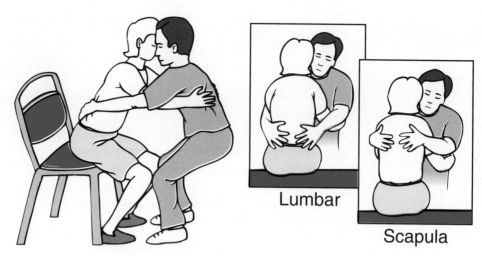

Figure 17-10 *The Pivot Transfer*

Lumbar

Scapula

EQUIPMENT	*Procedure 17-8: Assisting the Client Into a Shower Using a Shower Chair*

shower with
shower chair

If the client has a weak side (for example, as the result of a stroke), the client should have his or her stronger side nearest the tub.

1. Prepare as described earlier in this section. Make sure that the chair is parallel to tub.
2. Ask the client to push up from his or her chair, using the arm rests, and stand. Provide assistance as per the pivot transfer as required.
3. Ask the client to pivot and sit on the tub seat. Assist as required.
4. Ask the client to slide his or her strongest leg into tub first.

EQUIPMENT	*Procedure 17-9: Assisting the Client Out of a Shower Using a Shower Chair*

shower with
shower chair

1. Prepare as described earlier in this section. Make sure that the chair is parallel to tub.
2. Ask the client to slide to the end of the shower chair.
3. Ask the client to lift his or her weakest leg out of tub first. This will cause the client to pivot in the shower chair. Assist as required.
4. Ask the client to lift his or her strong leg out of the tub.
5. Ask the client to stand. Assist as required.
6. Ask the client to pivot, reach for chair armrests, and sit. Assist as per pivot transfer as required.

Procedure 17-10: Assisting a Client to Move from Chair to Toilet

Be aware that the configuration of the client's washroom, the type of assistive devices, as well as the client's degree of mobility will determine the exact procedure used. Adapt the approach to the client's situation while maintaining good body mechanics.

The following procedure assumes that the client can assist and that the bathroom has a grab bar affixed to the wall next to the toilet.

1. Prepare as described earlier in this section. Make sure that the chair is facing the toilet and is approximately 40 cm away from the bowl.
2. Ask the client to push up, using the chair's armrests. Assist as required.
3. As the client stands, ask the client to grip the grab bar with the hand nearest to the bar.
4. When the client is ready, ask him or her to grasp the bar with the other hand and to pivot around the bar to the toilet. Assist the client by placing your hands on the client's waist to provide support.
5. As the client pivots to the front of the toilet, ask the client to release his or her arm furthest from the grab bar. Support this arm as required.
6. Ask the client to sit on the toilet. Assist as per pivot transfer as required.
7. Reverse the procedure to transfer from toilet to chair.

Procedure 17-11: Assisting a Client Who Uses a Walker to Sit on a Chair or Toilet

1. Prepare as described earlier in this section.
2. Ask the client to get as close to the front of the chair or toilet as is possible.
3. Ask the client to back up to chair/toilet so that back of the client's knees touches the chair or the seat of the toilet.
4. If the chair or toilet has arm rests, ask the client to place his or her hands on the arm rests and sit down. If the chair or toilet has no arm rests, and there are no grab bars, assist the client as required.

Procedure 17-12: Assisting a Client Who Uses a Walker to Rise from a Chair or Toilet

1. Prepare as described earlier in this section.
2. Ensure that the walker is in front of the client and within the client's reach.
3. Ask the client to move as close to the front of the chair or toilet as is possible.
4. If the chair or toilet has arm rests, ask the client to place his or her hands on arm rests (or one hand on the walker and the other on the arm rest) and to push up to stand. If the chair or toilet has no arm rests, and there are no grab bars, assist the client as required.
5. Ask the client to place his or her hands on the walker.
6. Allow the client to get used to standing before attempting to move.

Procedure 17-13: Assisting a Client Who Uses a Walker to Transfer to Bed

1. Follow the basic rules for moving a person.
2. Ensure sheets and blankets are folded away from the area.
3. Ask the client to approach the bed with the walker, stopping about 50 cm in front

of the bed. The client should aim for the upper part of the bed.

4. Ask the client to pivot so that the client's back is facing the side of the bed.
5. Ask the client to step backward toward the bed, while using the walker.
6. Ask the client to place one hand on the bed and to sit on the edge of the bed, placing one hand on the walker and the other on the bed.
7. Ask the client to move each hip back alternately until both thighs are on the bed.
8. Ask the client to swing his or her legs into the bed. Assist as required.
9. Remove client's shoes before covering with sheets.

Using a Mechanical Lift

Some clients will require the use of a mechanical lift. There are many types available, each with its own specific procedure for use. Be certain you know how to safely operate any lift you are using.

Remember that the experience of being lifted by a mechanical lift is very different than when one is lifted by people. Clients often feel that they are "hanging" in space and may feel very vulnerable or frightened. Vision and balance problems may make these sensations very uncomfortable. Take the time to reassure the client.

EQUIPMENT

mechanical lift

Procedure 17-14: Basic Safety When Using A Mechanical Lift

1. Lock the lift's wheels once the lift is in position and *before* you attach the sling to the lift. Ensure that the lift's legs are positioned (and locked) in the position that offers the best base of support.
2. Ensure the sling is properly attached. Ensure that the hooks are attached so that the person is in a sitting position (not tilting back) when the lift is raised.
3. Ensure that sling hooks face to the outside as shown in Figure 17-11. This ensures that the hooks do not damage the client's skin.

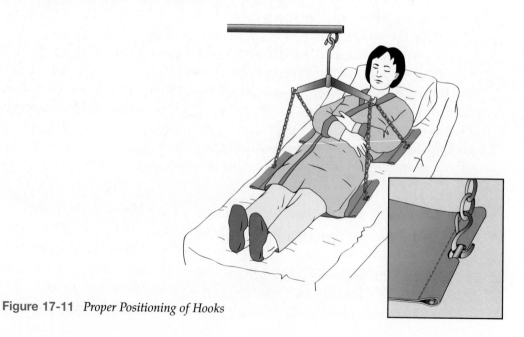

Figure 17-11 *Proper Positioning of Hooks*

4. Ask the client to cross arms over his or her chest.

5. Maintain eye contact with the client to decrease fear and anxiety. Reducing anxiety will also help to keep the client from swaying in the swing.

6. If you have locked the lift legs in step 1, move and lock the legs to a more centred position to make it easier to move the lift.

7. When you raise the sling, raise it only high enough to clear the surface of the bed or chair.

8. Release the brake on the lift and move to the desired location.

9. Apply brakes.

10. Slowly and steadily lower the client to the chair or bed surface.

11. Remove sling, if desired.

Mobility Aids

Many clients use **mobility aids** that are designed to improve a person's stability by expanding his or her base of support. In addition to making it possible for a person to move, aids serve four purposes: reduce weight-bearing; compensate for lost balance, strength, or coordination; reduce pain while walking; and enhance the person's sense of safety and security.

Canes, crutches, walkers, and rollators are common types of mobility aids. There are many variations within each type. In this section, we'll discuss the common uses of each type.

Canes

There are three types of canes: single point, tripod, and quad canes. Photo 17-4 shows a quad and a single point. Canes can help compensate for mild balance or leg weakness problems. Within this range, a quad cane provides the greatest support and stability, the tripod cane provides somewhat less. The single point cane provides the least amount of support and stability.

Many years ago, a client seldom used a cane unless he or she was advised by a health professional to do so. (In England many years ago, one had to have a permit to use a cane!) The person was usually fitted to the proper size and type of cane, as well as given instruction in its use. Today, many people simply purchase canes in the drugstore. As a result, the cane may be too short or tall or not the right type. As well, the person may not know how to use the cane properly.

Adjusting and Using a Cane

The cane should be adjusted so that the grip (the top of the cane handle) is level with the hip. Many canes are adjustable. They can be raised or lowered to accommodate people of different heights. Wooden canes are generally purchased at the proper height or are cut to the proper height. A rubber cane tip should be used on any cane. A bare cane tip presents a serious risk of slipping and causing the client to fall.

Photo 17-4
Types of Canes

Photo 17-5
Pronged Cane Tip. This tip provides grip in slippery conditions.

Some people who use a cane on slippery surfaces purchase a pronged tip for their cane. These tips have three or four metal prongs on the base and provide an improved grip on icy or snowy surfaces. Photo 17-5 shows a common type of pronged cane tip. Most pronged tips can be flipped up, allowing the person to use the cane on other surfaces without marring them.

A cane should be held on the strong side of the body. For example, if the person's left leg is weak, he or she would hold the cane in the right hand. The cane should be held so that the tip is about 15-25 cm to the side and approximately 15 cm in front of the person's foot.

A person walking with a cane should do so as follows:

1. Place the cane ahead approximately 30 cm.
2. Bring the weak leg up to be even with the cane.
3. Bring the strong leg forward and ahead of the cane.

Note that the adjustment and use of a cane is the same, no matter the type of cane used.

Crutches

Crutches provide more support and stability than a cane. Use of a crutch can allow the person to take all weight off of a leg (for example, if the person's leg was recently fractured and a walking cast was not applied). A person may use two crutches to remove some pressure from both legs. There are many types of crutches. Photo 17-6 shows one type. Some crutches have specific features designed to reduce the stress on arms or hands. Others have hinged tips to better simulate a natural walking rhythm.

Adjusting and Using Crutches

Photo 17-6
Adjustable crutches.

Like canes, crutches must be properly fitted. Crutch tops should three to four centimetres below the person's armpits when held in the standing position. Crutch grips should be adjusted so that the person's arm is at a 25°-30° angle when holding the grip. A person using crutches should not rest his or her armpits on the crutch tops. This can compress the nerves and blood vessels in the armpit and result in numbness of the arms and hands. This condition is sometimes called "crutch palsy". It almost always dsappears when the person stops resting on the crutch tops.

The usual procedure for walking with crutches is as follows:

1. Standing on the "good" leg, move both crutches and the weak leg ahead approximately 30 cm.
2. While bearing weight on the handgrips (not on the crutch tops), swing the good leg ahead of the crutches.
3. Standing on the good leg, move the crutches and weak leg ahead as in step one.

Walkers and Rollators

Walkers and rollators are four-point mobility aids. Walkers may have four legs, two legs and two wheels, or (less commonly) four wheels. Photo 17-7 shows these variations. Walkers equipped with wheels usually have a spring mechanism that prevents the wheels from moving when the person is leaning on the walker. This mechanism prevents the walker from rolling out from under the person.

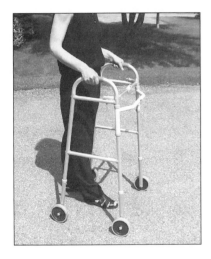 

Photo 17-7
Wheeled and standard walkers.

Rollators usually have four wheels. Rollators have hand brakes and a platform that can be used as a seat. Some have baskets, so that the person may easily carry items about. Photo 17-8 shows a common style.

Walking With a Walker or Rollator

To walk with a walker not equipped with wheels, the person lifts the walker and places it down about 15 cm in the direction the person wants to go. While holding on to the walker, the person then walks up to it. The process is repeated until the person reaches the desired location.

Walking with a rollator or a walker equipped with wheels is similar to walking with a shopping cart. The rollator or walker is pushed ahead as the person walks. (The person will have to release the handbrakes on the rollator to allow it to roll.)

Photo 17-8
A rollator. This device provides a seat and basket, making it ideal for shopping.

Questions for Review

1. Why is it important to encourage your client to move about?

2. How does moving people differ from moving objects?

3. What are good body mechanics?

4. What is a good base of support? How far apart should your feet be to ensure a good base of support?

5. Describe leverage.

6. How can you maintain good body mechanics when performing any task?

7. Name the twelve principles that should be followed when you are assisting a person with movement.

8. What is the Fowler's position? When is it used?

9. With a partner, demonstrate each positioning and transfer described in this chapter. Ask your partner to give you feedback on how he or she feels as you are assisting.

10. What is the general procedure for using a mechanical lift?

11. What is the proper procedure for walking with a cane? With a wheeled walker?

Questions for Discussion

1. How do you think you might feel if you had to depend upon the help of another person in order to get out of bed?

2. Consider the following case study. Then, discuss your answers to the questions at the end.

   Mrs. James has recently fractured her hip. She fell on black ice as she was getting her morning paper. Although her hip was repaired, she spent four weeks in hospital as a result of complications from the surgery. She spent eight weeks in a rehabilitation centre after discharge. She is now home and gradually regaining her ability. She now uses a cane "just to make sure" she won't fall. As well, she requires some help to get out of bed in the morning and to rise from a chair.

   One of your tasks is to assist Mrs. James as she again begins to shop and bank. She has not left her home since discharge from the rehabilitation centre. Although you have been gently encouraging her to go out with you, she politely refuses.

   How might Mrs. James be feeling? How might you apply the principles of assistance to this situation?

3. You work in an assisted living centre. You have a client who requires a great deal of assistance. In fact, the client is just at the point of needing a mechanical lift. The client repeatedly asks you to assist him without using the mechanical lift. What do you do? What factors must be considered? How do you think you might feel if you were in the client's place?

CHAPTER EIGHTEEN

Providing Physical Care

Learning Objectives

Through reading this chapter, you'll be able to:

1. Discuss the four main purposes of physical care.
2. Define RIDICUPS and apply its principles to providing physical care.
3. Describe changes in the integumentary system often associated with age.
4. Relate the purposes of a back rub and demonstrate a basic back rub.
5. List the steps involved in giving a client a bed bath, assisting a client in taking a sponge bath, a tub bath, or a shower.
6. List the steps in perineal care.
7. Discuss the signs and causes of pressure sores and the common measures taken to prevent them.
8. Describe the steps involved in performing or assisting a client to perform mouth and hair care.
9. Outline the proper steps for measuring temperature, pulse, and respiration.

Hair Care

Shaving the Client

Foot Care

Nail Care

Eye Care

Ear Care

Assisting the Client with the Use of a Bed Pan

Assisting the Client with Dressing

Bed Making

Measurement of Vital Signs

Measuring Blood Pressure

Measuring and Recording Intake and Output

Measuring Client Height and Weight

Terms You'll Use

Decubitus Ulcers   Sores caused when tissue is trapped between a hard surface and a bony prominence; also called *pressure sores*.

Ostomy   A surgical opening in the body.

Pulse   The rate at which blood is pumped through the heart.

Respiration   The act of inhaling and exhaling air; *breathing*.

RIDICUPS   An acronym describing the eight principles of personalized care: Respect, Independence, Dignity, Individuality, Communication, Understanding, Privacy, and Safety.

Temperature   The measurement of body heat.

Vital Signs   Measurements of temperature, pulse, blood pressure and respiration.

Purposes of Physical Care

Physical care includes the many tasks associated with cleanliness and good grooming. There are four purposes to physical care: client comfort, self-image, safety, and health.

Client comfort refers to both the physical and the psychological sensation of being clean. Think of how you feel when you've had a bath and are dressed in fresh clothes. You likely feel fresh and *good*. This is particularly important when the client has drainage from illness or an operation, if the client perspires as the result of the effort required to accomplish tasks, or when the client is in bed for an extended period of time.

A positive self-image refers to how the client sees him or herself as an attractive person. A positive self-image results from a combination of cleanliness and grooming. Some things may make it more difficult for a client to attain a positive self-image. A client may have an impairment or disfigurement that may make the client feel that he or she is ugly or "not presentable". Some clients may feel that the physical changes of age may make them unattractive. Assisting the client to feel good about their physical image through proper physical care and grooming is essential to client support (Photo 18-1).

Photo 18-1
A happy, well-groomed client.
Source: CHATS.

Stop and Reflect 18-1

Recall a time when you knew that you looked your best.

_____

_____

Remember how knowing that you looked your best made you feel?

_____

_____

_____

Client safety and health are promoted through the removal of dirt and microorganisms that may cause infection or illness. Improper cleansing can introduce microorganisms into areas of the body and promote infection. In order to ensure that this does not happen, you must carefully follow the principles for providing physical care discussed in this chapter.

Care Routines

Stop and Reflect 18-2

What are your physical care routines? Do you prefer to shower or to bathe? Do you do this task in the morning or the evening? Do you have a favourite soap, cream, or talc that you use?

_____

_____

_____

_____

In what order do you perform your physical care? Do you brush your teeth before or after you bathe? Do you fix your hair before or after you dress?

_____

_____

_____

_____

Have you ever had to alter this routine? If so, what was your reaction to the change?

_____

_____

_____

_____

Few things are as personal as the routines we each have for bathing, dressing, and grooming. Some of us prefer showers, others prefer baths. Some prefer to bathe in the morning, others at night. Some of us brush our teeth before we bathe, others do so after their bath. These routines are developed over many years of practice and are hard to change. Performing these routines in specific ways often gives us a sense of comfort.

Like you, your client will have preferences based upon his or her culture and past practices. It's important to respect your client's preferences for how physical care is done.

The Client's Skin

The skin forms the body's first defence against infection. It is also the largest organ in the body. The nerve endings embedded in the skin help us to sense pressure, heat, texture, and pain.

Many physical care routines involve *cleansing* the skin. Cleansing removes harmful microorganisms and can prevent infection. As well, the act of bathing allows for the skin to be massaged (such as when the client is helped to wash, to dry off, or to apply lotion). This, in turn, promotes circulation and helps to reduce the effects of pressure on circulation. Combined with proper positioning and frequent repositioning, skin care can prevent the development of pressure sores or help to heal existing sores.

As a person ages, the skin becomes thinner and less elastic. You may notice that the skin of some very old clients is almost transparent. As a result, an older person's skin is particularly susceptible to abrasions, bruising, or tearing. Observe these four guidelines when you are providing care to the client's skin.

1. **Remove any rings or other jewellery you are wearing to avoid catching and tearing the client's skin.** Make sure that your nails are cut short and filed smooth so as not to tear the client's skin.
2. **Be cautious when using rough sponges or cloths, as they can cause abrasions.** These items are often called loofah sponges or exfoliating sponges or pads.
3. **Never scrub a client's skin.** If a client has a stain that must be removed (such as ink from a pen), soak the area and gently rub it with a soapy cloth. Sometimes, a mark can be removed by applying a lotion on the spot and allowing it to absorb the stain.
4. **Always pat the client's skin dry.** Rubbing the client's skin to dry it can cause irritation and abrasions. It can also remove too much moisture from the client's skin, making it unnecessarily dry.

Pressure Sores

Pressure sores (also called **decubitus ulcers**) form when tissue is trapped between a hard surface (such as a chair seat or mattress) and a bony prominence (such as a hip bone, heel, or elbow). They can also form when braces or other appliances pinch and trap tissue. The pressure on the tiny blood vessels in the trapped tissue cause them to collapse, resulting in the death of the tissue. A client who is unable to move and read-just his or her position is at particular risk of having tissue trapped. Figure 18-1 illustrates the common pressure points.

Pressure sores develop in stages. In stage one, the area is reddened. In dark-complexioned clients, the area may appear drier, instead of red. In the second stage, tissue death has occurred. If left untreated, tissue death can be so extensive that the skin may die away allowing the bony prominence to become exposed. As well, the break in the skin can allow microorganisms to enter, resulting in an infection. Figure 18-2 shows the development of a pressure sore.

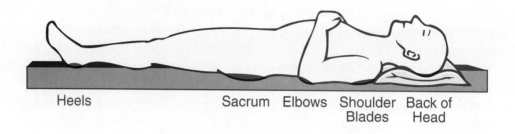

Heels   Sacrum   Elbows   Shoulder   Back of
                                                  Blades   Head

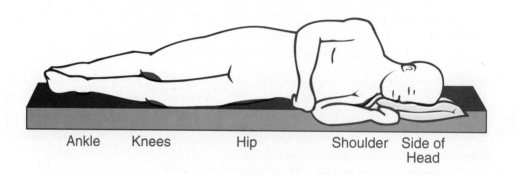

Ankle   Knees   Hip   Shoulder   Side of
                                                  Head

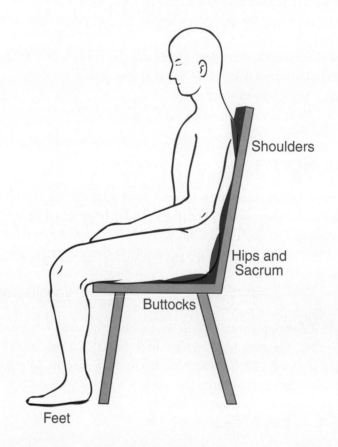

Shoulders

Hips and
Sacrum

Buttocks

Feet

Figure 18-1 *Pressure Points*

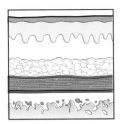 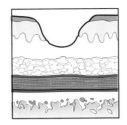 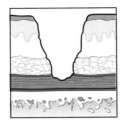 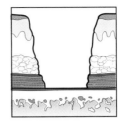

Figure 18-2 *The Stages of Pressure Sore Development*

Preventing Pressure Sores

You can do several things to prevent pressure sores. Table 18-1 lists some common methods to prevent sores. Vigilant observation of potential problem areas is also important, as many sores can be reversed if caught at the first stage.

TABLE 18-1	Preventing Pressure Sores

- Reposition the client to remove the pressure on specific areas. In general, a client should be repositioned at least once every two hours.

- Avoid shearing of the skin by keeping the head of the client's bed at 30° or lower when possible.

- Use proper lift and transfer techniques to avoid shearing and friction.

- Provide good skin care. Make sure that skin is clean and not left wet. If possible, apply talc or cornstarch to areas that tend to become damp.

- Dry skin is prone to chapping and cracking. Ask the client or your supervisor about applying a lotion to dry and rough areas.

- Ensure bedding is kept dry. Some clients may perspire and require frequent changes of linen.

- Ensure incontinent clients are kept dry and clean. Promptly change any wet or soiled incontinence briefs.

- Check with the client or your supervisor before using soap on fragile skin. Soap can dry and burn. If you do use soap, be certain to rinse it off thoroughly.

- Do not scrub the client's skin. Use lotion or oil to soften and remove dried material.

- Massage around pressure points to promote circulation.

- Use guaze, cloth, or a layer of clothing to limit skin-to-skin contact. Skin-to-skin contact promotes moisture and can foster bacterial growth.

- Use protective devices as prescribed.

- Immediately report reddened, abraded, or open areas to the appropriate person.

- Encourage clients who can do so to change position frequently.

Photo 18-2
A sheepskin pad.
Source: CHATS.

Photo 18-3
*An air-filled
mattress pad.*
Source: Maple Health
Centre.

Photo 18-4
A bed cradle.
Source: Maple Health
Centre.

Aids

There are a number of items that can help to relieve pressure: pads, special mattresses, and cradles.

Pads are usually made of a synthetic sheepskin that can be easily washed. Others are made of foam and usually cannot be washed. Gel-filled pads are commonly found in wheelchair seats and in some bed pads. These pads provide some cushioning to the pressure point, helping to avoid the pressure that causes the blood vessels to collapse. Some pads are made for a specific part of the body, such as an elbow or heel protector. Others are flat pads that cover a larger area of the bed or chair. Photo 18- 2 shows one type of sheepskin pad.

The choice of pad is determined by the area to be protected as well as how likely the pad will become soiled and require cleaning.

Air-filled, water-filled, and gel-filled mattresses are also used to help to relieve pressure points. Some of these mattresses are mechanical, cycling air in cylinders to alter the pressure. Others mould to the body and distribute the pressure across a larger area. Photo 18-3 shows an air-filled mattress pad.

Cradles are metal or wooden hoops that raise bedclothes off the client's legs and feet, relieving pressure on these extremities. Cradles are placed under the top sheet and blankets. Photo 18-4 shows a bed cradle.

RIDICUPS—Principles of Personalizing Physical Care

In addition to using proper and safe techniques to provide physical care, you must always *personalize* the care you provide. It is very important to identify the process your client uses (particularly if you are assisting the client and not performing the task for him or her).

RIDICUPS is an acronym that will help you to remember eight important principles of personalizing physical care. RIDICUPS stands for: Respect, Independence, Dignity, Individuality, Communication, Understanding, Privacy, and Safety (Figure 18-3). No matter what procedure you are performing, you must ensure that it meets the requirement of these eight principles. We'll look at each principle in this section.

Respect.   Does the procedure you are using demonstrate respect for the client? Does it take into account what he or she is able to do? Does it respect the client's preferences for when, where, and how the procedure is performed?

Independence.   Does the procedure promote the client's independence? Does it support the client's ability? Does it allow the client the time necessary to complete portions of the task?

Dignity.   Does the procedure help the client to avoid embarrassment? Is it done in a manner that minimizes discomfort?

Individuality.   Is the procedure adapted to meet the needs of the person? Are the client's preferences met? It's extremely important to avoid performing the task without thinking about the client's needs, no matter how many times you have performed it before.

Communication.   Does the procedure include communicating with the client? Does it include discussing the procedure to be performed and listening to the client's preferences and concerns? As you perform the procedure, do you read the client's body language and listen to the client's words (and adapt your approach as necessary)?

Understanding.   Does the procedure demonstrate an understanding of what it must be like for the client to undergo the procedure?

Privacy.   Does the procedure protect the client's privacy? Is it performed in an area away from other's view? Does it include proper draping to prevent unnecessary exposure of body parts?

Safety.   Is the procedure safe for both you and the client? Is the procedure complete? Does it leave the client in a comfortable state? Does it include proper body mechanics? Are proper infection control techniques used? Have you minimized any risks?

Figure 18-3 *RIDICUPS*

Personalizing care in this way takes practice. It's a lot to keep in mind all at the same time! The more you use the principles, the easier personalizing care will become.

Preparing to Provide Care

In addition to personalizing care, you must also take steps to prepare for the procedure, so that it will go smoothly and comfortably. There are four steps to preparing to provide care: knowing the *purpose, organizing* your approach, assembling the proper *equipment*, and knowing the basic *techniques* that are required in any procedure. We'll look at each step here.

Purpose. In addition to the basic purposes of care, are there other purposes the procedure must meet? Is the procedure especially important because of an event, (such as assisting a client to dress for a family wedding)? Is the procedure intended to assist the client to practise skills so as to become more independent?

Organization. You must have a thorough knowledge of the steps involved in the procedure, what equipment you will need, and when you will need it.

Equipment. You must assemble all necessary equipment and supplies *before* you begin the procedure. Make sure all equipment is clean and in good repair and that you know how to operate each item.

Techniques. Always perform the basic techniques with any procedure. There are four techniques: personalizing the procedure, discussing the procedure with the client, washing your hands, donning gloves or gown (if required).

Physical Care Procedures

Bathing the Adult Client

Bed Bath

Principles of bathing the client:
1. Always have the client assist wherever possible to increase the client's feelings of independence, maintain dignity, and increase self-esteem.
2. Ensure client privacy with proper draping, even if you are the only other person in the room.

Before beginning the procedure, be familiar with the following organizational steps:
1. Offer a bedpan or toilet prior to bath.
2. Position client; if the client is able to assist, he or she should be in a sitting position. If the client is unable to assist, he or she should be lying on his or her back closest to side of bed worker is on.
3. Raise the bed to working level (usually waist level).
4. Have clean pajamas or clothes readily available.
5. Keep the water warm (40.5-42° C or 105-110° F). Test water temperature with your wrist, never your hand, or a bath thermometer.
6. Change water as needed to maintain cleanliness and proper temperature.

7. Use a bath blanket (flannel or top sheet) to keep exposed areas covered during bath.
8. Fold the facecloth into a mitt for easier bathing. Figure 18-4 illustrates how this is done.
9. Always wash from clean to dirty areas.
10. Wash from distal (furthest from you) to proximal (closest to you) to avoid contaminating clean areas by reaching over them.
11. Always rinse soaped areas well to avoid drying the skin or soap irritation.
12. Wash perineal area last, using a clean washcloth.
13. Wear gloves to wash perineal area or any area of the skin with draining fluid.
14. Wash around areas with wound or skin dressings. If in doubt about how to cleanse near a wound or a dressing, ask for assistance.
15. Always observe the skin for any breaks, redness, swelling, or other abnormalities (e.g., changed moles, skin discolouration). Report any changes you observe to the appropriate person.

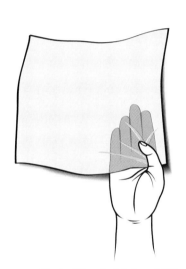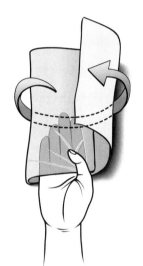

Figure 18-4   *How to Make a Mitt*

Procedure 18-1: Giving a Bed Bath

1. Place the bath blanket over the top linens and unfold so that the linens are completely covered. Pull the linens from underneath the bath blanket and leave at the bottom of the bed.
2. Remove the client's soiled gown or pajamas.
3. Place the basin of water on the over bed table and position close to the bed.
4. Wash the client's face or assist the client by starting with the eyes. Using a corner of the washcloth with no soap, wash from the inner corner to the outer. Use a second corner of the cloth to wash the other eye in the same way.
5. Gently wash the client's face, ears, and neck using soap only at the client's request.
6. Pat dry with the towel.
7. Place the towel lengthwise under the client's arm. Using a soap-lathered washcloth, wash from the hand to the shoulder using long, firm strokes. Rinse, dry well by patting.
8. Wash and dry the axilla (underarm). Repeat for the other arm. See Figure 18- 5.

EQUIPMENT

basin with warm water

2 facecloths, 1 towel

bar of soap

lotion for back rub

clean sheets (as needed)

clean gown, pajamas, or clothes

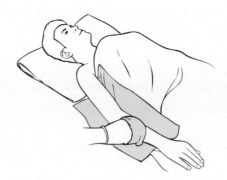

Figure 18-5 *Washing One Arm with a Towel Underneath*

9. Fold the bath blanket down to the client's pubic area. Lay the towel across the client's abdomen. Wash the chest and abdomen. Rinse and dry well.
10. Observe under the female client's breasts for redness. Report any unusual occurrences.
11. Lift the client's leg and place the towel lengthwise under it. Wash the client's leg from the ankles to the hip, using long, firm strokes. Rinse and dry well. Repeat with the other leg.
12. Wash the client's feet well, especially between the toes. It is often beneficial to soak the client's feet in a basin. (See the procedure for foot care.) Examine each foot for abrasions, redness, and the condition of the toenails. Rinse and dry well.
13. Discard the water and washcloth.
14. Rinse the wash basin and fill with clean, warm water. Select a fresh face cloth, forming it into a mitt.
15. Assist the client into a side-lying position away from the worker with bath blanket in place.
16. Place the towel lengthwise on the bed next to the client's back. See Figure 18-6d.

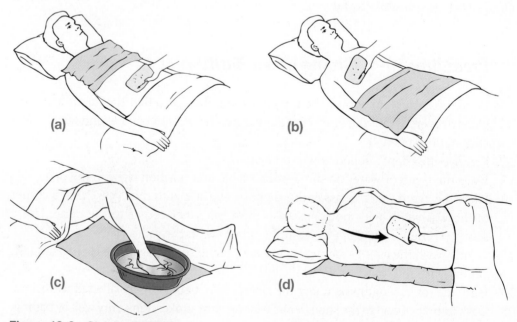

Figure 18-6 *Giving a Bed Bath*

17. Wash the client's back, using long, firm strokes, working from the shoulders to the buttocks. Rinse and dry.
18. Give a back rub at this time. (See the procedure for giving a back rub.)
19. Return the client to supine position. Fold bath blanket up to expose the pubic area. Place the towel between the client's legs. Put on gloves.
20. If the client is able to wash the perineal area independently, hand the soaped washcloth to client.
21. If the client is not able to wash the perineal area, proceed to wash the perineal area.
22. Perform peri-care as follows:

   a. Male:
   Grasp the shaft of the foreskin of the penis and retract the foreskin, if present. Wash the head of the penis in a circular motion and continue down the penis. Rinse. Dry well and replace the foreskin.
   Rinse the cloth, apply soap, and wash the scrotum, particularly between all folds of skin. Wash the rest of the perineal area around to the anus. Rinse and dry well.

   b. Female:
   Wash the outer area (labia majora), moving the washcloth from the pubis to the anus. Continue until the area is clean. Spread the inner lips (labia minora) with the non-dominant hand, directing the facecloth from the pubis to the anus. Use a fresh corner for each area washed. Rinse and dry well.

   c. Clients with Indwelling Catheters:
   Wash the perineal area as above. Using a clean corner of a facecloth, wash the catheter from the urethra entrance (meatus) down the tube. Repeat if necessary with another clean corner of the washcloth. Never put a dirty facecloth near the urethra entrance.

23. The bath is now complete. Apply back-rub lotion to elbows and heels, if needed.
24. Help the client put on a clean gown, pajamas, or clothes.
25. Assist the client up or into a comfortable position, if he or she is to remain in bed.
26. Lower the bed to the lowest position. Attach the call bell, if present.

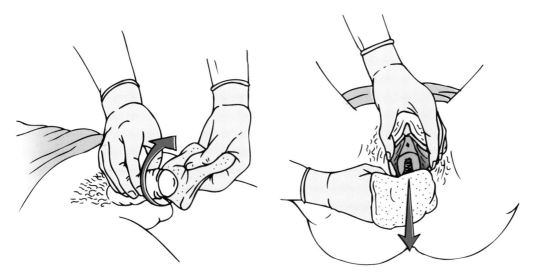

Figure 18-7 *Male and Female Peri-Care*

Tub Bath or Shower

The principles and organization are the same as for a bed bath.

EQUIPMENT

2 facecloths, 1 towel

bar of soap

lotion for back rub

clean sheets (as needed)

clean gown, pajamas, or clothes

Procedure 18-2: Tub Bath or Shower

1. Be sure tub or shower is cleaned and ready for use.
2. If the client shares a bath with others, place an "occupied" sign on the door.
3. Adjust water temperature in the shower or tub to 40.5-42° C (105-110° F).
4. For a tub bath, fill the tub with 30-40 cm of warm water.
5. Place a rubber bath mat in the tub.
6. Place a bath mat next to the tub or shower on the floor. If the client is unsteady on his or her feet, place a waterproof chair in the shower. (Some clients may have a bath seat installed in the tub, along with grab bars for the client to use.)
7. Have the client sit on the edge of the tub and swing his or her legs over the rim as described in Chapter 17. Provide assistance to the client as necessary.
8. If the client is able to bathe or shower alone, stay near the door so as to provide assistance if needed.
9. If the client is unable to bathe alone, bathe the client in the same order as described in the bed bath procedure.
10. Assist the client out of the tub, drain the water first, and follow the procedure outlined in Chapter 17.
11. Assist the client with drying off and dressing.
12. Clean the tub or shower according to client preference or agency policy.

Whirlpool or Hydraulic Tub

Residential Whirlpool Tubs Some clients may have a residential whirlpool tub. These tubs are often similar to a standard bathtub and the procedure used to assist the client into this type of bath is essentially the same. Remember the following:

1. Take care to ensure that the water level is above the whirlpool jets (the outlets on the sides of the tub that spray water). If it is not, water will spray out of the tub.
2. Ensure that the force of the jets is not too strong for client comfort. Adjust the jets by turning the air intake valves (usually located on the deck of the tub) to result in a comfortable degree of force.
3. Make sure that any bath salts or other bath supplies added to the water are safe for use in a whirlpool tub. Avoid any item that will make the tub surface slippery.
4. Be sure you know how to stop and start the whirlpool.
5. Run the whirlpool for no more than 15 minutes, unless instructed otherwise. Always stay with the client.
6. If the client complains of dizziness or lightheadedness, stop bathing and remove the client from the tub.
7. When the bath is finished, drain the tub before assisting the client to exit the tub.
8. Take particular care when assisting the client from the tub, as the whirlpool action may cause the client to be unusually weak.

9. Pat the client dry, apply lotion and assist with dressing.
10. Clean the tub as per instructions.

Commercial Whirlpool Tubs   Most long-term care facilities have commercial whirlpool tubs. These tubs are usually much higher than residential tubs and often require that clients use a bath lift to enter and exit the tub. Photo 18-5 illustrates this type of tub.

Procedure 18-3: Giving a Bath in a Commercial Whirlpool Tub

1. Fill the tub with warm water and be sure water is covering the jets in the tub.
2. Undress the client and place a towel over client's perineal area. Seat the client in the bath lift.
3. Follow the instructions for using the bath lift. Be sure safety waist belt is in place and is snug over the hips. Constantly reassure the client as hydraulic lift places him or her in the tub.
4. Turn jets on for no more than 10-15 minutes. Always stay with the client. Ensure that you know how to start and stop the whirlpool.
5. If the client complains of dizziness or lightheadedness, stop bathing and remove the client from the tub.
6. When the bath is complete, turn jets off and drain the water out of the tub.
7. Place towel over the client's back to prevent chilling and pat dry as soon as possible.
8. Remove the safety belt only when client is safe to move into chair.
9. Clean floor for water spills and clean tub according to agency policy.

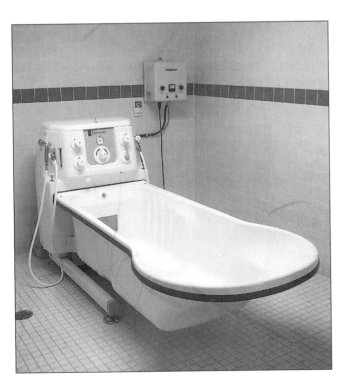

Photo 18-5
A commercial whirlpool tub.
Source: Maple Health Centre.

Special Situations

Possible Problems When Bathing a Client

If the Client Refuses Care

If the client refuses to have a bath, try to find out the reason for the refusal. Perhaps the bathroom is too cold or the client simply doesn't see the need for a bath. You may be able to fix the problem if you know what it is. You could raise the temperature of the bathroom, or place towels in the dryer so as to be warm when the client uses them. Sometimes, explaining the use of a bath for refreshment and hygienic reasons will help.

Some reasons are rooted in the client's discomfort with an unfamiliar person assisting him or her. Similarly, the client may feel awkward if the worker is of the opposite sex. Establishing a therapeutic worker-client relationship is the best approach. Make sure that your client knows that you understand his or her discomfort and that you are a professional. Work with the client to find an acceptable solution. You might suggest that the client wash his or her perineal area while you wait at the door. Perhaps a family member could assist in the procedure, particularly if the client is confused or disoriented.

In some cases, a workable solution will not be possible. If all attempts to resolve the issue fail, advise your supervisor of the situation. If the refusal stems from the fact that you are of the opposite sex, perhaps your agency can send a worker of the client's sex to assist with the bath or shower. **Never perform a bath or shower if the client openly refuses.**

If the Client Is Not Able to Tolerate a Suitable Position for the Bath   If the client is unable to sit or lay on his/her back or side for long periods of time due to disease, shortness of breath, or other conditions, you must adapt the procedure to fit the client's needs. There are several possibilities you might explore. A partial bath may be one solution. If another worker is available to assist, you may be able to work more quickly and complete the task before the client's tolerance is exceeded.

You may have to adapt your technique to whatever position the client is most comfortable maintaining. For example, a patient having shortness of breath when lying flat could be bathed in a sitting position.

If the Client Is Incontinent of Urine or of Stool While the Bath Is Being Performed   If the client is receiving a bed bath, change the sheets or pads. Use toilet tissue to remove excretions. Change the bath water and facecloths as necessary to prevent contamination.

If the client is receiving a tub bath, drain the tub. Place a towel over the client to avoid a chill. Remove excretions with tissue and dispose of in toilet. Assist the client to exit the tub and clean the tub prior to refilling and assisting the client to return to the bath. Use a fresh facecloth to avoid contamination.

If Secretions or Stool Are Hardened on the Perineal Area   Use an unscented back-rub lotion or petroleum jelly on a dampened facecloth to help remove the hardened secretions without damaging the skin. This procedure may have to be repeated several times. Never rub the skin so hard that it becomes irritated or begins to break down.

If the Male Client Has an Erection While the Penis Is Being Washed   Calmly and casually tell the client you will leave him alone for a few minutes. Stay professional. This is not usually something that the client has control over and it can be just as embarrassing to him as it is to you. By returning in a few minutes and continuing on with the bath, the situation will be easier for both of you.

Bathing a Client Who Has an Ostomy   An **ostomy** is a surgical opening in the body. Gentle washing of the stoma is necessary to maintain cleanliness and prevent bleeding of the surface tissue. Clients and their families are taught how to care for the ostomy immediately after surgery. If you are not permitted to replace the ostomy appliance, try to coordinate the bath with the family so that a family member can change the wafer of the ostomy appliance at the same time.

Initially, the stoma of the ostomy appears fragile and sometimes frightening, even to the experienced worker. The stoma is actually mucous membrane, with a consistency much the same as the vagina. There are no nerve endings in the stoma, so the client does not have feelings of pain in the stoma.

There are 3 types of ostomy. Contents will evacuate depending on the type:

- colostomy—formed stool contents empty once or twice a day
- ileostomy—loose stool contents may continually drain
- urostomy—continuous drainage of urine

If there is a chance of continuous drainage from the stoma when washing, apply gauze or tampon to the stoma when drying to prevent leakage onto the clean skin.

Procedure 18-4: Bathing a Client with an Ostomy

1. Check the service plan or any doctor's orders for bathing. Ask the client or the family (if appropriate) for any instructions they have received. If in doubt as to the procedure to be used, consult your supervisor.
2. Have the new appliance ready to apply.
3. Assure the client that washing around the stoma is important as any other part of the bathing routine.
4. Remove the old appliance by gently pulling down from one corner and by placing your hand under the appliance as it is lifted. See Figure 18-8.

EQUIPMENT

basin with warm water

2 facecloths, 1 towel

bar of soap

lotion for back rub

clean sheets (as needed)

clean gown, pajamas, or clothes

new ostomy appliance

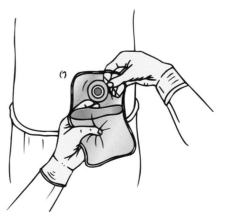

Figure 18-8 *Removing the Old Appliance*

5. Use a soaped facecloth and gently wash around the stoma to remove old glue or stool contents. Repeat until clean. Rinse well.
6. If the area is reddened or excoriated, report to the family or nurse for further treatment.
7. If the client is able to sit in the tub, fill tub up to just below the stoma level to avoid water going in the stoma. If the client is able to shower, ensure that the water is not directed into the stoma.
8. Be sure area around the stoma is dry prior to applying the new appliance.
9. Allow the client/family to assist whenever possible.

Performing a Back Rub

Most clients really look forward to a back rub. It can be performed at bath time or at bedtime or any other time in the day in order to promote relaxation for the client. The back rub has other benefits as well. It promotes dilation of the peripheral blood vessels which, in turn, enhances circulation. It also rids the surface of dead skin cells. The stimulation of the massaging technique causes relaxation of the muscles of the back and shoulders. It also provides for human contact. Figure 18-9 shows the basic motions of a back rub.

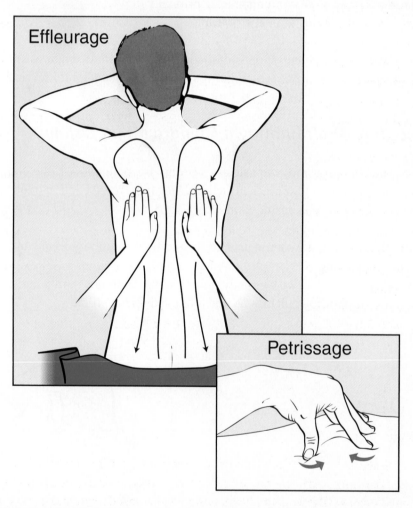

Figure 18-9 *Back Rub Technique*

Principles of giving a back rub:
1. Wash hands prior to and after giving a back rub.
2. Apply lubricant to your hands to reduce the friction created by one skin surface rubbing against another. Many clients have a lotion suitable for this purpose. You may need to apply lubricant several times to the client's back, depending on how dry his or her skin is.
3. You may use an unperfumed talcum powder or cornstarch if the client is perspiring and his or her skin is not otherwise dry.
4. Explain the procedure to the client.
5. Provide privacy. Ensure that other areas of the client's body are covered.
6. Raise the bed to working level (usually waist high).
7. Ensure that the client is in a comfortable position, preferably prone (on stomach) or side-lying if prone is not possible. If the client cannot lie down, you may be able to provide an upper back rub with the client seated in a chair, leaning forward with his or her arms on a table or other immoveable surface.

Procedure 18-5: Giving a Back Rub

EQUIPMENT

bath blanket or towel

skin lotion or oil

talcum powder (if needed)

1. Remove the client's gown, loosen ties, or remove pajama top.
2. Position the client with bedclothes pulled down to the top of the buttocks and bath blanket or towel over top of the bedclothes.
3. Apply a moderate amount of lotion to the worker's hands and rub hands together to warm lotion.
4. Start in lumbar region and smooth lotion toward shoulders.
5. Begin the massage with *effleurage* by stroking with both hands from the buttocks toward the shoulders and back again. Stroke firmly going up to the shoulders and lightly when moving back to the top of the buttocks.
6. Perform long strokes up the back and circular motions around the shoulders at least 8 to 10 times.
7. *Petrissage* may be used to knead the superficial tissues between the fingertips of both hands, moving toward the shoulders. Other techniques may be performed if extra training is provided.
8. Complete the massage by changing back to *effleurage* and stroking the back several more times.
9. Remove excess lubricant with the towel, if necessary.
10. Remove the bath blanket and replace the client's bedclothes.
11. Place the client in a comfortable position. Attach the call bell, if present.

Oral Care

Purpose

Oral care is essential to health and to a positive self-image. Whether the client has natural teeth or dentures, oral care must be performed daily. It is important that oral care be performed even when the client is unconscious. Diseased teeth and gums can make eating painful and even spread infection to other areas of the body.

The mucous membranes of the mouth are made up of delicate epithelial tissues which are prone to injury and infection, and so must be diligently cared for. If the client is able to move his hands and arms, minimal assistance in placing toothpaste on the brush or handing the client mouthwash may be all that is necessary. A client's teeth and oral surfaces should be cleansed after each meal and before bedtime. Oral care may be required more often if the client's mouth is dry due to disease, use of certain medications, or other reasons.

Cleaning Teeth

Principles of cleaning teeth:
1. Wash hands prior to and after procedure.
2. Use disposable gloves for oral care.
3. Use clean technique when cleaning the oral cavity.
4. Use only the client's personal toothbrush.
5. Allow the client to assist wherever able.
6. Use appropriate solution to cleanse mouth.
7. Gather all equipment.
8. Explain procedure to the client.
9. Raise the client to a sitting position if conscious and to side-lying position if the client is unconscious.
10. Identify full or partial dentures, bridges, or any loose teeth.
11. Be aware that the client may want to leave dentures out at night, so have a denture cup ready.

Different procedures are used for conscious and unconscious clients.

EQUIPMENT

toothbrush, tooth-paste, floss
(if available) for natural teeth

commercial tooth-ettes, if toothbrush not available

kidney basin or basin

towel, facecloth

mouthwash
(if used)

glass of water

Procedure 18-6: Providing Mouth Care for the Conscious, Alert Client

Figure 18-10 shows mouth care for the conscious and alert client.

1. Place a towel across the client's chest.
2. Assist the client to brush teeth, including the tongue.
3. Hold basin for the client to spit into.
4. Give several sips of water to rinse. Offer mouthwash.
5. If client's mouth is dry, avoid commercial mouthwashes. Use 5 to 15 ml (1 tsp. to 1 tbsp.) of baking soda to 250 ml (8 oz.) of water as a mouthwash to lubricate the mouth. Use as often as needed.
6. Offer the towel.
7. Remove and wash out soiled basin.
8. Leave client with fresh water.

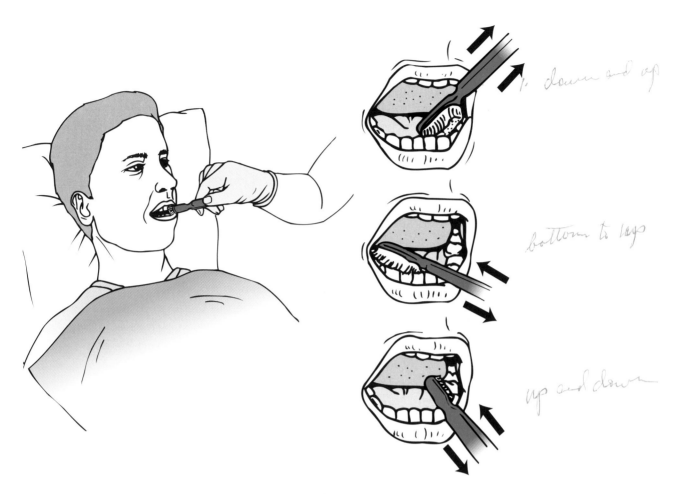

Figure 18-10 *Mouth Care for the Conscious and Alert Client*

Procedure 18-7: Providing Mouth Care for the Unconscious Client

Figure 18-11 shows mouthcare for the unconscious client.

1. Place the towel and kidney basin under side of mouth while client is on side.
2. Use gauze-covered tongue depressor to hold mouth open while brushing teeth. **Never put fingers in to the unconscious client's mouth as he/she may bite down due to the stimulation.**
3. Brush the teeth from the gum-line down to the tip of the teeth in an up-and-down fashion.
4. Brush on the inside of the teeth and then the outside.
5. Gently brush the tongue.
6. Use a bulb syringe to rinse the mouth, making sure no water goes down the client's throat.
7. Apply lubricant to the lips. Repeat as needed.

EQUIPMENT

toothbrush, toothpaste, floss (if available) for natural teeth

gauze-covered tongue depressor

bulb syringe

towel, facecloth

kidney basin

lubricant for lips (such as petroleum jelly or lip gloss)

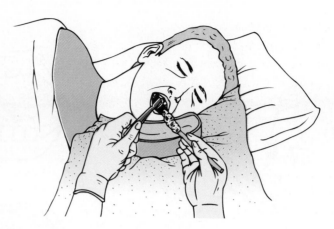

Figure 18-11 *Mouth Care for the Unconscious Client*

You may notice that the client's tongue is coated with white patches. This can be due to an infection or to dryness. Report the condition to the appropriate person so that the condition can be properly treated. If the condition is due to dryness, applying a 50-50 solution of hydrogen peroxide and water with a toothette every 1/2 hour throughout the day will remove the coating.

Assisting the Client with Cleaning Dentures

EQUIPMENT
kidney basin or denture cup
denture brush and paste
mouthwash
glass of water
denture adhesive
towel

Procedure 18-8: Cleaning Dentures

1. Assist the client to a sitting position.
2. Place the over-bed table in front of the client.
3. Place the denture cup or kidney basin close to the client and ask the client to remove his or her dentures.
4. If the client isn't able to remove the dentures, assist by grasping the upper denture with thumb and forefinger and gently wiggle to break the seal. Figure 18-12 illustrates this technique.

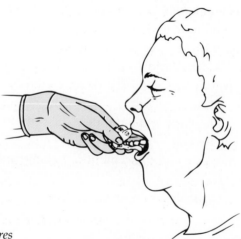

Figure 18-12 *Cleaning Dentures*

5. Lift out the bottom denture.
6. Place the dentures immediately into the basin to avoid breakage or dropping.
7. Take the dentures to the bathroom and place the basin in the sink under the tap.
8. Using the client's denture brush and paste, clean the dentures from the gumline to the tip of the teeth in an up-and-down fashion. Clean any debris or leftover food out of the crevices. **Always brush the dentures over the basin to avoid breakage by dropping.**
9. Rinse dentures well.
10. Return the dentures to the client. Before inserting, allow the client to rinse his or her mouth with mouthwash or fresh water.
11. Assist the client in replacing the dentures if required.
12. The client may want denture adhesive applied. If so, follow the directions for application.
13. If the client is having difficulty replacing the dentures, replace the top denture first. Then, using one finger, open the client's mouth wide and slip the bottom denture in sideways and then turn.
14. Wash client's face and dry with towel.
15. Leave the client in appropriate position.

It is not advisable to leave dentures in an unconscious client's mouth, due to the risk of choking or aspiration. Keep dentures stored in water in a denture cup. Advise the family and any other caregivers that the dentures are not in.

Hair Care

Purpose

Few things make a client feel better than having clean, well-groomed hair. Often when a client becomes very ill, hair care is neglected. The hair becomes soiled and tangled and may have exudate in it, due to excess perspiration or blood (such as from a head injury). It is uncomfortable, negatively affects the client's self-image, and can harbour microorganisms that may be harmful to the client.

After bathing the client, the hair should be combed or brushed into a style that pleases the client. Never cut the client's hair or place in an unfamiliar style without the client's or family's permission. If the hair is badly tangled, apply mineral oil and use a wide-tooth comb to remove tangles. Wash hair after the tangles are removed. Alternately, you can wash the client's hair, apply conditioner, and then use a wide-tooth comb to remove tangles.

Encourage the client to wash his/her hair as often as desired. If the client is able to wash independently, provide towels and shampoo. If the client is having a tub bath or shower, assist the client in washing his or her hair. Be sure to dry the client's hair well after shampooing or place a dry towel on the pillow to soak up any additional moisture. Dry shampoos are available in pharmacies if the client cannot have his or her head wet (for example, due to sutures).

Washing Hair Using a Bed Tray

shampoo tray

2 towels

2 facecloths

2 large buckets

1 small bucket

shampoo and
conditioner
(as per the client's
preferences)

Procedure 18-9: *Washing Hair Using a Bed Tray*

1. Lay the client flat and place a plastic sheet under the client's head.
2. Place the large bucket on the floor near the bed and underneath the spout of the shampoo tray.
3. Fill the other large bucket with warm water. Test temperature with wrist.
4. Place the client's head in the tray, putting a folded facecloth under the client's neck for added comfort. Figure 18-13 illustrates the proper position.
5. Give the client the other facecloth to hold over his or her eyes.
6. Wet the client's hair with water, using the small bucket.
7. Apply a small amount of shampoo to your hands and rub together to form lather.
8. Apply lather to the client's hair, massaging gently in a circular motion to increase the client's circulation. Be sure to wash all parts of the client's head by asking the client to turn his or her head as necessary.
9. Squeeze excess shampoo out of the hair and rinse well.
10. Repeat the shampoo if necessary for very soiled hair; however, check the client's comfort and general condition before going ahead. **If the client cannot tolerate lying flat for very long and becomes short of breath or generally distressed, stop the procedure and return the client to a sitting position.**
11. Dry the hair well, using a large towel.
12. Remove the shampoo tray and plastic sheet.
13. Replace wet towel with another towel and rub hair well to dry. Use a hair dryer if the client has one and can tolerate the heat and air flow. Be sure to set the dryer to a comfortable temperature so as not to burn the client's skin.

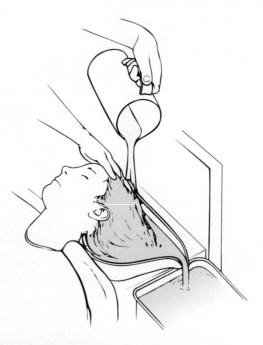

Figure 18-13 *Client Properly Positioned for a Bed Shampoo*

14. Comb and style hair according to the client's preference.
15. Clean up and remove the equipment. Clean the shampoo tray with appropriate disinfectant (if required or if it is to be used with another client).

This procedure may be adapted for use where there is no shampoo tray available. Use a firm plastic sheet, such as a vinyl tablecloth, folded in half. Roll a towel lengthwise to form a skinny "rope" and place inside the fold. Place the client's head on the centre of the roll and arrange the plastic sheet to form a trough to drain water from the bed. Figure 18-14 illustrates a homemade shampoo tray.

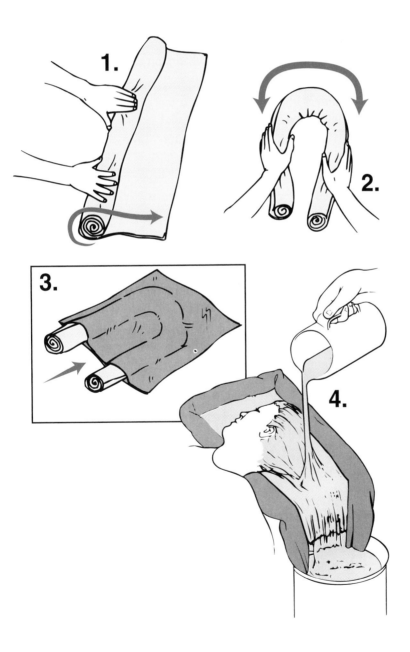

Figure 18-14 *Homemade Shampoo Tray*

Washing Hair at a Sink

Some clients prefer to have their hair washed under running water, even if they choose not to wash their hair when they bathe or shower. If the client can sit in a wheelchair or movable recliner chair, he or she may be able to have his or her hair washed at a sink. The client must also be able to hold his or her head forward or backward to accomplish the procedure. Make sure that you check with your supervisor before you wash the client's hair at the sink. An older person may have difficulty holding his or her head back, due to neck problems, or may have circulation problems that make holding his or her head back unadvisable.

Procedure 18-10: Washing Hair at a Sink

EQUIPMENT

shampoo and conditioner, as per client preference

2 washcloths

comb

2 large towels

hair dryer (if available)

1. Be sure that the client's chair cannot move before you proceed with the task.
2. If the client is going to hold his/her head forward over the sink, place a towel over the client's shoulders and give the client a facecloth to hold over his/her eyes.
3. If the client is facing away from the sink and is letting his head lay backward on the sink, place a folded facecloth on the edge of the sink for comfort.
4. Apply shampoo to your hands, work into a lather.
5. Apply lather to the client's hair, massaging gently in a circular motion to increase the client's circulation. Be sure to wash all parts of the client's head by asking the client to turn his or her head as necessary.
6. Squeeze excess shampoo out of the hair and rinse well.
7. Repeat the shampoo if necessary for very soiled hair, but check the client's comfort and general condition before going ahead.
8. Dry the hair well, using a large towel. Use a hair dryer if the client has one and can tolerate the heat and air flow. Be sure to set the dryer to a comfortable temperature so as not to burn the client's skin.
9. Comb and style hair according to the client's preference.
10. Assist the client to a comfortable position.

Photo 18-6
Client having hair washed at sink.
Source: CHATS.

Shaving the Client

Purpose

Men are used to shaving daily and when they are unable to do so because of illness or weakness, they do not feel clean or well-groomed. Most men have their own shaving equipment that they prefer to use. If the client lives in a long-term care facility, the desired equipment can be brought in from home by the family.

Prior to shaving a client, the worker must be aware of the client's general condition. This is particularly important if the client has a bleeding disorder (e.g., bleeding is difficult or slow to stop) or is taking medication to thin his blood (e.g., anti-coagulants). You must obtain approval to shave a client who has a bleeding disorder or is taking anti-coagulant medication.

Procedure 18-11: Shaving the Client

If the client is able to shave himself:
1. Assist the client to a sitting position in bed or a chair with a table in front and a mirror positioned so he can see with a good light in place.
2. Assist as needed.

If the client is unable to shave himself and uses an electric razor:
1. Apply pre-shave lotion, if desired by the client.
2. Plug in the razor and begin shaving by moving the head of the razor back and forth over the hair growth. Use your other hand to pull the skin taut as you shave.

If the client is unable to shave himself and uses a safety razor:
1. Apply a damp, hot facecloth to the client's face for five minutes prior to shaving to soften the bristles, especially if the growth is long.
2. Fill the basin with warm water.
3. Position the client in a suitable position to reach all areas of the face.
4. Apply shaving lather, cream, or soap evenly over the face.
5. Hold the skin taut with your nondominant hand and begin shaving, using short, even strokes (Figure 18-15).
6. Pull the razor blade lightly but firmly against the direction of the hair growth.
7. Rinse the razor frequently in the warm water.
8. Be sure not to shave off a moustache, beard, or sideburns unless the client or family has given permission.
9. After shaving is finished, wipe face with the wet facecloth and dry well with the towel.
10. If the client desires, apply aftershave lotion.
11. Observe for any nicks or scrapes. If present, apply a pressure bandage and report the occurrence to the appropriate person.

EQUIPMENT

For shaving with a safety razor:

shaving cream, lather or soap

facecloth and towel

wash basin with warm water

safety razor

mirror

aftershave lotion, if desired

For shaving with an electric razor:

pre-shave lotion (if available)

electric razor (check that cord is not frayed and that razor is in good working condition)

mirror

aftershave lotion, if desired

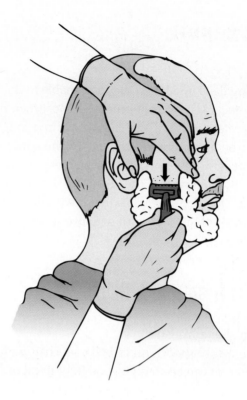

Figure 18-15 *Shaving the Client with a Safety Razor*

Foot Care

A client's feet should be inspected daily, especially if the client's circulation to the feet is impaired or the client is diabetic. Observe for any redness, irritation marks from shoes, colour of the feet, and any skin abnormalities. **Be sure to check between the toes for any crevices or cracks in the skin. These fissures could lead to infection.**

What makes up daily foot care will vary, depending upon the client's condition and preferences. If the client has dry skin, bathing the feet every day will excessively dry the feet, eventually cause cracking, and possibly lead to infection. In this case, a foot rub with lotion is soothing to the client. It also gives you a chance to inspect the client's feet.

Clients whose feet smell or are very moist from perspiration may be bathed. In these cases, the client is often advised to wear cotton socks and air his or her feet for some time every day. Moist, damp areas can attract a fungal infection.

Corns and bunions can interfere with normal walking and should be examined by a podiatrist or chiropodist. You should never attempt to trim a client's corns or to disturb a bunion.

Proper fitting shoes are an important part of foot care. Indentations in the client's foot that indicate that the client's shoes are too tight should be reported to the appropriate person. Decreased circulation may mean that a client does not feel the tightness.

Many clients enjoy a periodic foot soak. Use the following procedure if you are to soak your client's feet. If the client cannot sit in a chair, provide for a foot soak at the end of the bed bath.

Procedure 18-12: Providing Foot Care

If your client can sit in a chair:

1. Assist your client to a comfortable sitting position.
2. Place bath mat on floor in front of client.
3. Place basin on mat.
4. Dissolve soap in warm water of basin.
5. Follow steps 7-15 to complete the procedure.

If the client cannot sit up:

6. Position the basin at the foot of the bed.
7. Place client's feet in basin.
8. Place towel over client's feet to conserve heat.
9. Soak feet for 15-20 minutes. Add warm water as required to maintain proper temperature.
10. At end of soak period, wash feet with washcloth. Note any irregularities in each foot. Rinse feet and pat dry.
11. Using the orange stick, gently clean the toenails. **Do not cut toenails.**
12. If the client's skin is dry, apply lotion to tops and bottoms of feet. Avoid putting lotion between the toes as this can foster microorganisms. Wipe off any excess lotion to reduce the possibility of the client slipping.
13. If the client tends to perspire, apply a light dusting of talcum powder to the feet. Allow feet to air dry, if possible.
14. Assist client to put on socks and shoes or slippers.
15. Report long toenails and other irregularities to the appropriate person.

EQUIPMENT

basin with warm water, large enough to hold both of the client's feet

bath mat (on which to place the basin)

foot soap or mild soap (as per the client's preferences)

washcloth

2 towels

orange stick

Nail Care

Fingernails and toenails should be inspected daily, usually during the bathing routine. Normally, nails are smooth, transparent, and rounded over the edge of the fingers or toes. As a person ages, nails become harder and their care becomes more difficult. Some conditions cause the nails to become discoloured, thick, brittle, or to have different shapes. These conditions should be examined and treated by a specialist.

Your agency may allow you to cut the fingernails of a healthy client. Because of the risk of infection, you must never cut the nails of a diabetic client. Similarly, you should never cut the nails of a client who is taking anti-coagulants or has a bleeding abnormality.

EQUIPMENT

nail clippers or
sharp scissors

nail file or emery
board

orange stick

small basin
with warm water
and soap

towel

nail polish remover
(if required)

nail polish
(if required)

Procedure 18-13: Providing Nail Care

1. Position the client so the hands and feet can be soaked in a basin to soften the nails.
2. If the client is on bed rest, place the basin on the bed and soak hands while washing the client's arms and chest.
3. If the client is sitting in a chair, use the procedure defined earlier in this section to soak the client's feet.
4. After soaking, dry the hands and feet well. Inspect the hands, feet, and nails. Report if there is any redness, weeping areas, or other irregularities.
5. Remove old nail polish if necessary. Trim the fingernails if needed (and appropriate) by cutting straight across and avoiding cutting into the corners. Photo 18-7 illustrates proper nail cutting.

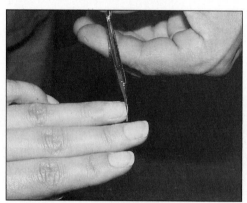

Photo 18-7
*Cutting nails
straight across.*

6. Clean under the fingernails with an orange stick.
7. File the edges of the fingernails until smooth with an emery board or a nail file.
8. Apply new nail polish if desired by the client.
9. Apply lotion to hands and feet when finished. Rub the lotion in by massaging in a gentle kneading fashion.

Eye Care

Routine Care

Normally the eyes do not require any other special care other than the routine used in the bathing procedure. You must observe for any drainage, noting the colour, consistency, and where it is coming from, as well as any redness, watering, or signs of irritation. Make note of any complaints from the client (such as itching or dryness) and report these, along with your observations, to the appropriate person.

If your client is very ill, you should watch to ensure that the eyelids are shutting. If they do not, the eye may tend to dry out. Report this observation so that special drops or care may be provided.

Eyeglass Care

Eyeglasses are made of many materials, each requiring a particular type of care. Make sure you know the correct procedure so that the lens will not be scratched or marred.

If there are no special instructions, clean eyeglasses with mild dish soap, rinse with clean water, and dry with a soft cloth. Do not use wipes or hand soap, as they will leave a film on the glass. If the client is not wearing his/her glasses, they should be stored in a proper case to prevent damage.

Contact lenses require special care. Make sure you know how to assist the client with lens care and, if you are required to do so, how to insert and remove them.

Artificial Eye Care

An artificial eye is made of glass or plastic and is very close to the actual shape and appearance of the normal eye. You must receive specific instructions on the care of the artificial eye if you are to provide this type of care.

Ear Care

Routine Care

Most ear care is performed through the bathing procedure. Care must be taken not to introduce any objects into the ear canal. Cotton swabs are a particular hazard, as they can puncture the ear drum. A buildup of wax (cerumen) may have to be removed through special procedures if it is affecting hearing capabilities. Report client complaints of pressure or pain in the ear, observations of excessive wax in the ear canal, or observations of diminished hearing acuity to the appropriate person.

Care for the external ear includes gentle washing of the ear lobe, behind the ear, and the folds of the outer ear.

Hearing Aid Care

There are four different types of hearing aids. Photo 18-8 illustrates two types. Although they look different, they all act in the same way. The tiny microphone in the aid picks up sound waves and amplifies them so that sound may be transmitted to the inner ear.

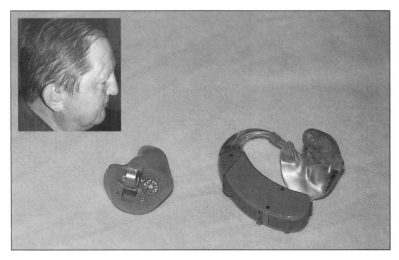

Photo 18-8

In-the-ear and behind-the-ear hearing aids.

Source: Robert Harmon.

The hearing aid is operated by a battery and has an "on-off" switch. Always turn off the aid when not in use and store in a case to prevent loss or damage. If the client will not be wearing the hearing aid for a few days, remove the battery from the aid and leave it in the storage case.

Clients who use bilateral aids (aids in both ears) have a distinct right ear aid and a left ear aid. Be sure to identify the right and left aids before assisting the client to place the aid in his or her ear. The aid must be properly placed to be comfortable and useful. Ask for specific instruction on how to properly insert your client's aid.

Some aids have an ear mould that is connected to the aid. This mould fits into the ear. You may carefully remove this mould from the aid and wash it with warm soapy water. Dry the ear mould well before connecting it to the aid and replacing it in the client's ear. Do not expose any of the other parts to moisture. Never allow a one-piece aid (sometimes called an *in-the-ear aid*) to become wet.

Assisting the Client with the Use of a Bed Pan

There are two common types of bed pans: standard pans and fracture pans. Photo 18-9 illustrates both types of pans. Fracture pans are used with clients who are recovering from a fractured hip. However, some clients without fractures may prefer a fracture pan.

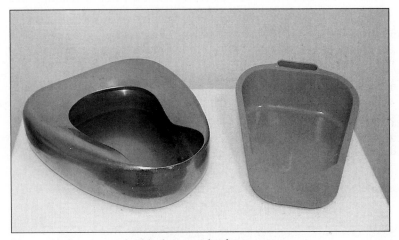

Photo 18-9   *A standard bed pan and a fracture pan.*

EQUIPMENT

bed pan

towel

toilet tissue

disposable gloves

Procedure 18-14: Assisting a Client with the Use of a Bed Pan

1. Provide privacy.
2. Identify what the person can do for him or herself; decide with the person what assistance you will provide.
3. Explain what you are going to do.
4. If you are using a stainless steel bed pan, warm it first by holding it under a running hot water tap.
5. Put on gloves.

6. Position the pan according to type. If you are using a fracture pan, place the smaller end under the buttocks. If you are using a standard pan, place the pan with the open end to the front.

7. Position the person on their back with bed flat. If able, ask the client to flex both knees. Place your hand under the person's lower back and assist him or her to raise the buttocks. Press the pan down into the bedding as you slide the pan under the person. Figure 18-16a and b illustrates this procedure.

8. If the person is unable to assist, turn the person onto the side away from you. Figure 18-17 illustrates the steps in positioning the pan.

9. Place bed pan firmly against the buttocks while remaining aware of the position of the pan.

10. Push the bed pan down and toward the person. Hold the bed pan securely and turn the person on their back.

11. Raise the head of the bed if possible. Positioning the person as close to upright as possible helps in elimination.

12. When the person is finished, lower the head of the bed.

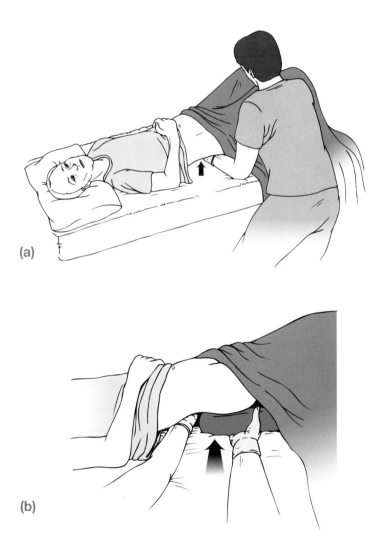

Figure 18-16   *Placement of the Bed Pan*

13. Provide tissue to the person if he or she is able to cleanse. If the client is unable, wipe the perineal area from front to back, taking care to gently remove all fluid and fecal matter. Drop used tissue into the pan.
14. Ask client to raise buttocks and remove pan. If the person is unable to raise the buttocks, hold bed pan securely, turn person away from you, and remove the pan.
15. Clean the genital area from front to back to remove any residual material. Give complete perineal care if necessary.
16. Empty bed pan and clean. Make sure the area under the rim is clean.
17. Return equipment to its proper place.
18. Make sure person is comfortable.
19. Remove gloves and wash your hands.

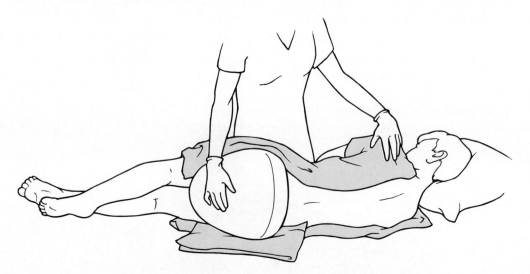

Figure 18-17   *Placing a Bed Pan When the Person Cannot Assist*

Assisting the Client with Dressing

How we dress is a reflection of how we see ourselves. Remember how you felt when you were well dressed? At other times, casual clothes may be the most appropriate.

Like you, the clothes your client wears depend mostly on his or her environment and preferences. Some clients will dress in casual clothes if their situation allows. Others may need to dress for work. Some clients always wear jewellery, others do so rarely. Health status affects the choice of clothing. If the client is not well, he or she may change into a clean gown or pajamas after bathing and remain in bed. The client should always have the opportunity to choose the clothing he or she wears. If, due to cognitive impairment, the client cannot make an appropriate choice (for example, selecting a shirt and sweater and nothing else), you can still offer appropriate choices (such as two appropriate dresses) from which the client can choose. Figure 18-18 shows the steps involved in dressing and undressing.

Whether it is due to disease, illness, or a physical impairment, the client may need assistance from the worker to get dressed. Assisting the client is much like dressing one-self. However, there are a few hints to help when there is physical impairment of limbs.

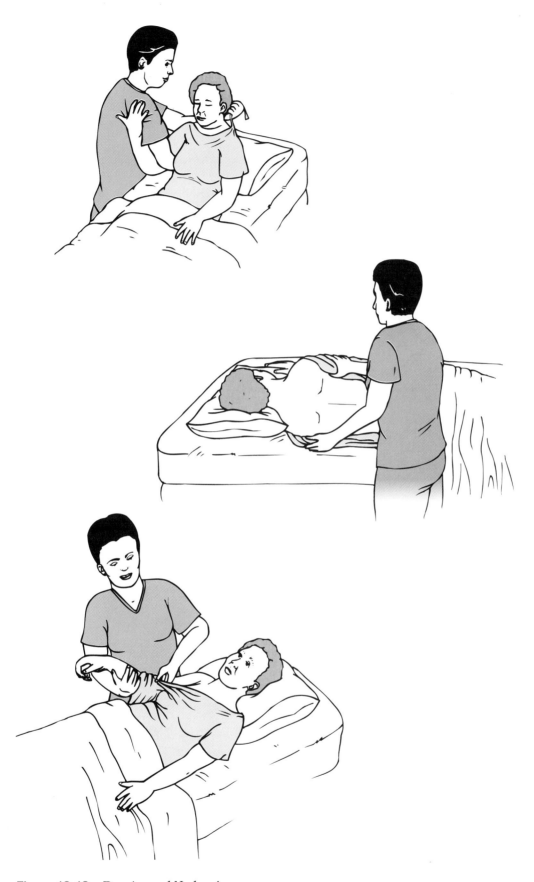

Figure 18-18 *Dressing and Undressing*

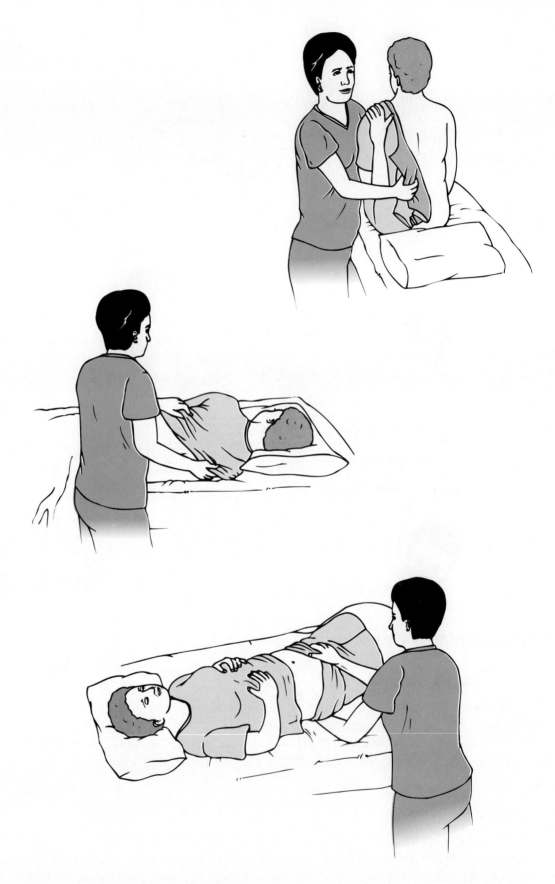

Figure 18-18 *Dressing and Undressing (continued)*

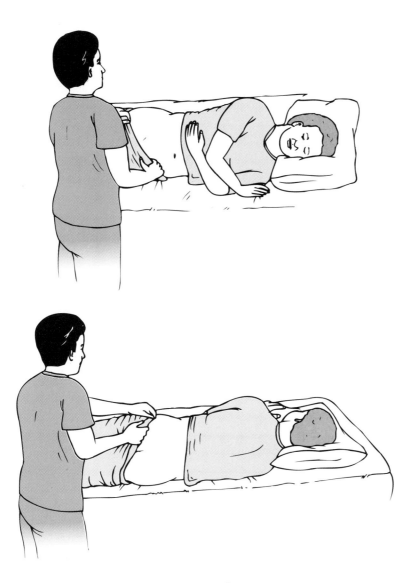

Figure 18-18 *Dressing and Undressing (continued)*

If the Client Is Unable to Move a Limb

1. Allow the client to help wherever he/she can to increase the client's feeling of self-worth.
2. Always remove the soiled gown or pajamas from the mobile limb first.
3. Always replace the new garment's sleeve or leg on the immobile limb first.
4. **Be sure to hold the immobile arm by the wrist or elbow or the immobile leg by the knee or ankle to prevent pressure or strain on the muscles.**

Elastic Stockings

A client may be instructed to wear special elastic stockings for many reasons. A client on prolonged bed rest, recovering from surgery, or who has poor peripheral circulation may benefit from the long-term use of elastic stockings. The worker should be familiar with the period during which the client is to wear the stockings.

Procedure 18-15: Removing Elastic Stockings

1. Gently pull down the stocking from the upper leg and roll it off of the foot.
2. Turn the stocking right side out and lay flat over a chair.
3. Repeat for the other leg.
4. Sometimes the client will have two pair so that one pair can be washed every day. Allow the skin to be exposed to the air for 10 to 15 minutes. This is a good time to bathe and observe the skin for any redness, irritation, etc.

Procedure 18-16: Replacing Elastic Stockings

1. Grasp the stocking and gather it in your hands.
2. Raise the client's foot by holding it at the heel.
3. Start by placing the stocking toe over the foot.
4. Gradually pull the stocking up over the heel, ankle, and the leg.
5. Be sure the stocking is placed evenly along the leg to maximize the distribution of the pressure.
6. Repeat for the other leg.
7. If the client's leg tends to perspire, a slight coating of talcum powder will allow easier replacing of the stocking.

Bed Making

Strictly speaking, bed making is not a component of physical care. However, it is an essential skill when the client is unable to leave his or her bed for extended periods of time.

Principles of making a bed (occupied or unoccupied):

1. Wash hands prior to and after making a bed; wear gloves if linen is soiled by body fluids.
2. Change only soiled linen or according to agency policy.
3. Bring only the required amount of clean linen into room to avoid contamination.
4. Do not let soiled linen touch your clothing.
5. If possible, have laundry cart close to bed; avoid putting soiled linen on the floor.
6. Stack clean linen on chair or over-bed table in the order you will use it.
7. Always raise bed to working level; use proper body mechanics at all times.
8. Lower the siderail on the side you are working on.
9. Do not shake sheets. Shaking can distribute dust and microorganisms into the air.
10. If you are making an occupied bed, explain to the client what you are doing.
11. Always keep the client covered.
12. Always attach the call bell (if available) when finished making the bed.
13. Leave the over-bed table in the client's reach when finished.

Procedure 18-17: Making an Unoccupied Bed

1. Loosen all soiled linen by pulling them away from the mattress.
2. If the top sheets are clean, remove by folding top to bottom and place on a nearby chair.
3. If linens are soiled with body fluids, put on gloves.
4. To remove soiled linen, take from top to bottom and roll into a ball. Place in laundry cart or hamper or take directly to client's washer.
5. Remove gloves.
6. Before placing clean linen on the bed, make sure that the mattress is pulled up toward the top of the bed as far as it will go. This will allow for better positioning of the client when the head of the bed is raised.
7. Apply a clean bottom sheet (or previous top sheet) by folding in half lengthwise on the bed.
8. Tuck one side in and repeat on the other side, making the bottom sheet snug. If a fitted sheet is not available, mitre the corners as in Photo 18-10.
9. Place the drawsheet on the centre of the bed, keeping the top edge at approximately the client's axilla. This will allow easier positioning of the client using the drawsheet as a lift sheet. Photo 18-11 illustrates proper placement.
10. Add the top sheet, blanket, and bedspread in the same fashion, going from side to side.
11. Smooth the top linens over the bed and tuck the ends under the mattress at the

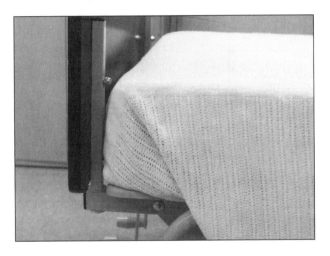

Photo 18-10 *Mitred corners.*

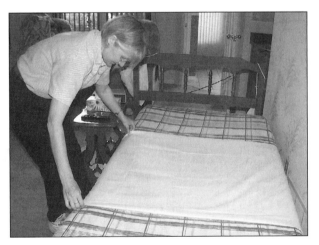

Photo 18-11 *Drawsheet in place. Source: CHATS.*

foot of the bed. Mitre the corners as in the previous diagram. Omit this step if your client prefers that the linens not be tucked in.
12. Fold back the top linens to make a 15 centimetre (about 6 inches) cuff at the head end.
13. If the client will be returning to the bed immediately, fan fold the top linen to the bottom of the bed.
14. Add a new pillowcase and position the pillow for the client's use.
15. Attach the call bell if present.
16. Remove the laundry cart and tidy the rest of the client's room.

EQUIPMENT

flat or fitted sheet to cover mattress

flat or top sheet

pillowcases

drawsheet

bedspread

blanket (optional)

bath blanket (to cover client if in bed)

laundry cart or laundry hamper

gloves (if required)

Procedure 18-18: Making an Occupied Bed

1. Loosen the soiled linens as in the unoccupied bed.
2. Place a bath blanket over the client.
3. Ask the client to hold the top edge while you reach underneath and pull the bedspread down to the bottom of the bed and off.
4. Fold the bedspread in half, if you are going to reuse it.
5. Repeat for the blanket and top sheet. If no bath blanket is available, leave the top sheet on the client to cover him during the bed change.
6. Have the client roll over to the side away from you. If the client is too ill, obtain help or position the client using pillows.
7. Lift the bottom sheet and the drawsheet from the side edge and tuck under the client.
8. Unfold the clean sheet lengthwise and place on the bed.
9. Lay the sheet so that there are 2.5 centimetres (about one inch) over the edge of the mattress at the foot at the bed.
10. Unfold the sheet so that half is on the bed and the other half is tucked under the client.
11. Repeat with the drawsheet, positioning it so the top edge will be under the client's axilla.
12. With the client covered with the top sheet or bath blanket, have him or her roll over to your side.
13. Explain to the client that he or she will have to roll over a lump of linen.
14. Grasping the siderail will make the client feel more secure. If the client is unable to roll, obtain help or raise the siderail and go to the other side of the bed.
15. Lower the rail and roll the client towards the other siderail and position with pillows.
16. Pull the soiled linen out from underneath the client and roll into a ball.
17. Place soiled linen in the laundry cart or hamper. Make sure you do not leave the client with the siderail down.
18. Find the edges of the clean linen and pull toward you. Smooth and straighten them.
19. Tuck the bottom sheet under the head of the bed and mitre the corner if necessary.
20. Tuck the rest of the sheet and the drawsheet under the length of the bed.
21. The client may prefer to roll back onto his or her back at this point to finish the bed.
22. Unfold the clean top linen over the client and remove the bath blanket.

Measurement of Vital Signs

Temperature, pulse, and respirations are important measurements of overall body status and are called **vital signs**. Often, when a client is ill, one or more of these signs will not be within a "normal" range. For example, if the client has the flu, his or her temperature may be raised. If the client's heart has an irregularity, the pulse will be irregular. If the client has pneumonia or another chest infection, respirations may be rapid and shallow. It is important for you to understand the normal range of these signs and how to measure them correctly. However, be aware that these are the only basic measurements. There are many more ways to determine the client's condition, particularly observing and listening to the client.

Temperature

Measurement of the total amount of body heat is called **temperature**. The temperature is maintained by a delicate balance of heat generation and heat loss. In a 24 hour period, it's normal for temperature to fluctuate slightly. Between midnight and 6 a.m., it drops slightly and it's at its highest between 4 p.m. and 8 p.m. Table 18-2 gives normal temperature ranges for temperatures taken at various sites on the body. Fever is a prolonged increase in temperature. Fever often accompanies illness or infection.

TABLE 18-2	Normal Temperature Ranges	
Location	**Normal Range**	
	Centigrade	**Fahrenheit**
Oral	36.5° to 37.5°	97.6° to 99.6°
Rectal	37.0° to 38.1°	98.6° to 100.6°
Axillary	36.0° to 37.0°	96.6° to 98.6°

Taking a Temperature

There are four sites used to take a temperature: under the tongue, the outer ear, the axilla, and the rectum. You must use the most appropriate area for each client. For example, an axillary temperature or outer ear temperature may be more appropriate when the client:

- is a baby or young child and cannot hold a glass thermometer in his/her mouth;
- is a confused or elderly client who may bite down on a glass thermometer;
- has just swallowed a hot or cold fluid; an oral temperature will not be accurate.

Some clients or facilities may have only certain types of thermometers. Table 18-3 illustrates three common types.

Principles of taking a temperature:
1. Wash hands prior to and after taking the temperature.
2. Assess which method of temperature-taking will be most accurate and safe for the client.
3. Avoid touching the end that goes into the body.

Procedure 18-19: Taking an Oral Temperature Using a Glass Thermometer

EQUIPMENT

clean glass thermometer

tissues

1. Take a clean glass thermometer and shake the mercury down until it is at the bottom of the scale on the thermometer. It may take several shakes to get it down. Be careful not to shake where you may hit something.

2. Place the thermometer under the tip of the client's tongue and ask the client to close his or her mouth, being careful not to bite down on the thermometer.
3. Leave in place for 3 minutes, or according to instructions.
4. Remove the thermometer after the correct time and wipe the end with a tissue.
5. Hold the thermometer at eye level, read immediately, and record.
6. Wash thermometer according to instructions.

TABLE 18-3	Types of Thermometers
Type	**Characteristics**
Glass Mercury Thermometer	• takes 3 minutes to work • is breakable • comes in oral and rectal types (rectal has a coloured end) • can be difficult to read for some people • at home, is cleansed in cold water, wiped with alcohol and stored in a clean container
Electronic Thermometer	• gives the temperature reading in a few seconds • is a probe that is attached to a portable machine • provides a digital reading in Celsius or Fahrenheit • has a sound or light to indicate reading done • has disposable plastic covers for each client • usually used in outer ear (tympanic) • may need regular maintenance to stay accurate
Chemical Probe Thermometer	• disposable, single-use device • series of dots change colour as temperature increases

EQUIPMENT

clean glass thermometer

petroleum jelly

gloves

tissues

Procedure 18-20: Taking a Rectal Temperature Using a Glass Thermometer

1. Take a clean glass thermometer and shake the mercury down until it is at the bottom of the scale on the thermometer. It may take several shakes to get it down. Be careful not to shake where you may hit something.
2. Lubricate the end of the thermometer with petroleum jelly for easier insertion.
3. Put on gloves.
4. Assist the client into a side-lying position.
5. Explain the procedure to the client.
6. Lower the pajamas and arrange the bed linens so the buttocks only are exposed.
7. For an infant, grasp both legs and raise up to expose the anus.
8. Place the tip of the thermometer to the anus and tell the client to take a deep breath.

9. Insert the thermometer gently into the anus, pointing it towards the client's umbilicus and sliding it along the rectal wall. Insert about 5-7.5 centimetres (about 2-3 inches) for adults and 1 centimetre (about 1/2 inch) for infants.
10. Hold it in place for 3 minutes or according to agency policy. **Never let go of the thermometer when it is in the anus.**
11. Remove the thermometer after the time limit and wipe from fingers to bulb with a tissue.
12. Read the thermometer.
13. Remove any extra lubricant from the client's anus and reposition his/her pajamas.
14. Record the temperature promptly.
15. Wash the thermometer as in instructions.

Procedure 18-21: Taking an Axillary Temperature Using a Glass Thermometer

EQUIPMENT

clean glass thermometer

towel

1. Take a clean glass thermometer and shake the mercury down until it is at the bottom of the scale on the thermometer. It may take several shakes to get it down. Be careful not to shake where you may hit something.
2. Position the client laying on the back or sitting up. If using this method for an infant, hold the infant on your lap.
3. Remove the client's clothing on the arm so it is easy to access the axilla.
4. Raise the client's arm and dry with a towel.
5. Place the bulb into the centre of the axilla.
6. Lower the client's arm and hold in place for 5 minutes or according to instructions.
7. Remove the thermometer.
8. Read and record.
9. Clean the thermometer according to instructions.

Procedure 18-22: Taking a Tympanic, Oral, Rectal, or Axillary Temperature Using an Electronic Thermometer

EQUIPMENT

electronic thermometer

probe covers

The electronic thermometer is most often used to take a tympanic temperature (in the outer ear). They are most often found in long-term care facilities, but some versions are becoming more common in clients' homes. In some facilities, electronic thermometers may be used for all types of temperature-taking. Be sure to know the policy for your agency. Photo 18-12 shows a typical electronic thermometer.

1. Take the probe handle out of the portable device.
2. Place a probe cover over the end.
3. Remove the hair from around the client's ear if it is in the way.

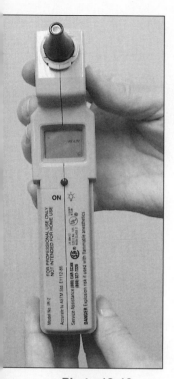

Photo 18-12
Electronic thermometer.

Source: Maple Health Centre.

4. Place the probe in the outer ear, making sure the probe is in contact with the skin.
5. Hold in place until the signal alerts that the temperature has been taken (usually 3 seconds or less).
6. Check the digital display.
7. Remove the probe from the ear and press the release button to allow the probe cover to be discharged.
8. Discard the probe cover.
9. Reconnect the probe to the portable device.
10. Record the temperature immediately.

Keep in mind that electronic thermometers can fail. If the reading is at all in doubt, repeat and, if still concerned, report and have thermometer checked. Be careful not to drop the device and store it carefully.

Pulse

Every time the heart beats, it is actually pushing a volume of blood through the rest of the heart and into the body. This is called a **pulse**. The pulse is indicative of metabolic conditions, the state of emotions, physiological responses to stress, exercise, blood loss, and other general conditions.

Health care workers can actually feel this push by feeling the pulse of the client. To feel a pulse, you must push an artery against a bone and feel with your fingertips the pulsing sensation. Each time a pulse is taken, it has a rate, a rhythm, and a quality all of which can be measured.

The rate is the number of times the heart beats in one minute. The normal rates are:

      Newborn infant — 120 to 140/min
      Child   — 100/min
      Adult   — 60 to 100/min

There are many factors determining the rate of the pulse. Each individual has a rate that is normal for him or her. A higher or lower than normal rate for the client should be reported.

The rhythm of the pulse tells us about the electrical impulses that stimulate the heart muscle to contract. Normally, the rhythm of the pulse is regular. A pulse that has an irregular beat or multiple beats and then long intervals in between may indicate a problem with the electrical system in the heart and should be reported.

The quality of the pulse is measured in how the pulse feels. A weak, thready pulse would indicate that there is a problem with the volume of blood being pumped. A bounding pulse could indicate such things as strenuous exercise, anger, or infection.

Where to Take a Pulse

There are several sites to take a pulse, but you are most likely to take the radial pulse. This pulse is the most common of all the areas and relatively easy to obtain. It is found on the inner aspect of the wrist on the radial bone below the base of the thumb.

Procedure 18-23: Taking a Pulse

1. Wash hands.
2. Explain to the client the procedure.
3. Place the first two fingers of your dominant hand on the client's radial artery.
4. Locate the pulsing artery.
5. Feel the sensations for a few seconds, noting the rhythm and quality.
6. Count the rate of the pulse by watching the watch for 60 seconds.
7. Once you get comfortable with the procedure, you may count the pulse for 15 seconds and multiply by 4, or 30 seconds and multiply by 2. **However, if there is any concern about the rate, rhythm, or quality of the client's pulse, always count for 60 seconds to be accurate.**
8. Record your findings immediately.
9. If you have any concerns about your findings, report them to the appropriate person.

EQUIPMENT

A watch with a second hand. The face of the watch must include all the numbers to make it easier to count the rate of the pulse.

 ## Stop and Reflect 18-3

Find your own pulse. How would you describe its rate, rhythm, and quality?

_____

_____

_____

Respiration

Respiration is a complex cycle that results in the delivery of oxygen to the cells by inspiration and the return of carbon dioxide to the air by expiration. A breath or respiration is made up of one inspiration and one expiration.

Normally, one breathes quietly and without effort. This can change with exercise, ambient temperature, metabolic changes, and disease. Respiration is monitored for rate, depth, pattern, and quality.

Rate of Respiration

Rate is the number of breaths or respirations the client makes in one minute. The usual adult rate is 14 to 18 respirations per minute. An infant's normal rate is 35 respirations per minute. A particular client's normal rate may vary somewhat. You should be familiar with the client's normal rate.

Infections, stress, and exertion can alter this rate. For instance, a person with a mild chest infection may have 22 respirations per minute but a person with severe pneumonia may have more than 40 respirations per minute. Some medications can actually depress the rate of respirations. It's important to have a measurement of the client's normal rates to be able to compare when the client is not well.

Depth of Respiration

To observe the depth of respirations, watch the client's chest. Normally, the chest moves slightly. If the chest barely moves at all, the respirations are called *shallow*. If the chest moves significantly, these respirations are called *deep*.

Pattern of Respiration

By watching respirations over a minute, you will notice that the rhythm and rate likely form a pattern. There are specific patterns that can occur, as follows:

hypoventilation	decrease in rate and depth
hyperventilation	increase in rate and depth
apnea	complete absence of respiration
Kussmaul's	increase in rate and depth with audible sighs or gasps
Cheyne-Stokes	a repeating cycle found in terminally ill clients where there is decreasing rate and depth followed by a period of apnea

Quality of Respirations

The quality of respirations is determined both by the client and the worker. How much effort is required by the client to breathe and the sounds made while breathing make up the quality. Increased movement of the chest with conscious effort by the client is called *laboured* breathing. A client who complains that he can't get his or her breath is having *dyspnea*. A person who has to sit in an upright position to breathe is having *orthopnea*.

There are several sounds that can be readily identified. *Stridor* is a high-pitched crowing sound during inspiration, usually occurring when there is an upper airway obstruction. A *wheeze* is a high-pitched whistling sound that occurs when the airways are partially obstructed, as in asthma.

EQUIPMENT

A watch with a second hand.

Procedure 18-24: Measuring Respirations

1. Hold the client's wrist over his/her chest and pretend to take the client's pulse.
2. Observe the rise and fall of the client's chest, making note of the depth, pattern, and quality.
3. Count the number of breaths in 30 seconds. Count for a full minute if there is concern as to the pattern. Never tell the client you are counting the respirations, as he/she could consciously alter the rate.
4. Record data immediately.
5. Always take the temperature, pulse, and respirations at the same time. Often the results are relative to each other and are more significant when reported together.

Measuring Blood Pressure

You may be asked to measure and record your client's blood pressure. This reading tells how much pressure is exerted on vessel walls when the heart is pumping blood (beating) and when it is resting (between beats). The most common way to take a blood pressure is to use a manual sphygmomanometer with a pressure cuff and a manometer. Photo 18-13 shows a common type of pressure cuff and manometer. Clients with hypertension may have a blood pressure machine in their home to monitor pressure.

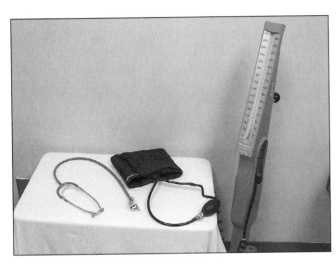

Photo 18-13
BP cuff and manometer.
Source: Maple Health Centre.

Blood pressure is usually measured at the brachial artery, in the client's upper arm. The cuff is placed on the client's upper arm and is manually inflated by the bulb pump to compress the brachial artery. A stethoscope is placed on the brachial artery. The air in the cuff is then slowly let out. As the pressure is decreased, the examiner can hear sounds through the stethoscope.

The pressure against the vessel wall when the heart is pumping is called the *systolic pressure*. The pressure against the vessel wall when the heart is between beats is the *diastolic pressure*. Blood pressure is recorded in the systolic measure over the diastolic measure. When written, the figures are separated by a forward slash. For example, a pressure of 110 systolic and 80 diastolic would be written as 110/80.

The average blood pressure for a normal adult ranges from 120/80 to 140/90. Any reading above the upper limit should be considered high and should be reported immediately. The person may require tests for hypertension (high blood pressure). Blood pressure can change throughout the day. It is often lower in the morning. As well, blood pressure changes as stress levels change throughout the day. When measuring blood pressure, it is important to take several readings over a specified period of time to indicate the person's normal reading and changes in a trend.

Some people live with a very low blood pressure such as 90/60. A lower than average pressure that is normal for the person is not a problem. However, anyone whose blood pressure is constantly falling from his or her normal over a period of a few hours could be considered hypotensive and may be considered at risk for shock and other conditions.

Measuring a client's blood pressure can be extremely difficult. An incorrect reading can put the client in jeopardy. You must be taught the procedure by a person familiar with measuring that client's blood pressure.

Measuring and Recording Intake and Output

It is often important to know what the client is eating and drinking, as well as how much of this material is being eliminated. You may be asked to measure and record client intake and output because your client has (or may have) a kidney problem or a digestive problem. Sometimes a client's fluid balance is critical to maintain health. For example, having too much fluid could be hard on the heart of someone with congestive heart failure. Conversely, having too little fluid could cause dehydration in a child with the flu.

Items that must be measured when the client drinks or eats them include:

- All fluids including milk, juice, coffee, tea, pop, water;
- All thick fluids such as gelatin, porridge, cream of wheat, ice cream, milkshakes; and
- All intravenous fluids.

The following types of output must be measured: urine, liquid stool, emesis or vomit, and liquid draining from a wound.

Each agency or facility has a special form to use for each client on a daily basis. You must be familiar with the form and what each agency uses for measurement. Many long-term care facilities have standard measurements for foods and liquids based upon the serving size each uses. Figure 18-19 illustrates a sample intake and output recording form. If you are measuring intake and output in the client's home, you must be careful to use clearly marked measuring cups for intake. Often, output is measured with a container provided specially for that purpose. A "hat" is a container used for collecting urinary output.

Intake and output is usually recorded for a period of a few days for adults. Infants are monitored hourly, as they can quickly become dehydrated. The health professional requesting the measurement will observe the daily pattern over the period to detect a trend.

In a healthy person, intake usually equals output. If this balance changes, a client can quickly become ill. It is **very important that the worker be accurate and consistent in measuring the client's intake and output, so that correct information is provided.**

LIONS GATE
H O S P I T A L

FLUID BALANCE /
IV THERAPY RECORD

INTAKE ☐   **OUTPUT** ☐

DATE: From 07:00 _____ to 07:00 _____

		INTAKE								OUTPUT								
		INTRAVENOUS						ORAL			URINE			OTHER FLUID LOSS				
														GASRIC			TUBE (Specify)	
START TIME	STOP TIME	SOLUTION VOLUME	RATE	INITIAL	TOTAL IV IN	TOTAL BLOOD IN	TIME	ORAL	TUBE	TIME	VOID	CATH.	EMESIS	N/G	BOWEL		
SUBTOTALS																	

12-H TOTAL:	IN:									OUT:							

START TIME	STOP TIME	SOLUTION VOLUME	RATE	INITIAL	TOTAL IV IN	TOTAL BLOOD IN	TIME	ORAL	TUBE	TIME	VOID	CATH.	EMESIS	N/G	BOWEL		
SUBTOTALS																	

12-H TOTAL:	IN:					OUT:		
24-H TOTAL:	IN:		OUT:		24-H BALANCE + or –			

A601 10M-S-T5
Rev. (03/91)

Figure 18-19   *Sample Intake and Output Recording Form*

Measuring Client Height and Weight

It's often important to measure the client's height and weight. As children are growing, these measurements are an indicator of growth and development. In adults, weight gain or loss are often associated with disease or illness and are indicators of the client's general well-being. For example, a client who has lost a lot of weight and is scheduled for serious surgery may not recover as well as someone who has maintained his or her normal weight. Also, a change in height in adults may indicate a problem in the spine. You must be able to accurately measure your client's height and weight.

Measuring Your Client's Weight

The equipment you use to weigh your client is usually determined by where he or she lives. Long-term care facilities have different types of scales, as Photo 18-14 illustrates.

Many different types of scales are used by clients living in the community. Make sure that the scale you are using weighs properly. Use an item of known weight (such as a 2 kilogram bag of sugar) to check the accuracy of the scale. If the scale does not seem to weigh properly, contact your supervisor.

Each time, before you weigh your client, check the scale to be sure it is balanced. If required, adjust according to the manufacturer's instructions. **Most scales measure in both kilograms and pounds. Be sure to always use the same measurement.** As well, always compare the weight you recorded with the previous two or three weights. If there is any discrepancy, reweigh the client or have the scales checked.

Photo 18-14   *Scales commonly used in long-term care facilities.*
Source: Maple Health Centre.

Procedure 18-25: Weighing Children and Adults

EQUIPMENT

scale

1. Weigh the client at the same time every day. Make sure that the weight time is recorded in the support plan, so that other workers involved will weigh the client at the same time.
2. Ask the client to wear the same type of clothes each time (such as pajamas or a gown) to make the weight more accurate. Remember that shoes can add over 0.5 kg to a client's weight. If the client is weighed wearing shoes one day and is weighed in stocking feet the next, the recorded weight will not be a true reflection of the client's weight.
3. Follow the instructions for using the particular scale. No matter the type of scale, assist the client to stand on the centre of the scale, or wheel the client's chair to the centre of the scale.
4. Read the client's weight.
5. Assist the client off the scale.
6. Record the client's weight.

Procedure 18-26: Weighing Infants

EQUIPMENT

scale

1. Undress the infant and weigh prior to a feeding.
2. Hold the infant steady with one hand while reading the scale. Never take your hand off of the infant, but take care to not alter the scale's weight.
3. Remove the infant.
4. Record the weight.

Procedure 18-27: Measuring Height

EQUIPMENT

scale with
height bar

1. Ask the client to remove shoes or slippers. Assist the client as required.
2. Raise the bar on the scale to well above the client's head (Photo 18-15).
3. Have the client stand straight on the scale platform and lower the bar so that it just touches the client's head.
4. Note the measurement.
5. Raise the head bar and assist the client off of the scale.
6. Lower the head bar back to its original position.
7. Record the measurement in inches or centimetres, depending on the agency policy.

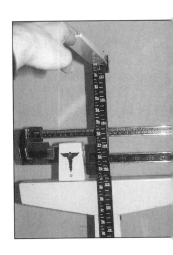

Photo 18-15 *Height bar on stand-on scale.*
Source: Maple Health Centre.

Questions for Review

1. What are the purposes of personal care?

2. Describe RIDICUPS and explain each component.

3. How does age affect a person's skin? What precautions should you take when caring for the skin of an older client?

4. Why is it good to give a back rub? How can you give a simple back rub?

5. What are the stages of a pressure sore?

6. How can you help prevent pressure sores?

Questions for Discussion

1. How do you think you might feel if you required someone's help to have a bath? If you bathed each other as part of a skill lab, recall how you felt. How would you feel if the person bathing you was of the opposite sex? What could the support worker do to make the procedure a positive experience for you?

2. You are assisting a client with morning care. The client complains that her toenails are too long and catch on her stockings. She asks you to cut them for her. What do you do?

3. Apply RIDICUPS to how you would prefer to be assisted with a bath. Compare your answers to those of your colleagues. In what ways are you similar? In what ways are you different?

CHAPTER NINETEEN

Common Impairments

Learning Objectives

Through reading this chapter, you'll be able to:

1. Define *functional impairment* and relate it to the concept of disability described in Chapter 13.
2. List the four common ways in which function can be impaired.
3. Discuss the role of the support worker in assisting the client to address common impairments.
4. Explain the eight questions that are useful to ask when observing how a client performs tasks.
5. Describe basic approaches that are useful in assisting the client with any common impairments.
6. Discuss in general terms the causes of common impairments, the body system each affects, the most frequent functional impairment each can create, and any specific techniques used to assist clients with the functional impairment.

Chapter At A Glance

Functional Impairment and Disability

Assisting the Client to Minimize the Effects of Impairments

Approaches Common to Any Assistance

Common Impairments

Terms You'll Use

Acquired Immune Deficiency Syndrome   A condition caused by the HIV virus in which the person experiences opportunistic diseases.

Arthritis   A condition that causes pain, stiffness, and sometimes swelling in or around joints. It can affect other tissues.

Cancer   A disease in which cells grow abnormally and out of control.

Cerebral Palsy   A condition that results from an anomaly or injury to the brain as it develops.

Chronic Obstructive Pulmonary Disease   A group of irreversible lung diseases.

Diabetes   A disease resulting from the pancreas' inability to produce enough insulin or to properly use the insulin that is produced.

Functional Impairment   The way in which a particular condition affects a client.

Hemiplegia   Partial or total paralysis of one side of the body.

Human Immunodeficiency Virus   The virus that causes AIDS.

Huntington's Disease   An inherited neurological disease.

Multiple Sclerosis   A central nervous system disease caused by the inflammation
and scarring of the myelin sheath that protects nerve fibres.

Muscular Dystrophy   A condition that causes muscle tissue to degenerate and be
replaced by fatty and connective tissue.

Osteoporosis A condition that causes bones to become less dense, brittle, and weak.

Parkinson's Disease   A neurological disorder that affects the ability to initiate
movement.

Post-Polio Syndrome   A condition that can occur in people who have had polio;
causes further weakening of the muscles injured by the virus.

Spinal Cord Injury   A condition caused by damage to the spinal cord, usually as
a result of injury to vertebrae.

Tuberculosis   A bacterial disease affecting the lungs.

Functional Impairment and Disability

Functional impairment refers to the way in which a particular condition affects a
client. This term means the same as the term *disability* we discussed in Chapter 13. The
phrase functional impairment is frequently used in health care and rehabilitation settings. It's useful for you to know this term.

As you'll recall, the disability or functional impairment a particular client experiences is directly related to the effects of the impairment (such as diminished endurance) and the extent to which the client's lifestyle is altered by those effects. Thus,
the functional impairment arising from the same cause will vary from client to client.

It's also important to keep in mind that many impairments can cause the same or
similar disability. For example, diminished endurance (tiring easily) can be the result
of a stroke, *multiple sclerosis*, *cancer*, or a heart condition. How you might assist the person will also be quite similar, despite the differences in the impairment that produced
the disability.

In this text, we'll group common impairments into four general categories. These
are: mobility impairments, fine motor skill impairments, endurance impairments, and

cognitive impairments. This chapter will discuss the effects of the first three categories. Cognitive impairment will be discussed in Chapter 22.

Mobility impairments include the vast number of movements that allow us to move from one place to another. Many things can cause mobility impairments: fractures, nerve or spinal cord damage, amputations, as well as neurological conditions.

Fine motor skills include the ability to use our hands and other body parts for fine movement. Examples include the ability to hold a pen or to turn a page. A person's ability to do this may be impaired by arthritis, polio, a stroke, or **spinal cord injury**, among other conditions.

Endurance describes the ability to maintain an activity over a period of time. As described above, many impairments can affect a client's endurance.

Consider the Whole Person

An impairment is not the only thing that can affect the client's ability to function. Consider Case Examples 19-1 and 19-2.

CASE EXAMPLE 19-1

Gareth Winter is a retired stockbroker. In years past, he was an avid photographer. His photos have twice won national awards and he spent many years travelling the world to take pictures.

Two years ago, he had a stroke. Although he has recovered a great deal of function, he is not able to take pictures as easily as he once did. His anguish at the change in his ability is obvious to anyone who works with him. As a result of the stroke, he no longer wants anything to do with photography. He does not like to have photographs around him, and has replaced all photos in his home with paintings. Even his daughter's portrait is a pastel drawing. He tells you that part of his joy in living was lost when he gave up photography.

CASE EXAMPLE 19-2

Meg McBride is a retired textile artist. In her 45-year career, she helped to design patterns for carpets and upholstery fabrics. She often designed patterns by working them out in petit-point (a very fine form of needle point).

Two years ago, she had a stroke much like the one Gareth Winter had. As a result, she has some difficulty holding and manipulating small objects and has begun doing needlework on a much larger canvas so that she can see the stitches and easily handle the needle. "At least I can still make beautiful designs," she tells you.

Notice how the same impairment affects the two people differently. In these cases, one person has adapted a previous activity to accommodate impairment and, as a result, experiences little disability. The other is not able to adapt (although it would be physically possible to do so) and, as a result, has experienced greater disability.

There are many things that can influence how (or if) a person experiences disability as the result of an impairment. Psychological response, the availability of resources to help overcome the effects of the impairment (such as the ability to remodel one's home to be accessible to a person using a wheelchair), the number of people the person has who provide support, as well as the number of changes and other impairments the client is experiencing can all influence the client's experience.

A person's psychological response to an impairment can help to determine the degree of disability experienced. This does not mean that a "good" attitude will enable a person to overcome the effects of any impairment. It simply means that the significance a person attaches to the impairment can affect the degree of disability the person experiences.

Remember that psychological responses can be very difficult to change, even if the person wants to change his or her response. It is extremely important to accept the client as he or she is, even if you feel that the client could see the impairment differently.

Assisting the Client to Minimize the Effects of Impairments

As a support worker, you will be called upon to assist the client to perform many routine functions. To do so effectively, you must know the client's priorities, his or her preferred methods of assistance, and appreciate how the client does the things he or she needs to do. As we discussed in Chapter 6, you may find that your client prefers that you do things that he or she is able to do. Your client has valid reasons for these preferences. You should not refuse to perform these tasks (unless your agency does not permit you to do them) or make the client feel bad that he or she does not do them.

There are eight questions you should always ask yourself when you are assisting a client. (Questions based upon the work of Jitka Zigola, *Doing Things*, 1988.)

1. WHAT tasks does the client see as *important* to do?
2. WHAT does the client *enjoy* doing?
3. WHAT is the client *able* to do?
4. HOW does the client do those things?
5. WHEN is it *easiest* for the client to perform the task?
6. WHICH parts of a task is the client *unable* to do?
7. WHY is the client unable to do those parts?
8. HOW does the client want *you* to assist?

Approaches Common to Any Assistance

Because many conditions result in similar impairments, there are some approaches that are often useful, regardless of the impairment.

1. **Talk with your client.** Communication is essential to any approach that you take. Approaches 2 to 7 provide specific examples of ways in which you can communicate.
2. **Take the time to learn the client's needs, preferences, and methods of doing things.** Use the eight questions listed in the previous section to help answer these questions.

3. **Follow the client's cues for pacing any task you do, or that you assist the client to do.**   Keep in mind that your client may find it difficult if you do tasks in too much of a hurry. Make sure that your body language does not indicate that you are impatient with your client's pace.

4. **Allow time for rest.**   Alternate activity and rest as the client's needs require. This is particularly necessary when the client is practising a task for the first time, when you are helping the client for the first time, or when the client is not feeling well.

5. **Break down the task into clear steps, based upon what the client can do.** This helps the client accomplish the portions of the task of which they are able.

6. **Take the time to learn how the client does things.**   Your client has had a great deal of experience in adapting to the effects of his or her impairment. You can often learn many good techniques this way.

7. **When you are assisting the client, plan the task with them.**   If possible, plan the tasks in a way that establishes a routine.

8. **Recognize that your client will have good days and bad days.**   Adapt your approach to your client's level of ability and interest.

9. **When possible, make use of labour-saving techniques.**   For example, place a sheet of waxed paper under mixing bowls to catch spills. Place newspapers under the vacuum when you change the bag. If your client permits, try using a cooking spray to make pots and pans easier to clean. Minimizing cleanup may encourage your client to do things he or she enjoys.

10. **Relax and encourage your client to do the same.**   Any task is easier when you can relax and even laugh a little.

11. **Work with the client.**   You are partners in getting the tasks done.

12. **The client's diagnosis is not as important as his or her functional ability.** Worry less about the medical diagnosis. Focus on the client's ability and where he or she needs help.

13. **Remember that an impairment is not necessarily an illness.**   There is a difference between having a physical impairment and having an illness (such as the flu). Your client will not appreciate being referred to as ill or sick if, in fact, he or she has a disability that is not caused by an illness.

14. **Not all tasks are an opportunity for rehabilitation.**   Respect your client's wishes for how—and how often—he or she practises tasks to develop a skill.

15. **Use available adaptive aids to make a task easier.**   Many clients have identified aids that assist them. Use these as the client wishes. If your client has a need for a particular adaptive aid, speak with your supervisor.

Common Impairments

This section covers many common diseases and other conditions. Each section briefly describes the process of the impairment, any known causes, and any hints specific to the impairment that may make proving support easier.

Please be aware that a client with a particular impairment will have had considerable advice from doctors, therapists, and other persons knowledgeable about the impairment. Many clients have done considerable research on their impairment and are quite knowledgeable. As well, each client will experience the impairment differently. Remember that your client is the expert in how he or she is affected by the impairment.

Cancer

Cancer is the term used to describe the abnormal and out-of-control growth of cells. A mass of these abnormal cells is called a *tumour*. We call a cancerous tumour a *malignant tumour*. Malignant tumours not only grow in size (as a result of the cell growth), but they can invade and damage healthy tissue. When a tumour spreads to other parts of the body, we say that it has *metastasized*.

There are over 100 different types of cancer. Most affect specific parts of the body. Some risk factors contribute more to one type of cancer than to another. For example, exposure to the sun increases one's risk of skin cancer. Smoking increases the risk of lung cancer; chewing tobacco increases the risk of mouth cancer. It's estimated that 5-10 percent of cancers are the result of inherited traits.

Over 125 000 cases of cancer are diagnosed each year in Canada (Canadian Cancer Society statistics). The Canadian Cancer Society estimates that 60-70 percent of cancers could be prevented if people adopted healthier lifestyles. Three behaviours are seen as significantly increasing a person's risk of cancer: smoking, a high-fat, low-fibre diet, and exposure to the sun.

Today, most cancers can be treated. Although treatment may not cure the cancer, it may lead to a longer and better quality of life for the person with the disease.

Early detection plays an important role in cancer treatment. In general, the earlier a cancer is detected and treated, the greater the person's chances of surviving the disease.

 Stop and Reflect 19-1

At the turn of the century, untanned skin was considered chic. Perhaps we should adopt that notion today!

Supporting the Person with Cancer

Because of the variety of cancers, it's important to keep in mind that each will have its own treatment plan. What is appropriate for one person is not necessarily appropriate for another.

You must also keep in mind that the person's level of ability may change in response to the effects of treatment as well as to changes in the person's condition. Chemotherapy and radiation therapy (two common forms of cancer treatment) can have significant side effects that will alter the person's ability. Some treatments (such as chemotherapy) may make the person more susceptible to infections. You must be careful to prevent transmitting infections to your client.

Be prepared to make the most of the client's "good" days. This may mean changing your schedule of tasks to do something that the client enjoys, even though the task would usually be done on another day.

Having cancer can be a frightening experience. Many people equate cancer with death, even if the particular type of cancer is treatable with a good chance for recovery. Your client may feel frightened or be angry. He or she may want to talk about the fears and other feelings. It is important to listen and to offer support. Your client may turn to you for advice. If this happens, offer your support for the decision the client makes, but do not offer advice as to what to do. Encourage your client to discuss these feelings with the doctor, health professional, or family.

Cancer treatments can cause physical changes that can be distressing to the client. Chemotherapy can cause hair loss. Radiation can alter appearance. Surgery can dramatically alter appearance. Your client may need special support and encouragement to cope with these changes in body image. Hairpieces, scarves, or other coverings may be used to mask hair loss. Cosmetics may be used to mask skin discolouration. Your client may use a prosthesis. Be aware that physical appearance is important to your client—assist him or her to look attractive.

Some clients will not acknowledge the diagnosis. Others will deny that they have the disease. Always respect your client's wishes. Do not force the client to discuss the disease if he or she does not want to.

Pain control is often an important component of support. While not all people with cancer experience pain, many do. Your client may use medications to control pain. He or she may also use nonmedicinal methods such as relaxation, distraction, or mental imagery to control pain. Some clients may benefit from massage.

CASE EXAMPLE 19-3

Mrs. Matthews is a 75-year-old resident of a retirement home. She was diagnosed with breast cancer six months ago. She has had a mastectomy (a removal of the breast) and is currently receiving chemotherapy.

Kara is one of Mrs. Matthews' support workers. She knows that Mrs. Matthews' immune system is weakened by the chemotherapy. She is particularly cautious to practise good infection control to avoid any transmission of germs that could harm Mrs. Matthews.

Mrs. Matthews often experiences some nausea after chemotherapy. Even so, her mouth becomes dry. Kara knows that sucking on ice chips moistens Mrs. Matthews' mouth without making her become more nauseous. She makes sure that Mrs. Matthews has a good supply of ice chips.

Mrs. Matthews' hair has thinned as a result of the treatment. As a result, she prefers to wear a wig when going out. Kara helps her to don the wig and to style it.

Stroke

It is very likely that you will work with a client who has had a stroke. The Heart and Stroke Foundation of Canada estimates that each year over 40 000 Canadians experience a stroke. A *stroke* (also called a *cerebral vascular accident* or CVA) is caused by an interruption of blood flow to the brain. This interruption causes death to the nerve cells nourished by the affected vessel. It is considered to be a cardiovascular problem because the impairment is caused by damage or disease of the blood vessels.

There are three main categories of causes: a blood clot in a blood vessel in the brain, hemorrhage (a burst or leaking blood vessel in the brain), or contusions (somewhat like a bruise in the brain). Two cardiovascular conditions contribute to many strokes: arteriosclerosis and atherosclerosis. Arteriosclerosis is a loss of thickening and loss of elasticity in vessel walls which narrows the vessel. Atherosclerosis is the buildup of plaque and other deposits on the inside of the blood vessel. Either condition can make it easy for matter to block the flow of blood in a vessel, causing the cells the vessel nourishes to die.

The effect a stroke has on a client will vary by the location and size of the stroke. Some strokes affect an area so small that the client may not even know that it has occurred. Others can cause significant changes in the person's ability or even death.

A stroke usually affects the structures in either the left or right hemisphere of the client's brain. Because the right hemisphere controls the body's left side and the left hemisphere controls the body's right side, physical effects are usually seen on the side of the body *opposite* the damaged hemisphere.

Many functions are controlled by a specific part of one hemisphere. For example, the ability to use language is usually found in the left side of the brain only. Table 19-1 illustrates the hemisphere of some common functions.

TABLE 19-1	Hemisphere Controlling Some Common Functions
Left Hemisphere	**Right Hemisphere**
▪ Language ▪ Difficulty controlling skilled movements, such as the ability to button a blouse, even though the body may be capable of making those movements ▪ Partial or total paralysis of the right side of the body (**hemiplegia**) ▪ Loss of sensation on the right side of the body	▪ Spatial-perceptual problems, such as an inability to identify objects, to distinguish an object from the background on which it sits, to judge distance, or to judge shapes ▪ Partial or total paralysis of the left side of the body (**hemiplegia**) ▪ Loss of sensation on the left side of the body ▪ Diminished or no awareness of the left side of the body, of the left side of the person's vision. This is called lateral neglect or left-sided neglect.

The location of the stroke may also affect the client's pattern of behaviour. The client with damage to the left hemisphere may become very cautious. The client with damage to the right hemisphere may become impulsive.

Many persons who have had a stroke experience some level of sadness or depression. Others may find that they cry easily, or experience strong emotions in response to everyday events, or experience rapid mood swings (such as being elated one moment and despondent the next). Researchers differ on the degree to which these emotional states are a result of a stroke or caused by the number of changes that the person has experienced as a result of the stroke. No matter the cause, it is important to be empathetic. Your client is not able to control the flow of emotions and needs your support.

Phases of Stroke Recovery

There are two general phases of stroke recovery. The first happens in the weeks and months after the stroke and can be fairly rapid. The second phase continues throughout the person's life. Although recovery in the second phase is usually much slower than in the first, recovery does continue to happen. For example, while 50 percent of persons who have had a stroke are incontinent (unable to control bowel or bladder function) in the first year after the stroke, only 14-23 percent remain so after the first year (*Heart and Stroke Foundation of Canada, 1999*). You should never assume that a client will not recover ability.

There are two aspects to recovery. The first aspect is to deal with the impairments (including perceptual problems) posed by the stroke. The second aspect is to make the psychological and social adjustment to the disability that the impairment creates. It's generally accepted that the psychological and social adjustment is more difficult for most clients.

Supporting the Person Who Has Had a Stroke

How you assist the client will depend upon the impairment the client has. It's very important to learn what disability the client experiences and what assistance is helpful to the client. Make sure that you follow the general approaches listed earlier in this chapter.

Here are some techniques useful in assisting the client who has had a stroke.

1. **The client may take a great deal of time to do tasks.**   This is particularly true of clients who are attempting a complex task or one that is new to them. Make sure you allow time for what the client is to do.
2. **Be aware that a client who is somewhat impulsive as the result of a stroke may appear very self-assured, even if he or she is not.**   Get to know what your client's behaviour signifies.
3. **If the client has hemiplegia, assist the client to dress the affected side first.**   For example, assist the client to put the *affected* arm in a sleeve first.
4. **Remember that language or perceptual problems are not dementia.**   The client will not necessarily have problems understanding, problem-solving, or sequencing tasks. Do not assume that the client is confused.
5. **A person with lateral neglect will not see items to their left, or even the left side of things.**   For example, your client may complain that his or her dinner plate is cleared when in fact only the right side of a plate is clean. Try turning the plate so that the remaining food is on the right. Similarly, placing often used items to the right of the client will help him or her to find them.
6. **If your client has a language problem, learn how to adapt your technique so as to be able to communicate effectively.**   Often, the client will share with you the techniques he or she has found useful. You may also find some useful hints in the guidelines for working with clients with aphasia discussed in Chapter 9.

Heart Disease

Like stroke, heart disease is a cardiovascular disease. Heart disease can result in a heart attack (also called a *cardiac arrest* or a *myocardial infarction*) or in chronic problems that can limit a person's activities.

A heart attack is a sudden condition that can result in death if not treated immediately. The Heart and Stroke Foundation of Canada estimates that 23 000 Canadians die of a heart attack each year, and that half of these people die before they reach hospital.

Heart disease can result in impairments that are not immediately life-threatening, but that can significantly limit the activity of the person. Sometimes, a person who has had a heart attack does not fully recover and must adjust to limitations imposed by his or her condition. Often, this means making lifestyle changes (such as stopping smoking or eating a low-fat diet) as well as reducing activity and stress to reduce strain on the heart.

Some people with heart disease also experience problems with circulation. This condition is called *peripheral vascular disease*. This condition can be very painful. As well, the person may be at increased risk for infection.

As with stroke, the leading causes of heart disease are arteriosclerosis and atherosclerosis. In the case of heart disease, the narrowing of the vessels makes the heart work harder and, over time, will weaken the heart. Try the exercise listed in Stop and Reflect 19-2 to get an idea of the effect of the narrowing of the vessels.

 Stop and Reflect 19-2

You can get an idea of how much harder your heart has to work to pump blood through narrowed blood vessels by trying this experiment.

Make a loose fist with your hand. Leave an opening about the size of a dime, as shown in Figure 1. Place your lips against the opening and blow.

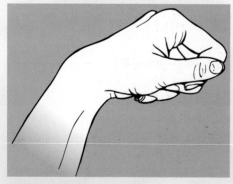

Figure 1

Now, make a tight fist, with your fingers curled so that they touch your palm. Try again to blow through the opening.

You likely found it much harder to blow through the closed fist. You probably had to blow very hard to get any air through at all.

Supporting the Person Who Has Heart Disease

Be aware that the person with a heart condition may not always look ill or disabled. A person with heart disease can be anxious about his or her condition. The person may fear being left alone in case he or she has a heart attack and there is no one there to help. A person who has survived a heart attack may feel particularly vulnerable. You may need to reassure the person that you are there.

It's important to identify your client's limits with regard to the type and duration of any activity. Realize that the person may tire quickly. Encourage the client to do what is comfortable for him or her. Help the client to pace his or her activities.

You should keep in mind that a client with a heart condition is at increased risk of a heart attack. It's important to know the warning signs of a heart attack so that you may provide help promptly. Common warning signs include:

- a sensation of heaviness or pressure in the chest area;
- shortness of breath;
- nausea and vomiting;
- sweating, cold, and clammy skin;
- acute and crushing chest pain;
- radiating pain (in the neck, arms, back, jaw);
- a feeling of fear and anxiety; and
- a denial of symptoms.

Arthritis

It's been said that if you live long enough, you'll likely develop some form of **arthritis**, a condition that causes inflammation of the joints or other tissues. The Arthritis Society estimates that 3.5 million Canadians have arthritis. The term arthritis actually includes over 100 different conditions. Table 19-2 illustrates some of the more common forms of arthritis.

TABLE 19-2	Common Forms of Arthritis	
Type	**Description**	**Common Treatment**
Osteoarthritis	The most common form of arthritis, osteoarthritis affects 2.7 million Canadians. It's often called *wear and tear* arthritis, but it is not caused by normal movement. Risk factors include injury, joint damage, excess weight, and heredity. It usually occurs in weight-bearing joints like the hips or knees, but can appear elsewhere. It is more common in older people, although people of almost any age can develop the condition.	Moderate activity usually helps this type of arthritis, as can the application of heat and cold. Proper positioning to reduce stress on joints. Many people benefit from the use of labour-saving devices like luggage carts, trolleys that can minimize the stress on affected joints. Medication is often used to control pain. ▶▶

TABLE 19-2	Common Forms of Arthritis *(continued)*	
Type	**Description**	**Common Treatment**
Fibromyalgia	Actually considered a *syndrome*, as the condition can present with a wide variety of symptoms. People with the syndrome experience widespread pain on both sides of the body. It may be difficult for the person to sleep, yet fatigue beyond that which could be accounted for by little sleep is also a symptom. Weakness, difficulty concentrating, and poor memory are also symptoms.	Exercise and physical therapy are beneficial. Pacing tasks, adapting to a slower pace, and balancing rest and activity are often of greatest benefit. Medication is often used to enable the client to sleep more soundly. Pain medication is not usually beneficial.
Lupus	Lupus refers to three types of conditions, of which Systemic Lupus Erythematosus is the most severe and most common. Lupus is an autoimmune disease. In this disease, the body's immune system malfunctions, and begins to attack the person's normal, healthy tissue. Many types of tissue can be attacked and become inflamed: the heart, lungs, joints, muscles, blood vessels, and the nervous system. Any one of any age can develop Lupus, but it is most common in women of childbearing age. Many people with Lupus experience "flare- ups" in which the effects of the condition are pronounced, mixed with periods of few or no symptoms. Exposure to the sun, excessive stress, and fatigue can all be triggers for these flare-ups.	Alteration of lifestyle to eliminate or reduce triggers. Medication can be useful in combatting many symptoms of the condition.
Rheumatoid Arthritis (RA)	Causes inflammation in the lining of the joints and, possibly, other internal organs. RA can affect people of any age, although it most often appears between the ages of 25 and 50 years. In children, the condition is now called *Childhood Arthritis*. Fatigue is often a result of RA. RA can have significant affects on the person's function.	Moderate exercise is often beneficial, but the optimal level of activity must be carefully determined. Low impact activities are best. Pacing tasks, avoiding repetitive movements, and using assistive devices like canes, and utensils with built-up handles, are all beneficial. Medication is useful in many cases.

Source: The Arthritis Society of Canada, 1999

Some degree of joint inflammation and pain are a part of all forms of arthritis. Figure 19-1 compares a normal joint to a joint affected by arthritis.

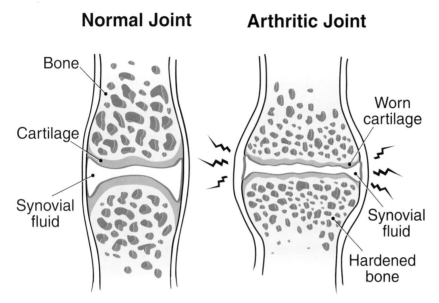

Figure 19-1 *Normal and Arthritic Joints*

Supporting the Person Who Has Arthritis

Arthritis encompasses many conditions, many of which have periods of acute (and often painful) symptoms. For this reason, it's important to take into account the client's level of ability each time you work with him or her. Helping the client to pace him or herself, to rest when required, and to enjoy good days are useful techniques.

CASE EXAMPLE 19-4

Mr. Gerard is 58 years old. He has had rheumatoid arthritis most of his adult life. As a result, he has lost some function in his arms, hips, knees, and hands.

Mr. Gerard's condition fluctuates. He often has long periods of time without significant pain. At these times, he is able to do almost all routine activities without problem. At other times, he experiences an exacerbation *(a flare-up of the disease) and can do very little for himself without pain.*

Julie, his support worker, knows that Mr. Gerard's condition can change from day to day. She is prepared to vary her tasks to best meet his level of ability.

Osteoporosis

The term **osteoporosis** literally means "porous bones" and causes bones to become brittle and weak. Although it can affect anyone, it is most common in women who have gone through menopause. In extreme cases, simple acts such as sneezing or rolling over in bed can break bones.

The condition occurs when bones lose calcium, something that happens as people age. The person's peak bone density is thought to occur around 20 years of age. If a person had low bone density as a young adult, he or she is more likely to develop osteoporosis as an older adult. This bone loss is often so slow and gradual that a diagnosis often is not made until the person has fractured a bone. Estrogen also plays a role in maintaining bone density in women.

Supporting the Person Who Has Osteoporosis

Assist the client by taking on the heavier or more demanding portions of a task, as the client will allow. Assist the client to assess and remove safety hazards that might cause the person to slip or fall. If within your tasks, keep walks and porches clear and free of ice in the winter (even if the client only goes outside to get the mail).

Post-Polio Syndrome

Post-Polio Syndrome is a condition that can occur in people who have had the poliomyelitis virus and results in a further weakening of the muscles initially injured by the virus. Post-Polio Syndrome can occur as many as 40 years after the original infection. Approximately 25 percent of the people who had the virus will develop it.

It's important to note that Post-Polio Syndrome is not a virus itself. It is not contagious. Although the exact mechanism is not known, it likely results from the way the body adapted nerve endings to recover from the virus. Common symptoms of the syndrome include joint pain, muscle pain, fatigue, and weakness, as well as problems with sleep, breathing, and swallowing.

CASE EXAMPLE 19-5

Mrs. Bibb is a 68-year-old woman who had polio as a teen. As a result, her left leg is weaker than the right and she has lost some fine motor control in both arms. With extensive rehabilitation, she was able to walk with a leg brace and two canes. She completed college and worked as a store manager while raising a family. She was most determined to remain independent.

As Mrs. Bibb grew older, she began to notice greater weakness in her left leg and in both arms. She began to tire much more easily and to experience pain in

her upper arms. At first Mrs. Bibb and her family thought that these changes were the result of "getting older". However, her doctor confirmed that they were due to Post-Polio Syndrome.

Once again, Mrs. Bibb has had to adjust to impairment. She has had to accept assistance from support workers. Sally, her support worker, is careful to respect Mrs. Bibb's independence. She plans work with Mrs. Bibb so that Mrs. Bibb may save her energy for the tasks most important for her.

The person who experiences Post-Polio Syndrome often benefits from pacing their activities to provide periods of rest as required, changing positions used to work, sleep, or eat. Some people benefit from water exercise routines and massage. Many times, adaptive aids can be of benefit.

It's important to bear in mind that this syndrome is not the result of aging or of a person's inability to cope with impairments. Assist the person to plan tasks to balance activity. Be prepared to take on parts of a task that cause the person pain. Most people with this syndrome will be able to define the tasks or parts of a task that they would like you to do. Work with your client to determine the best approach.

Multiple Sclerosis

Multiple sclerosis (MS) is a central nervous system disease that occurs when the myelin sheath (the protective coating that surrounds the nerve fibre) becomes inflamed and scarred. The term actually means "many scars". Nerve impulses do not get through the myelin sheath, or they produce a response that is different from what the person intended. The myelin sheath is much like the insulation on an electrical cord. If the insulation breaks, the wire shorts out and doesn't work.

Exactly what causes MS is not known. However, it is now thought to be an auto-immune disease, in which the person's body attacks its own myelin. This attack results in inflammation and scarring of the myelin. MS affects approximately twice as many women as men, mostly people between the ages of 20 and 40, although a rare, severe form can affect younger persons. It occurs more frequently in countries furthest from the equator. Canada has one of the highest rates of MS in the world.

There is no cure for MS. A number of therapies can be used to treat specific symptoms the person experiences.

The most common symptom of MS is fatigue. This fatigue is different than the fatigue that comes from lack of rest or overexertion. It is more intense and lasts longer. It's thought that the body requires more energy to transmit messages when the myelin sheath has been damaged. Problems with muscle control and vision are also common. About 10 percent of people with MS will experience some problems with memory. Approximately 15 percent will experience pain as the result of the disease.

People with MS experience periods in which their symptoms are severe. These are called *exacerbations*. Some things, such as having a child, can increase the risk of an exacerbation. However, many people have long periods of time when they have few or no symptoms.

In addition to the general approaches, keep the following in mind.

1. **A person with MS may be very disabled one day and fine the next.** Some exacerbations appear and disappear quite suddenly. Be prepared to accept rapid variations in your client's level of ability.
2. **Vision problems, although usually temporary, can be quite severe.** These include double vision, an involuntary jerking of the eyes that makes it impossible for the person to focus, or even total loss of vision for a period of time. Be aware that some clients may be very frightened by the changes, even if they have experienced them before. Provide support and assistance.

Parkinson's Disease

Parkinson's Disease is a progressive neurological disorder that affects the person's ability to initiate movement. It results from the death of cells in a part of the brain called the *substantia nigra*. These cells produce dopamine, a chemical which assists nerves to communicate. It most often affects people over 55 years of age, but can occur in younger people.

A tremor is one of the early signs of Parkinson's Disease. In later stages, it can significantly affect a person's ability to move as well as to speak. Some research has suggested that depression is more likely to occur in a person with Parkinson's Disease. However, Parkinson's Disease does not produce cognitive impairment.

Many people with Parkinson's Disease develop a rigid facial expression that does not easily change. This is called "masking" and can cause other people to believe erroneously that the person with Parkinson's does not understand what is going on around them.

At present, there is no known cause or cure. The effects of the disease can be controlled to some extent by medication. However, medication cannot stop the progression of the disease. Recently, surgical techniques have been used to relieve symptoms.

Supporting the Person Who Has Parkinson's Disease

There are many techniques that can assist the person with Parkinson's Disease. Keep in mind that your client will be the best source of information as to which techniques work best.

1. **Attempt only one task at a time.**   Attempting to pick up a pen while dialling a telephone number with the other will cause the hand that is dialling to stop working. This means that most tasks will take more time. Be patient.
2. **Pay particular attention to slight changes in the floor surface as your client walks.**   Door jambs, stoops, and even slight differences in the level of the sidewalk can cause a person with Parkinson's to trip and fall.

CASE EXAMPLE 19-6

Mr. Harris is 68 years old. He has had Parkinson's Disease for over 10 years. Medication has controlled most or Mr. Harris' symptoms; however, he does have difficulty starting to move (freezing). As well, his facial expression has become "mask-like" and his tremors are more noticeable.

Gerald assists Mr. Harris with bathing and other personal care. He also accompanies him shopping. Despite Mr. Harris' mobility problems, both he and Gerald realize how important it is for Mr. Harris to remain active. They plan out the activities beforehand to ensure that they are not rushed or doing too many things at once.

Gerald has noticed that people often speak to him instead of Mr. Harris. It seems as though others assume that, because of his facial expression, Mr. Harris is not able to answer. When this happens, Gerald turns to Mr. Harris for the answer. In this way, he encourages the other person to speak directly to Mr. Harris.

3. **Activity is essential for present and future health.** Because of the difficulty initiating activity, many people become less active. Help your client to start activities (most clients will have a preferred way of doing this) and encourage him or her to keep active. *Bicycling forward and backward no-one exercise*

4. **Be prepared to do difficult tasks without fuss.** For example, your client may not be able to butter toast. Be prepared to "fill in" for her or him if the inability is too frustrating.

Huntington's Disease

Huntington's Disease (HD) is a progressive neurological disease that eventually affects all the person's abilities: physical and cognitive. An older name for this disease was *Huntington's Chorea.* The term *chorea* means dance, and it referred to the uncontrolled movements that people with HD develop.

The disease is caused by a single gene and is passed down from one generation to the next. The child of a person with HD has a 50 percent chance of developing the disease. A test is available that will determine whether a child of a person with HD carries the gene, but it is not given unless the person agrees to pre- and post-test counselling.

HD usually appears in middle age, although one rare form appears in school-age people. The duration of HD ranges from 10-20 years. In general, the earlier the disease appears, the quicker it progresses. There are no medications or treatments that can stop the progression of the disease. Some medications are used to treat the physical and cognitive effects of the disease.

Supporting the Person Who Has Huntington's Disease

1. **Help the person participate in everyday communication.** Although HD affects both physical and cognitive function, it is impossible to know how much the person understands. A person may well understand the communication but be unable to easily speak and participate. Help the person by restating what he or she has said so that he or she knows you have understood.

2. **Help the person to maintain adequate nutrition.** People with HD can burn over 5000 calories per day. Remember that the person may have trouble chewing and swallowing. Cut foods into small pieces to reduce the amount of chewing required. Sometimes, puréed food is easier to eat. Thin or thicken liquids for easier swallowing.

3. **Learn about and make use of the adaptation the client and family have made to make the environment safer.** For example, some people with HD sleep on a mattress placed on the floor. This helps to minimize the risk of injury if the person's movements propel him or her out of bed. Others have removed obstacles or bric-a-brac to lessen the possibility of injury. Make sure that you do not place items in areas that could pose a hazard to the person.

4. **Do your best to keep a calm environment.** The effects of HD worsen when the person is anxious.

Muscular Dystrophy

The name *muscular dystrophy* (MD) actually refers to a group of conditions. Each condition is caused by a defect in a specific gene. Most people think that MD is a children's disease, but different forms of the disease can affect people of any age. In general, **MD** causes muscle tissue to degenerate and be replaced by fatty and connective tissue. There is no loss of intellectual function in the person with MD.

The age of onset, the muscles affected, and the rate at which the disease progresses vary from form to form. Some forms are inherited, others appear in people who do not have a family history of the disease.

Supporting the Person Who Has Muscular Dystrophy

Because of the number of forms of MD, as well as the variations in the ways each form can progress, it's vitally important to learn what works for the client. As with most other conditions, your client will know very well what works best for him or her. Discuss methods and techniques with your client.

Cerebral Palsy

Cerebral palsy (CP) is the term used to describe a group of disorders that result from an anomaly or an injury to the brain as it develops. While many infants are born with CP, the condition may occur after birth and up to three years of age. The condition is not progressive: it will not get worse.

A person may experience a wide range of problems with physical sensation and motor skills. Some people with CP experience a great deal of muscle rigidity. This is called *spasticity*. Some people may experience learning disabilities or developmental problems. Many people with cerebral palsy have difficulty producing speech.

Supporting the Person with Cerebral Palsy

1. **Do not assume that your client has difficulty understanding simply because he or she has difficulty speaking.**   A speech problem is a motor skill problem, not a cognitive one. Treat the person as the adult he or she is.
2. **Learn from your client.**   Many clients with CP can give specific instructions as to how you should assist.

CASE EXAMPLE 19-7

Kathy James is a 24-year-old woman with CP. She has significant problems with walking and speaking. Despite these impairments, she has completed a degree in mathematics and works for a research company.

Like anyone her age, Kathy enjoys going out. She is fond of bluegrass music and tries to see new plays as they come to town. In order to do this, Kathy has set up a network of support. Gail, her attendant, assists her with dressing and getting ready for work each weekday morning. Cassie and Erin assist Kathy morning and night on weekends.

Kathy enjoys a friendship with all three attendants. She has selected all three not only for their skills but their personalities. She and Cassie attend plays; Gail and Kathy head for music clubs periodically. Kathy has introduced all three women to her other friends. In this way, she finds the need for support less intrusive.

Spinal Cord Injury

Spinal cord injuries are caused by a number of things that damage the spinal cord, usually the result of an injury to the vertebrae in the back or neck. When the vertebrae are damaged, parts of the bone may irritate, sever, puncture or compress the spinal cord. When this happens, the nerves in the spinal cord are damaged and they no longer carry nerve impulses as they did before.

Sometimes, damage is full (e.g., all the nerves in the spinal column at a specific point are damaged). When the damage to the spinal cord is complete, no impulses can travel from the brain to beyond that point. Any muscle groups controlled by nerves that are damaged will not function and the person will not have any sensation in the affected areas. If there is partial damage, some, but not all, movement and sensation may be affected.

The loss of movement caused by spinal cord injury is called *paraplegia*. This term is often used to describe the injury a person has when he or she has sensation and use of the upper part of the body but not the lower part. *Quadriplegia* is the term used to describe the condition where a person has lost sensation and use of the upper part of the body as well as the lower.

Motor vehicle accidents account for most spinal cord injuries. Sports and workplace injuries account for approximately 25 percent of the injuries. It is a condition that usually affects young people aged 18 to 35.

Supporting the Person Who Has a Spinal Cord Injury

Most clients with a spinal cord injury will need help with specific physical tasks. Aside from the impairment, the person may be quite physically fit and able—perhaps more so than you (Photo 19-1)! Most clients will discuss with you the tasks they need done and how they would like you to do them. This can involve learning special techniques.

Depending upon the extent of the disability, the client may ask you to assist with skin care and positioning. Skin breakdown is a serious problem for anyone who cannot easily move about. If your client does not have sensation, he or she may rely upon you to observe for skin problems.

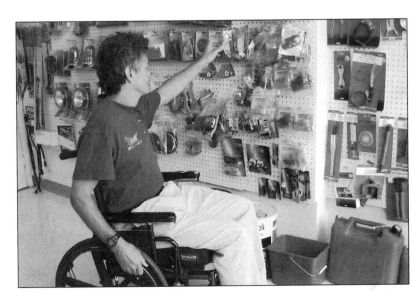

Photo 19-1

Most people with a spinal cord injury live full lives.

Chronic Obstructive Pulmonary Disease (COPD)

Chronic Obstructive Pulmonary Disease (COPD) is the name given to a group of lung (pulmonary) diseases that are irreversible. The two most common diseases are emphysema and chronic bronchitis. Both diseases cause the airways in the lungs to become obstructed. In chronic bronchitis, the airways become partially blocked with mucus. Emphysema results in an enlargement of the air sacs in the lungs that causes the airways to collapse. COPD causes shortness of breath and, as the body has to work harder to get oxygen, can have negative effects on the cardiovascular system as well.

COPD occurs as the result of damage to the lungs over a long period of time. It happens slowly and is often not noticed until the effects have become disabling. While over 80 percent of COPD cases are caused by smoking, exposure to chemical fumes, organic dust or mining dust can also cause the condition. A very rare form of emphysema is linked to an inherited lack of a specific protein.

While COPD cannot be cured, it can be controlled to some extent. Medications can help open airways. Techniques can help the person breathe more effectively and help clear the lungs of mucus. Even proper sitting and standing can help the person cope with the effects of the condition.

Supporting the Person Who Has COPD

1. **As with many conditions, pacing is important.**   Shortness of breath can be severe and occur very suddenly. Many persons with moderate COPD may not be able to walk 10 metres without stopping to rest.
2. **Encourage the person to sit while performing activities.**   Sitting takes less energy than standing.
3. **Adapt tasks so that the client avoids bending or lifting.**
4. **Plan tasks so that you can help with the more physically demanding components.**
5. **If your client allows, help him or her to organize their belongings so that what is needed is within easy reach.** This is particularly important if the client will be using the items when you are not there.

Tuberculosis

Tuberculosis (TB) is a disease caused by bacteria that affects the lungs. A person can contract TB only through exposure to a person who has *active* or *infectious* TB. It usually takes prolonged exposure to TB to put a person at risk.

It's important to be aware that exposure to TB does not mean that the person has the active disease, even if a Mantoux test (a screening test for TB) is positive. Only 10 percent of the people exposed to active TB will develop the active form. The remaining 90 percent will not develop the active form of the disease, do not become ill, and cannot affect others.

TB is considered to be more common in long-term care facilities. This is due in part to the fact that many people with weakened immune systems live in close proximity to one another. Many infections can spread more easily in these situations. For this reason, most health care workers are regularly tested for exposure to TB.

Active TB can be treated by a course of medications given over a long period of time. People exposed to TB but who do not have the active form usually take preventative medication for six months to one year. This substantially reduces their chances of developing active TB.

Diabetes

Diabetes is a disease that results from the pancreas' inability to produce enough insulin or to properly use insulin that is produced. A person with diabetes cannot metabolize food properly and may be at risk for cardiovascular and kidney problems. Diabetes also causes vision problems, due to the changes in the circulation of blood in the retina of the eye.

There are three types of diabetes: Type 1, Type 2, and Gestational. Type 1 diabetes occurs when the body does not produce insulin, or does not produce enough insulin. This type accounts for about 10 percent of the cases. Most children who develop diabetes have Type 1. Type 2 diabetes is sometimes called *late-onset diabetes*, as it tends to occur in people over 45 years of age. It can be the result of insufficient insulin, or from the body's inability to use the insulin that the pancreas does make. Gestational diabetes is a form of the disease that develops when a woman is pregnant. It usually disappears after the pregnancy is over, but may result in an increased risk of both mother and child developing diabetes at a later date.

Diabetes cannot be cured. The condition requires close monitoring of blood sugar levels, food intake, and activity. Medication may have to be taken orally or by injection each day. Even when treated, diabetes can have devastating effects on a person's circulatory system. As a result, even a small wound may pose serious risk to the person. It may not heal or gangrene may set in. Diabetics also are at an increased risk of kidney and vision problems.

Diabetes can have a dramatic affect on the person's life. Even such simple things as joining a friend at a coffee shop for a snack may require planning. Daily blood tests may be required. Some people are able to control their condition by careful management of their diet. Others must take daily doses of insulin to control blood sugar levels. Insulin must be injected to be effective, and most people who take insulin learn to self-inject. Others train a family member to assist. Some people must take two or more injections per day.

People with diabetes must also guard against two conditions related to the amount of sugar in the blood: *hyperglycemia* (high blood sugar) and *hypoglycemia* (low blood sugar). Hypoglycemia is also known as *insulin shock*. Hyperglycemia can result in a *diabetic coma*. Both conditions are serious and can result in death if not treated. Table 19-3 summarizes the causes and symptoms of each condition. Note that some of the symptoms are identical.

Supporting the Person Who Has Diabetes

Each person has his or her own regime for managing diabetes. It's important to know your client's regime and what you can do to help him or her maintain it. This may include preparing special meals or helping the client to find acceptable alternates to favourite foods. If part of the client's diabetes management plan involves losing

TABLE 19-3	Hypoglycemia and Hyperglycemia		
Condition	Causes	Symptoms	Possible Remedy
Hypoglycemia (Insulin Shock)	Too much insulin Omitting a meal Eating too little food Increased exercise Vomiting	Weakness Headache Low blood pressure Dizziness Rapid pulse Perspiration Trembling Hunger Cold, clammy skin Confusion Convulsions Unconsciousness	Orange juice Hard candy
Hyperglycemia (Diabetic Coma)	Insufficient insulin Eating too much Too little exercise Stress Undiagnosed or untreated diabetes Infection	Weakness Headache Low blood pressure Rapid and weak pulse Drowsiness Thirst Flushed face Frequent urination Slow, laboured breathing Dry skin Nausea or vomiting Coma	Insulin

weight, you might be asked to assist your client to prepare low-calorie meals or to take part in an exercise program. You might be asked to help the client test urine. You will not usually be expected to administer insulin. Speak with your supervisor if your client or another caregiver asks you to administer any medication.

Human Immunodeficiency Virus

Human immunodeficiency virus (HIV) is the virus that causes **AIDS** (Acquired Immune Deficiency Syndrome). HIV attacks the body's immune system, making the person susceptible to many infections and diseases. These are called *opportunistic infections and diseases*. When a person develops these conditions, her or she is considered to have AIDS. Over time, these infections and diseases result in the person's death. There is no cure for HIV or AIDS, although the opportunistic conditions can usually be treated or prevented to some degree.

HIV cannot be spread by social contact. Hugging, holding hands, and touching do not spread the disease. Insect bites cannot transmit the virus. HIV can be spread by the exchange of body fluids: semen, vaginal secretions, and blood. A person can contract HIV by having unprotected sex with an infected person, by using needles that have been used by an infected person (and not sterilized), by having a transfusion of infected blood or blood products, or a puncture of the skin or mucous membrane by an infected object (such as a needle-stick).

Supporting the Person Who Has HIV

1. **Keep in mind that you may pose a risk to your client.**   The person who has HIV is susceptible to many infections. Colds, viruses, and other infections that you can easily fight off could be quite serious for your client. Use universal precautions to protect both of you.
2. **Keep the disease in perspective.**   HIV is a serious disease that can be transmitted. However, proper precautions can ensure that the virus is not transmitted. Do not focus so much on your client's condition that you cease to see her or him as a person.

Questions for Review

1. Describe functional impairment. How does it relate to the concept of disability?

2. What are the four common types of impairments?

3. You have a new client who needs physical assistance due to arthritis. What eight questions should you ask yourself in order to learn how to best assist the client?

4. What approaches should be used, no matter what assistance you are providing?

5. What are the three main types (categories) of a stroke?

6. What cardiovascular conditions contribute to an increased risk of a stroke?

7. What functions are commonly controlled by the left hemisphere of the brain? The right hemisphere?

8. What are the warning signs of a heart attack?

9. What is the most common symptom of multiple sclerosis?

10. What techniques may assist the client with Parkinson's Disease?

11. What techniques may assist the client with COPD?

12. What two things should you keep in mind when you are supporting the client with HIV or AIDS?

CHAPTER TWENTY

Infant and Child Care

Learning Objectives

Through reading this chapter, you'll be able to:

1. List the six common situations in which the support worker may provide support to infants and children.
2. Describe the role of the support worker in providing support to the family with infants and children.
3. Outline the child's stages of development from birth to age one.
4. Demonstrate well infant care.
5. Describe the characteristics of support provided to new mothers.
6. Identify selected conditions that may require children to have support needs.
7. Discuss the characteristics of support provided to children with developmental or physical disabilities.

Terms You'll Use

Autism   A condition that results from structural disorders in parts of the brain.

Circumcision   The surgical removal of the foreskin of the penis.

Cleft Lip   A fissure or opening in the upper lip.

Cleft Palate   A condition in which there is no passageway between the naso-pharynx and the nose.

Club Foot   A malformation of the bones of the foot, causing it to twist inward or outward.

Congenital Hip Dysplasia   A condition reulting in partial or total hip dislocation.

Down Syndrome   A genetic condition produced by an abnormality in chromosome 21.

Engorgement   A painful overfilling of the breasts.

Fetal Alcohol Effect (FAE)   A disorder that can occur when a woman drinks alcohol during pregnancy; milder than FAS.

Fetal Alcohol Syndrome (FAS)   A disorder can occur when a woman drinks alcohol during pregnancy; more serious than FAE.

Fragile X Syndrome   A genetic disorder caused by a weakness or break in a portion of a child's X chromosome.

Hydrocephalus   A condition related to an increase intracranial fluid in the brain that causes increased head size and pressure in the brain.

Jaundice   A condition that causes yellowing of the skin.

Milestones   Sets of abilities that a child is expected to attain by a certain age.

Multiple Births   The birth of more than one baby during one pregnancy.

Parent   A person who has the primary responsibility of caring for a child.

Phenylketonuria   A disease caused by the absence of a liver enzyme.

Postpartum Depression   A depression which can occur in women who have recently had a baby.

Spina Bifida   A condition caused by a defect in the way the spinal column has formed.

Common Situations

The support provided to a family usually falls into one of these six categories. Keep in mind that some support may address more than one type of need.

1. **Support to the new parent or parents of multiple births.**   You may be asked to provide support to new parents of **multiple births**, which refers to the birth of twins, triplets, or quadruplets. This type of support usually focusses on helping with infant care, with any other children in the home, as well as with the new mother as she recovers from childbirth.

2. **Support to the infant and parents of a premature infant.**   You may be asked to assist with care for the infant or to undertake household tasks so that the parents may care for the child. Many premature babies have medical conditions that are treated by a professional member of the support team. You may be asked to assist with care appropriate for a support worker to perform.

3. **Support to a infant or child with a physical or developmental disability.**   You may be asked to assist with care for the infant or to undertake household tasks so that the parents may care for the child. Many infants or children with disabilities have conditions that are treated by a professional member of the support team. You may be asked to assist with care appropriate for a support worker to perform.

4. **Support for the parent with physical disabilities.**   You may be asked to assist a parent who cannot perform all parenting activities as the result of a physical disability. You may be asked to perform specific infant and child care tasks, to assist the parent perform tasks (such as bathing an infant) that he or she cannot do alone, or be asked to perform specific household tasks so that the parent can devote time to child care.

5. **Support for the parent who lacks parenting skills or experience.**   You may be asked to assist a parent who does not have parenting skills. The parent may be a spouse who has to assume parenting because the primary care giver is ill or away. The parent could also be a young person who has no experience or self-confidence. In these situations, you may spend a great deal of time teaching the parent to care for the infant or child, as well as coaching the parent as he or she practises skills.

6. **Support for the parent who has difficulty coping with the demands of parenting.** You may be asked to assist a parent who has difficulty coping for many reasons. The parent may have multiple sources of stress: a mental health condition, a substance abuse problem, or a history of abuse. In these situations, you may provide emotional support, coach the parent as he or she practises skills, as well as complete household tasks so that the parent does not become overwhelmed.

Establishing a Relationship with Parents

In this section, we'll use the term **parent** to refer to any person who has the primary responsibility of caring for the child. This may include grandparents, aunts, uncles, and mothers and fathers. Also, families come in many types such as single-parent, nuclear (a mother and father with children), extended (a nuclear family with grandparents or other relatives in the same home), among many others.

The role of a parent is a special one. It implies a special love, closeness, and caring between the child and the parent. Consider the situation in Stop and Reflect 20-1.

Many times, the parent you are assisting has mixed feelings about your help. The parent may feel that he or she is a "bad" parent because of a need for assistance. The parent may be concerned that their child will begin to rely upon you instead of him or her. Occasionally, a parent will feel that you are there to judge him or her in some way.

You must do your utmost to put the parent at ease. If possible, you should have the opportunity to go over the support plan *before* you first visit. This allows you to get an accurate description of the purpose of your support, as well as the specific tasks you may be asked to perform.

As you make your first few visits, you will need to take time to get to know the parent and others involved in the child's care. It's particularly important to establish how you can work together to best meet the child's needs. Keep in mind that you are not there to comment on how the family is organized. You must respect the ways in which family members relate to one another, even if it is not the way that you would prefer.

Stop and Reflect 20-1

If you are a parent, recall a time that your child had a minor injury (such as a cut, scrape, or bruise).

_____

_____

_____

How did you feel when your child asked or reached out to you for comfort?

_____

_____

_____

How do you think that you would feel if your child had reached out to someone else for comfort?

_____

_____

_____

Infant and Child Development

The period between birth and age three is one of extensive growth and development. At birth, the nervous system is relatively mature and directs most of the newborn's activity. The newborn displays many reflexes that attest to the maturity of the nervous system. Table 20-1 describes some of the more common ones.

TABLE 20-1	Common Reflexes in the Newborn
Reflex	**Happens when**
Moro	The crib is jarred and the infant startles by drawing its legs up and folding its arms on its chest.
Rooting	The infant's cheek is touched, the infant moves its head toward the source looking for food.
Sucking	The infant's lips are touched, it begins to suck.
Tonic Neck	The infant is sleeping, the head is turned to one side and one arm is raised over its head, as if the infant is "fencing".
Grasp	The infant's hands are touched and the fingers grasp your fingers.
Blink	The infant's bridge of nose is touched, he or she blinks.

The newborn can also hear, taste, smell, and see and fixate on objects.

At full term, all of the body's systems are working, but are immature. Keep these things in mind as you care for a newborn.

1. Full expansion of the lungs does not take place for a few days after birth in an infant carried to full term. A premature infant's lungs may be very immature.
2. Infants cannot easily regulate or conserve their body temperature. Therefore, room temperature should be kept at 20°C to 22°C as infants lose temperature very quickly.
3. The immaturity of the infant's musculoskeletal system means that movements are random and uncoordinated. However, an infant should never be limp.
4. It is common for an infant's eyes to be crossed at birth, as the eye muscles are immature. This should correct itself as the infant grows.
5. Immature kidneys cannot hold a great deal of water. Therefore, it is not unusual for the infant to have several wet diapers each day.
6. The infant's immune system is immature at birth. Take steps to prevent any infectious contacts.
7. At birth, small pimples (called *milia*) are evident on nose and chin; these will disappear in the first few weeks.
8. The infant's skin peels within the first few weeks.

9. Stools are initially black-green and tarry; they change within the first week to bright yellow, soft, and pasty for breast-fed infants. Bottle-fed infant stools are yellowish-brown and are usually firmer than those of breast-fed infants. It is normal for a newborn to strain when having a bowel movement.

10. Hiccups occur often. Burping the infant and offering warm water helps to calm them.

Conditions That Require Special Care

There are other conditions which may require special care.

1. **Circumcision** (the surgical removal of the foreskin of the penis) may be performed prior to discharge from hospital. If so, there may be special instructions for bathing and monitoring urine output.

2. **Jaundice** (yellowing of the skin) can occur for a variety reasons. If you notice any yellowing of the infant's skin or eyes, report the observation to your supervisor.

Developmental Milestones

Researchers have developed **milestones**—a set of abilities that a child is expected to attain by a certain age. It's important to remember that milestones are guidelines, not absolute deadlines. Each child will be somewhat different, attaining some milestones ahead of schedule and others somewhat later. These minor variations are not usually a cause for concern. However, a consistent delay in developing abilities is something to discuss with your supervisor. Table 20-2 describes some common milestones from birth to one year.

Caregiving Tips

Research suggests that the more you interact with the infant, the more complete the infant's development will be. Keep these guidelines in mind to make the most of the time with the child.

1. **It's important to spend time with the infant.**   This stimulates many senses and encourages awareness.

2. **Learn and follow the infant's schedule.**   Most infants will fall into a routine after a period of time. Don't be alarmed if the routine differs from infant to infant.

3. **Respond to the infant's cries.**   The cry is the only way the infant can communicate his or her needs. Responding also makes the infant feel secure ("my needs will be met").

4. **Hold and cuddle the infant when feeding him or her.**   Physical contact is very important to a child's development. Holding the infant means that you are not propping a bottle up with a pillow, an action that can lead to choking and later, tooth decay.

5. **Make use of the pre-crawling period (birth to 5 months or so) to child-proof everything.**   Safely store *all* household chemicals and cooking supplies. Be aware

TABLE 20-2		Milestones from Birth to One Year	
Age	Physical Development	Cognitive Development	Social Development
Birth to 4 months	<ul><li>lifts head and chest when lying on stomach</li><li>follows a moving object or person with eyes</li><li>grasps rattle or finger</li><li>wiggles and kicks</li><li>rolls over (stomach to back)</li><li>sits up with support</li><li>plays with fingers, hands, toes</li></ul>	<ul><li>explores objects with mouth</li><li>can discriminate between people, places, shapes, and colours</li><li>turns head toward bright colours and lights</li><li>responds to a shaking rattle or bell</li></ul>	<ul><li>cries (with tears) to communicate pain, fear, hunger, discomfort, fatigue, or loneliness</li><li>stops crying when lifted or touched</li><li>babbles and coos</li><li>loves to be touched and held close</li><li>responds to voices</li><li>returns a smile</li><li>responds to 'peek-a-boo' and other simple games</li></ul>
4 to 8 months	<ul><li>develops a pattern for feeding, sleeping</li><li>rolls from back to stomach and stomach to back</li><li>sits alone without support</li><li>holds head erect</li><li>raises up into crawling position; may rock back and forth, but not move forward</li><li>uses finger and thumb to pick up an objects</li><li>transfers objects from one hand to the other</li><li>first teeth begin to appear</li><li>drools, mouths, and chews on objects</li><li>drinks from a cup with help</li><li>reaches for cup or spoon</li><li>closes mouth firmly or turns head when not hungry</li></ul>	<ul><li>develops ability to think</li><li>learns through smelling, tasting, touching, seeing, hearing</li><li>can focus eyes on and reach for small objects</li><li>plays at length with one or two items</li><li>uses voice to indicate pleasure or displeasure</li><li>can assign simple words to people and objects (e.g., "dada" or "mama")</li><li>recognizes and seeks familiar voices</li><li>looks for ball rolled out of sight</li><li>seeks toys hidden out of sight (e.g., under a blanket, basket, or container)</li><li>recognizes names of family members</li></ul>	<ul><li>cries in different tones or pattern to indicate hunger, fear, loneliness, and other needs</li><li>responds to own name</li><li>responds differently to strangers and family members</li><li>imitates sounds, actions, and facial expressions of others</li><li>squeals, laughs, babbles, or smiles in response to others</li><li>smiles at own reflection in mirror</li><li>raises arms to be held</li><li>shows mild to severe anxiety at separation from parent</li></ul>

TABLE 20-2	Milestones from Birth to One Year *(continued)*		
Age	Physical Development	Cognitive Development	Social Development
8 to 12 months	▪ needs 2-3 meals per day ▪ enjoys drinking from a cup ▪ begins to eat finger foods ▪ enjoys opening and closing doors ▪ crawls well ▪ pulls self to a standing position ▪ stands alone holding onto furniture for support ▪ walks holding onto furniture or with help ▪ prefers one hand over the other	▪ says first words ▪ interested in picture books ▪ pays attention to conversations ▪ claps hands, waves bye, if prompted ▪ likes to place objects inside one another ▪ uses 3-4 word speech ▪ responds to own name ▪ likes to watch self in mirror	▪ imitates adult actions such as drinking from a cup, talking on phone ▪ expresses fear or anxiety toward strangers ("makes strange") ▪ wants caregiver or parent to be in constant sight ▪ may become attached to a favourite toy or blanket ▪ offers toys or objects to others but expects them to be given right back

Handwritten margin note: talking, walking — milestones at 12 months

that ingesting even a "safe" substance (such as vinegar) can be harmful to an infant. Install safety latches on cabinets and place covers on electrical outlets. Pad sharp corners of tables or shelves or remove them from the area in which the child plays. Remove fragile, breakable items from lower shelves and low tabletops.

6. **Provide good stimulation.**   Provide bright colours and a variety of objects to look at and handle. These need not be expensive toys. Clean, bright socks or wash cloths, small plastic containers, plastic measuring cups, a kettle spoon, or a spatula will often do. Big pictures cut from packaging can also amuse. Simple music (played on a radio or stereo) provides auditory stimulation.

7. **As the child grows, offer variety in tastes, temperature, texture, and aroma.** Infants are often very sensitive to tastes. Even foods that do not seem spicy to you may be too spicy to the infant, so experiment with caution.

8. **Talk and read to the infant.**   This helps the infant to learn language.

9. **Play games like peek-a-boo and pat-a-cake.**   This encourages intellectual and motor skill development as well as promotes social interaction.

10. **Provide a safe area for the infant to crawl about.**

Infant Care

This section includes procedures for many types of infant care. There may be a number of safe variations for each procedure and some procedures will have to be adapted to take into account the specific setting. If you are assisting a parent, make sure not to discourage him or her from performing tasks. Do your utmost to follow the style of care provided by the parent—if it is safe.

Bathing the Newborn

Bathing is a wonderful opportunity to spend time with the infant. Parents will usually pick the best time of the day to bathe their infant, based upon the needs of the infant and others in the household.

Preparing the Environment

a. Make sure that the room is warm and all windows are closed to prevent drafts.
b. Remove any jewellery to prevent scratching the infant's skin.
c. Bathe the infant before a feeding. Bathing stimulates the infant to feed better. Bathing before a feeding can also prevent vomiting or bowel movements during the bath.

EQUIPMENT
bassinet, basin, or infant tub
towel and washcloth
baby soap
diaper
alcohol swab (optional) or cotton swab with rubbing alcohol
petroleum jelly
brush or comb
clean clothing
blanket

Procedure 20-1: Bathing the Newborn

1. Wash your hands.
2. Fill the basin or tub with lukewarm water. Always test the water with your wrist. Never add warm or hot water while the infant is in basin or tub.
3. Undress the infant and immediately wrap in towel to prevent chilling. Support the infant under your nondominant arm and close to your body in a football fashion. Figure 20-1a illustrates this position.
4. Use clean washcloth without soap to wash eyes, face, and ears.
   a. Gently wipe each eye from inner corner to outer corner. Use a separate corner of washcloth for each eye. This prevents spread of bacteria from one eye to the other.
   b. Wash off particles at entrance to the nose. Do no use cotton-tipped swabs as they may push mucus further in to the nose or cause damage to the nasal lining.
   c. Do not use cotton-tipped swabs to clean the ear canal as they may push wax further into the canal and damage it. Wax will work itself out naturally. Be very careful in handling a premature infant's ears as they are very soft.
5. While holding the infant's head over the tub, use a washcloth and soap to wash the hair. Hair can be washed daily or twice a week. Wash the hair quickly as the infant rapidly loses heat through its head. Massage the scalp gently in a circular fashion. Avoiding the soft spot is not necessary, but be sure to use gentle motions. Be careful not to get soap into the infant's eyes.

Figure 20-1a   *Proper support for an infant.*

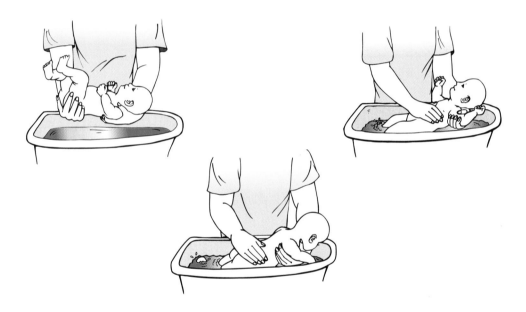

Figure 20-1b   *Supporting the infant in the tub.*

6. Lather and rinse thoroughly. It is important to get all of the soap out to prevent irritation from soap residue.
7. Dry the hair thoroughly with the towel.
8. Unwrap the infant and place him or her into the tub, supporting the upper torso and head at all times with your arm. Figure 20-1b illustrates the positions. (Do not immerse the infant totally into the tub until the umbilical cord has fallen off.)
9. Using your right hand, wash the infant with soaped hand or washcloth, starting at the neck and working down. Pay special attention to the creases.
10. Turn the infant over with head to the side and wash its back.
11. Rinse well.

12. Wash genitalia as follows:
    1. Female genitalia: Wash from front to back to prevent spreading anal bacteria into the urinary system and the vagina. The female infant may have a scant amount of bloody vaginal discharge which is normal due to the hormones received from her mother.
    2. Male genitalia: Do not retract the foreskin of the uncircumcised penis as it is attached firmly to the head of the penis. The foreskin will retract naturally at about five years old. Wash the penis and scrotum gently, paying special attention to keeping the creases clean.
13. Dry the infant thoroughly with the towel, with special attention to the creases.

Caring for the Umbilical Cord Stump

Some physicians recommend that the umbilical cord stump be wiped with rubbing alcohol to aid in drying. This will help it fall off within a week or so after birth. If this is the case, wipe after each bath and diaper change. Be sure to wipe the base of the cord itself, not the infant's skin. If the cord area becomes red or has an odour or discharge, notify the parents and advise them to contact the infant's doctor.

Dressing the Infant

After drying the infant well, dress him or her in clean clothing. Clothing should be weather-appropriate and unrestrictive. Be aware that an overdressed infant can overheat quickly and that an underdressed infant can lose heat quickly. A good guideline is to dress the infant in the same amount of clothing as an adult.

For the first week after birth, it is sometimes recommended to wrap the infant snugly in a blanket. This gives the infant a secure feeling and makes it easy to position the infant on his or her side or back. Avoid placing the infant on his or her stomach until the infant's physician advises it is safe. An infant under one year of age should never be placed on his or her stomach to sleep.

Feeding the Infant

Usually after the bath, the infant is ready to eat. If the infant is breast-fed, assist the mother into breast-feeding position. If bottle-fed, prepare a bottle for the infant.

Assisting the Mother with Breast Feedings

Breast-feeding is a wonderful experience for mother and infant. Most mothers receive help from post-partum nurses in the hospital prior to discharge, but she will still require support and encouragement when she returns home. A mother's milk is not present until approximately the third day after birth. At that time, the milk is usually present and the infant can receive adequate nutrition. The infant is receiving adequate nutrition from mother when the infant:

1. appears comfortable at the breast;
2. latches on easily;

3. is satisfied after feeding;
4. is sleeping well (4-5 hours);
5. has 6-8 wet diapers per day;
6. has one or more stools per day; and
7. is gaining weight.

A breast-feeding mother must maintain a nutritious diet. In most cases an additional intake of 500 calories a day over the mother's normal intake is required. A nursing mother should avoid gassy foods that are passed to the infant, such as cabbage, beans, or broccoli. She should also avoid all medication and alcohol; these will be passed to the infant.

Breast-feeding is done on demand but usually every 2-3 hours. Frequent breast-feeding prevents **engorgement**, a painful overfilling of the breasts.

Procedure 20-2: Assisting the Mother with Breast Feedings

1. Wash hands prior to assisting mother.
2. Help her into a comfortable position. No one position is necessarily better than another, as long as the mother is comfortable. Some mothers find the use of a nursing pillow useful. It is most important that the mother is comfortable and relaxed during feeding to promote the let-down reflex and allow a good flow of milk.
3. Bring the infant to the mother's breast to avoid strain on the mother's back.
4. Advise the mother to brush the infant's cheek with the nipple. This causes the infant to turn toward the nipple (the rooting reflex).
5. Advise the mother to guide the infant's mouth toward the nipple so that it can latch onto the whole nipple and areola. If the infant sucks only on the nipple, the nipple becomes cracked and sore. Figure 20-2 illustrates the proper position and shows an incorrect position.
6. As the infant nurses, watch to ensure that the infant's nose is not covered by the mother's breast.

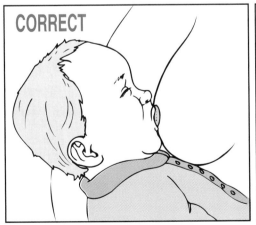
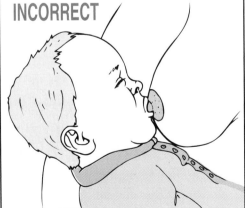

Figure 20-2   *Infant Latching onto Nipple*

7. The infant should feed from both breasts at each feeding. Burp the infant after finishing feeding from the first breast. An infant receives most of each breast's milk within five minutes, but 10-30 minutes of sucking stimulates the breast to produce more milk. As well, alternating the breasts (starting one feeding with the right breast, the next with the left) allows for equal replenishing of breast milk.

8. To remove the infant from the breast, advise the mother to insert her finger into the infant's mouth to break the suction.

Preparing Formula

If a mother decides to bottle-feed, a commercially prepared formula is often recommended by the physician. Formula may come in many forms from ready-to-use in cans to powder that must be mixed.

Formulas that must be mixed have simple instructions on the can. These instructions must be followed exactly. The formula must be used within the time limit set in the instructions. Stale prepared formula loses nutritional value and can become contaminated. It must be discarded to prevent infection in the infant.

Most mothers prefer to heat formula, but it is fine to feed the infant formula at room temperature. Avoid heating the bottle in the microwave, as this form of heating can destroy nutrients. If you heat formula, use a pan of water into which you place the formula in a heat-proof container. Do not heat plastic bottles in a pan as they will melt. Pour the warmed formula into a bottle, placing a nipple and bottle ring on top.

Always test the formula on your wrist before feeding the infant to make sure it is not too hot. This is also an opportunity to check that the nipple hole is the correct size. If it is, the formula should come out in drops, but not flow steadily. An infant can tire easily if the hole is too small or receive too much formula and choke if it is too big.

Bottle-fed infants usually feed every 3-4 hours. Each feeding should take 15-20 minutes.

Procedure 20-3: Bottle Feeding

1. Assist the mother to find a comfortable position. If you are feeding the infant, hold the infant in your nondominant arm. Make sure that the infant's head is higher than its torso.
2. Tilt the bottle so that the nipple fills with formula.
3. Place the nipple in the infant's mouth. You will know you have the right position when you can feel the infant sucking on the nipple.
4. Burp the infant after each 15 to 30 ml (one-half to one ounce) of formula is taken. You can burp the baby over your shoulder or over your lap as shown in Figures 20-3 and 20-4.
5. Continue to feed until the infant takes no more formula. Do not allow formula to pool in the baby's mouth as it can cause choking.
6. Discard unused formula after each feeding.
7. Document the amount of formula the infant drank.
8. Change the infant if required.
9. Place the infant on his or her side to promote digestion.

Figure 20-3   *Burping the Infant on the Shoulder*

Figure 20-4   *Burping the Infant on the Lap*

Diapering the Infant

Parents may choose to use cloth or disposable diapers. They may also choose a diaper service to deliver and pick up cloth diapers. The choice of which type to use is a personal decision and is often based upon cost, comfort, convenience, and environmental factors. You should not attempt to convince parents to use a type you prefer.

The infant should be changed several times a day, prior to feedings, after feedings, and at any other time necessary. Infants frequently wet and soil diapers. As the infant gets older, diaper wetting and soiling will become less frequent.

Procedure 20-4: Diapering the Infant

1. Wash your hands.
2. Lay the infant on the change table. Always have one hand on the infant when on the change table to prevent falls.
3. Undo the diaper (unpin or open velcro if cloth diaper, pull adhesive tab on disposable diaper). Close pins and make sure they are well out of infant's reach.
4. Pull the front of the diaper down between the infant's legs.
5. Wipe the infant from front to back with clean area on inner front of the diaper.
6. Roll the front of the diaper so that the inner portion is inside.
7. Pull the back of the diaper so that it is away from the side of the infant.
8. Lift up the infant's buttocks by holding the infant's legs and lifting up.
9. Wipe off soil with a cloth.
10. Remove the soiled diaper from under the infant.

EQUIPMENT

diaper (if cloth, fold as per parent's instructions)

wet washcloths or wipes

petroleum jelly, diaper cream, or other ointment as used by parents

11. Lower the infant to the table.

12. Wrap the diaper and set it aside, out of the infant's reach.

13. Lift the infant's legs as in step 8. Using baby wipes or a wet washcloth, cleanse the genital area. Always wipe from front to back. If the infant is very soiled or has a rash, use a mild soap with the washcloth. Wet wipes do not need additional soap. Rinse well and pat dry.

14. Apply cream if used.

15. Lift up the infant's legs as per step 8. Place a fresh diaper under the infant's buttocks. Disposable diapers and fitted cloth diapers have a front and back. Disposable diapers have tape tabs on the back. Fitted cloth diapers are usually larger in the back. Make sure that you position the diaper properly.

16. Lower the infant's legs and bring the front of the diaper up between the legs.

17. Fasten the diaper securely. If pins are used, insert them from the front to the back.

18. Make sure that the diaper is snug around the hips and abdomen. If the umbilical cord stump is present, fold the diaper edge so that it is below the stump to prevent irritation.

19. Place the baby in a safe place.

20. Dispose of diaper according to type. Wrap disposable diapers up tightly and dispose of promptly. Flush cloth diaper in toilet to remove excess soil and place in diaper pail.

21. Wash hands.

22. Report any unusual bowel movement or rash to parent and, if appropriate, your supervisor.

Infants and Children with Special Needs

There are many conditions that cause an infant to have special needs. Some result in effects to physical development, others on cognitive development. Some conditions affect both physical and cognitive development.

Providing Support to the Child with Special Needs

In many cases, the child's family will have gained extensive knowledge of their child's condition and will be quite involved in their child's support. In some cases, you may be assisting a family just learning to cope with a condition. The family is an integral part of the support team: you must work together to support the child. It's likely that you will follow a specific support plan developed for the child. It's also possible that you will be asked to perform household tasks so that a parent can devote more time to working with the child. You must be prepared to adapt your role and to be flexible in order to be effective.

In this section, we'll discuss some of the more common conditions. Table 20-3 describes other conditions you might encounter.

Autism

Autism is a condition that results from structural disorders in parts of the brain. It occurs in about one in every 500 births. While current research has linked some cases to specific gene mutations, the cause of autism is not known. We do know that it is biological and not related to a poor environment or bad parenting.

Children with autism usually begin to develop symptoms by age three. There are many possible symptoms. It's quite possible that two children with autism will have very different symptoms. Approximately two-thirds of children with autism have below-average intelligence. A child may possess extraordinary ability in a specific task (such as mathematics) even though he or she might not possess average intelligence overall.

Most children with autism have difficulty forming and maintaining social relationships. They avoid interaction with others and usually play alone. Many of them have an altered response to sensory stimulation (sights, sounds, tastes, and touch). They may be overly sensitive to sensory stimulation or appear to ignore all stimulation. Many autistic children have a focussed or narrow attention span and repetitive behaviour.

There is no cure for autism. Treatment is usually centred on encouraging social interaction and addressing specific problem behaviours. Some children with autism undergo intensive one-to-one therapy. Therapy started when the child is very young can help to minimize symptoms. You may be asked to assist in specific play therapy or to work with the child to help change how he or she responds to sounds or sights.

Children with autism do not grow "out" of the condition. Some adults with autism are able to live and work independently. Others require support with everyday activities.

Cerebral Palsy

We discussed cerebral palsy (CP) in Chapter 19. If you choose to provide support to children, it's quite likely that you will be assigned to assist a child with special needs at some time in your career. CP affects one child in every 1000 births. There are four types of CP, each the cause of a malformation or injury to the brain before, during, or shortly after birth. People with CP usually have difficulty with muscle control (having muscle tone that is too tight or too loose). Sensory problems, developmental problems, learning disabilities, and speech problems may also occur.

Down Syndrome

Down Syndrome is a genetic condition produced by an abnormality in chromosome 21. Down Syndrome actually refers to three conditions. The most common is when there is an extra copy of chromosome 21 in each cell. It occurs in one of every 800-1000 births.

Children with Down Syndrome often have distinctive physical features. Some of the more common features include: small nose, wide-set eyes, an upward slant to the eyes, small hands and feet, short stature, and low muscle tone. Most children with Down Syndrome have mild to moderate mental retardation and often have heart and respiratory problems as well as reduced resistance to disease. They are at increased risk for developing Alzheimer Disease or leukemia as adults.

Fetal Alcohol Effect and Fetal Alcohol Syndrome

Fetal Alcohol Effect and **Fetal Alcohol Syndrome** are two disorders that can result from a woman drinking alcohol when pregnant. Fetal Alcohol Effect (FAE) is a milder and much more common form of the two disorders. Both FAE and Fetal Alcohol Syndrome (FAS) can produce physical and psychological impairments. Many people with FAE or FAS will require support all their lives. It is estimated that one in 750 children born has FAE or FAS.

Children with either disorder can have difficulty learning. Many have difficulty paying attention to tasks or are easily distracted. The ability to problem-solve and to learn from previous mistakes is often impaired as well. Some children act impulsively or are extremely stubborn. FAE or FAS may also be linked to learning and attention disorders.

Children with FAE/FAS can benefit from therapy aimed at helping them learn life skills and practise problem-solving. Children with FAE/FAS often benefit from a consistent routine free of overstimulation and distraction.

Fragile X Syndrome

Fragile X Syndrome is a genetic disorder caused by a weakness or a break in a portion of a child's X chromosome. It is an inherited condition and is thought to be the leading cause of inherited learning disabilities and mental retardation.

Children with Fragile X Syndrome often have distinctive facial characteristics such as a long, narrow face, prominent jaw, flat feet, or prominent ears. Psychological problems, including learning disabilities, autism-like symptoms, anxiety, or a dislike of being held or touched, can also appear. Speech and language problems are almost always present.

Children with Fragile X Syndrome are often helped by speech and language therapy. You may be asked to help with any exercises the therapist prescribes. Children with Fragile X Syndrome are often helped by a consistent routine that limits distraction and overstimulation.

Spina Bifida

Spina Bifida is a condition caused by a defect in the way the spinal column has formed. This defect can leave a gap in the spinal column and cause the spinal cord to attach to the spinal column. Most often, the condition involves vertebrae at or below waist level.

There are three main types of Spina Bifida: Spina Bifida Occulta, Spina Bifida Cystica and Cranium Bifida. The most common is Spina Bifida Occulta (Occulta means hidden). Some studies suggest that 5-10 percent of the population has this condition. The vast majority of people with this condition have no symptoms. In fact, they may not even know that they have the condition until an x-ray for other reasons brings the condition to light.

A small number of people with Spina Bifida Occulta do experience physical problems such as loss of sensation in the legs, bowel problems, and incontinence. Sometimes, the condition is noticed when the child has a growth spurt. Surgery can reduce or eliminate the symptoms. Figure 20-5 illustrates the spine of a person with Spina Bifida Occulta.

Spina Bifida Cystica occurs when the gap in the spinal column is so large that a sac forms in the column. In many cases, this sac contains nerves and part of the spinal cord. When it does, there is usually loss of sensation and paralysis below the damaged vertebrae. Incontinence and bowel problems are almost always present. However, the exact impairment will depend upon the location of the sac as well as the nerves affected. In a few cases, the sac contains fluid only and does not cause significant impairment. Figures 20-6 and 20-7 illustrate the two types of Spina Bifida Cystica.

Cranium Bifida occurs when the bones of the skull fail to develop properly. This can cause brain damage and, in severe cases, death.

Table 20-3 lists other conditions that can affect development in children.

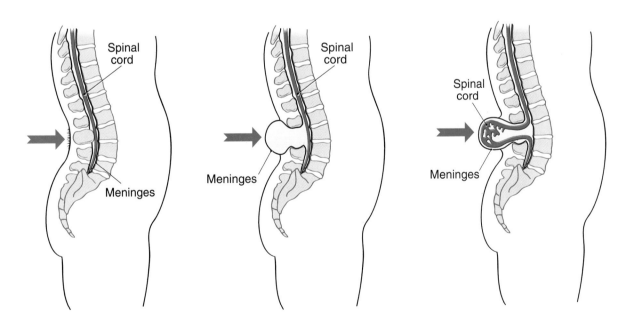

Figure 20-5
Spina Bifida Occulta

Figure 20-6
*Spina Bifida Cystica
(Melomeningocele)*

Figure 20-7
*Spina Bifida Cystica
(Meningocele)*

TABLE 20-3	Other Conditions That Can Affect Development	
Condition	**Cause**	**Affect**
Hydrocephalus	Increase of intracranial fluid in the brain, causing an increased head size and pressure changes in the brain.	Can result in cognitive delays. Hydrocephalus can be treated and impairment diminished.
Cleft Lip	A fissure or opening in the upper lip.	Affects speech and appearance. Can be corrected surgically.
Cleft Palate	A more serious condition in which there is a passageway between the naso-pharnyx and the nose.	Condition complicates feeding and leads to infections. Can be corrected surgically.
Club Foot	A malformation of the bones in which one foot is twisted inward or outward.	Affects gait. Can be corrected surgically.
Congenital Hip Dysplasia	Partial or total hip dislocation.	Affects gait and posture. Some forms can be corrected surgically, others may only be partially corrected.
Phenylketonuria	A disease caused by the absence of a liver (hepatic) enzyme.	If not treated can result in cognitive delays.

Postpartum Depression

It is normal for a new mother to experience emotional feelings after the delivery of her child. A woman's hormones shift very rapidly after delivery. This can cause mood swings.

Two conditions, postpartum blues and *postpartum depression*, are more serious forms of this mood swing. These conditions can produce depression or feelings of sadness in women who have recently delivered a baby.

Postpartum Blues

Researchers estimate that over 75 percent of all new mothers experience postpartum blues. This condition usually occurs within the first ten days after delivery and is related to the rapid drop of estrogen and progesterone levels in the woman's body. A mother with postpartum blues may feel irritable, tired, and down. She may cry for no apparent reason.

Postpartum blues can last for two to three weeks. In most women, it will disappear over time. Reassure the new mother that this condition is quite normal and will pass with time. Work with the new mother to divide tasks so that she can rest or get out of the house for a bit.

Postpartum Depression

Postpartum depression is a serious depression in women who have recently had babies. It affects about 10 percent of new mothers and is more serious than postpartum blues. It results from a combination of biological and psychological factors. Sometimes, postpartum depression occurs in a woman who has experienced depression prior to or during her pregnancy. Many symptoms of postpartum depression can also be those of extreme fatigue. You should report to your supervisor any observation of the following.

1. A lack of enjoyment in life;
2. Disinterest in others;
3. Loss of normal give-and-take in relationships;
4. Feelings of inadequacy and inability to cope;
5. Loss of mental concentration;
6. Disturbed sleep; or
7. Constant fatigue and feelings of ill health.

As a support worker, you may be asked to assist the mother by taking on a number of routine activities so that she can rest. Actively listening, encouraging, and supporting the new mother may also provide some support. In some cases, the mother may require medication.

A more serious form of postpartum depression is that of postpartum psychosis. This condition affects less than one mother in 1000. A mother with postpartum psychosis is not in touch with reality and could harm or neglect her infant. Some mothers with this condition contemplate suicide. You must immediately report to your supervisor any observations of potential harm or neglect as well as any expressed thoughts of suicide. If the mother attempts to harm her infant or herself, you must contact emergency services immediately.

Questions for Review

1. What are the six types of situations in which you may be asked to assist a family with children?

2. What are six common reflexes in the newborn?

3. What milestones would you expect a child to attain by eight months of age?

Questions for Discussion

1. Why is it important to establish a good relationship with the parents? What concerns might the parents have about receiving support?

2. You have been assigned to Mrs. Green, a new mother of premature triplets. Two of the triplets are home. The third is still in hospital. Mrs. Green spends time at the hospital every day, in part so that she can breast feed the infant. You are assigned to a 6-hour shift. The first three hours are spent with the infants at home while Mrs. Green is at the hospital. Mrs. Green is at home for the second three hours.

   What sorts of tasks would you expect to do? Why?

3. Your client, a new mother, has been crying a great deal for the past month and a half. She seems very tired. When you ask how she is, she tells you that she never realized that being a parent would be so difficult. What should you do?

PART FIVE

ASSISTING IN
SPECIAL SITUATIONS

Source: CHATS.

CHAPTER TWENTY-ONE

Mental Health

Terms You'll Use

Anxiety Disorders   A group of conditions in which anxiety becomes extremely disabling over a long period of time.

Bipolar Disorder   A condition in which a person has alternating periods of hyperactivity and depression; also called *manic depression*.

Continuum   Range.

Depression   A range of conditions from a feeling of sadness to a clinical syndrome.

Mental Health   The ability to deal with the conditions of life effectively.

Mental Health Conditions   Conditions that affect a person's self-concept, behaviour, thoughts, or feelings to such an extent that they interfere with the person's ability to deal with situations effectively.

Multiple Loss   The loss of more than one thing at a time.

Omnipotent   The state of being above all harm.

Paranoia   A range of conditions in which a person believes that he or she is being persecuted or threatened.

Risk Factors   Factors that put a person's mental health at risk.

Schizophrenia   A chronic mental health condition that affects a person's ability to take part in everyday activities. The condition may cause delusions, hallucinations, and disordered thinking.

Substance Abuse   The intentional misuse of medications, illicit drugs, or alcohol.

What Is Mental Health?

In understanding *mental health*, it's helpful to review the definition of health in general. As we discussed in Chapter 13, health can be defined as optimum physical, social, and emotional well-being, not just the absence of disease.

Thus, **mental health** refers to having a sense of well-being—having the ability to deal with the conditions of life effectively. Having good mental health can be said to mean that the person is able to adjust to changes in his or her life and is able to make some changes which will maintain or improve his or her quality of life. Being in good mental health is not the same as simply not having a mental illness in much the same way that being physically healthy is not the same as not being sick.

Researchers have proposed six characteristics of mental health. These are presented in Table 21-1.

TABLE 21-1	Characteristics of Mental Health

Self-acceptance—to have a positive, yet realistic, appreciation of yourself.

To have positive relationships—to make and keep friends, get along with people in a social situation, avoid relationships that are harmful to yourself or others.

To be able to make decisions for yourself—without feeling obligated to conform to the expectations of other people.

To feel that you are basically in control of your own life—to have confidence that you can cope with setbacks or get through hard times.

To have a purpose in life—to have goals, a sense of direction, and a sense that life is worth living.

To have a sense of ongoing development—to be open to new ideas and new skills.

Source: National Advisory Council on Aging, *Mental Health and Aging,* Paper #10 in the *Writings on Gerontology* series, March, 1991.

Mental health is not an "either/or" situation. It is defined by how well we are able to function and how satisfied we are with how we function. Health is thus measured in degrees, not by whether or not a factor is fully met. Figure 21-1 illustrates the **continuum**, or range, of mental health.

Most of us have at least one of the four factors, yet we see ourselves as mentally healthy. For example, we all have some anxieties and challenges or feel sad or stressed sometimes, yet are still able to relate to others as well as do what we need and want to do. It's quite normal to have changes in mood or energy level from day to day. It's also normal to feel stressed or down for a brief period of time or to be angry or frustrated over something.

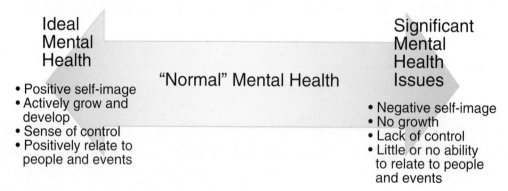

Ideal
Mental
Health

- Positive self-image
- Actively grow and develop
- Sense of control
- Positively relate to people and events

"Normal" Mental Health

Significant
Mental
Health
Issues

- Negative self-image
- No growth
- Lack of control
- Little or no ability to relate to people and events

Figure 21-1 *The Continuum of Mental Health*

Mental Health Across the Life Span

People of any age can experience *mental health conditions*. Some conditions are more common at certain ages. In general, however, older adults do face more problems, losses, and challenges than do people of other ages. Many of these conditions, losses, and challenges can put older adults at greater risk of developing a mental health condition.

Risk Factors

Several social factors which can put a person's mental health at risk have been identified and are called **risk factors**. These include:

- **A recent loss of spouse or close family member.**   The loss of a spouse is considered to be one of the greatest, if not the greatest, loss one might experience. However, the loss of a close family member, or even an exceptionally close friend may also be extremely significant. These losses often bring with them other changes: financial, social, and lifestyle.

- **Being socially isolated.**   Social contacts may decline as people get older. About 30 percent of seniors report spending most of their time alone (Stone & Fletcher, 1986). Friends and family members die, making family size smaller, which means that there are fewer family supports or opportunities for contacts. Social contracts can also diminish if a person has a condition that limits his or her ability to get about, particularly in a Canadian winter. Living alone puts a person at greater risk for isolation.

- **Having a physical disability or poor health.**   Chronic conditions, including physical impairments, have been linked to *depression, anxiety*, and *substance abuse*.
- **Low income**.   Having limited finances can limit a person's social activity. Unexpected costs—for home repairs, for example, can mean significant stress for a person on a limited budget.
- **Sensory defects.**   Vision and hearing problems have been linked to anxiety and even paranoid behaviours. Significant sensory loss may increase social isolation by making it difficult to talk with others or get out to events.
- **Stressful life events.**   Changes in roles, finances, health, and losses are often stressful. Even "positive" stresses, such as a new job or a move to a new location, can cause stress.

CASE EXAMPLE 21-1

Mrs. Emma Chang and her husband Robert, both 78, lived together in the home they had owned since their marriage. They managed well on their Old Age Security and Mr. Chang's private pension. Mrs. Chang has had arthritis for a number of years, but had been able to manage with Mr. Chang's help.

When Mr. Chang died suddenly, Mrs. Chang was not comfortable living on her own and, without her husband's pension, could not really afford to keep up their home. She felt that she had to sell her home and move into an apartment. The only suitable apartment Mrs. Chang could find was in a neighbourhood several blocks from her old home. She now rarely goes out as the neighbourhood is not familiar and she knows no one there.

In this case, her husband's death has caused Mrs. Chang to experience a number of other losses. She lost not only her spouse, but her home, and some of her financial security—all in a very short period of time. This is a common event among older people and is often called **multiple loss**.

Mental Health Conditions

Mental health conditions (also called *mental problems, mental illnesses*, or *psychiatric disorders*) are conditions that affect a person's self-concept, behaviour, thoughts, or feelings to such an extent that they interfere with the person's ability to do what he or she wants or needs to do. For example, a person may have extreme feelings of sadness or worthlessness that make it very difficult or impossible for the person to function.

The term mental health condition can be described as a situation where a person's ability to adapt is affected or limited in some way that affects the person's well-being. Generally, mental health conditions affect the person over a period of time, not just once or once in a while.

Most of us have experienced a problem coping with something. Perhaps you can recall a situation when you simply had too much going on and that last thing was just one thing too many. You might have burst into tears. Perhaps you lost your temper.

Whatever happened, you were probably able to get through it and found the next day better. Does this mean you have a mental health condition? Probably not.

Mental health conditions can be caused by any one of four factors: social causes (such as isolation), biological causes (such as the lack of a specific chemical in the brain), psychological factors (such as extreme stress or emotional trauma), and genetic factors. Sometimes, more than one factor is involved.

Warning Signs of Mental Health Conditions

Mental health conditions often change a person's behaviour. Table 21-2 lists some behaviours that can be warning signs of a mental health condition. It's important to remember that these signs can be a symptom of many conditions, not just mental health conditions. As well, these signs are usually *changes* in the client's usual behaviour. Speak with your supervisor if you notice that any of these signs are present for a prolonged period of time.

TABLE 21-2	Signs of a Mental Health Condition
Warning Signs of Mental Health Condition in Adults	
confused thinking	prolonged sadness or irritability
feelings of extreme highs and lows	excessive fears, worries, or anxieties
social withdrawal	dramatic changes in eating or sleeping habits
strong feelings of anger	
growing inability to cope with daily problems and activities	delusions or hallucinations
	suicidal thoughts
denial of obvious problems	numerous unexplained physical ailments
substance abuse	
Warning Signs of Mental Health Condition in Younger Children	
changes in school performance	frequent temper tantrums
excessive worry or anxiety	hyperactivity
persistent nightmares	persistent disobedience or aggression
Warning Signs of Mental Health Condition in Older Children and Pre-adolescents	
substance abuse	excessive complaints of physical ailments
change in sleeping and/or eating habits	
defiance of authority, truancy, theft, and/or vandalism	prolonged negative mood, often accompanied by poor appetite or thoughts of death
intense fear of weight gain	
inability to cope with problems and daily activities	frequent outbursts of anger

Source: Adapted from the National Mental Health Association, 1999.

Responding to Warning Signs

1. **Be sensitive to changes in behaviour, particularly if you have not noticed the behaviour before, such as a client who suddenly seems more anxious than usual.** Look for cause and effect: does a particular event or situation seem to cause the behaviour?
2. **Tell your supervisor about the behaviour.** Be careful to describe it, not to evaluate it. Instead of saying, "Mrs. G. was really paranoid when we were shopping," say, "Mrs. G. accused me of wanting to leave her alone in the store."
3. **Identify with your supervisor the steps to take if the person is in danger of hurting themselves or another person.**

Common Mental Health Conditions

In this chapter, we'll discuss five common mental health conditions: *depression, schizophrenia,* bipolar disorder, *anxiety,* and paranoia. As you read the following information, be aware that each condition may affect one person differently than it does another. The information presented here provides some general information. You must be careful to follow the support plan developed for your client.

Depression

 Stop and Reflect 21-1

Take a minute and think back to a time in the past when you experienced feelings of sadness. Perhaps you described it as depression at the time, perhaps not. Keeping that experience in mind, consider the following questions:

1. At the time, were you aware of having other feelings? If so, what were they?

_____

_____

_____

2. How did you express those feelings to others? What did you do or say?

_____

_____

_____

3. At the time, were you aware of the cause of these feelings?

_____

▶▶

4. What helped you to get over these feelings? (Others, time, thinking about it differently, etc.)

_____

_____

_____

Keep these things in mind as you read on.

Most of us have used the term *depression*, whether about ourselves or others. We've had a bad afternoon, day, or week. We're frustrated at events—or overwhelmed by them. We might feel helpless or hopeless. For most of us, this is a temporary state—after a bit, the feelings lift and we go on. The situation you described above probably did not last a long time—although it might have seemed to be.

Depression is used to describe a wide range of conditions, from a casual feeling (such as "I was so depressed about that assignment") to what is called a clinical syndrome or depressive episode—a diagnosis that a doctor or psychiatrist might make. Most of this section is concerned with the feeling-state type of depression.

Depression as a Feeling State

This is probably the most common use of the term depression. The feelings are not so strong as to keep us from doing most of our usual activities, although we might not have the usual interest or energy. Usually, these feelings are a reaction to something that has happened to us. These causes can range from things that are fairly minor—a cold that has dragged on a long time, for example—to things that are much more significant, such as the loss of a loved one.

As well, we are generally aware of these causes. Think back to your situation. Were you aware of the cause(s) of your feelings at the time? Chances are that you were, although you might not have always connected your reactions to the event. For example, you might have found it strange that you didn't have your usual interest in something, only later realizing that the lack of interest was related to the sadness.

Depression as a Clinical Syndrome

Depression as a clinical syndrome is far less common. In this situation, the feelings of sadness are often quite extreme—the person may feel unable to do anything at all. They may lose interest in most activities or not have the energy to act. This type of depression usually lasts much longer than the feeling-state type—sometimes months or years. The person may not be able to identify any reason or cause for the condition. This type of depression must be diagnosed by a physician or psychiatrist. It is a serious condition, but can be treated by a combination of medication and counselling.

When you are working with a client who has been diagnosed as having this type of depression, it is very important to learn what approaches are best to use with the client and to follow those approaches carefully.

Signs and Symptoms of Depression

One of the most difficult problems in identifying any type of depression is that the list of signs and symptoms of depression includes things that are opposites. For example, both weight gain and weigh loss can be a symptom, as can an inability to sleep or an inability to remain awake. Sometimes, the symptoms don't seem to be consistent with our idea of what depression is. For example, we don't normally associate frustration with depression, yet it is often present in people who are also depressed. Finally, many of these symptoms are also symptoms of other conditions.

Go back to your situation. Did you experience other feelings? What were they? You probably weren't only sad, but had a number of other feelings as well. These might have included anger, guilt, frustration, or anxiety. You may have shown these feelings in a variety of ways. Perhaps you cried a lot. You might have withdrawn from others, or found yourself unable to relax. Perhaps you lost all interest in food; maybe you ate much more than usual.

Beyond that, depression is a condition we define by how severe a symptom or set of symptoms is, not just whether or not it's present. We don't have a list of symptoms that we can simply check off to identify the condition like we could if the person had, for example, chicken pox. All of the following things can be symptoms of depression:

TABLE 21-2	Possible Symptoms of Depression
weight loss	weight gain
lethargy—too tired to move	hyperactivity—can't settle down
feelings of worthlessness/hopelessness	blames self for things, angry, frustrated
lack of emotions—flat affect	crying easily
sadness	loss of interest in others
headaches	constipation
dizziness	rapid heart beat

Can you see the difficulty? All of us have experienced some of these symptoms, yet very few of us would consider ourselves to be depressed in any sense of the word. Some of these symptoms are opposites of others; some are also symptoms of a great many other conditions. All of this makes depression difficult to identify.

Depression and the Older Person

Older people, like people of any age, can become depressed. Like other ages, older people can experience the short-term feeling-state kind of depression as well as the clinical syndrome. As above, we'll focus on the feeling-state type for now.

Social Attitudes and Depression

Despite the fact that depression is one of the most common mental health conditions among older people, attitudes about the condition can make it harder to identify. Many older people feel that a "mental illness" is an embarrassment and are very reluctant to discuss it. As well, people who work with older people sometimes overlook or misinterpret possible symptoms of depression. This can happen because the worker might:

1. Accept the signs and symptoms as things that can't be changed because they come with growing old.
2. Feel that the person's losses aren't really that significant or that the person could "shake these feelings off" if they really wanted to.
3. Confuse the symptoms of depression with those of cognitive impairment (dementia). At first glance, many symptoms of depression do seem to be much like the symptoms of cognitive impairment. However, they are not, as the following table shows:

TABLE 21-3	Dementia and Depression
Dementia	**Depression**
Client tries to hide cognitive losses, or seems unaware.	Client complains of memory loss or other cognitive losses and is upset over them.
Symptoms progress slowly.	Symptoms progress fairly quickly.
Client tries to answer, but may give vague answers or answers that aren't quite right.	"Don't know" types of answers are common.
Client tries hard to perform tasks well and is frustrated when can't do them.	Client makes little effort to perform, seems not to care.
The client's emotions seem to change easily—one minute upset, the next OK.	The client's mood is consistently sad.
Attention and concentration may be impaired.	Attention and concentration are usually present.

Supporting the Person with Depression

Many clients who are depressed will have a support plan that identifies specific responses to the client's needs. Be sure to follow the client's support plan. The following are general guidelines only.

1. **Accept the client where she/he is.**   If you make the client feel that he or she must behave in a specific way to gain your acceptance, you won't likely be able to establish rapport.
2. **Keep the client at the centre of the activity.**   The client who helps plan things will have more desire to follow the plan.

3. **Be prepared to accept "objective" inconsistencies.** Look for the meaning behind the behaviour and base your interaction on that. A person may tell you that your visit 'doesn't matter', yet you know that they look for you to come. Respond to what they mean, not always what is said.

4. **Recognize you client's need for control.** Situations often rob clients of the ability to make decisions or control a situation. The perception of loss of control can, in some clients, be sufficient to withdraw.

5. **Display your faith in the client's ability to act effectively in the situation, to the degree possible.** This includes the offering of structured choices (where neither option is incorrect) if necessary.

6. **Present challenges which are appropriate.** A rule of thumb is to begin with the most complex task that the person is assured of completing. Positive experiences encourage positive approaches.

7. **Some challenges begin with simple interaction.** Display your interest by showing pleasure at the relationship with the client.

8. **Support self-esteem by direct reinforcement of the person.** Comment on current attributes, activities. If there are none obvious, comment upon those past and still possible.

9. **Encourage physical activity where possible.** There are demonstrated relationships between physical activity and outlook.

10. **Use strength of the interpersonal relationship to help compensate for needs.** Faith in you may be transferred through you to another person or activity. (I believe in you, you believe in X, I believe in X.)

Suicide

Suicide is more common among older people and people who have recently experienced significant physical disability. Studies done in the United States indicate that 25 percent of the suicides that happen there each year are committed by people over 65, even though people over 65 represent only about 11 percent of the total population. We also know that older people who attempt suicide are more likely to be successful in taking their life.

Finally, we know that older people who talk about suicide or make comments like "I may as well do myself in" should *always* be taken seriously. Never assume that a person who says things like this is just trying to get attention or to scare you.

If your client does say these things, listen carefully and with concern, but don't try to argue with the client or tell them that they 'couldn't mean that'. Always report these situations to your supervisor immediately.

Schizophrenia

Schizophrenia is a chronic mental health condition that often has significant effects on a person's ability to take part in everyday activities. Schizophrenia is thought to be caused by biological factors, although it appears that a person can inherit a likelihood of developing the condition.

Schizophrenia can cause the person to have delusions (false ideas or beliefs), hallucinations (hearing, seeing, feeling, smelling, or even tasting things that do not really exist), and disordered thinking (rambling, disconnected, or incoherent speech). The person can also lose motivation, interest, and any ability to express emotion. These experiences can be frightening to both the person and those around him or her. They can cause the person to withdraw from social contact.

Schizophrenia usually appears in people aged 20 to 30. Men often show symptoms at an earlier age than do women. There are four major types of schizophrenia. These are:

Catatonic Schizophrenia. A severe form in which the person is withdrawn and mute.

Disorganized Schizophrenia. A form that results in incoherent speech and behaviour, but does not usually cause the person to experience delusions.

Paranoid Schizophrenia. A form that causes the person to feel persecuted or suspicious, or to have delusions of grandeur (such as being very powerful or rich).

Residual Schizophrenia. A form that causes the person to have no interest in life or motivation to act. Delusions or hallucinations are usually not present, or have ceased.

Medication is the most common treatment for schizophrenia, although counselling may help the person to cope with everyday life. Many medications are available to treat schizophrenia. Most treatments cannot fully control the symptoms and many medications have significant side-effects. Only about 20 percent of the people diagnosed with schizophrenia recover.

Supporting the Person with Schizophrenia

Most clients with schizophrenia will have a support plan that identifies specific responses to the client's needs. Be sure to follow the client's support plan. The following are general guidelines only.

1. **Help the person to stick with his or her medication regimen.** Regularly and conscientiously taking medication can control many symptoms.
2. **Follow a consistent routine for all activities.** This can reduce anxiety and promote a sense of control.
3. **Have patience.** Do not become anxious or frustrated: this will only heighten the client's anxiety.
4. **Actively listen to the client and support his or her efforts to cope.**
5. **Keep things simple.** Do one task at a time. Use short sentences. Make it easy for the client to follow what you are saying: do not abruptly change topics.
6. **Do not argue with a person about whether or not a delusion is real.** The delusion *is* real to the person experiencing it. Comfort the person if the delusion is frightening to him or her.

Bipolar Disorder

Bipolar disorder is commonly known as *manic depression* and occurs when people experience periods of hyperactivity (called *mania*) that alternate with periods of depression. There are many variations of this disorder, but virtually all cause the person to alternate (or cycle) between mania and depression. How frequently these cycles occur depends upon the variation. Some people experience 8-10 cycles in a lifetime, others rapidly move from mania to depression several times a day.

The symptoms of depression in bipolar disorders are almost identical to those of a clinical depression, although they are less likely to be as severe. Manic phases often follow immediately after a period of depression. A manic phase is sometimes seen as recovery, as the person has renewed interest in activity, in life, and is often quite social. The person soon becomes irritable, and may not sleep much at all. Some people in the manic phase feel that they are **omnipotent**—above all harm. The person may talk rapidly, may hallucinate, or have rambling, incoherent speech. People with bipolar disorder have a greater risk of suicide.

Bipolar disorder is thought to be the result of a chemical imbalance in the brain. Medication often offers effective treatment. Some studies suggest that maintaining a consistent sleep routine can reduce the number of cycles the person experiences.

Supporting the Person with Bipolar Disorder

Most clients with bipolar disorder will have a support plan that identifies specific responses to the client's needs. Be sure to follow the client's support plan. The following are general guidelines only.

1. **Help the person to stick with his or her medication regimen.**   Regularly and conscientiously taking medication can control many symptoms.
2. **Follow a consistent routine for all activities, particularly sleep.**
3. **Actively listen to the client and support his or her efforts to cope.**

Paranoia

Like the term depression, we often use the words paranoia or paranoid in many ways. We may say that someone who thinks someone is talking about him or her is paranoid. We may also think that someone who fears that "someone" will hurt him or her is paranoid.

The term **paranoia** is used to describe many conditions—from those above to the psychiatric condition *paraphrenia*, a condition in which the person has delusions (false beliefs) and is constantly feeling persecuted.

Paraphrenia is relatively rare among older adults. Where this condition exists, it is often something diagnosed earlier in the person's life. This condition may affect people with another form of mental illness or dementia.

More common is what we might call "paranoid behaviour". For example, we might say that someone who accuses people of taking things is "paranoid". Like paraphrenia, this type of behaviour often happens when a person has another condition, such as dementia or delirium (acute confusion). It's important to remember that while paranoid behaviours can be a sign of another condition, they do not mean the person has a delirium or dementia.

Sometimes, the paranoid behaviour is related to other things. Research has shown us that people with hearing loss may seem "paranoid". For example, they may think that people are talking about them. People with vision problems may also seem paranoid. They may fear someone whose face they cannot clearly see, for example. These changes more likely are due to the difficulties the person has in seeing and hearing well, not to a mental health condition. Unfamiliar places or people and unexpected events may cause a person to become suspicious or paranoid.

Supporting the Person with Paranoia

Most clients with paranoia will have a support plan that identifies specific responses to the client's needs. Be sure to follow the client's support plan. The following are general guidelines only.

1. **Don't argue with the person.**   It seldom works and may make the person very angry with you.
2. **Focus on areas where the person is not paranoid.**   Some people may feel very positive about their sister, but be very (unrealistically) suspicious about their brother. Trying not to dwell on the negative situation may help.
3. **Remember that this behaviour may be related to sensory loss.**   Help the person to remember to put on their glasses, use their hearing aid, if they have one. Use techniques to enhance vision and hearing.
4. **Explain noises or sights that have been misinterpreted.**   For example, "That noise was a car backfiring." Or, "The wrapping sound was me opening this package."
5. **If the behaviour is related to a lost item: help look for misplaced articles, don't scold the person for losing things.**   If something is frequently lost and can easily be replaced (e.g., a favourite mug), you might suggest that the family get an extra one. If need be, learn where favourite hiding places are.
6. **Don't forget that even the most suspicious person may actually be a victim.** Advise your supervisor of any situation that seems based upon fact.
7. **If possible, use distractions such as music, going for a walk, etc.**
8. **Keep a consistent routine.** This may reduce uncertainty and reassure some persons.

Anxiety and Anxiety Disorders

Anxiety as a Normal Emotion

Everyone feels anxious at one time or another (think back to the night before you wrote your first test). An older person may feel anxious about becoming ill or dependent upon other people. A person who has recently had a car accident may feel very anxious about driving again. For most of us, anxiety allows us to generate energy, focus our efforts, and move into action.

Anxiety as a Disabling Condition

Sometimes, anxiety keeps us from taking any action at all. This may be due to an extreme reaction to a situation, such as being so anxious about speaking in front of a large group that a person cannot talk at all. This type of anxiety can also come from drug or alcohol abuse or as a side-effect of some medications. Sometimes, anxiety increases for a period of time when the person stops taking certain medications, such as Valium. This type of anxiety is not usually considered a mental illness, although a person may benefit from treatment. It is common in older adults. Studies estimate that between 10 and 20 percent of older adults living in the community have symptoms severe enough to require treatment.

Anxiety disorders are a group of conditions in which anxiety becomes extremely disabling over a long period of time. There is usually no identifiable reason for the anxiety. People with anxiety disorders may experience panic attacks with significant physical symptoms (such as shortness of breath, dizziness, a racing heart beat, or chest pain). The person may become unable to do everyday activities, such as going to the mailbox or grocery shopping. Anxiety disorders are the result of biological and psychological causes. They most often appear in persons who are between 20 and 30 years of age.

Anxiety disorders can be treated with medication and a specific type of counselling. It helps the person to change the way he or she sees the anxiety and includes specific ways that the person can reduce the anxiety.

Supporting the Person with Anxiety or an Anxiety Disorder

Most clients with anxiety or anxiety disorders will have a support plan that identifies specific responses to the client's needs. Be sure to follow the client's support plan. The following are general guidelines only.

1. **If the person has a specific technique that they use to address the anxiety, remind or help the person to use it.**
2. **Help the person to relax.**   If the person is in a public place, try to move to a quieter spot.
3. **Do not tell the person that he or she should not be anxious.**   Remember that the person knows this, but is still having difficulty. Be calm and reassuring.

Substance Abuse and Misuse

Substance abuse refers to the *intentional* misuse of medications, illicit drugs, or alcohol. Substance *misuse* is the unintentional misuse of medications. People of any age, sex, or income level can have a substance abuse or misuse problem.

Recent research has identified that alcohol abuse is not uncommon among older adults. Alcohol abuse among older persons is grouped into two types: early-onset (when alcohol has been a problem since early or middle adulthood) and late-onset (alcohol problems that arise in response to stressors in late life). Social isolation, multiple losses, and lack of coping mechanisms all contribute to late-onset alcohol abuse. In some cases, others may influence the person's consumption.

Alcohol Abuse

Symptoms of alcohol abuse include many symptoms common to other conditions: frequent falls, tremors, memory problems, difficulty focussing one's attention, and confusion. This can lead others involved with the person to overlook a potential condition. You should advise your supervisor if you note any of these symptoms. As these symptoms can indicate many conditions, you should report your observations, not make a conclusion about a person's alcohol use.

Supporting the Person with an Alcohol Problem

If your client has an identified support plan, be sure to follow it. The following are general guidelines only.

1. **Reduce social isolation.** Many studies have linked social isolation with alcohol abuse. Spending time with the client and helping him or her to renew or maintain social contacts may provide valuable connections with others and reduce isolation.
2. **Assist the client to find ways to overcome challenges of later life.** Assisting a client to manage his or her household, to shop or even to prepare a meal may reinforce the client's sense of control and ability to cope and reduce the need to escape.
3. **Assist the client to find creative positive ways of coping with stressors.** A walk, a creative activity, even a telephone contact may provide a more positive alternative to alcohol consumption.
4. **You cannot force a client to change his or her behaviour.** You should never attempt to coerce or force a client to alter his or her alcohol consumption. Speak with your supervisor if you have concerns about your client's alcohol consumption.

Medication Misuse and Abuse

Medication abuse or misuse among older adults may be higher than for any other age group. This is likely due in part to the number of drugs prescribed to older adults, as well as to misunderstandings about how a drug is to be taken.

Sometimes, a person unknowingly takes too many medications because he or she has received prescriptions from more than one doctor (for example, a family doctor and a specialist). In this instance, neither doctor may know that the other has prescribed medications for the person.

The symptoms of medication misuse vary, depending upon the medications used and the amounts taken. You should be alert for any change in your client's condition that appears to be the result of medication. Report any changes to your supervisor.

Supporting the Person Who Has
or May Have a Medication Use Problem

If your client has an identified support plan, be sure to follow it. Do not advise the client on the proper use of medications: this is a task for the client's pharmacist or physician.

1. **Discuss any medication problem you observe with your supervisor.**   For example, vision problems may make it difficult for a client to see that he or she has taken the right medication at the right time. A client who is forgetful may not remember that he or she has already taken medication and repeat the dose.
2. **Be alert to the signs of medication misuse if requested.**   As signs vary with the specific medication, you may have to discuss the possible signs with your supervisor or other person responsible for the client's medication.

Questions for Review

1. Describe the continuum of mental health.

2. What six factors can put older adults at risk to develop a mental health condition?

3. Are the warning signs of a mental health condition the same in children as in adults? If not, how are they different?

4. What should you do if you observe any of the warning signs?

5. What are the two types of depression? How are they different?

6. What are some common signs of depression?

7. Why is depression often overlooked in older adults? State at least two reasons.

8. Depression and dementia have similar symptoms. How might you tell the difference between the two?

9. What can you do to assist a client who is depressed?

10. Is suicide a problem among older adults? Why or why not?

11. What five things can you do to assist a client diagnosed with schizophrenia?

12. What is bipolar disorder? By what other name is it sometimes called?

Questions for Discussion

1. How might you support the person who has a degree of paranoia?

2. Can anxiety actually *help* you to function? When is anxiety helpful? When can anxiety make it *harder* for you to function?

3. Your client is a single woman. You are aware that she has abused alcohol in the past and that reducing the possibility for abuse is part of her service plan. What can you do to assist your client to reduce alcohol abuse?

4. You work in a long-term care facility. You are out to dinner with friends when you see one of your residents out to dinner with his family. You stop to say hello and you notice that he is drinking a beer. Residents cannot have alcohol in your facility unless it is allowed by a doctor. You don't know if this resident has permission. What do you think that you should do? Why? Does the resident have the right to drink alcohol when he or she is out of the facility?

CHAPTER TWENTY-TWO

Cognition and Cognitive Impairment

Learning Objectives

Through reading this chapter, you'll be able to:

1. Describe cognition and cognitive impairment.
2. List the six types of function affected by cognitive impairment.
3. Outline the three major causes of cognitive impairment.
4. Identify common reversible and irreversible causes of cognitive impairment.
5. Describe the six fundamental principles of providing support to a client with a cognitive impairment.
6. Explain common approaches to communicating with a client with cognitive impairment.
7. Discuss common approaches to assisting a client to perform tasks.
8. Identify challenging behaviours and describe common approaches to addressing these behaviours.

Acquired Brain Injury   Brain injury that occurs as the result of trauma, anoxia, hemorrhage, seizure, or toxins.

Cognition   The ability to process information; includes six cognitive processes.

Cognitive Impairment   A condition that disrupts the way the brain works to think, use language, remember, and coordinate movements.

Cognitive Processes   The six factors that contribute to cognition: perceiving, recognizing, interpreting, and organizing information; judging; and reasoning.

Delirium A reversible cognitive impairment often related to extremely high fever.

Dementia   A term used to describe the types of cognitive impairment.

Early-Onset Dementia   Dementia that occurs in younger people.

Heterotopic Ossification   Abnormal bone growth in joints after a brain injury.

Irreversible   Not curable or capable of being restored to a previous state.

Progressive   Worsens over time.

Reversible   Curable or capable of being restored to a previous state.

Traumatic Brain Injury   Brain injury caused by traumatic events such as motor vehicle accidents, gunshot wounds, and falls.

What Is Cognition?

There are many definitions of *cognition*. For the purposes of this text, we'll define **cognition** as including six general **cognitive processes**: perceiving, recognizing, interpreting, and organizing information; judging; and reasoning. Cognition also controls motor functions, helping a person to decide how to move, as well as how to sequence the movements into purposeful action. In other words, cognition controls all we do.

The brain is the control centre of the body. It is a complex organ and researchers are just beginning to understand how it works. Much is yet to be discovered. We do know that different areas of the brain are responsible for different cognitive processes. Some functions are held in a relatively well-defined area of the brain. Others appear to be spread out over larger areas. Figure 22-1 illustrates the functions controlled by specific areas of the brain.

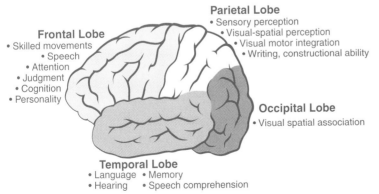

Parietal Lobe
• Sensory perception
• Visual-spatial perception
• Visual motor integration
• Writing, constructional ability

Frontal Lobe
• Skilled movements
• Speech
• Attention
• Judgment
• Cognition
• Personality

Occipital Lobe
• Visual spatial association

Temporal Lobe
• Language • Memory
• Hearing • Speech comprehension

Figure 22-1 *Functions Controlled by Specific Areas of the Brain*

Cognitive processes change over time. Adults process information differently than do infants or children. Most researchers agree that older adults process information differently than younger adults. Despite these differences, most people do not experience a significant decline in cognitive function over their lifetimes.

Cognitive Impairment

Cognitive impairment is the term used to describe conditions which disrupt the way the brain works to think, remember, use language, and coordinate movements. Cognitive impairment is often called *dementia*, particularly when it occurs in older adults.

There are over 100 conditions which can produce cognitive impairment. These conditions can be broken into two general categories: reversible and irreversible conditions. Reversible conditions can be partially or fully cured by treatment. Examples of reversible conditions include **delirium** (a condition often caused by an extremely high fever) and overmedication.

Other conditions produce **irreversible** impairment—which cannot be cured. These include many traumas, vascular dementia, and *senile dementia of the Alzheimer type*. These conditions affect the structure of the brain, damaging and destroying brain cells. Many conditions that produce irreversible impairment are also **progressive**: they become worse over time. Table 22-1 lists common categories of conditions.

TABLE 22-1	Common Conditions Causing Cognitive Impairment	
Irreversible and Progressive	**Irreversible and Non-Progressive**	**Reversible**
Alzheimer Disease *(Senile Dementia of the Alzheimer Type)*	Trauma	Infection
	Hemorrhage	Drug Toxicity
Vascular Dementia	Subdural Hematoma *(a bruise under the skull)*	Vitamin Deficiency
Creutzfeldt-Jakob's Disease		Tumour
Huntington's Disease		Depression
Parkinson's Disease		Normal Pressure Hydrocephalus
Alcohol-related Dementia		Congestive Heart Failure
Aids-Related Dementia		Thyroid Disease
Frontal-Lobe Dementia		Metabolic Disorders

It's important to remember that a person can have both an irreversible cognitive impairment (like Alzheimer Disease) and a **reversible**, or curable, cognitive impairment (from an illness or overmedication, for example). Treating the reversible impairment may reduce the symptoms of the disease and help the person to function better. You should never overlook symptoms of a possible reversible impairment.

What Is Confusion?

Have you ever said that someone was confused? What made you say that about the person?

_____

_____

_____

_____

Look at your answer. Did you say that the person was confused because of something they did—like answering a question inappropriately or losing something?

Confusion is not cognitive impairment. Sometimes hearing loss, stress, or a person who just isn't paying attention can result in a behaviour that seems wrong. A person with cognitive impairment is often confused, but a person who appears confused doesn't always have a cognitive impairment.

What Is Dementia?

As we discussed earlier, **dementia** is a term that is often used to describe many types of cognitive impairment when they occur in older adults. The term dementia is used to refer to a group of diseases that are all very similar. Some rare forms of dementia can occur in people as young as age 30. When it occurs in a younger person, the condition is called **early-onset dementia**.

About 250 000 Canadians have some type of irreversible dementia. The risk of dementia increases with age. About 8 percent of the population over 65 has some form of dementia, and this rises to 35 percent of people over 85 (*Canadian Study on Health and Aging*, 1994). Despite the fact that it is more common in people over 85, dementia is *not* a normal part of aging.

Remember that the terms *acquired brain injury* or *traumatic brain injury* are used to describe cognitive impairment in a person of any age when the impairment is caused by a trauma. The impairment caused by trauma differs from that caused by non-traumatic causes. We'll look at these conditions in a separate section in this chapter.

Alzheimer Disease

Alzheimer Disease is the most common cause of dementia in older people. It probably accounts for 75 percent of all irreversible dementias.

The disease is named after Dr. Alois Alzheimer, a German doctor who first de-scribed the disease in 1906. Dr. Alzheimer noticed changes in the brain tissue of a woman who had died of an unusual mental illness. Upon an autopsy, he found abnormal clumps (now called senile plaques) and tangled bundles of fibres (now called neurofibrillary tangles) in the brain. These plaques and tangles are considered to be the hallmarks or characteristics of Alzheimer Disease.

Scientists also have found other changes in the brains of people with Alzheimer Disease. There is a loss of nerve cells in areas of the brain that are vital to memory and other mental abilities. There also are lower levels of the chemicals in the brain that carry complex messages back and forth between the billions of nerve cells. Alzheimer Disease may disrupt normal thinking and memory by blocking these messages between nerve cells.

Causes of Alzheimer Disease and Other Irreversible Dementias

We don't know for certain what causes Alzheimer Disease. We do know that some things increase a person's risk of developing it. The major risk factors are age and family history. Another possible risk factor is a serious head injury. Researchers are also examining the possibility that metals (such as aluminum, zinc, and lead) may cause the disease.

It's important to remember that Alzheimer Disease is probably not caused by any single factor. It is more likely to be the result of several factors that act differently in each person. For example, genetic factors alone may not be enough to cause the disease. Other risk factors may combine with a person's genetic makeup to increase his or her chance of developing the disease.

Other dementias may be the result of poor circulation in the brain, heavy metal poisoning, or metabolic conditions.

Symptoms

Usually, irreversible dementias begin slowly. The only symptom at first may be mild forgetfulness. The person may lose keys or misplace his or her wallet. Because forgetfulness is something that happens to us all at some time, this symptom may not be noticed by the person or those around him or her.

Later, memory loss becomes more obvious. The person may have trouble remembering recent events, where familiar things are located (such as the post office or the grocery store), or even the names of familiar people or things. The person may have difficulty solving simple problems. At this stage, driving a car is difficult and dangerous, although the person may not realize it.

As the disease goes on, the symptoms become serious enough to cause concern. For example, the person with dementia may not remember how to do simple, everyday tasks, like brushing his or her teeth or combing his or her hair. The person can no longer think clearly and may begin to have problems speaking, understanding, reading, or writing.

In the later stages, the person with dementia may become anxious or aggressive or wander away from home. It is at this later stage that families often begin to consider admitting the person to a long-term care facility. Despite this, the Canadian Study on

Health and Aging estimates that 50 percent of all people with dementia live in the community. Most of these people live with family members, often with a husband or wife.

Diagnosis

We don't have a test that will tell us for sure that a person has Alzheimer Disease or most other irreversible dementias. A firm diagnosis of the disease can only be made by examining brain tissue for tangles and plaques. However, doctors use a number of things to help to diagnose probable Alzheimer Disease. They often look for other causes for the dementia—like overmedication, sensory problems, or illnesses. They also often run a series of medical tests. Doctors at specialized centres can diagnose "probable Alzheimer Disease" correctly 80 to 90 percent of the time.

Duration of the Condition

The course the disease takes and how fast changes occur vary from person to person, as well as from one type of dementia to another. Some people may live as little as five years after the diagnosis, while others may live with it for as many as 20 years. Some people may lose abilities very quickly; others may see a decline over a much longer period of time.

Treatment

At present, there is no treatment that can cure or stop the progression of Alzheimer Disease or most other irreversible dementias. However, some new medications seem to help the person to think more clearly.

Also, some medications may help control symptoms of dementia such as sleeplessness, agitation, wandering, anxiety, and depression. Treating these symptoms often makes the person more comfortable and makes his or her care easier for caregivers to provide. Medications may not help in all cases, however, and may make the symptoms worse for some people.

It is important to be aware that symptoms may also be the result of other causes and that they may respond to treatment. Sometimes, the treatment is simple. For example, a person who has a dementia and wears glasses will generally be more responsive if he or she is wearing her glasses. The person will be able to see better. This means that it's more likely that information will reach the person's brain more clearly which, in turn, can help him or her to function.

Caring for the Person with Dementia
Fundamental Principles of Support

There are six fundamental principles you must keep in mind when working with a client with dementia. Relate the first three principles to what you would have done in response to Stop and Reflect 22-2.

Stop and Reflect 22-2

Consider the following situation. You are home alone on a stormy night. No one else is expected to be at home. It is 2:30 a.m. when you hear pounding on the front door. You go to answer the door. You try to switch on the outside light, but it does not turn on. In the brief glare of a flash of lightning, you see a person in a dark, hooded sweater. You do not recognize the person.

How do you feel? What are you thinking? Will you open the door?

_____

_____

_____

_____

You ask the person at the door to tell you who they are. When the person speaks, you realize it is one of your friends who lives nearby.

How do you feel now? Have your feelings changed from the ones you had before you knew who the person was? Would you open the door?

_____

_____

_____

_____

1. **Every action has a purpose to the person performing the action.** Even the most aimless activity is purposeful to the person who is performing it. For example, studies have shown that clients who wander do so for a number of reasons: to get exercise, to relieve boredom, or to be with others. Whether or not you understand the client's purpose does not matter.

2. **Every action has meaning for the person doing it.** No activity is meaningless.

3. **The world, as the person perceives it, is as real to him or her as our world is to us.** For example, a client may refuse to enter an elevator because he or she sees the elevator is a small, dark hole and the client fears that he or she will fall. Do your best to see what the client might see. This will help you to understand the behaviour. Never argue with a client about what he or she perceives.

4. **The person may lose words, but never lose feelings.** The ability to experience emotions remains with the client long after he or she loses the ability to verbally communicate. Use nonverbal forms of communication to help get your message across.

5. **You are the person who must adapt and change.** The client with dementia has little, if any, ability to adapt his or her behaviour. You must adapt your approach to the client's needs.

6. **Your approach to the client will determine whether or not communication is successful.**

Communication

Communication with the person with dementia is one of the most important parts of caring for the person (Photo 22-1). It can also be one of the most challenging. The person may not be able to find the right words or many words at all. This can be painful, frustrating, and embarrassing for the person and for the caregiver.

As we discussed in Chapter 8, nonverbal components of communication (body language) can often be more significant than the words used. In communication with clients with dementia, body language may be the most significant component of communication. This is because the person gradually loses the ability to understand concepts and words. The person may also be less able to tell that someone is trying to get his or her attention and may have difficulty following a conversation.

You should focus on four things when communicating with a person with dementia: the setting, your approach, the message, and the client's response. Remember that the person will pay attention to your body language, no matter what you are saying. Make sure that you know how you look and act as you speak with the client. The following tips can make communication easier.

Photo 22-1
Good communication requires patience and creativity when there are barriers to overcome.
Source: CHATS.

The Setting

1. **Talk to the person in a place free from distractions.** Move away from background noise (such as an open window, air conditioner, television, or a crowded room).
2. **Do not position yourself between the person and a window.** The glare from the window will make it impossible for the person to see your face. This can frighten the person.

Your Approach

1. **Approach the person from the front.** Many people with dementia ignore their peripheral (side) vision.
2. **Approach the person slowly.** Walking quickly up to a person may startle or frighten him or her.
3. **Do not invade the person's personal space.** Doing so will make the person uncomfortable and hamper his or her ability to understand your message.
4. **Identify yourself at the beginning of your conversation.** Allow time for the person to acknowledge you. If possible, gain eye contact before proceeding.
5. **Use a calm and gentle approach.** Don't demand that a person do something. Make sure that your body language does not convey that you are upset or in a hurry.
6. **Make sure that you are at eye level.** Crouch, sit, or kneel in front of the person if necessary.
7. **Try using touch to help convey your message, if acceptable to the client.** Be aware that touch may not be helpful to communication with every person.
8. **Make sure your body language is in tune with your words.** Remember that the person will take his or her cue from your body language.
9. **Don't patronize or talk down to the client.** The person will sense your tone and respond negatively.

Your Message

1. **Use short sentences with simple words.**   Long sentences or words with many syllables will make it harder for the person to follow your message.
2. **Speak slowly.**   Consciously slow down your rate of speech.
3. **Keep your tone gentle and normal.**   Avoid shouting or speaking forcefully. (This is harder to do when you are speaking slowly.)
4. **Make time for social pleasantries before beginning a task or asking for information.**   Most people with dementia retain social skills well into the later stages of the condition. Allowing the person to use these familiar skills can help to put the person at ease and make the remaining communication easier.
5. **Use concrete terms and words you know are familiar to the client.**   If possible, use words the client uses.
6. **Allow the person time to understand what you've said before continuing.**   It is very frustrating for the person to have too little time to understand. As a result, the person may cease trying to communicate at all.
7. **Give the person time to answer a question before going on to another.**   This encourages the person to participate in the conversation.
8. **Ask simple questions which have a "yes" or "no" answer.**
9. **Don't order the person to do something.**   The person is still an adult and should be asked and encouraged, not ordered.
10. **Don't argue with the person about their statements.**   If something is incorrect, gently state the correct information. In some cases, it may be better to distract the person by changing the subject. Whatever you do, try to avoid embarrassing the client. For example, if a client says that another person's purse is hers, you might gently respond that although the purse looks like the client's it actually belongs to another person.
11. **Use notes if the person can read and follow them.**   Some people can follow only printed notes. If you use a note, make sure that it is clear. List any steps the person is to take in the order the person is to do them.
12. **Be flexible.**   If the client has difficulty understanding a word or phrase, try a different one that means the same as the first.
13. **Be patient.**   Communication takes time.
14. **Remember that an ill or tired person will not hear as well.**   Take this into account as you decide how much you will attempt to get across at one time.

The Client's Responses

1. **Be sensitive to the person's body language and the tone of his or her words.** This is often the first indication you will have of how well your message is getting through.
2. **Acknowledge and respect the person's feelings.**
3. **Actively and carefully listen to what the person is trying to say.**   This will do two things. First, it will enhance the likelihood that you will understand. Second, your body language will also let the person know that you are interested in his or her thoughts.
4. **Be aware that the person may only be able to speak in concrete terms.**   In particular, the ability to make comparisons may be lost. The person who says to

you "I was hit by a Mack truck" likely means that the person *feels* like he or she was hit, not that the event actually happened.

5. **Focus on a word or phrase that makes sense or seems to be 'key' to the client's message.** Often, once you have a key word or phrase, you can make guesses and ask questions to get the whole message.

6. **Ask family and friends about possible meanings of words or phrases you don't understand.**

CASE EXAMPLE 22-1

Mrs. Lavigne is a resident of a long-term care facility. She has vascular dementia. Support workers have noticed that she calls every female who helps her "Claire". At first, staff members assume that she is confused. One day, a support worker asks Mrs.

Lavigne's family about the name. She learns that "Claire" is the first name of the niece who cared for Mrs. Lavigne before she moved into the facility. Thus, "Claire" is the name Mrs. Lavigne uses to refer to any woman who helps her.

Communicating with Others When the Client Is Present

There will be times when you and your client are with other people. Make sure that you include the client in any conversation to the extent that he or she can participate. Even if the client cannot take active part in the conversation, attempt to include the person by making sure he or she is physically a part of the group (Photo 22-2). These tips can help you keep the person included.

1. **Don't ask questions that rely on a good memory.** This relies upon an ability that is not strong. This can be frustrating and embarrassing for the client.

2. **Don't talk to others about the person in front of the person.** Respect the person's presence. If there is information about the client that you must convey to another, do so when the person is out of the room.

3. **Don't ignore the person.** The person will notice the lack of inclusion. If possible, ask the person questions that you know he or she can answer to help keep the person part of the conversation.

Photo 22-2
Support the client to do their best. Here, a worker encourages discussion.
Source: CHATS.

Supporting a Client with the Performance of Tasks

As a support worker, you often will be required to assist a client with routine tasks of living. The eight questions we described in Chapter 19 can be a good starting point for determining what the client can do and when the client will need help. Table 22-2 recaps these eight questions.

TABLE 22-2	Assessing a Client's Ability to Perform Tasks

- WHAT tasks does the client see as important to do?
- WHAT does the client enjoy doing?
- WHAT is the client able to do?
- HOW does the client do those things?
- WHEN is it easiest for the client to perform the task?
- WHICH parts of a task is the client unable to do?
- WHY is the client unable to do those parts?
- HOW does the client want you to assist?

In addition to the eight questions, there are several steps you can take to make the process easier for you both.

1. **Focus on familiar skills or tasks.** Familiar is easier and can boost the person's self-esteem.
2. **Break the task down into simple steps.** Small simple tasks are much easier to do.
3. **Give choices whenever you can.** We all like to have control over the things we do.
4. **Allow plenty of time for tasks to be done.** All cognitive processes will take longer. If the client feels pressured to respond quickly, anxiety may further hamper ability.
5. **Allow time to rest when needed.** The client will not be able to function well when tired or overstimulated.
6. **Follow the client's cues.** Learn what parts of the task are frustrating or impossible. Plan on completing these steps before the client becomes frustrated.
7. **Sincerely praise any success.** Genuine praise lifts anyone's spirits. Make sure that your praise is appropriate for an adult.

Challenging Behaviours

Often, people with dementia develop some behaviours that are hard for us to understand. These behaviours include wandering, becoming angry, becoming frightened, refusing to take a bath, or even refusing to go into a room. The behaviours seem to happen without warning and may last a few minutes or a long time. These are called *challenging behaviours.* You may hear other people refer to these behaviours as problem behaviours or difficult behaviours. They should not be seen as problems or difficulties, they simply are behaviours caregivers must strive to understand. They pose a *challenge* to caregivers who must unravel the meaning of the behaviour, the cause of the behaviour, as well as determine what, if anything, can alter the behaviour.

Understanding the A-B-Cs of Behaviours

One helpful way of looking at actions is to use the A-B-C (Action, Because, and Communication) approach. This approach is based upon the belief that no action or behaviour just happens. Each is a product of some reason or stimulus. Additionally, each action is affected by others' responses to the behaviour.

This approach asks the caregiver to look at each challenging behaviour in terms of what causes (or seems to cause) the behaviour and what the caregiver's response communicates to the client.

Table 22-3 describes the Action, Because, and Communication. Through this method, the caregiver may be able to figure out what triggers the behaviour. The caregiver may also be able to determine what may be changed in order to reduce the incidence of the behaviour. Let's take a look at each of these steps.

TABLE 22-3	The A-B-Cs of Behaviour

Action

- What you see the person doing
- May include signals before the behaviour
- Generally, the action is the event to which we react

Because

- The reason or "why"
- What thing that triggers or cues the behaviour
- Often not readily seen

Communication

- How we respond to the behaviour
- How we signal that we have "understood"
- Communication can be used to encourage or discourage the behaviour

The Action

This is the actions or behaviours that you see, such as wandering, yelling, or striking out at another person. Some actions are preceded by other actions, called warning signs or signals. For example, a client who is about to strike out may narrow his or her eyes. Determining warning signs can help you to prevent an undesired behaviour from happening.

The Because

The because is the reason for the behaviour. Because they trigger the behaviour and occur before the behaviour happens, we often overlook these things. The because is important. If you can determine what triggers an undesirable behaviour, you may be able to remove the trigger and stop the behaviour from happening.

There are four main sources of triggers. Examining each as a potential source of the action may help you to define the likely reason.

1. **Emotional and Physical Health.**   A person who is ill, in pain, tired, already frightened or upset may react unpredictably. Sometimes, the trigger is a biological need. For example, a person who wanders may have to use the washroom. Similarly, emotional needs can trigger behaviours. A person who needs the comfort of others may refuse to leave an area where other people are present.

2. **Environment.**   Sometimes, the environment is too busy, too noisy, even too hot or too cold. Environmental distractions can overstimulate the person, causing the person to react unpredictably. A loss of personal space can cause a person to strike out at another. A confusing environment can heighten a person's disorientation and trigger anxiety or fear. For example, a resident of a long-term care facility who cannot tell which room is his or hers may end up in other residents' rooms, causing upset to all concerned. Placing a distinctive wreath on the resident's door may help the resident to find the right room more easily.

CASE EXAMPLE 22-2

A facility noticed that cognitively-impaired residents regularly refused to enter a particular elevator in the home. This elevator was in a wing that had been recently renovated. The problem was not noticed until after the renovation. Staff members decided to observe resident behaviour to see if they could find out what the problem was. They soon realized that a black rubber strip placed at the entrance to the elevator was apparently frightening the residents. It appeared as though residents felt that the black strip was a hole into which they might fall. Replacing the strip with a brighter coloured one solved the problem.

3. **Tasks or Demands.**   A task that is too complex or that needs to be done too quickly may overwhelm the person and trigger anger or anxiety. Similarly, too much to do at any one time may overwhelm the person.

4. **Communication.**   Difficulty in understanding communication or in making oneself understood can trigger anxiety or aggression.

Once you've determined the possible triggers, you can attempt to eliminate or change them so that they do not provoke the behaviour. Preventing the behaviour will likely save the client a great deal of distress as well as make your job easier.

The Communication

You will not be able to prevent every challenging behaviour. There will be situations when you will have to respond to an unexpected and challenging situation. How you respond to a challenging behaviour is important as it can either reduce the behaviour or make it worse. This section discusses some common behaviours and possible responses.

Wandering

CASE EXAMPLE 22-3

Madeline Green often wanders throughout the halls of the long-term care facility where she lives. The support workers who care for her have determined that Mrs. Green's wandering is related to a need for exercise and a need to see other people.

Occasionally, support workers have to stop Mrs. Green, in order to bring her to the dining room or to help her get ready for bed. The support workers have found that trying to stop Mrs. Green makes her upset and can cause her to yell at the staff.

The support workers have learned to walk with Mrs. Green for a bit as they gently guide her in the direction they desire her to go. When the workers approach Mrs. Green is this manner, she rarely becomes upset. In fact, she seems to enjoy the workers' company as they walk.

Wandering can often be linked to a specific event, such as the need to use the bathroom, the desire to see others, or to get exercise. Remember that the activity has meaning for the person. Try to identify what it is that the person is wandering in order to do. If you cannot determine this, or if the wandering seems to be in response to a need for exercise or stimulation, the best approach may be to provide a safe area in which he or she can wander. If you must stop a wandering client, try to distract him or her or gently guide the person in the desired direction. A restraint should *not* be used to control wandering as it can cause the client to become very angry and aggressive.

Anger or Aggression

Anger and aggression are usually signs that the person is frightened and feels the need to defend or protect him or herself. These behaviours can be linked to many causes. The environment can be too stimulating, the environment may be unfamiliar, or there may be many unfamiliar people or sounds in a familiar setting. Losing sight of a familiar person or object can cause the person to feel suddenly alone and insecure. Sudden movements or startling noises (such as a yell or scream) may put the person on guard. Even the difficulty of adapting to varying levels of light (such as when the person leaves a brightly lit hallway to enter a dark room) may upset the person as he or she cannot see well enough to become comfortable with the surroundings.

Physical causes can also trigger anger or aggression. Fatigue or sleep deprivation can cause the person to become angry when bothered (much as it might cause you to become irritable). Physical discomfort (such as that caused by pain or even constipation) can trigger anger. Other potential triggers include the side-effects of medications, hallucinations, or sensory loss.

Anger or aggression can be triggered for psychological reasons as well. The person may be reacting to the pressure of too many demands at once. The person may be frustrated in response to a lack of ability or upset over a change in routine. As well, many people with a dementia can easily adopt the emotions of others (for example, becoming angry if there is another angry person in the area). Inappropriate communication, such as being scolded, confronted, or treated in an offensive manner, can cause the person to become angry or aggressive.

The best response to angry or aggressive behaviour is to eliminate the trigger. Attempt to determine the reason for the anger or aggression. Can you eliminate or reduce it?

Sometimes, you can minimize an angry or aggressive outburst if you can "catch" it as it begins. Many times, a person's body language will warn of anger before it happens. Get to know these signs. As well, avoid surprising a client. Surprise often turns to fear when the person cannot easily understand what is going on.

If you must respond to a client who is angry or aggressive, use these guidelines.

1. **Use a quiet approach.**   Be gentle and calm. Do not yell or be forceful.
2. **Do not ridicule or attempt to "laugh off" the situation.**   Your actions will tell the person that you are making fun of him or her.
3. **Make sure that the person's surroundings are calm and quiet.**   Turn off radios or televisions. Ask others nearby to leave the area, if possible.
4. **Don't overwhelm the person with too many commands, too many words, or speech that is too rapid.**   This simply heightens the person's sense of a loss of control and may heighten the anger.
5. **Listen to the person's words and body language.**   He or she may say or do something that indicates the source of the anger. As well, the act of calmly listening and attempting to understand may calm the person.
6. **Don't challenge the person.**   Attempting to reason with the person, or to force the person to do something may provoke more anger or even physical violence.

CASE EXAMPLE 22-4

Mr. Green has Alzheimer Disease. He is in the middle stages of the disease. He lives at home while he awaits admission to a long-term care facility. He receives support service five days per week. Mr. Green can very quickly become angry if he is startled or if someone near him is moving very quickly. In particular, he will become angry if someone tries to quickly make him do something. He will strike out at a support worker who insists he do something.

Support workers have learned that they can best assist Mr. Green by gently asking him to participate. If he refuses, the support worker does not press the issue. She leaves him alone for a few moments. When she returns, Mr. Green is often no longer angry.

7. **Distract the person if possible.** You can sometimes reduce the anger by causing the person to focus on something else.
8. **Give the person private space when necessary.** Leave the room, if possible. Ask others to do the same. Give the person a few minutes to calm down before returning.
9. **Avoid restraining the person.** The use of a restraint will almost certainly be seen as a sign of aggression. It usually heightens the person's anger. Try leaving the person alone in a room instead.
10. **Use touch carefully.** To an angry person, touch can be perceived as a sign of aggression.
11. **Do not argue with the person.** Instead, gently repeat information.
12. **Never approach anger with anger.**

Catastrophic Reactions

A catastrophic reaction is an overreaction to a situation. The person is not able to control these reactions which are often unpredictable, although the reaction may occasionally be preceded by flushing, restlessness, or a refusal to receive care.

When you respond to the client, you must be aware that the behaviour is not willful. Attempt to reduce the resident's feelings of anxiety and panic by providing comfort and support.

You may be able to prevent some catastrophic reactions by maintaining familiar routines and a quiet environment. Interpersonal approaches can also help. Always approach the person from the front and remain in his or her field of vision. Introduce new persons and situations carefully and slowly. Avoid attempting to force the person to do things beyond his or her capacity.

Delusions, Paranoia, Hallucinations

Remember that delusions, paranoia, or hallucinations are the person's reality. Telling a person that what they see, hear, or believe is wrong will not help. Focus your efforts on preventing frightening episodes by ensuring that the person feels safe and secure. Try to create a calm and nonthreatening environment. You should also attempt to identify any physical causes of hallucinatory behaviour (such as fever, dehydration, or poor nutrition).

If a person is experiencing delusions, paranoia, or hallucinations, try the following:

1. **Do not argue or try to rationalize with the person.** This will only upset the person.
2. **Reassure or distract the person if he or she feels threatened.** Some hallucinations may not be threatening to the person.
3. **Ensure that the person is not misinterpreting the situation.** It may help to explain that what the person sees as a dead body is actually a pile of laundry on the floor. If the person cannot accept your explanation, do not argue.
4. **If the person is not in distress or causing others distress, ignore the behaviour.**
5. **Problems in hearing or vision may contribute hallucinations and paranoia.** Monitor the person for physical causes of the behaviour and report as necessary.

Acquired Brain Injury

Acquired brain injury refers to brain injuries that occur as the result of any one of the following five factors.

Trauma.   This includes injuries caused by motor vehicle accidents, by being hit with a pole, brick, or bat, by sustaining a fall, as well as gunshot wounds.

Anoxia.   Injury caused by the lack of oxygen in the brain (such as that caused by carbon monoxide poisoning, a cardiac arrest, or an airway obstruction).

Vascular.   Injuries caused by a hemorrhage, the result of surgery, or a vascular malformation. Some definitions also include strokes in this category. Others exclude all strokes except those caused by a hemorrhage.

Seizure.   Injury caused by seizures.

Toxins.   Injury caused by substance abuse, ingestion of lead, or inhaling volatile agents (such as glue or gasoline).

Acquired brain injuries do not include conditions that are inherited, that are present at birth, or are progressive. Acquired brain injuries are not caused by dementias.

The majority of acquired brain injuries are the result of motor vehicle accidents. More men than women are affected by this type. Most accident-related brain injury occurs in people between the ages of 16 and 24 years of age. Falls account for a significant number of brain injuries. In fact, falls are among the leading causes of acquired brain injuries among older adults.

The Effect of Brain Injuries

The effect of a brain injury will depend upon the size and location of the injury, as well as whether or not the person has experienced any secondary problems such as infection, problems that arise from the brain's reaction to the injury (such as changes in the blood vessels affected, swelling, bruising), or increased pressure in the brain. Cells damaged by the primary injury can release chemicals and other products that cause additional damage. In many cases, the secondary effects can be more damaging than the initial injury.

Keep in mind that the person's ability to recover may change from day to day or even hour to hour. What could be done easily at one time may be impossible just hours later. Identifying when, where, and with whom the person is most able is important to understanding when a particular task is appropriate and when it is too difficult.

Loss of memory is one of the most common effects. The person may find it difficult to remember common and familiar information, such as people's names. New information, such as remembering details of a phone message or an appointment, may be difficult. The person may become lost in familiar territory or forget where he or she left things.

CASE EXAMPLE 22-5

Greg Martin is a 34-year-old who sustained a head injury in a car accident two years ago. Until the accident, he was a senior sales representative for a utility company. Although Greg had few physical injuries from the accident, his brain injury impaired his ability to coordinate his activities. He finds it difficult to drive.

A year ago, Greg's employer offered him a job that did not require him to drive. However, Greg has memory problems that are minor on one day and very significant on the next. As a result, he was not able to do the tasks required. He received a disability pension and "retired".

Greg has found his inability to work frustrating. He has always kept busy. Now, sometimes even the simplest things are impossible for him to do. He does enjoy working in a volunteer position with a local agency. He is able to go to the agency on his "good" days.

Greg uses support services to help him organize himself, to get ready for his volunteer work, and to help him manage his banking and bill-paying. His support workers adapt to the dramatic changes in Greg's ability from day to day. They also recognize that Greg is an intelligent person who has significant impairments in some abilities.

Brain injury can also affect the person's ability to plan, initiate, or properly organize activities. Simple, once-familiar tasks, such as getting a glass of milk, may become very frustrating. Problem-solving abilities may also be impaired. A person may make quick and poor judgments or not react at all to a situation. Common social skills may also be lost, making it difficult and embarrassing for the person to take part in social activities.

There also may be losses in the ability to focus one's attention, to respond quickly to a situation, to sequence physical movements, as well as to control impulses. Hearing, vision, and perception may become altered, either as a result of the primary injury or a secondary injury.

The person also may experience loss of the ability to actually control movement. In some cases, the person may develop abnormal bone growth in certain joints (such as the hips, shoulders, knees, and elbows). This bone growth is called **heterotopic ossification** and is a secondary effect of the brain injury.

Supporting a Person with a Brain Injury

Supporting a person with a brain injury is a complex and daunting task. Most people who sustain a moderate or severe injury will have to make adaptations and adjustments throughout their lives. Even people who have made significant recovery will have to cope with problems related to the injury.

Each person's situation will be different. People with the same type of injury will often require different coping and support strategies. It is extremely important that a support plan be developed with the person and that the plan be followed by all persons supporting the person.

You may find that some strategies used to support a person with a brain injury are similar to those used for other conditions such as stroke or dementia. Do not assume from this that the person's brain injury is the same as the other condition. It is not.

In many cases, the person will have family support. Note that the family will also be making adjustments as it learns to get along with the changes the injury has brought about. Like your client, the family may show a mixture of joy (that the person has survived) and grief (that the person has changed). Support the client and family members as they deal with these emotions.

Questions for Review

1. What six processes make up cognition?

2. What are the two main categories of cognitive impairments?

3. Do all irreversible cognitive impairments continue to get worse with time? If not, which conditions are nonprogressive?

4. Is confusion the same as cognitive impairment? Why or why not?

5. What do we call dementia that occurs in a younger person?

6. What is the most common cause of irreversible dementia?

7. What six principles are fundamental to the support of the person with dementia?

8. Are all hallucinations distressing to a person? Why or why not?

9. What causes an acquired brain injury?

10. You are assigned to a client who has an acquired brain injury. What should you keep in mind as you work with this client?

Questions for Discussion

1. You are assigned to a client with dementia to complete his or her care. How might you assess the client's ability to do the tasks involved? How might you support the client to perform the tasks of which he or she is capable?

2. You are to take your client for a walk. When you get into the hallway, the client looks from side to side, backs up, and refuses to enter the doorway. Use the A-B-C approach to identify what might be the cause of the situation and report on your response. Discuss your approach with your colleagues.

3. Today, you are preparing Mr. Urich for a bath. When you approach him with the towels, he begins to scream at you. He raises his fist to strike out. What do you do?

4. You have been assigned to assist a client with Alzheimer Disease. What can you do to make communication with the client easier?

CHAPTER TWENTY-THREE

Abuse

Terms You'll Use

Abuse   Harm to a victim caused by anyone upon whom the victim relies for basic needs or support.

Cycle of Abuse   A term used to describe the three phases of abuse; abuse, remorse, and anger escalation.

Failure to Thrive   The condition of abuse that causes a child to fail to grow and develop.

Infantilize   The treatment of an adult like a child.

Neglect   The intentional or unintentional failure to provide the essentials of life.

Abuse

Stop and Reflect 23-1

When I hear the term *abuse* I think of the following things:

_____

_____

_____

_____

The emotions I associate with the term *abuse* are:

_____

_____

If I am faced with a situation that I think might be abusive, my first reaction is (or would be) to:

_____

_____

_____

If I had to identify factors that might be linked to abuse, I would list the following:

_____

_____

_____

_____

What came to your mind when you thought of the term *abuse*? Many people first think of physical violence. However, the definition is much broader than just physical abuse. **Abuse** can be defined as *any* harm to the victim caused by anyone upon whom the victim relies for basic needs or support. Abuse occurs in relationships where the victim is under the control or influence of the offender. The definition of abuse generally does not include self-neglect or victimization by an unknown assailant.

Some types of abuse are easier to define than others. Physical and financial abuse are sometimes much easier to identify than are other types of abuse. Sometimes people (even professionals trained to work with situations of abuse) can disagree on whether a specific situation is abusive. Sometimes the person others see as a victim does not agree that abuse has taken place. All these issues can make it difficult to determine what, if anything, should be done.

Abuse can occur across the life span. Children and spouses as well as older adults can be abused. People of any financial status may be abused. Sometimes, more than one type of abuse occurs within the same family.

Abuse is an issue that often provokes strong feelings. Review your answer to Stop and Reflect 23-1 about the emotions you associate with abuse. Did you have feelings of anger? Perhaps you felt sadness or even embarrassment for a victim. People in abusive relationships often are embarrassed to admit that it is happening, or are ashamed of their behaviour. Some victims may feel that they have done something to provoke the abuse, that the abuse is somehow their fault. Some (both abusers and victims) may be afraid of what may happen if the abuse is reported or discovered.

The Effect of Abuse

In addition to the effects directly related to the abusive actions, the experience of being abused may affect the person's emotional, social, physical, and sexual development, and well-being. The effect abuse has on a person is most often determined by four factors: the nature and severity of the abuse, the abuser's relationship to the victim, the type(s) of threat or coercion used, and the quality of the intervention made by others to stop the abuse.

The Role of the Support Worker

If you were faced with a situation you felt might be abusive, what would your first reaction be? You might have said "to stop the abuse," or "to help the person leave the situation," or even "to make the abuser stop." You might have very strong feelings about your need to help. While you have a role to play in helping the victim of abuse, you are not responsible to deal directly with the abuse (or suspected abuse), unless the victim is in a life-threatening situation in your presence.

As a support worker, your responsibilities are threefold. First, you are responsible for accurately reporting any observations or suspicions of abuse to your supervisor immediately, so that your supervisor may take the appropriate action. Second, you are responsible for providing emotional support to the client. Third, if you are assigned to a client who has been abused, you are responsible to follow the support plan established to support the client. The last section of this chapter discusses how you might fulfill these responsibilities.

Forms of Abuse

There are four major forms of abuse: psychological, physical, financial, and neglect. All forms of abuse involve one person exercising power over the other. A person might not experience all types of abuse, but most abuse also causes psychological harm.

Psychological Abuse

Psychological abuse is sometimes called *verbal abuse*. Because it attacks a person's needs to feel safe, secure, and to belong, psychological abuse can be very damaging to the person. Someone who abuses another in this manner may humiliate the person (such as intentionally embarrassing the person in front of others), insult the person by calling the person "stupid", "a moron", or "an idiot". Some people **infantilize** an adult by treating him or her like a child.

Another form of psychological abuse includes not speaking to the person, ignoring the person, or behaving as though the person wasn't there. It also includes isolating the person by not allowing him or her to take part in conversations and activities or by not allowing the person to have visitors. A third form consists of saying things to frighten or threaten the person.

Physical Abuse

Physical abuse occurs when a person experiences actual physical harm. The harm can take many forms: slapping, pushing, kicking, pinching, hitting, or beating. It can also take the form of intentionally rough treatment, such as pulling hair, allowing someone to drop when they are being helped from a bed to a chair, and using bath water that is far too hot or cold. Chemically or physically restraining a person is also a form of physical abuse.

Sexual assault (assault, harassment, or use of the person as a subject of pornography) without the person's knowledge and consent is also a form of physical abuse.

Financial Abuse

Financial abuse includes the misuse or theft of a person's money or possessions. It includes forcing a person to sell property, stealing their money or personal possessions, forging a person's signature on pension cheques to obtain their money, as well as using a legitimately obtained power of attorney to improperly use the client's resources or dispose of their property.

Neglect

Neglect is defined as the intentional or *unintentional* failure to provide the person with the essentials of life. This can include abandoning (even for short periods of time) a

CASE EXAMPLE 23-1

Mrs. Sarah McGillvray has always lived in another province. Because of increasing health problems, she recently moved to the area to be close to her son, his wife, and three teenaged daughters. Mrs. McGillvray's family was unprepared to help her meet her care needs. They were not able to arrange for the time to take her to many medical appointments. They also did not know how to help her find friends and social activities in her new home.

As Mrs. McGillvray's condition worsened, tension grew. Mrs. McGillvray was asked to eat in her room, not with the rest of the family. When her calls to friends at "home" increased the telephone bill, the calls were limited to no more than five minutes once each week.

person who cannot safely be left at home or denying a dependent person food, liquid, medication, or access to health services (such as taking the person to the doctor or allowing health professionals to visit). Neglect can also occur when the person is left in an unclean or unsafe environment or when a person is not allowed to have the stimulation of social contacts, entertainment, or exercise.

Sometimes, neglect comes from the caregiver not performing the duties required to appropriately care for a person. The person might be careless, forget, or not learn the proper methods of caring for specific needs (such as how to properly apply a dressing).

When an infant, child, or frail older adult is involved, neglect can be particularly serious due to the victim's size and the extent to which the victim depends upon the person. Neglect can easily be fatal in infants or very dependent older people, for example, if the caregiver does not even feed the person. Neglect also includes the denial of necessary affection.

The Cycle of Abuse

Once an abusive incident happens, it usually happens again and again, unless something is done to stop it. This is called the **cycle of abuse**. It has three phases: the incident phase, the guilt or remorse phase, and the anger escalation phase. Figure 23-1 illustrates these phases.

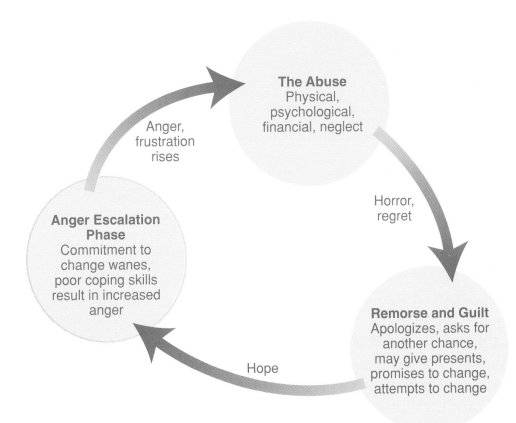

Figure 23-1 *Cycle of Abuse*

The Incident Phase

This is when the abusive incident or incidents occur. Keep in mind that the abuse takes place even if the person who has been abused does not know that it has happened. In cases of financial abuse or neglect, the person who has been abused may not be aware at all.

The Guilt or Remorse Phase

This is when the abuser reacts to the event. Many abusers will react with guilt or remorse. The person may vow not to abuse again, and may make this promise to the victim. It's important to be aware that the abuser may have genuine guilt or remorse. The abuser may truly believe that he or she will be able to break the cycle. However, it is unlikely that the cycle will be broken unless help is sought.

The client may truly believe that the abuser will change based upon his or her change in behaviour. This may allow the person to deny a problem for an extended period of time.

The Anger Escalation Phase

The anger escalation phase is when the abuser's commitment to changing wanes and poor coping skills give way to another incident of abuse. Without assistance, this phase culminates in another abusive incident, starting the cycle anew.

Child Abuse

Most information on child abuse is divided into two types: physical abuse and sexual abuse. Researchers estimate that about 10 percent of all children experience physical abuse by a parent or caretaker. It's estimated that about one in five male children and one in four female children will experience unwanted sexual acts.

We sometimes have an image of a child abuser as a stranger. This is not usually the case. Most abusers are people known to the child. Only a small percentage are strangers. Researchers suggest that the abuser may have been a victim and that the likelihood of abuse may increase with stress, economic, or internal pressures.

Indicators of Abuse

Remember that the presence of certain behaviours does not necessarily mean that abuse is occurring. There may be other reasons for these behaviours. Report your observations to your supervisor immediately if you notice any of these indicators. Your province may require you to report suspected child abuse to a local or provincial authority.

Indicators of Psychological Abuse

The following behaviours *may* be associated with psychological abuse.

The adult abuser may use the child as a scapegoat, blaming the child for things that are beyond the child's control. The adult may tell the child that he or she is bad or tell other people (in the child's presence) that the child is bad. The adult may reject the child, withhold affection, or isolate the child from other children or all other people. The adult may use power to coerce the child to do something, such as bribing, manipulating, or intimidating.

The child may have a variety of responses. He or she may appear depressed, withdrawn, aggressive, or display extreme attention-seeking behaviours. The child may attempt too hard to please others, be overly compliant, or extremely well-mannered.

Children may also have physical problems, such as an inability to control their bowel or bladder. The child may also have frequent psychosomatic complaints (complaints of physical problems for which a physical cause cannot be found).

Physical Abuse

In addition to bruises, cuts, burns, and other physical injuries, there may be other indicators of physical abuse. It is extremely important to keep in mind that many of these indicators may be the result of other causes, not abuse.

The adult may have little or no knowledge of child development and express difficulty coping with the child or show little or no affection toward the child. The adult may indicate that the child is injury-prone. The adult may also lie about the child's injuries, give inconsistent explanations about injuries, or even delay seeking treatment.

The child may have several injuries at various stages of healing. He or she may "forget" how injuries happened or have explanations inconsistent with the injuries. The child may be wary of adults or cringe if touched unexpectedly. Some children may display extreme behaviours, such as extreme aggression, withdrawal, overt compliance, or excessive eagerness to please others.

Failure to Thrive

In extreme cases, the abuse may cause the child to fail to grow and develop. This condition is called **failure to thrive**. This is an extremely dangerous form of child abuse which can be life-threatening.

The adult may reject the child or ignore the child's attempts to be affectionate. The adult may indicate that the child was and is unwanted or label the child difficult to care for.

The child may appear lethargic, to move very little, or to be disinterested in the surroundings. It is not uncommon for these children to display little anxiety or cry very little, if at all. The child may appear pale and extremely thin, with an extremely low body-fat ratio. Some children will stop growing altogether. Most of these children will not have met developmental milestones normal for children their age.

Spousal Abuse

CASE EXAMPLE 23-2

Carrie Worth is a 32-year-old woman with three children, all under five years of age. She is recovering from a severe fracture of her left leg. She fractured her leg when her husband threw her down the basement stairs. When hospital emergency room staff ask her about the incident, she tells them, "He had a right to be angry. I burned the mashed potatoes and dinner was late." Hospital staff encourage her to enter a shelter, but she refuses. She returns home with her husband.

Both men and women can be victims of spousal abuse, although women are most often the victims. It's estimated that almost 50 percent of women have experienced some form of abuse. Unlike children, we see adults as able to make decisions and take action. It may be difficult to understand why the victim does not simply leave an abusive relationship. You must become aware that there may be many factors that make it difficult for the victim to leave.

The abuser may intimidate and isolate the victim, gradually stripping the victim of all outside contacts and supports. The victim may believe that he or she is incapable of leaving the relationship.

Abusers may exert control over the victim through the victim's children, by using the children to convey messages, by threatening to take the children away, or by attempting to make the victim feel guilty about all the "upset" the victim has caused. The abuser may also threaten to withdraw economic support, prevent the victim from getting a job, or prohibit the victim access to family funds.

Indicators of Spousal Abuse

Psychological Abuse

It's very likely that indicators of psychological abuse will accompany indicators of physical or financial abuse. Isolation, lack of social contacts, loss of contact with family as well as a reliance upon the abuser for the necessities of life may all be present. The victim may feel helpless or state that the abuse was deserved.

Physical Abuse

Indicators of physical abuse include old and new injuries. In many cases, recent injuries are more severe than earlier injuries. The victim may deny the injuries, or have explanations for their cause that do not make sense. He or she may cover injuries with clothing or makeup.

Elder Abuse

Although both men and women can be victims of elder abuse, a typical victim is likely to be over 75, and female. She is likely to be widowed or single. While the victim may have progressive physical or mental impairments, most are competent. Most victims are socially isolated and increasingly dependent upon the abuser to meet their needs. The victim may take on the role of a child. Many victims of elder abuse deny the abuse and, even if they don't, are reluctant to report the abuse. Some may feel that the abuse is deserved.

The abuser is usually middle-aged, and often is the child of the victim. The abuser is frequently experiencing stress (such as financial, medical, marital, substance abuse, or unemployment). The abuser may feel that increasing demands of the caretaking role deplete family resources and often resents the need to care for the parent. The abuser may also feel dependent upon the victim for emotional or financial support.

Potential Indicators of Elder Abuse

Caregiver Characteristics

The following caregiver behaviours may indicate an abusive (or potentially abusive) situation. As with all indicators, you must not make the assumption that the presence of one or more means that abuse is present. Discuss any observations with your supervisor.

A caregiver may respond defensively when asked about the health of the older adult. The caregiver may make excuses or be hostile, suspicious, or evasive about explanations. The caregiver may not want the older adult to be interviewed alone.

The caregiver may appear excessively concerned or unconcerned about the older person. He or she may "blame" the elder for conditions—forgetfulness or incontinence—yet refuse to permit hospitalization or diagnostic tests.

The caregiver may show signs of stress, often as the result of needlessly taking on all the older adult's care without help. He or she may have been a caregiver for an extended period of time and may appear tired. The caregiver may have been forced (or felt forced) take on the caregiving situation and, as a result, may resent having to provide care.

Victim Characteristics

The older adult may show signs of neglect (unclean, thin, or dehydrated) or physical abuse. He or she may have medical needs that have not been addressed.

The older adult may withdraw from contact with others or be anxious or fearful of communication. He or she may be unwilling to discuss the relationship with the caregiver or any problems in caregiving. The older adult may be demanding or hostile and may be verbally abusive.

Some older adults may express fear of having "no place to go" or fear that they will have to leave their home if abuse is discovered. There may be evidence that a competent person has lost control over his or her financial affairs.

Indicators of Elder Abuse

The indicators of elder abuse are virtually identical to those of spousal abuse.

Psychological Abuse

It's very likely that indicators of psychological abuse will accompany indicators of physical or financial abuse. Isolation, lack of social contacts, loss of contact with family, as well as a reliance upon the abuser for the necessities of life may all be present. The victim may feel helpless or state that the abuse was deserved.

Physical Abuse

Indicators of physical abuse include old and new injuries. In many cases, recent injuries are more severe than earlier injuries. The victim may deny the injuries or have explanations for their cause that do not make sense. He or she may cover injuries with clothing or makeup.

Neglect and Failure to Thrive

An adult who suffers neglect will show many of the same symptoms of a neglected infant or child. The adult may shun communication, show no interest in others, or even seem to fear contact. There may be evidence of poor personal care and lack of medical attention.

What to Do

It is extremely important to be aware of the scope of your role in reporting observations and supporting the client. Your agency will have specific guidelines for providing support in these cases. The ten guidelines below provide some general guidance as to assistance you can provide.

1. **Report suspicions of abuse to your supervisor.**   Do not assume that someone else will do it.

2. **If asked, assist the abuser in obtaining help.**   Contact your supervisor to determine the specific steps you should take when assisting the abuser.

3. **Find out what resources for victims of abuse exist in your area.**   Make sure that you have telephone numbers available if a client should ask for them.

4. **Observe for indicators and report your observations to your supervisor immediately.**

5. **Listen to the client.** Do not judge the client or insist that he or she do something.

6. **Offer information if the client wants it.**

7. **Support the client in taking action, but do not insist that the client do so.** Recognize that a competent abused person has a right to maintain his or her lifestyle—you cannot force the client to make changes he or she does not want.

8. **Do not assume that one person's method of addressing an abusive situation will apply to all others.** What has worked for someone else—or even for you— may not be right for the person. Do not insist that a person take a particular approach.

9. **Maintain your relationship with the client, even if other types of assistance are refused.** The client still needs your support. If you withdraw support, the client may find it very difficult if he or she does decide to seek help at a later date.

Questions for Review

1. What are the four general types of abuse? What are the signs of each type?

2. Describe the cycle of abuse.

3. What factors can make it difficult for a person to admit that he or she has been abused?

4. Identify indicators of abuse in infants and children.

5. Why is neglect so dangerous? What three types of people are most at risk of neglect?

6. What are indicators of spousal abuse?

7. What are the indicators of elder abuse?

Questions for Discussion

1. Is the existence of abuse always easy to define? What factors can make it difficult for the people involved to agree that abuse exists?

2. Imagine that a client tells you that he is being abused by his family. He says that his daughter is making him sign over his Canada Pension cheque. He tells you that he doesn't know what she does with the money and when he asks his daughter, she yells at him. What are your feelings? What should you do? Why?

3. Review this case study. As a support worker, what steps would you take?

   You are assigned to assist Sandy Rendor to care for her newborn twin girls. She also has a 2-year-old daughter and a 4-year-old son. The twins were born prematurely and spent some time in hospital. One was in critical condition for a while. They are both now home, but still are frail. Both babies require monitoring to ensure that they do not stop breathing. Sandy's husband, Dale, travels a great deal, so the primary responsibility for care rests with Sandy.

   Today, as you are assisting Sandy with the laundry, the 4-year-old comes into the room holding one of the twins' breathing monitors. It is supposed to be on the baby, as she is napping. The 4-year-old says: "Baby's sleeping, mom—this could wake her up." You know that he has heard the alarm sound.

   Sandy yells at the 4-year-old, grabbing the monitor from him. She grabs his arm and tells him he's a bad boy and to never do that again. You are surprised at the level of her anger, as she is normally a loving parent.

CHAPTER TWENTY-FOUR

Palliative Care

Learning Objectives

Through reading this chapter, you'll be able to:

1. Describe the range of attitudes Canadians have toward death.
2. Define palliation and palliative care.
3. Discuss the role of the support worker providing palliative care.
4. Outline the impact of life-threatening illness on the client, the client's family, and the support worker.
5. Explain the client's rights with regard to treatment and resuscitation.
6. Demonstrate specific techniques (within the scope of support work) to promote comfort and help alleviate pain.
7. Describe signs of apparent death and care of the body after death.
8. Define grief and discuss aspects of grief work.

Chapter At A Glance

Attitudes Toward Dying and Death

Culture, Life-Threatening Illness, Dying, and Bereavement

Palliative Care (or Palliation)

The Role of the Support Worker in Palliative Care

The Impact of Life-Threatening Illness

Living Wills and Do Not Resuscitate Orders

Promoting Comfort and Reducing Pain

When Death Is Near

At the Time of Death

Care of the Body After Death

Grief and Grief Work

> ## Terms You'll Use
>
> **Anticipatory Grief**   The sense of loss, grieving, and preparing to move on that can occur before an expected loss happens.
>
> **Do Not Resuscitate Orders**   A document that states a person is not to receive life-sustaining measures.
>
> **Grief Work**   Tasks associated with moving through the phases of grieving.
>
> **Hospice**   How many terminally ill people receive support and care.
>
> **Life-Threatening Illness**   An illness that is likely to cause death.
>
> **Living Will**   A document that gives specific instructions as to the care and treatment a person wants; also called an *advance directive*.
>
> **Palliative Care**   Active and compassionate care with the purpose to provide comfort and control pain, not to cure.

Attitudes Toward Dying and Death

The experience of dying and death is intensely personal. No two people—even two siblings who experience the death of a parent—will see the experience in the same way. Our responses are the result of our personalities, culture, coping mechanisms, experiences with previous deaths, as well as the social supports we have to assist us.

Nonetheless, Canada is seen as a death-ignoring society. By this we mean that, although we all are aware that people die, as a society we do not see death as a natural consequence of living. Researchers attribute this to two things: that we have moved death from the person's home to the institution and that we have developed technology to treat many conditions, leading to a belief that death can be avoided in many cases. Let's look at each of these more closely.

Where People Die

At the turn of the century, most deaths occurred at home. People did not go to hospital to die. Care was provided in the person's home, often by family members who learned how to provide the necessary care. This gave people the opportunity to see death as a natural occurrence as well as to be able to assist in making a person comfortable.

Gradually, people began to go to institutions such as hospitals or long-term care facilities near the end of their lives. In part, this was due to advances in treatment that were available only in hospital. Additionally, Canadians were increasingly becoming two-career families, leaving no one at home to care for a dying person.

Today, we estimate that about 70 percent of people who die do so in a hospital or long-term care facility. This has made death less familiar to people and, therefore, somewhat frightening.

Treatment Advances

Many treatment advances have occurred in the last century. As a result, many conditions once thought incurable can now be cured. This has altered how we see illness and death, making it easier to believe that almost everything can be cured. It is called the *medicalization of death* and has had the effect of making dying and death seem to be something beyond the scope of families, requiring it to be managed by only professionals.

The Hospice Movement

The hospice movement is dedicated to the compassionate care of people who are dying. Canada's hospice movement is based on the St. Christopher's Hospice of London, England that was founded by Cicely Saunders in 1967. A **hospice** is a residence where terminally ill people can receive support and care. There are only a few hospice residences. In Canada, the hospice movement provides support to many people who choose to die in their homes.

The hospice movement has been instrumental in changing Canadian attitudes about dying and death. Because of this movement, people are once again seeing death as a natural part of life. People who are terminally ill are now more likely to remain at home. Families are becoming more involved in the support of the dying person. As a result, support workers are frequently involved in supporting both the client and his or her family.

Stop and Reflect 24-1

How do you see death?

_____

_____

_____

From whom did you learn about death?

_____

_____

To what extent are your views about death influenced by your culture?

_____

_____

_____

To what extent are your views about death influenced by your personal experiences?

_____

_____

_____

Your Own Attitudes

Support workers providing palliative care must carefully examine their beliefs and attitudes about death prior to working with clients requiring this care. It is extremely important that the worker ensures that personal attitudes, fears, or anxieties do not interfere with the ability to care for the client.

Culture, Life-Threatening Illness, Dying, and Bereavement

Canada is a multicultural country. Death is a significant event in most cultures, but there are many ways in which death is viewed. This challenges us to both question and adapt our approaches to better meet the needs of people who view dying and death differently.

CASE EXAMPLE 24-1

An older Asian woman feels that her cancer is punishment for not having cared for her mother when her mother was ill many years ago. She feels that she is *not deserving of care and asks her support workers to leave because of this.*

■

As you'll recall from our discussion in Chapter 6, each person is the product of a unique *personal culture*. A person's views on *life-threatening illness*, dying, death and bereavement may be heavily influenced by religion, previous experiences, as well as ethnic practices (Figure 24-1).

It is not helpful to assume that people will act a certain way or hold certain beliefs just because they are members of a particular ethnic group. You must learn how your client sees the situation, what he or she feels is appropriate treatment, and how the

Figure 24-1   *Perceptions of Life-Threatening Illness, Dying, and Death Are Influenced by Many Things*

client sees your role. Equally important is how the client sees the role of the family, as well as the type and extent of emotional and spiritual support the client desires.

Even people who have not observed religious or ethnic practices throughout their lives may turn to these practices and rituals when faced with a life-threatening situation. As a support worker, you role is to support the client and the client's family, however new or different the practices they choose to observe might be.

Palliative Care (or Palliation)

There are many definitions of palliative care (also called palliation). For our purposes, we will define **palliative care** as active and compassionate care whose purpose is to provide comfort and control pain so that the person may live life fully until he or she dies. It is not to cure or to prolong life.

Palliative care implies four things: that death is a natural process, that the person is entitled to measures that support comfort and reduce pain and other symptoms, that the person has the right to maintain his or her lifestyle as he or she chooses until death, and that the person has the right to die with dignity. Many hospice services have formalized their thoughts about the rights of the dying person. Exhibit 24-1 contains a sample "Bill of Rights".

THE DYING PERSON'S BILL OF RIGHTS

1. I have the right to be treated as a living human being until I die.
2. I have the right to maintain a sense of hopefulness, however changing its focus may be.
3. I have the right to be cared for by those who can maintain a sense of hopefulness, however changing this might be.
4. I have the right to express my feelings and emotions about my approaching death, in my own way.
5. I have the right to participate in decisions concerning my case.
6. I have the right to expect continuing medical and nursing attention even though "cure" goals must be changed to "comfort" goals.
7. I have the right not to die alone.
8. I have the right to be free from pain.
9. I have the right to have my questions answered honestly.
10. I have the right not to be deceived.
11. I have the right to have help from and for family in accepting my death.
12. I have the right to die in peace and dignity.
13. I have the right to retain my individuality and not be judged for my decisions, which may be contrary to the beliefs of others.
14. I have the right to discuss and enlarge my religious and/or spiritual experiences, regardless of what they may mean to others.
15. I have the right to expect that the sanctity of the human body will be respected after death.
16. I have the right to be cared for by caring, sensitive, knowledgeable people who will attempt to understand my needs and will be able to gain some satisfaction in helping me face my death.

Exhibit 24-1 *A Dying Person's Bill of Rights*

The Role of the Support Worker in Palliative Care

As a support worker, you will likely be asked to support both the client and his or her family. You will likely assist clients with personal care as well as provide social and emotional support. You may provide respite services (such as assisting the client so that another caregiver can get needed rest or recreation). You may help with household tasks so that a family member is free to provide the client's personal care.

In most cases, you will be part of a team comprising the client, the client's family, friends and other supports, other caregivers, and the person's doctor. You will work closely with the other team members to ensure that the client receives the support he or she desires. It is particularly important that you share information with all other team members.

Erica Huber is a support worker with Hometown Support Services. She is assigned to provide palliative care to Mr. Stokes, a client. Erica is a part of a team that is made up of Mr. Stokes, his wife and daughter, a visiting nurse, and two hospice volunteers.

When she was first assigned to Mr. Stokes, Erica spent a bit of time getting to know him. Erica learned Mr. Stokes' preferences as well as his expectations of

her. She was also able to get a sense of how Mr. Stokes' condition affects him.

Erica knows Mr. Stokes will often share information with her that he would like to be passed on to other team members. She makes sure to carefully listen to him as well as to pass on significant information to other team members.

The Impact of Life-Threatening Illness

The Client

Although each person and situation is different, most people experience a range of emotions when faced with a **life-threatening illness**, or an illness that is likely to cause death. Denial, anger, bargaining, and acceptance are the emotions that have historically been associated with dying, but we now know that the person may experience many other emotions as well. A client may also experience despair, fear, uncertainty, or hope. Sometimes, a client experiences many strong emotions, or experiences a single emotion for a period of time. He or she may also alternate between emotions (for example, between despair and hope).

The client may also question his or her faith or purpose in life. She or he may search for meaning in past activities or need to know that he or she will leave a legacy for others.

The client faces many changes in his or her life as a result of the illness. The client may not have the energy to maintain social relationships or take part in activities he or she once enjoyed. Sometimes, friends drift away, perhaps because they are uncomfortable with the client's illness or because the client can no longer take part in the activities they once shared. A client whose illness has forced him or her to leave work may have to deal with financial uncertainty, as well as the concern that family members may not have the resources necessary to live comfortably.

People with a life-threatening illness have the same range of needs as anyone. However, their priorities may be very different. Exhibit 24-2 illustrates a list of needs identified by people with life-threatening illness. As you read this list, make note of how many needs relate to everyday activities. As a support worker, it's likely that you will have a great opportunity to assist a client attain what is important to him or her.

Needs of the Dying Person

Psychological Needs

To be heard
To be with people I wish
To know that the person's life has made a difference
To be a part of their community
To be loved
To be touched
To make peace

Spiritual Needs

To participate in the rituals that are a part of one's beliefs
To have spiritual beliefs recognized and respected
To have access to religious symbols (Bibles, rosaries, statues, etc.)
To have visits with a member of the clergy, if desired

Physical Needs

To be free from pain, as much as is possible
To have needs for food, water, and body function met
To be as comfortable as possible
To be touched as desired

Most Importantly, the Person Needs to Live Until They Die

Exhibit 24-2 *The Needs of the Dying Person*

The Family

Like clients, each family member will react differently to the diagnosis of a life-threatening illness. It is not uncommon for family members' reactions to be different than the client's. For example, a client may be accepting of a diagnosis although the family members are not. Like clients, family members may experience many feelings and may alternate among many of them.

For many families, the time after a diagnosis is made is one of many changes. The client may have many new needs. There may be a number of other caregivers involved in the client's support. Familiar patterns of activity (ways of doing things) change, and there is usually a period of uncertainty as family members get used to new roles and activity. Sometimes, the family becomes very protective of the client and must balance their need to keep the client "safe" with respect for the client's need to make decisions and take risks.

Everyone may need time to come to terms with the diagnosis and its meaning. Family members may find it hard to balance the client's need for support with their own needs for support. The family may also have to deal with **anticipatory grief**—the sense of loss, grieving, and preparing to move on that occurs before an expected loss happens. Anticipatory grief can cause the family members to distance themselves from the client.

As a support worker, you will likely be involved in supporting the family. Family members may need to discuss the way the client's illness affects them and how they must adapt to those changes. Be assured that each client and family will come to their own unique way of responding. No single way is the "right" or "best" one. You must be nonjudgmental as you listen and provide support.

The Support Worker

CASE EXAMPLE 24-3

Jenna Mace assisted Mr. Moreau and his family as Mr. Moreau was dying of cancer. As one of two support workers assigned to Mr. Moreau, Jenna came to know him well. As she was often the worker assigned to overnight shifts, Jenna and Mr. Moreau spent a great deal of time talking. Mr. Moreau shared his family photographs with her and told her many stories of growing up in a farming community.

After a period of remission, Mr. Moreau's condition suddenly and dramatically worsened. Within one week, he was dead. Jenna found that she experienced shock and grief at the sudden loss of the client she had come to know so well.

You must not overlook the effect that supporting a terminally ill client has on you. Even though you are not a family member, you will get to know the client very well. You will establish a relationship with the client that will require you to share a bit of yourself, even as you maintain professional boundaries. It's very likely that you will feel a sense of anxiety at the impending loss of the relationship.

Make certain that you have a support system that can assist you as you assist your client. You may want to speak with your supervisor to see if you can discuss issues in palliative care with other workers who provide this type of support.

Living Wills and Do Not Resuscitate Orders

A client receiving palliative care has likely made a decision to cease extensive treatment aimed at attaining a cure. Some clients have made this decision informally with their loved ones. In these cases, all caregivers understand the client's wishes and act accordingly, even though there is no written document that outlines them.

Some clients, particularly those who are in long-term care facilities or hospitals, may choose a more formal way of stating their desires. Two common ways are through *living wills* and *do not resuscitate orders*. Each province has specific legislation governing these documents.

A **living will** (also called an *advance directive*) is a document that gives specific instructions as to the care and treatment a person wants. The living will is used if a client cannot tell others what treatment he or she wants. Some people name a person in the living will who is responsible to advise caregivers of the person's treatment wishes. Many living wills are used to indicate the type of treatment a client with a life-threatening illness does not want.

A **do not resuscitate order** is a document that states that a person is not to receive heroic measures to sustain his or her life. A do not resuscitate order is concerned only with life-sustaining measures, while a living will may address other forms of treatment.

When these documents are written to conform to legal requirements and are in place, their contents must be respected. Your agency will have specific guidelines for following the instructions in a living will or do not resuscitate order. Make sure that you know your agency's procedures.

As a rule, you should not witness any living will or do not resuscitate order. It may seem to others that you could have influenced the client to write or sign the document. If you are asked to witness, you might suggest that one of the client's friends or neighbours be asked instead.

Promoting Comfort and Reducing Pain

Comfort takes many forms. It can be physical, as in freedom from pain. It can be emotional, as in being in the company of someone who genuinely cares. With all that the client is experiencing, comfort may be difficult to attain.

Many clients with a life-threatening illness will experience physical pain. In some cases, the pain is mild or moderate and is not always present. In other cases, pain may be severe and constant.

Many clients may receive medication for pain. If so, there should be a person who is responsible for monitoring the medication. Usually, you will not be expected to take responsibility for a client's medication. However, there may be a number of other things that you can do to promote comfort and reduce pain.

Promoting Comfort

A Positive Self-Image

Having a life-threatening illness can be very destructive to a client's self-image. First, the effects of the illness or treatment may alter a client's appearance. For example, there may be visible scarring from surgery or hair loss from chemotherapy. Some medications may cause the person to develop reddened or flaky skin. Second, the client's ability to maintain personal hygiene may be compromised by the illness, the treatment, or both.

You can promote a positive self-image by helping the client to bathe, dress, and groom in whatever way makes him or her comfortable. Many clients may not have the stamina for a daily bath. However, most will appreciate daily sponge baths, clean clothing, and having their hair neatly styled.

Communication

Do you remember the last time you really communicated with someone? Can you recall the satisfaction you got from knowing that the other person was "on the same wavelength"? The ability to establish rapport, actively listen, and relate to another person can provide great comfort.

Through the practice of good communication skills, you can make sure that your client feels that he or she has been listened to by someone who is genuinely interested. You can also ensure that your client has the opportunity to spend time alone with friends.

Basic Nutrition and Personal Care

Stop and Reflect 24-2

Recall a time when you were ill with the flu or a cold. Focus for a moment on the physical discomfort associated with the illness.

How did you feel?

_____

_____

_____

_____

What made you feel better?

_____

_____

_____

_____

Chances are that you felt out of sorts when you were ill. An ill client, particularly one who spends a great deal of time in bed, may share many of those feelings. Scratchy, wrinkled sheets can irritate fragile skin. A client may also experience a variety of physical irritants: his or her mouth may become dry, the tongue may become coated, or dried secretions may collect in the corners of the mouth. Poor swallowing may allow particles of food to stick on the client's teeth.

Techniques to Support Client Comfort

There are many techniques you can use to promote client comfort. Table 24-1 identifies some useful techniques.

TABLE 24-1	
Area of Concern	Comfort Measure
Confusion, possibly due to drugs or pain	Reassure the client, be patient, provide orientation information, but don't force the client to accept the information.
Constipation, possibly due to inactivity, weakness, or dehydration	Help the client maintain an upright position for bowel movements, if possible. Increase mobility, if possible. Increase fluid intake.
Difficulty swallowing	Moisten dry foods. Substitute more easily swallowed foods for those that are difficult. Chop or purée foods.
Dry, irritated or sore mouth Dry or coated tongue	Assist the client to brush teeth or provide mouth care. Encourage client to rinse mouth frequently. Encourage client to suck on ice chips, frozen juice cubes, or popsicles. Avoid acidic drinks or fruits if mouth has sores. Use lip gloss or petroleum jelly to keep lips moist. Ensure tongue is brushed or cleaned.
Lack of interest in eating, possibly due to fear of vomiting; drugs; chemotherapy; dry mouth; diarrhea; or constipation	Respond to the factor causing the lack of interest.
Nausea or vomiting	Provide smaller meals. Encourage starchy foods: crackers, pasta, rice, potatoes. Offer clear fluids. Avoid spicy, greasy, or overly sweet foods. Offer cold foods (cold foods do not have as much of an aroma and may not trigger nausea).

Pain Control

While medications are often the most effective means of controlling pain, there are other techniques for controlling pain. In particular, four techniques may be of benefit to clients: massage, relaxation techniques, visualization, and music.

Massage.   A back rub or hand or foot massage may provide great comfort to the client. Even clients who decline most touch may appreciate a massage if offered. Do not force a client to accept a massage, however.

Relaxation Techniques.   These techniques cause the person to focus on body rhythms and away from pain. Table 24-2 outlines a simple relaxation technique.

TABLE 24-2	A Simple Relaxation Technique

1. Find a quiet spot where you are not likely to be distracted.

2. Get into a position that is comfortable. This can be sitting, reclining, or lying down. Use a pillow to provide support if required.

3. Close your eyes if you wish.

4. Breathe in deeply. As you do, tense your muscles.

5. Keep your muscles tense for a few seconds as you hold your breath.

6. Exhale and relax your muscles.

7. Repeat the process for 5-10 minutes.

Visualization.   Imagining oneself in a pleasant place or reliving a pleasant experience can provide respite from pain.

Music.   Music can lift spirits and distract a person, minimizing the sensation of pain. Any type of music or sound that relaxes the client is appropriate, whether it is new age, rap, or jazz.

The suggestions in this section are general ideas. Many clients have developed their own measures. It's important to learn effective comfort and pain control approaches from your client, his or her family, as well as other caregivers.

It is helpful to learn about the quality of the pain that the client feels. Knowing some basic information about the type, frequency, and severity of the pain, as well as what makes the pain worse or better can help you to comfort your client. Often this information is recorded in the client's support plan. If not, talk to your supervisor about obtaining this information. Report to your supervisor your observations about when pain begins, how long it lasts, what makes it better or worse, as well as how severe it is.

When Death Is Near

It is likely that you will be asked to assist at a time when your client is near death. There may be a number of physical signs that death is near. It is important to remember that the dying person is often conscious to the very end.

Concepts

1. **Senses are dulled and finally fail to respond.**   Do not assume that the person cannot hear, however. This sense may remain after all others diminish.
2. **The person's pulse and respirations gradually change.**   Sometimes, there is a marked change from laboured breathing to a peaceful rhythm.
3. **Urine output diminishes.**   If output ceases, death is likely within 48-72 hours.
4. **The sensation of pain likely is diminished and the person may seem more "content".**
5. **Sensation and ability to move diminish first in the client's legs, then in the arms.**
6. **Body surfaces cool as peripheral circulation diminishes.**   The client's skin will often feel cold and clammy to the touch.
7. **Despite being cool to the touch, most dying persons do not feel cold.**   In fact, any restlessness is often caused by the sensation of heat.

Techniques

The following techniques may be helpful. Always take your cues from the client. A technique that calms a client is useful, no matter where the idea came from.

1. Offer lighter-weight clothing to help minimize the sensation of heat. You may have to explain to family that although the client feels cold to the touch, his or her internal temperature is quite warm.
2. Providing for fresh-air circulation helps to reduce the sensation of heat as well as to diminish any odours.
3. Some people are more comfortable when sheets are not tucked in. Sometimes, leaving the client's feet exposed can help to reduce the sensation of heat.
4. Reposition the person frequently to prevent sore spots.
5. The room should not be darkened unless it appears to comfort the client.
6. Encourage family to be seated near the client's head and to touch the client (if this has been acceptable in the past). The nearness and physical contact helps to compensate for diminished sensory perception and to promote a sense of connection.

At the Time of Death

At the time of death, the client's respirations and pulse will cease. Unless asked to do otherwise, allow the family time with the client.

The client's support plan should offer detailed information as to the actions to be taken at the time of death. It is extremely important to make sure all tasks are defined beforehand, so that there is no confusion.

It's often helpful if the support worker makes any calls or handles any tasks identified in the support plan that a family member does not want to do. This allows the family to focus on their grieving.

Care of the Body After Death

It is usually acceptable to straighten the sheets and cover the client's body to ensure modesty. Client preferences as well as agency policy will determine what, if any, additional care is provided to the client's body. Make sure you know your agency's policy beforehand.

Grief and Grief Work

The pain of grief is as much a part of life as the joy of love.
It is, perhaps, the price we pay for love, the cost of commitment.

Parkes

It is normal to feel loss when a client dies. The process of grieving allows us to deal with the loss, to work through the changes the loss has brought about, to begin to adapt to the new reality, and, finally, to begin to create a new life for ourselves. **Grief work** is defined as the tasks that are associated with moving through these phases.

As a support worker who has supported a client who has died, your grief work is twofold. You must support the client's family and loved ones in their grief, as well as work through the stages of your own.

Each person's grief is unique. It results from the unique relationship between the person and the client. However, there is a general pattern to the process of grieving. Knowing that one's reactions are "normal" may be a comfort to some people. The three phases most people experience are: numbness, confronting, and redefining.

It is important to remember that people do not move through these phases in an orderly fashion. For example, a person may still experience periods of denial long after the death. It is not uncommon for a person to "automatically" telephone the deceased person on a birthday or anniversary, only realizing the error when the person does not answer.

Phase One—Numbness

The first phase is one of shock and denial. The person may say something like, "I can't believe that he is gone." The person may appear shocked or overwhelmed. Sometimes, the person seems to behave almost as if nothing happened. Attention and concentration are usually diminished and the person may find it incredibly difficult to do routine things like eating or dressing. The person may have no appetite and find it difficult to sleep.

At the same time, there is often a great deal of activity in the home. Family, friends, and neighbours may visit. Arrangements may have to be made. There are many details to which to attend. These tasks can provide a purpose—in effect, a ready-made list of things to do. In turn, this allows the person some time to adjust to the loss.

The task of this phase is to move from the initial shock to acceptance of the death. As a support worker, you can help the person by listening without challenging, by making sure that support is available, and by making sure that the necessities of life are provided. Perhaps you have taken part in the ritual of bringing food to the family of the deceased person. This helps to provide the grieving person nourishment, as well as provide a way for others to help.

Phase Two—Confronting the Loss and Pain

As the activity in the home subsides and the shock wears off, the person can begin to focus on the pain of the loss. This can be a time of uncertainty, a time in which the person questions his or her ability to "go on". It may also be a time of desiring to maintain contact with the deceased person's memory by doing things like going to the restaurant the deceased person really liked.

The task of this phase is to work through the uncertainty and yearning. This also involves rediscovering one's strengths as a way of preparing to go on. As the survivors may not be receiving support services, it may not be possible for you to assist them through this phase. If you are present, your task is to help the person balance the grieving with periods of time devoted to maintaining the person's health and well-being. This is often called "taking a break from grieving," as it allows the person to regain energy necessary to deal with this phase. It's often helpful to assist the person to focus on the strengths he or she does have that can be of help.

Phase Three—Redefining and Reconnecting

The third phase of grief deals with the survivor's gradual focus on life without the deceased person. It is in this phase that the person begins to believe that they will have a life and begins to focus on making plans, forming new relationships, and re-connecting with old relationships.

The task involved in this phase is to reinvest energies into new goals, activities, and relationships. A support worker involved with the survivor during this phase should assist the person to believe in his or her strengths and abilities. The support worker should also offer encouragement to reconnect with old friends as well as take steps to make new ones.

The Support Worker's Grief

It's not unusual for you to experience aspects of these three phases as well, although they will not be as intense as they are for a loved one. It's not uncommon to feel shock, as well as a loss of purpose in the period right after the death. You must be sensitive to your needs and ensure that you have proper support. If your agency provides palliative care to many clients, it may offer support groups or other help for workers who have experienced a client's death.

Questions for Review

1. What factors have shaped our attitudes toward death?

2. What is the *hospice movement*? How has it changed Canadian attitudes toward death?

3. You are assigned to assist a person who is dying. What might you expect your role to be?

4. Do people with a life-threatening illness have the same needs as other people? Why or why not?

5. How can a life-threatening illness affect the family of the client?

6. What are living wills and do not resuscitate orders called in your province? What are your responsibilities with regard to these documents?

7. Medication is the only thing that can reduce pain. Do you agree? Why or why not?

8. What are four signs that death is near?

9. What can you do to promote client comfort at the time near death?

10. What are the phases of grief work? What are the tasks (grief work) of each phase?

Questions for Discussion

1. What is a *good death*? Is your definition the same as that of your colleagues?

2. Are there times when it is better for a person to go to hospital to die? Under what circumstances might this be a good choice?

3. You have been assigned to assist Mrs. Ross, a 58-year-old woman who has breast cancer that has metastasized. Her doctor has advised her that further treatment would not be effective. Mrs. Ross tells you that she has made peace with the prognosis and has put her affairs in order.

   Mrs. Ross has two children who are at university 2000 kilometres away. Her husband's job requires him to travel and he is often away. Mrs. Ross is an independent woman who does not want to disrupt her family members' lives. An architect, she has always been active in professional associations and has socialized with a small group of friends. Since her diagnosis, however, she has become less and less active. She tells you that part of the reason for this is that she has little energy for socializing. She also says that she feels that she is "not a pretty sight" and is uncomfortable with going out. Mrs. Ross' hair did not grow back well after chemotherapy and is patchy. As well, she is uncomfortable with her breast prosthesis, and prefers not to wear it. She seems to miss the social interaction and often seems lonely and sad.

   Explain how her behaviour relates to the process and stages of dying.

   What are your thoughts and feelings? Explain how they relate to your beliefs about illness, health care, and death.

   Describe the approaches that you should take to help Mrs. Ross.

CHAPTER TWENTY-FIVE

Assisting with Medications

Learning Objectives

Through reading this chapter, you'll be able to:

1. Define what items are considered drugs and the conditions under which you may assist a client to take medications.

2. Outline the four general ways in which you may assist a client to take medication and describe any special precautions you must take when using each.

3. Specify the information you must have in order to safely administer medication to a client.

4. List the five "rights" of medication administration.

5. Explain the difference between over-the-counter and prescription drugs and between generic and brand-name drugs.

6. Identify and describe common medication terminology and the information found on a prescription drug label.

7. Accurately measure liquid medications.

8. Demonstrate the proper administration of: oral and topical medications, eye, ear, and nose drops.

9. Outline the steps to take if a problem arises.

Terms You'll Use

Buccal Tablet   A dose of medication that is dissolved in the mouth and absorbs through the mucous membrane of the mouth.

Dossette   A container that holds individual doses of medication.

Drug   An agent that alters the body's mechanisms.

Generic Name   The name of the active ingredient in a drug.

Herbal Medications   Substances that contain naturally occurring chemicals.

Narcotics   Drugs that dull the senses to provide pain relief and are very addictive.

Over-the-Counter Medications   Drugs that can be purchased and used without a prescription.

Proprietary Medications   Drugs that a person can buy to treat minor conditions or symptoms of a condition.

Prescription Drugs   Drugs that are prescribed by a doctor for the treatment of specific conditions.

Sublingual Tablet   A dose of medication that is dissolved under the tongue and absorbs through the mucous membrane of the mouth.

Syringe   A hollow tube that can be filled with a medication for adminstration.

What Is a Drug?

When we hear the term "drug", we often think of prescription medications but there are many more items that are actually drugs. For the purposes of this text, we'll define a **drug** as an agent that alters the body's mechanism. This definition includes:

- *prescription drugs*
- *over-the-counter* (nonprescription) *drugs*
- vitamins and minerals
- *herbal medications*
- alcohol
- tobacco

Prescription drugs. **Prescription drugs** are those that must be prescribed by a doctor (or, in some cases, dentist or other specific health professional). Prescription drugs are approved by Health Canada. Many drugs are approved for the treatment of specific ailments or conditions and cannot be prescribed for other conditions.

Controlled drugs and *narcotics* are two special types of prescription drugs. These drugs are seen as having the potential for dependency or abuse if their use is not carefully controlled.

Controlled drugs include many antidepressants. Prescriptions for these drugs can be refilled, but it is expected that the doctor will keep very close supervision of the person taking the medication. **Narcotics** are drugs that dull the senses to provide pain relief and that have great potential for addiction. Narcotic prescriptions cannot be refilled. The doctor must write a new prescription each time the prescription runs out.

Over-the-counter medications. Over-the-counter medications are those that can be purchased and used without a prescription. Many remedies, pain medications, and ointments are available over the counter. In some cases, the over-the-counter drug is a low-dose version of a prescription medication. Over-the-counter medications usually have a product code that begins with the letters DIN.

Over-the-counter medications include a group of medications called **proprietary medications**, drugs that a person can buy to treat a minor condition or minor symptoms of a condition. In Canada, these drugs have a product code that starts with the letters GP.

Be aware that over-the-counter drugs can be harmful if taken improperly. Taking too much medication, taking it with other medications, or combining it with alcohol or certain foods all can cause serious side-effects.

Vitamins and minerals. Vitamins and minerals are regulated by Health Canada. Although they are sold as over-the-counter medications, some vitamins and minerals can be harmful in large quantities or when combined with other drugs. In some cases, the effect of large doses of a vitamin or mineral is simply not known.

Herbal medications. Herbal medications are those that contain naturally occurring chemicals and can be just as potent as prescription medications. In fact, the chemicals found in some herbal medications are the same as those found in prescription medications. For example, the chemical found in the herb foxglove is the same as that found in the heart medication digitalis (a medication that slows and strengthens heart rate). Because herbal medications are regulated as food supplements, the quality and potency may vary widely from one manufacturer to another.

Alcohol. Alcohol is classified as a drug, although it is regulated differently than are other drugs. Alcohol can alter or heighten the effects of other medication. Alcohol is also seen as potentially addictive and has a potential for abuse. Excessive consumption of alcohol can cause alcohol poisoning or death.

Tobacco. Among many other chemicals, tobacco contains nicotine, an addictive agent that stimulates the central nervous system. Nicotine also can have adverse affects on the cardiovascular system. In Canada, tobacco is regulated under separate legislation.

Generic and Name-Brand Drugs

Every drug has a **generic name**, the name of the active ingredient in the drug. When a drug is first brought to market, it is protected by a patent issued to the manufacturer who discovered the drug. The manufacturer gives the drug a *brand name* which is trademarked, meaning that only that manufacturer can use that brand name to describe the drug.

The trademark does not expire, but the drug patent lasts for a period of time and cannot usually be renewed. After the drug patent expires, other manufacturers can duplicate the drug. For example, a common pain reliever is ASA or *acetylsalicylic acid*. The name *aspirin* is the brand name that the manufacturer, Bayer, has patented for its brand of ASA. After the patent expires, many manufacturers can make the same drug, but only the manufacturer that holds the trademark may use that brand name.

A drug whose patent has expired may be sold by the original manufacturer as well as a number of other manufacturers. Those other manufacturers give their own name to their version of the drug. For example, the generic drug *furosemide* is sold under four different brand names.

A generic drug must have the same active ingredient as the brand-name version. However, the inert ingredients (the things that make a pill easier to swallow or that coat a pill) may be different. Some people may be sensitive to an inert ingredient and thus respond differently to different versions of the same generic drug.

A client's doctor may allow a pharmacist to substitute a generic version for a brand-name version. Because the name of the drug may be different, you must be cautious that any drug you are asked to administer is, in fact, the drug in the container.

Role of Other Professionals

Chances are, you have taken a medication prescribed by your doctor. At least three people are involved in the proper use of a medication:

- the doctor who prescribes the proper medication;
- the pharmacist who fills the prescription accurately; and
- the person who takes the medication properly.

If the client requires assistance with medication, there will be other support workers involved, depending upon the type of assistance needed. Often, a family member and a nurse are involved. As a support worker, you may be asked to assist a client. Remember that every person involved has an equally important role in ensuring that the medication is properly taken.

Assisting a Client with Taking Medication

When we speak of assisting with taking medications, we are speaking of *administering* or assisting a client with administering medication. Administration means the act of taking a medication. When we take medication, we are considered to be *self-administering* the medication.

Your ability to assist a client with medication will be determined by three things:

- the type of medication/the way it is administered;
- the setting (such as a client's home, a long-term care facility, or a rest home); and
- the specific assistance you provide.

Each province has legislation that restricts who may administer some types of medication. For example, in most cases many provinces require that specific registered health professionals administer injected medications. Many provinces require that a registered nurse administer medications in a long-term care facility. Beyond the restrictions posed by legislation, your agency's policy will also determine how you can assist a client to take medication. You always must be careful to follow your agency's policies. Be aware that agencies will vary in how they allow a worker to assist a client. If you work for more than one agency, you may find that one allows you to assist in ways that are prohibited by the other.

Types of Assistance

There are four general types of assistance. You may assist a client by:

- reminding him or her to take medication, when the client is physically able to take the medication;
- providing some help with physical tasks, such as helping the client to open a bottle or blister pack, when the client asks you to do so;
- handing the clients the contents of a **dossette** or individual dose blister pack at the proper time; or
- opening the prescription or over-the-counter medication bottle, pouring out the proper amount of medication, and giving the medication to the client.

Each level of assistance requires you to ensure that the action you are taking is correct. For example, if your role is to remind the client to take a medication, you must do so at the proper time. The more involved in assisting your client, the more responsibility you will bear in making sure the act is done accurately.

What You Need to Know to Assist the Client

There is specific information you must know in order to safely assist a client to take his or her medications. You must know:

1. Any pertinent information about the client, such as allergies or health concerns that may be affected by the medication.
2. What other medications the client is taking, when they are taken, and if any of these medications may affect the effect of the medication you are asked to give the client.
3. Foods or beverages that may affect the purpose of the drug or cause side-effects.
4. The reason the client is taking the drug.
5. The effects that should be expected (such as reduced joint pain) and action to take if the expected results do not appear.
6. What side-effects may arise and what to do if they do arise.
7. The time the drug is to be administered, the correct dosage, and the method to be used to administer the medication (for example, orally or by ear or nose drops).
8. What to do if the client refuses the medication or skips a dose.

9. The name of the person to contact if any problems arise.
10. The records to be kept and the procedure to be used for recording.

If you are uncertain as to whether a drug can be safely given, contact the designated person or your supervisor as your agency requires. Do not give the medication unless you are certain that it is safe to do so.

The Five "Rights" of Medication Administration

In addition to all the information you must know in order to assist the client, you must know and follow the five "rights": the right person, the right drug, the right dose, the right time, and by the right method. Each of these "rights" is explained in this section. Small errors in medication can have significant effects on the client. Keep your mind on your work. If it is difficult to concentrate due to noise or commotion, move to a quiet area if possible.

The Right Person

In a client's home, this is usually obvious. However, if you are in a group home or assisted living situation, make sure that you have the proper client. Ask the client his or her name. If the client's chart has a photo, compare it to the client.

The Right Drug

How you check for the right drug depends upon the container from which you will remove the drug.

If removing the drug from its prescription bottle:

1. **Check the prescription label.**   Figure 25-1 illustrates a typical drug label. Ensure that the drug is prescribed for the person and that the date on which it was dispensed is within the last six months. If the drug is older, verify its use with the appropriate person.

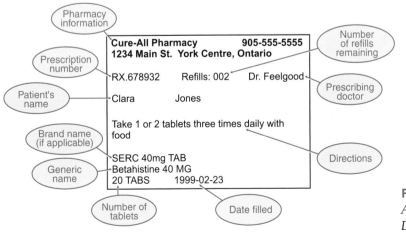

Figure 25-1

A Prescription Drug Label

2. **Check that the drug name and strength listed on the bottle are the same as the drug name and strength listed in the support plan.**
3. **Check that the pills in the bottle are all the same.**   If not, contact the appropriate person before giving the medication.
4. **Check the pills to ensure that they are not split, chalky, wet, or discoloured.** If any of these conditions exist, contact your supervisor.

If removing drugs stored in a dossette:

1. **If possible, review the contents of the dossette with the person responsible for filling it.**   Know which medications should be given during your visit.
2. **Store the dossette properly until use.**   Make sure that the dossette is not left where its contents can be tampered with by others in the setting or by the client. Do not leave the dossette in direct sunlight (for example, on a window sill).
3. **If you have any concerns about the contents of the dossette, contact the appropriate person before administering the medication.**

The Right Dose

1. **Read and reread the order written in the support plan.**
2. **Confirm any changes in the usual dose (e.g., two tablets instead of one, or a different strength of drug).**
3. **Compare the information on the prescription bottle with the strength listed on the support plan.**
4. **Know the meaning of abbreviations for medications.** (Table 25-1 lists common abbreviations.)
5. **Make sure that you measure liquids accurately and that you use the correct number of pills.**   When measuring liquids, make sure that you are using the proper system of measurement (imperial or metric). Do not use household spoons to measure, as they vary widely in size.
6. **Make sure that the person takes all of the medication.**

The Right Time

1. **Double-check the time of administration on the support plan.**
2. **Know the meaning of common terminology related to frequency.** (Table 25-1 lists common short forms for timing.)
3. **Make sure that the client's meals are timed so that the client takes the medication on an empty stomach, with meals, or after eating, as required.**
4. **Make sure that medications ordered for the same time can be safely given together.** If not, make sure that you know which medication must be given first and how much time must elapse between administering the medications.
5. **If going out with a client, make sure that medication to be taken while out is checked before departure and brought with the client.**

The Right Method

1. **Make sure you know how to administer the drug.**
2. **Make sure that you are familiar with any special measuring devices prior to using them.**
3. **Carefully follow any instructions for preparation.**   Be aware that some pills can be crushed and mixed with jelly or applesauce to make them easier to swallow, but others cannot. If you don't know if a client's pills can be crushed or mixed, contact the appropriate person.
4. **Do not handle medications with your bare hands.**   Pour liquids directly into the measuring device. If the device has been washed, ensure that it is dry before using. Water left in the device may reduce the amount of medication.
5. **Pour the required number of pills into the inverted top of the pill container and then into the client's hand.**   If using a dossette, check the contents of the appropriate vial, then pour directly into the client's hand.

TABLE 25-1	Sample Prescription Abbreviations

This table lists some sample abbreviations. **Before you use any abbreviation, make sure that you find out if your agency approves of it.** The use of an incorrect or misunderstood abbreviation can pose a significant danger to a client.

Abbreviation	Means
a.c.	before meals or food
ad lib.	at pleasure
amp.	ampoule
b.i.d.	twice daily
caps.	capsule
fl., fld.	fluid
fort.	strong
gtt.	drops
h.s.	at bedtime
i.c.	between meals
liq.	liquid
NPO	nothing by mouth
p.c.	after meals or food
per os.	by mouth
p.r.n.	when or as required, whenever necessary
q.i.d.	four times daily
qh, q1h	every hour
q2h	every two hours
q.s.	a sufficient quantity
stat.	at once
t.i.d., t.d.	three times daily
t.i.d.a.c.	three times daily before meals
ung.	ointment

Administering Medications

Pills and Capsules

EQUIPMENT

medication

liquid for
swallowing

Procedure 25-1: Administering Pills and Capsules That Are to Be Swallowed

1. Follow the five rights listed earlier.
2. Wash your hands.
3. Explain to the client what you are doing.
4. Assist the client to sit up, if possible. Prop with pillows or raise the head of the bed if necessary.
5. Pour the correct amount of pills or capsules into the inverted cap of the prescription bottle. Check again to ensure that number and strength are correct.
6. Pour into client's hand.
7. Ask client to put pill or capsule into mouth. Ask client to place on the top of his or her tongue. Watch to see that the client does so.
8. Offer a full glass of water, juice, or other liquid to help the client swallow the medication. Make sure liquid offered is not contraindicated.
9. Remain with the client until the medication is swallowed.
10. If the client vomits immediately after taking the medication, check the emesis for the pill. Contact the appropriate person for directions.
11. Record as per the agency's requirements.

EQUIPMENT

medication

Procedure 25-2: Administering Buccal Tablets

Buccal tablets work best when allowed to dissolve and be absorbed into the mucous membrane of the mouth by being placed in the pouch between the teeth and the cheek (Figure 25-2).

1. Follow the five rights listed earlier.
2. Wash your hands.
3. Explain to the client what you are doing.

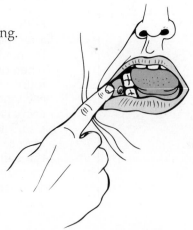

Figure 25-2   *Placement of a Buccal Tablet*

4. Assist the client to sit up, if possible. Prop with pillows or raise the head of the bed if necessary.
5. Pour the correct amount of pills or capsules into the inverted cap of the prescription bottle. Check again to ensure that number and strength are correct.
6. Pour into client's hand.
7. Ask client to put pill or capsule into the pouch between the mouth and the cheek.
8. Ask client to close mouth and let tablet dissolve completely. Remind client not to swallow or chew the tablet. Do not give liquids or foods while tablet is dissolving.
9. If necessary, ask client to open mouth and pull cheek to the side so that you can ensure that the pill has dissolved.
10. Record as per the agency's requirements.

Procedure 25-3: *Administering Sublingual Tablets*

EQUIPMENT

medication

Sublingual tablets work best when allowed to dissolve and be absorbed into the mucous membrane of the mouth by being placed under the tongue (Figure 25-3).

1. Follow the five rights listed earlier.
2. Wash your hands.
3. Explain to the client what you are doing.
4. Assist the client to sit up, if possible. Prop with pillows or raise the head of the bed if necessary.
5. Pour the correct amount of pills or capsules into the inverted cap of the prescription bottle. Check again to ensure that number and strength are correct.
6. Pour into client's hand.
7. Ask client to put pill or capsule under the tongue.
8. Ask client to close mouth and let tablet dissolve completely. Remind client not to swallow or chew the tablet. Do not give liquids or foods while tablet is dissolving.
9. If necessary, ask client to open mouth and lift tongue so that you can ensure that the pill has dissolved.
10. Record as per the agency's requirements.

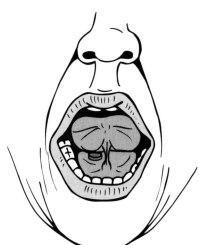

Figure 25-3   *Placement of a Sublingual Tablet*

Oral Liquid Medications

If at all possible, use a calibrated spoon, cup, or oral *syringe* when giving liquid medications. A calibrated dose cup may be provided with the medication. A **syringe** is a hollow tube that can be filled with a medication and then administered. You should wash the cup, spoon, or syringe after use and dry it thoroughly. It is always best to use the cup, spoon, dropper, or syringe that the pharmacist provided with the medication. If no device was provided, ask the pharmacist for one or for advice.

Measuring Oral Liquid Medications Using an Oral Syringe

1. Follow the five rights listed earlier.
2. Wash your hands.
3. Explain to the client what you are doing.
4. Shake the medication unless the instructions advise otherwise. If the medication tends to foam when shaken, be careful not to shake the liquid too vigorously.

EQUIPMENT

oral syringe

bottle adapter

Procedure 25-4: Filling the Syringe Using a Bottle Adapter

1. Many oral syringes come with an adapter that fits into the top of the bottle. Ensure that the adapter is clean. Dampen the adapter with tap water to make it more easily fit into the mouth of the medication bottle and insert it. Ensure that the adapter fits snugly.
2. If the oral syringe has a cap, remove it. Insert the tip of the oral syringe into the upper part of the adapter, as shown in Figure 25-4.
3. Make sure that you can easily read the markings on the syringe. Turn the syringe if necessary.
4. Hold the bottle and syringe vertically with the bottle upside down at the top as shown in Figure 25-4.

Figure 25-4   *Measuring Oral Liquids into a Syringe*

5. Draw the syringe's plunger out. This will draw the medication into the syringe. Make sure that you keep the tip of the syringe firmly inserted in the adapter so as to prevent air from entering the syringe.

6. If air enters the syringe, depress the plunger fully and draw the liquid into the syringe again.

7. Carefully measure the amount of medication as per the support plan. It's often easier to get the exact amount if you slightly overfill the syringe, then depress the plunger until only the correct amount is remaining.

8. Carefully remove the syringe from the adapter. Avoid touching the syringe's tip to avoid contamination.

Procedure 25-5: Filling a Syringe Without a Bottle Adapter

EQUIPMENT

syringe

clean cup or glass

medication

1. Pour a small amount of the medication into a clean cup or glass. Do not pour an excessive amount, as you will not be able to return the excess to the medication bottle.

2. Place the syringe upright into the liquid. Do not push the syringe to the bottom of the cup as this will make it very difficult for you to draw up the liquid.

3. Draw the syringe's plunger out. This will draw the medication into the syringe. Make sure that you keep the tip of the syringe in the liquid to prevent air from entering the syringe.

4. If air enters the syringe, depress the plunger fully and draw the liquid into the syringe again.

5. Carefully measure the amount of medication as per the support plan. It's often easier to get the exact amount if you slightly overfill the syringe, then depress the plunger until only the correct amount is remaining.

6. Remove the syringe from the cup. Avoid touching any surface with the syringe's tip to avoid contamination.

Procedure 25-6: Administering Liquid Medications to an Adult Using an Oral Syringe

EQUIPMENT

filled oral syringe

1. Ask the client to sit upright. If necessary, assist the client or raise the head of the bed.

2. Slide the oral syringe tip along the inside cheek or point toward the back of the mouth. To avoid choking, make sure that the tip of the syringe is not far from the surface of the mouth.

3. Slowly depress the plunger. Allow the person to swallow the liquid normally.

4. If permissible, offer liquid to drink.

Procedure 25-7: Administering Liquid Medication to an Infant Using an Oral Syringe

EQUIPMENT

filled oral syringe

1. Hold the infant as though you were feeding him or her a bottle. Make sure that the infant's head and neck are well supported.

2. Use your thumb to gently push down on the infant's chin to open the infant's mouth.

3. Slide the oral syringe tip along the inside cheek or point toward the back of the mouth (Figure 25-5). To avoid choking, make sure that the tip of the syringe is not far from the surface of the mouth.

4. Slowly depress the plunger to flow the liquid into the infant's mouth. Allow the infant to swallow the liquid normally. You may have to pause once or twice to allow the infant to swallow.

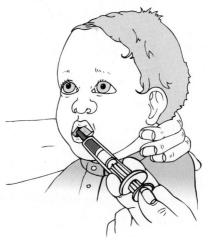

Figure 25-5   *Administering Liquid Medications to an Infant Using an Oral Syringe*

Procedure 25-8: Cleaning the Syringe

EQUIPMENT

oral syringe

clean water

towel for drying

1. Pull the plunger out of the barrel of the syringe.
2. Wash and thoroughly rinse all parts.
3. Shake the barrel out to remove excess water and position upright to drain any remaining water.
4. Dry the plunger completely.
5. Store the parts in a clean area until the next use. Do not reassemble the syringe until both barrel and plunger are completely dry.
6. Wash and thoroughly rinse the cup or adapter. Shake the adapter to remove excess water. Dry the cup. Store with the syringe.

Procedure 25-9: Administering Oral Liquid Medication Using a Medicine Spoon or Cup

EQUIPMENT

medicine cup or spoon

medication

1. Follow the five rights listed earlier.
2. Wash your hands.
3. Explain to the client what you are doing.
4. Make sure that you can easily see the measurement markings on the spoon or cup.
5. Slowly pour medication into the spoon or cup until you reach the prescribed amount.
6. Ask the client to sit upright. If necessary, assist the person or raise the head of the bed.

7. Place the rim of the spoon or cup in the client's mouth.
8. Slowly tilt the spoon or cup so that the liquid runs into the client's mouth (Figure 25-6). Pause to allow the client time to swallow if necessary.
9. Make sure that the client receives all the medication.
10. If permissible, offer liquid to drink.
11. Wash, rinse, and dry the spoon or cup.

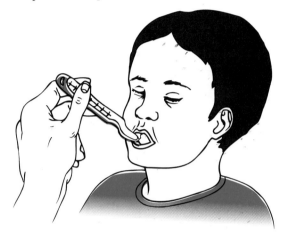

Figure 25-6 *Administering Oral Liquid Medications Using a Medication Spoon*

Procedure 25-10: *Administering Oral Liquid Medication Using a Built-In Dropper*

EQUIPMENT

medication with built-in dropper

Some medications require that you administer a specific number of drops of medication. These medications are often packaged in a bottle with a dropper built into the cap.
1. Follow the five rights listed earlier.
2. Wash your hands.
3. Explain to the client what you are doing.
4. Open the bottle.
5. Make sure that the tip of the dropper is in the liquid. Squeeze the bulb on the dropper to expel the air in the dropper.
6. Release the bulb, allowing liquid to rise into the dropper.
7. Administer the proper number of drops onto the client's tongue.

Procedure 25-11: *Administering Oral Liquid Medication Using a Calibrated Dropper*

EQUIPMENT

medication

calibrated dropper

1. Follow the five rights listed earlier.
2. Wash your hands.
3. Explain to the client what you are doing.
4. Open the bottle.
5. Make sure that the tip of the dropper is in the liquid. Squeeze the bulb on the dropper to expel the air in the dropper.

6. Release the bulb, allowing liquid to rise into the dropper.
7. Remove the dropper from the liquid when you have drawn the prescribed amount. If you have drawn too much, carefully squeeze out the excess amount.
8. Administer the medication in the same manner as described in the procedure for administering medication with an oral syringe.

Transdermal Patch

Transdermal patches provide a constant flow of medication to a client. These patches release medication slowly, so that the amount administered is constant over the period of time that the patch is applied. The medication is absorbed through the skin. In order to make sure that the amount of medication remains constant, the patch should be applied at the same time each day.

EQUIPMENT

transdermal patch

water and soap to wash skin

towel for drying

Procedure 25-12: Applying a Transdermal Patch

1. Follow the five rights listed earlier.
2. Wash your hands.
3. Explain to the client what you are doing.
4. Identify the area to which the patch is to be applied. Be aware that some patches must be applied to a specific area of the body.
5. Do not apply the patch to skin that is broken, scratched, or has a rash or scar tissue as these things can affect the absorption of the medication. Avoid skin folds and areas that usually are moist as the patch may not adhere securely. Avoid hairy areas as the patch may not adhere securely or work properly. As well, removing a patch from a hairy area can be painful.
6. Rotate patch locations to avoid skin irritation.
7. Wash and dry your hands thoroughly.
8. Wash the client's skin where the patch is to be applied. Thoroughly dry the area.
9. Open the package containing one patch (Figure 25-7). Be careful not to tear the patch.
10. Remove the backing from the patch. Do not touch the sticky side.
11. Apply the patch so that there are no wrinkles. Press the patch in place and maintain pressure on the patch for 10-15 seconds to ensure that the patch adheres properly and is secure.
12. Dispose of the wrapper and wash your hands.

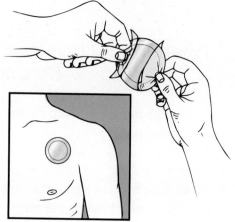

Figure 25-7   *Applying a Transdermal Patch*

Medicated Creams, Ointments, Gels, and Lotions

Procedure 25-13: *Applying Medicated Creams, Ointments, Gels, and Lotions*

1. Follow the five rights listed earlier.
2. Wash your hands.
3. Explain to the client what you are doing.
4. Wash your hands before applying the medication. If recommended or applying the medication to broken skin, wear gloves.
5. Wash the area of the client's skin where the medication is to be applied. Pat off excess water, but leave the skin moist.
6. Apply a small amount of the medication to the client's skin. Remember that a thick layer of medication is no more effective than a thin layer.
7. Spread the medication over the designated area.
8. Do not cover with gauze or a bandage unless required.
9. Cap the medication.
10. Wash your hands.

EQUIPMENT

medication

gloves

water and soap for washing

towel

guaze or bandage if required

Eye Drops and Ointments

Procedure 25-14: *Administering Eye Drops*

1. Follow the five rights listed earlier.
2. Wash your hands.
3. Explain to the client what you are doing.
4. Ask the client to lie down or to tilt his or her head back.
5. Ask the client to look up at the ceiling.
6. Open the eye drops. Do not allow the tip of the eye drop bottle to touch any surface.
7. Gently pull down the lower eyelid to form a pouch between the lid and the client's eye (Figure 25-8).

EQUIPMENT

eye drop medication

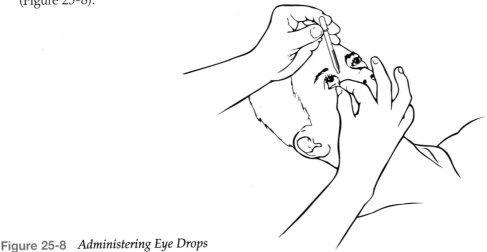

Figure 25-8 *Administering Eye Drops*

8. Position the eye drops at the side of the client's eye. Do not allow the tip of the eye drop bottle to touch the eye. You may find it easier to control the position of the bottle if you rest the palm of your hand on the client's forehead.

9. Squeeze the bottle slightly to administer the prescribed number of drops into the pouch.

10. Ask the client to close her or his eyes and place light pressure on the inner corners of the eye to prevent the drops from leaving the eye. Ask the client to avoid rubbing or squeezing his or her eye shut to avoid forcing the medication out of the eye.

11. Recap the bottle.

12. Wash your hands.

EQUIPMENT

eye ointment

Procedure 25-15: Administering an Eye Ointment

1. Follow the five rights listed earlier.
2. Wash your hands.
3. Explain to the client what you are doing.
4. Ask the client to lie down or to tilt his or her head back.
5. Ask the client to look up at the ceiling.
6. Open the eye ointment. Do not allow the tip of the tube to touch any surface.
7. Gently pull down the lower eyelid to form a pouch between the lid and the client's eye (Figure 25-9).
8. Squeeze the tube gently to place the prescribed amount of ointment in the pouch at the side of the client's eye. Do not allow the tip of the tube to touch the eye. You may find it easier to control the position of the tube if you rest the palm of your hand on the client's forehead.

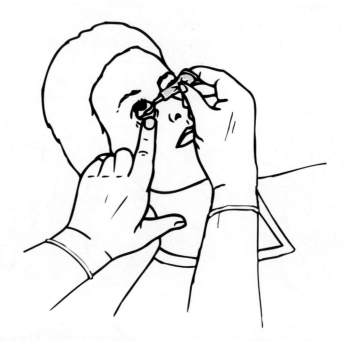

Figure 25-9 *Administering Eye Ointment*

9. Ask the client to close her or his eyes and place light pressure on the inner corners of the eye to prevent the drops from leaving the eye. Ask the client to avoid rubbing or squeezing his or her eye shut to avoid forcing the medication out of the eye.
10. Recap the bottle.
11. Wash your hands.

Ear Drops

Procedure 25-16: Administering Ear Drops

1. Follow the five rights listed earlier.
2. Wash your hands.
3. Explain to the client what you are doing.
4. Ask the client to lie down or to tilt his or her head so that the ear to be treated is facing up.
5. Shake the ear drops. Warm the bottle in your hands before opening.
6. Open the bottle and squeeze the dropper to draw the medication into the dropper.
7. If you are administering the ear drops to an infant or toddler, pull the ear *down* and back slightly to straighten the ear canal (Figure 25-10). If you are administering the drops to a child, youth or adult, pull the ear *up* and back slightly to straighten the ear canal (Figure 25-11).
8. Administer the prescribed number of drops into the ear canal. Do not insert the dropper into the ear canal or allow the dropper to touch any surface.
9. Ask the client to keep the treated ear "up" for 5-10 minutes to allow the drops to be absorbed. If both of the client's ears must be treated, allow 10-15 minutes between each ear to allow the drops to be absorbed in each ear.
10. Dry excess medication from the client's ear lobe.
11. Wash your hands.

EQUIPMENT

ear drops

towel

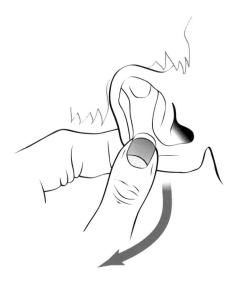

Figure 25-10 *Administering Ear Drops to Infants*

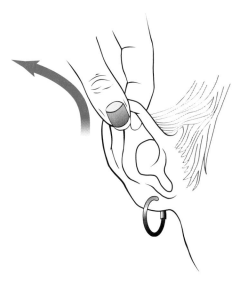

Figure 25-11 *Administering Ear Drops to Children and Adults*

Nose Drops

EQUIPMENT	*Procedure 25-17: Administering Nose Drops*

EQUIPMENT

nose drops

tissues

1. Follow the five rights listed earlier.
2. Wash your hands.
3. Explain to the client what you are doing.
4. Ask your client to gently blow his or her nose to clear the nostrils.
5. Ask the client to sit in a chair and tilt his or her head backward. If more comfortable for the client, he or she can lie on a bed with a pillow under the shoulders so that the head can tip back. A small child or infant can lay on the worker's lap with his or her head tilted back and neck supported.
6. Shake the nose drops. Warm the bottle in your hands before opening.
7. Open the bottle and squeeze the dropper to draw the medication into the dropper.
8. Administer the prescribed number of drops into each nostril (Figure 25-12). Do not allow the dropper to touch any surface.

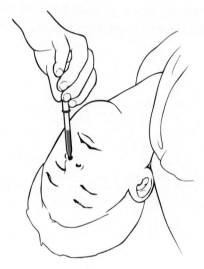

Figure 25-12
*Administering
Nose Drops*

9. Ask the client to bend forward, with his or her head toward the knees. Ask the client to hold this position for 5-10 seconds, then sit upright for 5 minutes. This helps the drops reach the desired spot.
10. Wash your hands.

If Problems Arise

When you are asked to administer medication you should know the name and telephone number of the person to call if a problem arises. You should contact that person and your supervisor if any of the following occur:

1. The client refuses to take the medication, or says that the medication is not the correct one.
2. The client appears to have taken too much medication.
3. The client has skipped a dose of medication.

Questions for Review

1. Are herbal medicines drugs?

2. If taken incorrectly, can over-the-counter medications be as harmful as a prescription medication?

3. Is a generic drug *exactly* the same as the name-brand version? Why or why not?

4. What are the four types of assistance?

5. You have been asked to administer medication to Mr. London. What ten things must you know before you can safely do this?

6. What are the five rights of medication administration?

7. What provincial legislation (if any) limits your ability to administer medication? What is this legislation called? What branch of the government administers it?

Questions for Discussion

1. How do you feel about assisting a client to take medication? What types of assistance are easier for you to provide? Which are harder to do?

2. You have been asked to give Mrs. Jaeger her medication. When you bring it to her, she says, "That's not the right pill." The medication in the bottle is identical to the pill you gave her. The name on the label of the bottle matches the name of the drug you are to give. What do you do?

3. You are assigned to assist Mr. Cadieux. Your assignment does not include assisting Mr. Cadieux with medication. However, when you open the refrigerator to get Mr. Cadieux' lunch, you find a cup with two pills in it. A note in the cup says, "Make sure Mr. Cadieux takes these pills. They are *essential.*" What do you do? Why?

PART SIX

GAINING EMPLOYMENT

Source: Interface Personnel.

Preparing for Work

Through reading this chapter, you'll be able to:

1. Define employability.
2. Describe the work settings most appropriate for you.
3. Use the seven-step method to prepare a résumé that includes the proper content, is well organized, and is formatted so as to be attractive and easy to read.
4. Accurately complete a standard job application.
5. Conduct an effective job search.

Chapter At A Glance

Employability

Work Settings

Your Résumé

The Job Application

Terms You'll Use

Academic Skills   Skills that provide the basic foundation to get, keep, and progress in a job.

Chronological Résumé   A résumé that organizes the information in each section by date.

Employability   The ability to do the tasks of a job.

Functional Résumé   A résumé that groups skills and experiences gained from a variety of employment situations.

Personal Management Skills   The combination of skills, attitudes, and behaviours required to get, keep, and progress in a job.

Police Record Check   A check done to provide proof that a person has not been convicted of a crime that would affect that person's employability.

References   People who have agreed to give information regarding your abilities to potential employers.

Teamwork Skills   Skills that are needed to work with others in a job.

Employability

Employability is having the ability to do the tasks of a job is just a part of what you need to gain employment. Employers want employees who are also adaptable, take responsibility for their actions, as well as communicate and work well with others. These types of skills are classified into three groups: *academic skills*, *personal management skills*, and *teamwork skills*. Table 26-1 describes these three types of skills (Conference Board of Canada, 1993).

TABLE 26-1 Employability		
Academic Skills	**Personal Management Skills**	**Teamwork Skills**
Those skills which provide the basic foundation to get, keep, and progress in a job and to achieve the best results	The combination of skills, attitudes, and behaviours required to get, keep, and progress in a job and to achieve the best results	Those skills needed to work with others in a job and to achieve the best results
Canadian employers need a person who can: **Communicate** ■ Understand and speak the languages in which business is conducted ■ Listen to understand and learn ■ Read, comprehend, and use written materials including graphs, charts, and displays ■ Write effectively in the languages in which business is conducted **Think** ■ Think critically and act logically to evaluate situations, solve problems, and make decisions ■ Understand and solve problems involving mathematics and use the results ■ Use technology, instruments, tools, and information systems effectively ■ Access and apply specialized knowledge from various fields (skilled trades, technology, physical sciences, arts, and social sciences) **Learn** ■ Continue to learn for life	Canadian employers need a person who can demonstrate: **Positive Attitudes and Behaviours** ■ Self-esteem and confidence ■ Honesty, integrity, and personal ethics ■ A positive attitude toward learning, growth, and personal health ■ Initiative, energy, and persistence to get the job done **Responsibility** ■ The ability to set goals and priorities in work and personal life ■ The ability to plan and manage time, money, and other resources to achieve goals ■ Accountability for actions taken **Adaptability** ■ A positive attitude toward change ■ Recognition of and respect for people's diversity and individual differences ■ The ability to identify and suggest new ideas to get the job done—creativity	Canadian employers need a person who can: **Work with Others** ■ Understand and contribute to the organization's goals ■ Understand and work within the culture of the group ■ Plan and make decisions with others and support the outcomes ■ Respect the thoughts and opinions of others in the group ■ Exercise "give and take" to achieve group results ■ Seek a team approach as appropriate ■ Lead when appropriate, mobilizing the group for high performance

Source: Employability Skills Profile: What Are Employers Looking For? Brochure 1999 E/F (Ottawa: The Conference Board of Canada, 1999).

As you can see, these skills are complementary, but different. Many of these skills are discussed in this text and covered in your training. To succeed as a personal support worker, you must excel in all three types of skills.

Work Settings

Where do you want to work? In Chapter 2, we discussed the various types of work settings. Depending upon where you live, there may be many types of work settings readily available to you.

What's Available?
Seeking Out the Opportunities

A good first step to starting your job search is finding out what opportunities are available in your community. There are several ways to do this.

1. **Ask family and friends who work in health care or support services for their recommendations.**   This often is a good method of finding out a bit about an agency as well.
2. **Check with your teacher or your school's career counsellor.**   Many teachers work (or have worked) in the field. Career counsellors are usually in contact with area employers. Teachers and counsellors can be a rich source of information and advice.
3. **Contact the local home care program for information on area agencies.**   Many home care agencies produce lists of agencies and facilities for clients.
4. **Visit your local library or information centre.**   Libraries and these centres often have information on the services available in your area.
5. **Look in the yellow pages.**   Many agencies are found under the headings of "Home Health Care", "Home Health Services", "Nursing Homes", "Retirement Homes", and "Nursing Services".
6. **Check employment ads in your local newspapers.**   Most agencies regularly advertise for staff.
7. **Contact your local Canada Employment Centre.**   These offices often have information about area employers, even if the employers have not posted jobs with the Centre.
8. **Attend job fairs held in your community.**   Job fairs are usually advertised in local newspapers, on the community information channel of your local cable company, or even by flyers posted in local stores. These fairs usually provide an opportunity to learn about a number of agencies in a very short period of time.

Keep in mind that any time you visit an employer, attend a job fair, or visit an agency to make enquiries about potential employers, *you* are making an impression. Make sure that you dress professionally and appropriately for the visit. Do not take children or friends with you. Chapter 27 discusses professional appearance and behaviour in greater detail.

What Do I Want to Know?

When you are first seeking out the opportunities in your area, there are several questions you will want to answer.

1. What kinds of work do support workers do in the agency?
2. What types of clients does the agency serve?
3. Where is the agency located? Does the agency serve clients at other centres or in their homes?
4. Are there many types of jobs that support workers do? Do support workers have the opportunity to work in more than one type of job?
5. What types of training, experience, skills, and abilities does the agency look for in a support worker?
6. What are the hours of work? Do support workers work different shifts? Weekends? Holidays?
7. Do most of the support workers work full time or part time?
8. Does the agency encourage support workers to take additional training? If so, what opportunities are available?
9. What kind of supervision and guidance do support workers have?
10. What is the agency's mission or philosophy?
11. What is the agency's reputation?

What If the Agency Isn't Hiring?

It's likely that your search will turn up agencies that are not hiring support workers at that time. This is fine. You still can learn about the agency and perhaps submit an application for consideration in the future.

Getting the Right Fit

Once you have gathered information about the agencies in your area, you can begin to identify those that are most promising. The questions posed in Chapter 2 will assist you in refining your search. For each agency, answer the following.

1. Does the type of work interest me? Am I excited by the job?
2. Can I perform the tasks required? Do I have all the training I'll need? If not, will the agency provide the necessary training?
3. Do I like working with people in that kind of work setting?
4. Can I get to the work site? Can I travel from client to client if the job requires it? Do I *like* the amount of travel required?
5. Am I comfortable with the agency or client? Will I be proud to work for them?
6. Are the wages and benefits (if any) competitive?
7. Is there an opportunity to learn additional skills and take on different responsibilities if I would like to?

Police Record Checks

Many agencies now require that employees provide a **police record check** that provides proof that the person has not been convicted of a crime that would affect the employee's ability to work as a support worker. Exactly what convictions would affect a person's ability to work as a support worker will depend upon the specific job. For example, a conviction for impaired driving may not matter in some cases, but probably would matter if the position applied for involved driving clients.

Each agency has its own policy with regard to police record checks. Generally, the agency considering you for employment will tell you where you must go to obtain the record check. In some areas, record checks are handled by the local police department. In other areas, the provincial police or the Royal Canadian Mounted Police (RCMP) handles these requests. Most police departments charge a fee to provide a record check. Some will reduce the fee if you are requesting the record check in order to apply for a job.

If you have a criminal record *for which you have not received a pardon*, any convictions will be listed on the form you receive from the police department. You must be prepared to discuss any items appearing on your record. Note that you may apply for a *pardon* to remove a conviction from your record. Pardons are obtained through the Federal Government and are usually limited to convictions that occurred many years ago. Contact your local police department for information on how to apply for a pardon.

Your Résumé

What Is a Résumé?

A résumé advertises your skills and experience to a prospective employer. Its purpose is to make the employer so interested in you that you are granted an interview.

If the résumé is to be effective, it must highlight your skills and make it easy for the employer to see how you might contribute to the organization. The résumé must include the information an employer will want to see, be well organized, and be formatted so as to be professional, attractive, and easy to read.

The Seven-Step Method

Developing your résumé has seven steps: information gathering, focussing, organizing, summarizing, checking, formatting, and printing. Let's take a look at each of these steps.

Information Gathering

Most employers want to know the relevant skills and experience you would bring to the job. Gather information for this section by writing down your previous and current experience, using the categories in this section. For now, don't worry about organizing the information too much, simply write down the details.

Education

Answer these five questions.

1. Do you have a certificate or diploma in support work or a similar field?
2. What is the exact name of the certificate (for example, *Support Service Worker* or *Personal Support Worker*)?
3. From what educational institution did you get your certificate or diploma? In what year?
4. Do you have a high school diploma? When and where did you get these certificates?
5. Are there other relevant certificates you have attained (for example, a certificate in palliative care or mental health support)? When and where did you get these certificates?

As you gather this information, focus on any items that may be attractive to an employer. Did you complete a field placement in a setting that gave you special skills, such as an Alzheimer's day centre, an infant stimulation program, or a palliative care centre? Did you take classes from someone who is well known in the field? Did you receive any awards or honours for your work?

At first glance, you may feel that including your high school diploma is unnecessary. It may be. Include the diploma if it was recently granted and you feel that it will demonstrate your commitment to learning and attest to your self-discipline. For example, if you returned to school as an adult and completed your diploma while working, you are demonstrating that you can set realistic goals, balance priorities, and achieve success under difficult circumstances. These are qualities that most employers desire.

Experience

Experience is gained through paid employment and volunteer work. It also includes experience you have gained from work not directly related to your career. For example, you might have gained valuable problem-solving skills through volunteer work with an organization like the Girl Guides, Block Parents, or Big Sisters. Ask yourself if the experience is something that you could use as a support worker. If the experience is relevant, jot it down.

Abilities and Skills

Skills are techniques that you have developed. Abilities are often traits that you may have had all of your life. As you identified your experience, you likely began to identify abilities you have used and skills you have gained. For example, you may have been able to creatively tailor your approach to your client's needs. Or, you may have developed problem-solving or teamwork skills. Make a list of these abilities and skills.

Interests

You may want to consider including a brief description of your interests or hobbies. Sometimes, these help to give a more complete picture of you as a person. Interests and hobbies can also tell a bit about your self-discipline, commitment, and organization.

Make sure that you are specific in your description, and include only two or three significant interests. For example, if you are a long-distance runner, you might say, "I am a long-distance runner who has completed 15 races in the past three years."

Focussing

What do you offer an employer? Look at the answers you've written down during the information-gathering phase. Compare what you offer to the things you have learned employers look for in a support worker. You might want to ask your instructor or another person who knows you well to look over your answers and give you other ideas. The employability listed earlier in this chapter may also help you recognize attributes you have. Make a list of the information that is most relevant to potential employers.

It's important to be specific about your attributes. If you can communicate well with clients who have some type of dementia, say so. Don't use a vague phrase like "good communication skills" if you can give a really relevant example.

Organizing

You now have all the information you need to develop your résumé. In the organizing phase, you'll put this information in order so that the most important information is the easiest to find.

There are two basic methods of organizing your information. The first method organizes information *chronologically*, starting with the most recent information. The second résumé organizes information by *function*. Each method has its particular uses. In this section, we'll discuss each in terms of what it is and when you should consider using it.

Chronological Résumé

In a **chronological résumé**, you organize the information in each section by date. It is most appropriate when your work experience is in the same field as is the job you'd like to get, and most of your work experience has been with one or two employers over that period of time. For example, you would use a chronological résumé when you have worked as a support worker for a period of time and you are applying for a similar position. As this method illustrates your work history, it's not a good choice if you have held positions with a number of employers.

Exhibit 26-1 illustrates a sample chronological résumé. Refer to this figure as we discuss the various components.

A chronological résumé usually begins with a section on work experience. Within this section, list the positions you have held, starting with the most recent employer. If you are working in the field, you should include information about your present employment first. For each employment situation, state the position held, the employer, and the dates of employment. In a sentence or two, describe the most significant aspects of your work for that employer. Any skills you developed are usually listed with the employment, although they can be summarized in a separate section.

A section on education usually follows the section on work experience. The most recent certificate or diploma is usually listed first, unless there is a specific certificate or diploma you know the employer prefers. For example, if you are applying for a support worker position, you might list a support worker certificate first, even though you may have taken other certificates more recently.

After the section on education you may choose to list skills and interests in separate sections.

AUDREY O'SHEA

123 Anywhere Road · Anytown, British Columbia V7B 1J2 · 604-555-1234

Objective

To secure a full-time or part-time position providing personal support to clients who live in the community.

Qualification a

Our

Employment

SOUTHWESTERN HOME HEALTH & SUPPORT	Central, B.C.
HOMEMAKER	MAY, 1997 -PRESENT

I provide assistance with: personal care (bathing, dressing, grooming, eating, etc.) and exercise and ambulation, including follow-up on physiotherapy/ occupational therapy orders as appropriate. I also provide relief for care givers of clients with dementia.

MID-REGIONAL MS SUPPORT SERVICES	Burnaby, B.C.
ATTENDANT	JANUARY, 1994 -MAY, 1997

Responsible to tailor approach and service to clients with Multiple Sclerosis whose needs often varied from day to day. Demonstrated creativity and flexibility in determining with clients what tasks were to be performed and how they were to be done.

VILLA LIVING CENTRE	North Vancouver, B.C.
HEALTH CARE AIDE	JUNE, 1990 - MAY, 1997

Responsible to assist 15 cognitively-impaired residents with routine activities of living. Developed strong communication, problem-solving and time management skills.

Education

PERSONAL SUPPORT WORKER CERTIFICATE	November, 1998	
Bytown College		*Bytown, B.C.*

SECONDARY SCHOOL DIPLOMA	June, 1996
Bytown District School Board	*Bytown, B.C.*

Skills & Abilities

- Manage multiple demands
- Flexible
- Work in a variety of settings
- Organized
- Responsible
- Reliable
- Strong problem-solving skills
- Thorough

I speak the following languages:

English	·	Gujrapi
Katcsi	·	Swahili

Exhibit 26-1   *A Sample Chronological Résumé*

Functional Résumé

A **functional résumé** groups skills and experiences gained from a variety of employment situations. It is most appropriate when you have had a number of positions, have gaps in your work history, have had positions that vary in responsibility or skills, or have held a number of part-time positions in the field. Exhibit 26-2 illustrates a functional résumé created by a person who holds three part-time positions in the field.

In this method, the skills gained through the various positions are identified at the beginning of the résumé. Skills should be organized to highlight the most significant skills. (The résumé in Exhibit 26-2 includes a section on the type of clients with whom the worker has experience, as this is seen as important to employers.) Sources of the experience are listed after the skill set, but without describing which skills came from each setting. Education and interests follow experience.

Summarizing

Summarizing includes three components: identifying data, career objective, and a summary statement.

Identifying Information

You must include some identifying data: your name, address, telephone number, as well as a statement that you are legally able to work in Canada. You should not include your social insurance number, any information about your age, race, citizenship, marital status, children, or religious affiliation. Because your age can be determined from some provincial driver's licence numbers, you should not include your licence number on your résumé.

Place the identifying information at the top of the first page of the résumé. Centre the information or use a bold or larger typeface to make sure your name stands out.

Career Objectives and Summary Statements

Including a career objective or summary statement is optional. Many résumés include a career objective (as illustrated in Exhibits 26-1 and 26-2). Others include a summary of the candidate's significant background. The choice of including one or both is a personal one. Use the guidelines below to determine whether you should include these items.

Career Objective

A career objective is useful only when it indicates a specific objective that meets a unique employment need. Avoid vague objectives like, "To use my skills in a community agency." Table 26-2 lists sample specific objectives.

TABLE 26-2	Examples of Specific Objectives
"Providing personal support to clients with dementia in a day program setting."	
"Assisting with recreation programs in a long-term care facility."	
"Working with clients receiving palliative care service at home."	

AUDREY O'SHEA
123 Anywhere Road · Anytown, British Columbia V7B 1J2 · 604-555-1234

Objective

To secure a full-time or part-time position providing personal support to clients who live in the community.

Skills and Abilities

- Manage multiple demands
- Flexible
- Responsible
- Work in a variety of settings
- Organized
- Calming
- Reliable
- Thorough
- Caring
- Strong problem-solving skills
- Gentle
- Professional

I have worked successfully with clients in a variety of settings:
- Palliative
- Cognitively Impaired
- Rehabilitation
- Clients with Chronic Pain
- Post-Surgical Recovery

I speak the following languages:
- English
- Gujrapi
- Katcsi

Employment

I currently work with three local agencies on an on-call basis. With each, I provide the following:
- Assistance with personal care (bathing, dressing, grooming, eating, etc.)
- Assistance with exercise and ambulation, including follow-up on physiotherapy/occupational therapy orders as appropriate.
- Assess changes in client condition and report observations to supervisor
- Care giver relief
- Housekeeping and meal preparation

The agencies with which I currently work are:

SOUTHWESTERN HOME HEALTH & SUPPORT HOMEMAKER	Central, B.C. MAY, 1997 -PRESENT
MID-REGIONAL MS SUPPORT SERVICES ATTENDANT	Burnaby, B.C. JANUARY, 1994 -MAY, 1997
VILLA LIVING CENTRE HEALTH CARE AIDE	North Vancouver, B.C. JUNE, 1990 - MAY, 1997

Education

PERSONAL SUPPORT WORKER CERTIFICATE *Bytown College*	November, 1998 *Bytown,B.C.*
SECONDARY SCHOOL DIPLOMA *Bytown District School Board*	June, 1996 *Bytown, B.C.*

Exhibit 26-2   *A Functional Résumé*

If you have more than one specific area of interest, you might consider creating a separate résumé for each area. If your résumé was created on a computer, it is often very easy to create two résumés from the same information.

Summary Statement

Summary statements are statements that give a brief overview of your relevant background. These statements are usually placed at the beginning of the résumé, just after the career objective.

Include a summary statement only if you want to highlight an aspect of your background that is truly desirable to an employer or that gives a context to your application. For example, if you have specialized in working with children with multiple needs and are applying to work in an agency serving children, you might create a summary statement that highlights your years of experience and training in that capacity

A summary statement should not be used to highlight general skills or to highlight interests or attitudes. Table 26-3 illustrates some well-defined—and some ill-defined—summary statements.

TABLE 26-3	Summary Statements
Try This...	**Not This...**
To indicate expertise in a specific field:	*Not focussed on a specific need:*
Over the past 10 years, I have focussed my training and work in the area of dementia care. I have received three awards for my work with clients.	I am an outgoing person who is interested in clients. I enjoy working with people who need assistance.
To explain a career shift:	*Not directly related to the profession:*
After 15 years in accounting, I left the field to train in personal support. This change has enabled me to use my interpersonal and problem-solving skills to assist people to live independently.	I have won several awards for my artwork in local competitions.

Formatting and Printing

Formatting includes the layout and typesetting that helps to make your résumé look professional. Proper formatting makes it easy for the reader to find the information he or she is seeking. Printing means the way the résumé is copied.

Formatting and printing make the first impression on your reader. A neat, well-formatted résumé will encourage the reader to consider what you have to say. A poorly laid out or printed résumé will not be considered. Remember that the average employer spends only a few seconds looking at each résumé he or she receives. If your résumé doesn't catch the employer's eye, you won't be considered for the position.

Director of Admissions
Forget School of Massage
123 4th St. NW
Calgary, Alberta
N4B 4R5

28 January, 1991

RE: Rebecca Smith

To Whom it May Concern:

I am pleased to provide a letter of reference for **Rebecca Smith**, a graduate of the Support Worker Programme offered by our school. I was the primary instructor for the programme, and as such, was aware of Rebecca's proficiency in both theoretical and practical components.

Rebecca clearly demonstrated interest and ability in class. She was quick to absorb new material, and was well able to apply it in the appropriate context. She was self-directed, yet willing and able to work with others as the situation required. Her overall average for the programme was 91%. I would have no doubt about her ability to undertake and succeed at additional academic training.

In addition to the above, Rebecca also possesses a sensitivity toward others, as well as a patient nature--both of particular value in her current profession. She also demonstrates a strength of character and a sense of purpose in her activity.

I would strongly recommend Rebecca for admission to your programme.

Sincerely,

Marilyn Garast
Instructor, Support Worker Programme
Continuing Education Department

Director of Admissions
Sutherland Chan School of Massage
TORONTO, Ontario

28 January, 1991

To Whom it May Concern:

I am pleased to provide a letter of reference for Rebecca Smith, a graduate of the Support Worker Programme offered by our school. I was the primary instructor for the programme, and as such, was aware of Rebecca's proficiency in both theoretical and practical components. Rebecca clearly demonstrated interest and ability in class. She was quick to absorb new material, and was well able to apply it in the appropriate context. She was self-directed, yet willing and able to work with others as the situation required. Her overall average for the programme was 91%. I would have no doubt about her ability to undertake and succeed at additional academic training. In addition to the above, Rebecca also possesses a sensitivity toward others, as well as a patient nature--both of particular value in her current profession. She also demonstrates a strength of character and a sense of purpose in her activity. I would strongly recommend Rebecca for admission to your programme.

Sincerely,

Marilyn Garast
Instructor, Support Worker Programme
Continuing Education Department

Exhibit 26-1 *Which would you prefer to read?*

Formatting

Many computer programs such as *WordPerfect®*, *Microsoft Word®*, or *WordPro®* have predefined layouts that you can use to create a professional-looking résumé. If you have a computer, or have access to one at school, you may be able to use one of these layouts. Ask a colleague or teacher for help in using the layout. Remember to save your work on a disk so that you can easily edit the information.

If you have access to a computer but do not want to use a predefined layout, consider using a layout that you have seen and like. You might copy a layout used by a colleague or use one found in a résumé-preparation handbook (usually available at your local library).

A third option is to have your résumé formatted by a professional typist or résumé preparer. You might be able to have this done through the career centre at your school. Typists and professional preparers charge for their services. Make sure that you know what you will receive and how much it will cost before arranging for the service. Career centres may charge a nominal fee for their service. Be aware that you are responsible for the accuracy of the information in your résumé, even if you use a professional résumé service to prepare it.

No matter who formats your résumé, make sure that the résumé uses professional and easy to read typefaces. Use no more than two typefaces, preferably one for the section headings and another for the information under each heading. Do not use script fonts, headline fonts, or other decorative fonts. Table 26-4 illustrates some good—and not so good—choices.

TABLE 26-4	
Use This...	Not This...
I have worked as a support worker (Times New Roman typeface)	**I have worked as a support worker (ad lib typeface)**
I have worked as a support worker (Arial typeface)	*I have worked as a support worker (Snell Black typeface)*

Checking

Before you print your résumé, take a good look at it. Make sure that it is attractive, clear, and complete. Use the following questions to examine your résumé's components.

1. Are my name, address, and telephone number at the top of the first page of the résumé? Are they correct? Are they in slightly larger type and easy to read?
2. Does the typeface and size make the résumé look professional and easy to read?
3. Is the résumé free from spelling and typographical errors? Remember that a computer spell-checker will not flag a word that is spelled correctly, even if it is not the right word. Make sure that another person reads over your résumé to catch all these errors.
4. If you stated a career objective, is it specific enough to be useful without being so specific that you might be excluded from consideration from a position you might want? Is your objective no longer than two sentences?
5. If you stated a summary, does it reflect the events in your career that are most significant to the position for which you are applying? Is your summary no longer than two sentences?
6. Have you included all information that would be significant to a potential employer? Have you removed any "extra" information that is not essential?
7. Does your résumé use a consistent writing style from beginning to end?
8. Have you included the names and contact information of persons who have agreed to give professional, academic, and personal references on your behalf? Make sure that you obtain each person's permission before you include his or her name as a **reference**.

Printing

Your résumé should be printed on high-quality paper in a light colour (grey, off-white, or white), using a laser or ink-jet printer. Avoid using a dot-matrix printer or a low-quality printer that smears ink or prints poorly.

If possible, have several copies of your résumé printed on a laser printer or good-quality ink-jet printer. If this is not possible, then make sure that you make copies on a high-quality photocopier. Many office supply stores now offer high-quality printing and copying at reasonable prices.

The Job Application

Most employers require applicants to complete a job application, even if the applicant has submitted a résumé. An employer may do this for several reasons: to make sure that all applicants submit information in the same format; to make sure that specific information is provided by all applicants; and even to make sure that applicants can understand and complete a simple form.

You must be prepared to complete an application. Although most employers design their own form, most forms ask for similar information. Use the sample application form in Exhibit 26-3 to make sure you have the information you need to complete a basic application form.

Remember that you must be truthful and accurate in your answers. If an answer to a question points up a shortcoming (for example, if you were fired from a recent job), answer the question honestly and attach an explanation if necessary.

Application For Employment
Omega Support Services Association

Last Name	First Name		
Address:	City		Postal Code
Telephone #:			
Are you legally eligible to work in Canada? ☐ YES ☐ NO			
Are you willing to travel within our organization's service area? ☐ YES ☐ NO			

To help us determine your qualifications, please provide information related to your employment, academic and other achievements, including volunteer work. Your resume or other additional information may be attached to this application.

Work Related Skills
Describe any of your work related skills, experience, or training you feel relate to the for which you are applying.

Employment Please list most recent/current employer first.

Employer Name	Address	When Employed?
Position	Duties	Reason for Leaving
Salary	Name of Supervisor	Telephone Number
Employer Name	Address	When Employed?
Position	Duties	Reason for Leaving
Salary	Name of Supervisor	Telephone Number
Employer Name	Address	When employed?
Position	Duties	Reason for Leaving
Salary	Name of Supervisor	Telephone Number

Exhibit 26-3   *Sample Application Form*

Education	Please list most relevant education first.		
School	Programme	Completed?	☐ YES ☐ NO
Certificate or Diploma Granted:		Date Granted:	
School	Programme	Completed?	☐ YES ☐ NO
Certificate or Diploma Granted:		Date Granted:	
School	Programme	Completed?	☐ YES ☐ NO
Certificate or Diploma Granted:		Date Granted:	

Other courses, workshops, seminars or certificates

Course Name	School	Date

References

For employment references we may approach:

Your present/last employer?   ☐ Yes   ☐ No
Your former employer(s)?   ☐ Yes   ☐ No

Please list additional references here:

Name	Telephone Number	Relationship to Applicant
Name	Telephone Number	Relationship to Applicant
Name	Telephone Number	Relationship to Applicant

Personal Interests and Activities

I hereby declare that the foregoing information is true and complete to my knowledge. I understand that a false statement may disqualify me from employment, or cause my dismissal.

Signature _____

Have you attached an additional sheet?   ☐ YES   ☐ NO

Date _____

Exhibit 26-3   *Sample Application Form (continued)*

Questions for Review

1. What is employability? Why is it important?

2. What do you need to do to prepare a résumé that includes the proper content, is well organized, and is formatted so as to be attractive and easy to read?

3. What makes up an effective job search?

Questions for Discussion

1. What work settings are most appropriate for you? What makes a particular setting a good one for you? Compare your answers with those of your colleagues.

2. When you are preparing your résumé, is it ever a good idea to leave out information about your work or education? Why or why not?

3. You were out of the work force for seven years when your children were young. How might you describe this period in your résumé?

Presenting Yourself to an Employer

Chapter At A Glance

Professional Appearance and Behaviour

Contacting Prospective Employers

Your Cover Letter

The Interview

The Offer of Employment

When You Have Not Been Offered Employment

Terms You'll Use

Attire   Clothing.

Conditional Offer of Employment   An offer of employment that is conditional upon you providing certain documents before you can be hired.

Probationary Period   A trial period of employment.

Professional Appearance   All aspects of how you appear, including clothing, cleanliness, and the attention paid to the details of grooming.

Professional Behaviour   Conducting yourself in a polite and businesslike manner.

Professional Appearance and Behaviour

You must take every opportunity to make a positive impression on a potential employer. Remember that even the most casual contact, such as dropping in to the agency to obtain a brochure, gives the employer an opportunity to see you. How you dress, how you act, who is with you, will all be observed. These observations form the employer's first impression of you. First impressions are lasting impressions. It is difficult for most people to change their first impression. If you look and behave in a professional manner, you will make a positive impression. If your appearance or behaviour is unprofessional, you will make a negative impression.

What Is Professional Appearance?

Professional appearance includes all aspects of how you appear: your clothing, your cleanliness, the attention you pay to the details of your grooming. Use the following guidelines to help you attain a professional appearance. Photo 27-1 shows a professional-looking applicant.

Photo 27-1
*Professional
Appearance*

Source: Interface
Personnel.

Clothing

1. You should dress in a business-type **attire**. This means a dress, a suit, or coordinated shirt with pants or a skirt. Do not wear casual clothing such as T-shirts, track suits, tube tops, jeans, or shorts. Select clothing that fits properly and make sure that any undergarment (such as a slip or bra strap) does not show.
2. All clothing should be clean, without stains, and in good repair. Replace missing buttons and repair sagging hems.
3. Hosiery should be appropriate and in good repair. Stockings should be free of holes and runs. Avoid ankle socks and gym socks as they are too casual.
4. Shoes should be polished and in good condition. Do not wear casual shoes such as running shoes or sandals.

Grooming

1. You must be clean and fresh. Shower or bathe before your interview. Wash your hands just before the interview so that they are clean.
2. Make sure that your hair is freshly washed and neat. Keep hair ornaments (barrettes, bows, clips, or headbands) to a minimum.
3. Makeup should be subtle.
4. Wear minimal jewellery. Avoid large rings, earrings, or bracelets. Remove obvious body ornaments, such as tongue studs, eyebrow studs, and nose rings.
5. Make sure that your nails are clean and neatly trimmed. If you wear nail polish, choose a neutral colour.
6. Make sure your teeth are clean and your breath is fresh. If you have eaten or smoked, chew a breath mint before the interview.

Professional Behaviour

Professional behaviour means conducting yourself in a polite and businesslike manner. Observe the following guidelines to help ensure a good impression:

1. Do not take children, family members, or friends along to the interview.
2. Arrive 5-10 minutes early for any scheduled appointment. Avoid dropping in to the agency at busy times, even if you are just picking up or dropping off information.
3. Make sure that you have a clean, unwrinkled copy of your résumé to leave with the prospective employer. Invest in a portfolio to protect your résumés from damage.
4. Make sure you have a pen that writes cleanly. Bring a spare in the event that the first runs dry. Make sure the ink is blue or black. Do not use red, green, violet, or fluorescent inks to fill out forms.
5. Neatly and fully complete any forms given to you to fill out. Complete the form on site, unless you are told that the form may be taken home.
6. Make your communication respectful. For example, if you have someone who is picking you up at the conclusion of the visit, politely ask the employer if you can tell that person how long you might be. *Don't* say something like, "Will this be long? I have someone waiting for me."
7. If you carry a cell phone, turn it off during an interview.
8. Thank the employer for his or her time.

Contacting Prospective Employers

Submitting an Unsolicited Application or Résumé

You need not wait until you see an advertisement to make an application or submit a résumé for employment. Many agencies accept applications or résumés at any time, even though some accept them only at specific times. Be sure to call the agency first to see if it is accepting applications or résumés.

When you submit an unsolicited application or résumé, make sure that you include a cover letter. Your cover letter should follow the format described later in this chapter. It should indicate that you are aware that the agency is not currently hiring and that you wish to have your application on file if a position becomes available.

Responding to an Advertisement

Employers may post advertisements in local newspapers, at the local Canada Employment Centre, at schools, or even on the public service boards in supermarkets and shopping centres. Get into the habit of checking the locations where employers in your area post advertisements.

An advertisement for a support worker position will usually contain some information about the duties involved, the experience and academic requirements, as well as the procedure to follow to submit a résumé or application. The information contained in the advertisement can give valuable clues as to how you should present yourself to the employer. Let's take a look at the components of a sample advertisement, using Exhibit 27-1 as an illustration.

Employer

Who is advertising? In this case, it is Omega Support Services Association. In order to personalize your cover letter, you will want to find out the name of the person who will receive your résumé. If possible, find out this information through a colleague or friend who works at the agency, not by calling the agency. The agency may receive many such calls and become a bit frustrated at the time it takes to respond to each one.

Type of Position

What positions are being offered? In this instance, both assisted living and outreach positions are available. You would have to decide whether you are interested in applying for either or both. Your interest would be reflected in your cover letter.

Omega Support Services Association
is seeking
Support Workers (with certificate)

We have immediate openings in our outreach and assisted living programs for support workers (with certificate). The successful candidates will be enthusiastic and have experience working with clients with a wide range of disabilities. Experience in providing support in a community setting and in working with clients with communication disorders is preferred.
A car is essential for the outreach position.

You may apply in person at:

12345 Bytown Road
Anytown, B.C.
on **October 15 & 16, between the hours of 1-4 p.m. only**

Please bring résumé and copy of all relevant certificates.

Exhibit 27-1   *Sample Advertisement*

What Requirements Does the Agency Have?

Requirements are "must-haves". These are usually stated as "necessary for the position," "essential," or "at a minimum, the candidate must have." Make sure you distinguish the requirements from the preferred characteristics.

Omega Support Services requires four things for either position: enthusiasm, a certificate as a Support Worker, experience working with people with a wide range of disabilities, and the ability to start as soon as possible. The outreach position also requires that the candidates have a vehicle. All other characteristics are *preferences*.

In general, you must make sure that you possess the requirements stated before you apply. An agency may feel that you did not take the time to read its advertisement thoroughly, or that you are wasting its time if you apply without the necessary qualifications. Your cover letter should state that you have the requirements.

What Qualities Does the Agency Desire?

Many agencies will list *preferred* characteristics in their advertisements. Preferred characteristics are things that will cause the agency to prefer one applicant over another, but that are not absolute requirements. In Exhibit 27-1, experience in community settings and experience with clients who have a communication disorder are preferred characteristics.

If you have one or more of the preferred characteristics, highlight this information in your cover letter.

Keep in mind that the agency may not state in its advertisement all the characteristics it prefers. This is where any prior knowledge you have about the agency can be useful. For example, you may learn from colleagues that Omega Support Services emphasizes teamwork. Even though this is not explicitly stated in the advertisement, you might refer to this in your cover letter.

How Do Candidates Apply?

Be certain to carefully follow the instructions for making applications. The agency may have arranged for extra staff members to be present to process the applications and have made other preparations to receive applications in a specific way. If you do not follow the agency's instructions, you run the risk of irritating the people you want to hire you. In some cases, your application may not be considered if you do not submit it in accordance with the stated instructions.

Omega Support Services wants candidates to apply in person between 1 p.m. and 4 p.m. on October 15 and 16. Thus, you could visit the agency on either date. In order to allow for ample time for your application to be reviewed, you should arrive no later than 3:30 p.m.

Some agencies will ask that you fax or mail a résumé. In most cases, you can drop off a résumé instead. If so, you can use the visit to make a positive impression. If the agency does not want résumés submitted in any other way, respect its wishes.

Your Cover Letter

When you submit a résumé, you should always include a cover letter. This letter should be no longer than one page, and should be typewritten. It should also meet the following criteria.

1. It is addressed to the appropriate person, by name. For example, if the person hiring support workers is Jane Harberry, the Coordinator, you should address your cover letter to "Ms. Jane Harberry". Take the time to find out the name of the person and make sure that you have the correct spelling of the person's name.
2. It highlights your skills and abilities that directly relate to the position for which you are applying.
3. It focusses on how you can contribute to the agency, not on the challenges and opportunities you expect the agency to give you.
4. It does not contain misleading information.
5. It is grammatically correct and has no spelling or typographical errors.
6. It is typed on the same paper as you used for your résumé.
7. It is signed in blue or black ink.

The Interview

The interview provides you and the employer the opportunity to find out more about each other. It is also your opportunity to show how well you can contribute to the agency.

Plan Ahead

If you have planned ahead, you will have investigated the agency as a part of the job search described in Chapter 26. You will have learned about the agency, its clients, services, and philosophy. If not, you should take the time to learn about the agency *before* you go to the interview.

Your initial investigation probably answered many questions. It likely raised some questions about the agency. These questions may be ones to ask in the interview. Review these questions with a teacher or trusted friend before the interview.

Another aspect of planning ahead is knowing your own strengths and weaknesses. What parts of your career have been most satisfying for you? Are there types of work you do better than others? Reviewing this information in your mind will help prepare you for any questions.

Arrive on Time

Make sure that you allow plenty of time to get to the interview. If you are unfamiliar with the area, consider taking a trial trip from your home to the site. Plan to arrive at least 10 minutes before the scheduled appointment time. This will allow you a few minutes to collect your thoughts before the interview begins.

Allow Plenty of Time

Allow plenty of time for the interview. If you have a friend waiting for you, make sure that the person knows that you may be an hour or more, particularly if the interview goes well.

During the Interview

Be Confident

It's normal to be a bit nervous in an interview. However, you don't want to let any nervousness get in the way of giving your best impression. In particular, you want to put forth an image of confidence. Make sure that your body language says that you are comfortable and confident of your skills and that you are interested and excited about the potential opportunity. If you have a "nervous habit", such as playing with your pen or picking at your cuticles, make sure that you do your best to control it.

Prepare for Commonly Asked Questions

Most interviewers have questions they prefer to use in an interview. If possible, find out what questions are likely to be asked (colleagues and friends who have interviewed with the same agency can be a good source of information). Prepare for these questions, but also be prepared for other questions as well. Some common questions include the following ones.

1. What interests you about working for our agency?
2. What type of client poses the greatest challenge to you and why?
3. What do you plan to do five years from now?
4. What makes you feel that you are particularly well suited to this type of work?

You may be asked "what would you do" questions. These are often case studies where you are asked to describe the action you might take in a situation. Be aware that the agency probably has a policy that they would ask staff to follow in the situation. Consider beginning your response to questions like these with a phrase such as, "As an employee, I would follow your procedure for handling this type of situation. Without knowing your procedure I would likely do the following." Then, outline what you would do. This allows you to demonstrate good problem-solving skills without appearing to go against an agency's policy.

Answer Questions Directly and Honestly

When you are asked a question, make sure that you answer the question directly and honestly. If the answer leads to a weakness, own up to it. For example, you might be asked why you left a previous position. If you were fired because you were often late, you must be forthright. If you have corrected the problem, make sure that you use the opportunity to include this information. For example, you might say something like, "I was fired from that position because I was frequently late. Afterward, I made certain that I did not allow other things to interfere with my ability to get to work on time. I have not been late for work since then."

Handle the Conclusion of the Interview Professionally

You will often have the opportunity to ask questions at the end of the interview. This is an appropriate time to ask any remaining questions you have about the position. It is *not* an appropriate time to ask about salary or benefits.

At the conclusion of the interview, remember to thank the interviewer for his or her time. At that time, you may ask when you can expect to hear the agency's decision. Be careful to word your question carefully so that it does not sound as though you are demanding that the person contact you. Consider using this type of question: "Do you have an idea of when you'll be making your decision? Or, "Would it be appropriate for me to contact you in the next week or so?"

Follow-Up

It's always a good idea to write a brief note of thanks to the interviewer. Exhibit 27-2 shows a typical thank-you note. The note shows that you appreciate the amount of time and effort that the interview process takes. It also shows that you pay attention to details and are organized in your job search. This note should be sent to the person who interviewed you no later than two days after the interview. The note should be handwritten on a blank note card. Do not send a letter or a thank-you card that has a printed verse inside.

Dear Ms. Harberry,

Thank you for your time Monday. I really appreciated the opportunity to interview for the outreach support worker position in your new program. From what you told me, I'm sure that the program will make it much easier for clients to remain in their own homes.

Thank you again for your time.

Sarah Jones

Exhibit 27-2   *A Typical Note*

Your note should express your appreciation for the interviewer's time. You should also include a sentence about something that impressed you about the agency, or about the way the interviewed conducted the interview. Make sure that any compliment you offer is specific and genuine. For example, you might say, "The way you asked questions really put me at ease" or "I was impressed with the way you have involved clients in the development of the assisted living project." It's usually a good idea to write out a rough draft of your note on plain paper first. Make any changes before you write the final version on the card. Make sure that you sign your name on the card.

The Offer of Employment

When Will I Hear?

While it's possible that you will be offered employment at the conclusion of the interview, an offer is most likely to come after the agency has held all the interviews scheduled for a particular period of time. Don't be disappointed if your interview does not conclude with an immediate job offer.

Conditional Offer of Employment

If you are offered employment, it is likely to be a **conditional offer**. This means that you must provide certain documents before you can be hired. The most common conditions are: a medical report that certifies that you are able to perform the duties of the position; a police record check that shows no offences unacceptable to the employer; and a medical report verifying that you are free from infectious diseases. You will usually have to supply the required information before you can begin to work for the agency.

Probationary Periods

Employers usually make an initial offer of employment on a trial basis. This situation is called a **probationary period**. Most provinces have legislation that governs this *probationary period*, but it is usually a few months long. This gives both you and the agency the opportunity to see how well your employment works out. Usually, if the probationary period is successful, you become a regular employee.

Your Responsibilities

It is particularly important to submit all required documents as soon as possible so that you can begin work. If your agency requires that a particular form be completed, obtain the form and get it to the proper person as soon as you can.

You will likely have to complete tax forms and other payroll documents. Have all the information that is required when you complete the form and make sure that any information you write down is correct and legible.

When You Have Not Been Offered Employment

Not every interview will result in an offer of employment. This may be for several reasons: the agency had more qualified applicants than it could hire; your skills were not exactly what the agency was seeking; or you were simply not the strongest candidate.

You should follow up with the agency to see if you can learn why you were not the appropriate candidate and what you can do to improve your chances for employment.

Most agencies will share their impressions with you provided that you let them know that you are seeking for ways to improve your interview skills and nothing more.

If you are able to discuss your performance with the interviewer, keep in mind that you are there to learn, not to debate the interviewer's opinion. Listen carefully to what the person has to say. Focus on how you can improve your skills. Take notes, if possible, and ask questions so that you fully understand what the interviewer is saying. At the conclusion, thank the interviewer for his or her time. Be sure to send a written thank-you note as soon as possible after the session.

When you return home, review the notes that you have made. Make the changes that you need to make. If the interviewer made suggestions as to how you may better answer interview questions, practise these suggestions with a friend.

Questions for Review

1. Describe how you would dress to give a professional appearance.

2. What are eight ways you can demonstrate professional behaviour when contacting the employer?

3. What five types of information must you find in an advertisement?

4. Why should you send a cover letter with any résumé or application?

Questions for Discussion

1. You are being interviewed for a job in a new long-term care facility. The clients will all be over 90 and many will have a cognitive impairment. How would you answer the following questions?

   a. What do you see yourself doing two years from now?

   b. What interests you most about this position?

   c. Working with clients with cognitive impairment poses real challenges to support staff. Describe how your training and experience has prepared you for this role.

2. Generate a list of interview questions you feel an employer is likely to ask. Share your questions with your colleagues. Then, use these questions to help each other practise responding.

3. You are in an interview. The employer asks you why you left a position you held two years ago. You were not the right person for that position and were let go before your probationary period was over. How do you respond to the employer's question?

Appendix A
Canadian Charter of Rights and Freedoms

Schedule B

Constitution Act, 1982 (79)

Enacted as Schedule B to the Canada Act 1982 (U.K.) 1982, c. 11, which came into force on April 17, 1982

PART I

Canadian Charter of Rights and Freedoms

Whereas Canada is founded upon principles that recognize the supremacy of God and the rule of law:

Guarantee of Rights and Freedoms

Rights and freedoms in Canada

1. The Canadian Charter of Rights and Freedoms guarantees the rights and freedoms set out in it subject only to such reasonable limits prescribed by law as can be demonstrably justified in a free and democratic society.

Fundamental Freedoms

Fundamental freedoms

2. Everyone has the following fundamental freedoms:
   a) freedom of conscience and religion;
   b) freedom of thought, belief, opinion and expression, including freedom of the press and other media of communication;
   c) freedom of peaceful assembly; and
   d) freedom of association.

Democratic Rights

Democratic rights of citizens

3. Every citizen of Canada has the right to vote in an election of members of the House of Commons or of a legislative assembly and to be qualified for membership therein.

Maximum duration of legislative bodies

4. (1) No House of Commons and no legislative assembly shall continue for longer than five years from the date fixed for the return of the writs of a general election of its members.
   (2) In time of real or apprehended war, invasion or insurrection, a House of Commons may be continued by Parliament and a legislative assembly may be

continued by the legislature beyond five years if such continuation is not opposed by the votes of more than one-third of the members of the House of Commons or the legislative assembly, as the case may be.

Continuation in special circumstances

5. There shall be a sitting of Parliament and of legislative each legislature at least once every twelve months.

Annual sitting of legislative bodies

Mobility Rights

6. (1) Every citizen of Canada has the right to enter, remain in and leave Canada.

Mobility of citizens

   (2) Every citizen of Canada and every person who has the status of a permanent resident of Canada has the right

      a) to move to and take up residence in any province; and

      b) to pursue the gaining of a livelihood in any province.

Rights to move and gain livelihood

   (3) The rights specified in subsection (2) are subject to

      a) any laws or practices of general application in force in a province other than those that discriminate among persons primarily on the basis of province of present or previous residence; and

Limitation

      b) any laws providing for reasonable residency requirements as a qualification for the receipt of publicly provided social services.

   (4) Subsections (2) and (3) do not preclude any law, program or activity that has as its object the amelioration in a province of conditions of individuals in that province who are socially or economically disadvantaged if the rate of employment in that province is below the rate of employment in Canada.

Affirmative action programs

Legal Rights

7. Everyone has the right to life, liberty and security of the person and the right not to be deprived thereof except in accordance with the principles of fundamental justice.

Life, liberty and security of person

8. Everyone has the right to be secure against unreasonable search or seizure.

Search or seizure

9. Everyone has the right not to be arbitrarily detained or imprisoned.

Detention or imprisonment

10. Everyone has the right on arrest or detention

    a) to be informed promptly of the reasons therefor;

    b) to retain and instruct counsel without delay and to be informed of that right; and

    c) to have the validity of the detention determined by way of *habeas corpus* and to be released if the detention is not lawful.

Arrest or detention

11. Any person charged with an offence has the right

    a) to be informed without unreasonable delay of the specific offence;

    b) to be tried within a reasonable time;

    c) not to be compelled to be a witness in proceedings against that person in respect of the offence;

Proceedings in criminal and penal matters

d) to be presumed innocent until proven guilty according to law in a fair and public hearing by an independent and impartial tribunal;

e) not to be denied reasonable bail without just cause;

f) except in the case of an offence under military law tried before a military tribunal, to the benefit of trial by jury where the maximum punishment for the offence is imprisonment for five years or a more severe punishment;

g) not to be found guilty on account of any act or omission unless, at the time of the act or omission, it constituted an offence under Canadian or international law or was criminal according to the general principles of law recognized by the community of nations;

h) if finally acquitted of the offence, not to be tried for it again and, if finally found guilty and punished for the offence, not to be tried or punished for it again; and

i) if found guilty of the offence and if the punishment for the offence has been varied between the time of commission and the time of sentencing, to the benefit of the lesser punishment.

Treatment or punishment

12. Everyone has the right not to be subjected to any cruel and unusual treatment or punishment.

Self-crimination

13. A witness who testifies in any proceedings has the right not to have any incriminating evidence so given used to incriminate that witness in any other proceedings, except in a prosecution for perjury or for the giving of contradictory evidence.

Interpreter

14. A party or witness in any proceedings who does not understand or speak the language in which the proceedings are conducted or who is deaf has the right to the assistance of an interpreter.

Equality Rights

Equality before and under law and equal protection and benefit of law

15. (1) Every individual is equal before and under the law and has the right to the equal protection and equal benefit of the law without discrimination and, in particular, without discrimination based on race, national or ethnic origin, colour, religion, sex, age or mental or physical disability.

Affirmative action programs

(2) Subsection (1) does not preclude any law, program or activity that has as its object the amelioration of conditions of disadvantaged individuals or groups including those that are disadvantaged because of race, national or ethnic origin, colour, religion, sex, age or mental or physical disability.

Official Languages of Canada

Official languages of Canada

16. (1) English and French are the official languages of Canada and have equality of status and equal rights and privileges as to their use in all institutions of the Parliament and government of Canada.

Official languages of New Brunswick

(2) English and French are the official languages of New Brunswick and have equality of status and equal rights and privileges as to their use in all institutions of the legislature and government of New Brunswick.

(3) Nothing in this Charter limits the authority of Parliament or a legislature to advance the equality of status or use of English and French.

Advancement of status and use

16.1 (1) The English linguistic community and the French linguistic community in New Brunswick have equality of status and equal rights and privileges, including the right to distinct educational institutions and such distinct cultural institutions as are necessary for the preservation and promotion of those communities.

English and French linguistic communities in New Brunswick

(2) The role of the legislature and government of New Brunswick to preserve and promote the status, rights and privileges referred to in subsection (1) is affirmed.

Role of the legislature and government of New Brunswick

17. (1) Everyone has the right to use English or French in any debates and other proceedings of Parliament.

Proceedings of Parliament

(2) Everyone has the right to use English or French in any debates and other proceedings of the legislature of New Brunswick.

Proceedings of the New Brunswick legislature

18. (1) The statutes, records and journals of Parliament shall be printed and published in English and French and both language versions are equally authoritative.

Parliamentary statutes and records

(2) The statutes, records and journals of the legislature of New Brunswick shall be printed and published in English and French and both language versions are equally authoritative.

New Brunswick statutes and records

19. (1) Either English or French may be used by any person in, or in any pleading in or process issuing from, any court established by Parliament.

Proceedings in courts established by Parliament

(2) Either English or French may be used by any person in, or in any pleading in or process issuing from, any court of New Brunswick.

Proceedings in New Brunswick courts

20. (1) Any member of the public in Canada has the right to communicate with, and to receive available services from, any head or central office of an institution of the Parliament or government of Canada in English or French, and has the same right with respect to any other office of any such institution where

a) there is a significant demand for communications with and services from that office in such language; or

b) due to the nature of the office, it is reasonable that communications with and services from that office be available in both English and French.

Communications by public with federal institutions

(2) Any member of the public in New Brunswick has the right to communicate with, and to receive available services from, any office of an institution of the legislature or government of New Brunswick in English or French.

Communications by public with New Brunswick institutions

21. Nothing in sections 16 to 20 abrogates or derogates from any right, privilege or obligation with respect to the English and French languages, or either of them, that exists or is continued by virtue of any other provision of the Constitution of Canada.

Continuation of existing constitutional provisions

22. Nothing in sections 16 to 20 abrogates or derogates from any legal or customary right or privilege acquired or enjoyed either before or after the coming into force of this Charter with respect to any language that is not English or French.

Rights and privileges preserved

Minority Language Educational Rights

Language of
instruction

23. (1) Citizens of Canada

a) whose first language learned and still understood is that of the English or French linguistic minority population of the province in which they reside, or

b) who have received their primary school instruction in Canada in English or French and reside in a province where the language in which they received that instruction is the language of the English or French linguistic minority population of the province, have the right to have their children receive primary and secondary school instruction in that language in that province.

Continuity
of language
instruction

(2) Citizens of Canada of whom any child has received or is receiving primary or secondary school instruction in English or French in Canada, have the right to have all their children receive primary and secondary school instruction in the same language.

Application
where numbers
warrant

(3) The right of citizens of Canada under subsections (1) and (2) to have their children receive primary and secondary school instruction in the language of the English or French linguistic minority population of a province

a) applies wherever in the province the number of children of citizens who have such a right is sufficient to warrant the provision to them out of public funds of minority language instruction; and

b) includes, where the number of those children so warrants, the right to have them receive that instruction in minority language educational facilities provided out of public funds.

Enforcement

Enforcement of
guaranteed rights
and freedoms

24. (1) Anyone whose rights or freedoms, as guaranteed by this Charter, have been infringed or denied may apply to a court of competent jurisdiction to obtain such remedy as the court considers appropriate and just in the circumstances.

Exclusion of evidence
bringing administration
of justice into disrepute

(2) Where, in proceedings under subsection (1), a court concludes that evidence was obtained in a manner that infringed or denied any rights or freedoms guaranteed by this Charter, the evidence shall be excluded if it is established that, having regard to all the circumstances, the admission of it in the proceedings would bring the administration of justice into disrepute.

General

Aboriginal rights
and freedoms not
affected by Charter

25. The guarantee in this Charter of certain rights and freedoms shall not be construed so as to abrogate or derogate from any aboriginal, treaty or other rights or freedoms that pertain to the aboriginal peoples of Canada including

a) any rights or freedoms that have been recognized by the Royal Proclamation of October 7, 1763; and

b) any rights or freedoms that now exist by way of land claims agreements or may be so acquired.

Other rights and
freedoms not
affected by Charter

26. The guarantee in this Charter of certain rights and freedoms shall not be construed as denying the existence of any other rights or freedoms that exist in Canada.

27. This Charter shall be interpreted in a manner consistent with the preservation and enhancement of the multicultural heritage of Canadians.

Multicultural heritage

28. Notwithstanding anything in this Charter, the rights and freedoms referred to in it are guaranteed equally to male and female persons.

Rights guaranteed equally to both sexes

29. Nothing in this Charter abrogates or derogates from any rights or privileges guaranteed by or under the Constitution of Canada in respect of denominational, separate or dissentient schools.(93)

Rights respecting certain schools preserved

30. A reference in this Charter to a Province or to the legislative assembly or legislature of a province shall be deemed to include a reference to the Yukon Territory and the Northwest Territories, or to the appropriate legislative authority thereof, as the case may be.

Application to territories and territorial authorities

31. Nothing in this Charter extends the legislative powers of any body or authority.

Legislative powers not extended

Application of Charter

32. (1) This Charter applies

Application of Charter

a) to the Parliament and government of Canada in respect of all matters within the authority of Parliament including all matters relating to the Yukon Territory and Northwest Territories; and

b) to the legislature and government of each province in respect of all matters within the authority of the legislature of each province.

(2) Notwithstanding subsection (1), section 15 shall not have effect until three years after this section comes into force.

Exception

33. (1) Parliament or the legislature of a province may expressly declare in an Act of Parliament or of the legislature, as the case may be, that the Act or a provision thereof shall operate notwithstanding a provision included in section 2 or sections 7 to 15 of this Charter.

Exception where express declaration

(2) An Act or a provision of an Act in respect of which a declaration made under this section is in effect shall have such operation as it would have but for the provision of this Charter referred to in the declaration.

Operation of exception

(3) A declaration made under subsection (1) shall cease to have effect five years after it comes into force or on such earlier date as may be specified in the declaration.

Five year limitation

(4) Parliament or the legislature of a province may re-enact a declaration made under subsection (1).

Re-enactment

(5) Subsection (3) applies in respect of a re-enactment made under subsection (4).

Five year limitation

Citation

34. This Part may be cited as the *Canadian Charter of Rights and Freedoms.*

Citation

Appendix B
National and Provincial Long-Term Care Associations

All provinces have long-term care services. However, the exact services each province provides are different. The following list provides information on selected provincial and national associations. It is current as of early 2000. Please note that this is not an exhaustive list. There may be other associations or organizations in your area.

National

Canadian Association for Community Care
Suite 520, 1 Nicholas Street
Ottawa, Ontario
K1N 7B7
tel.: (613) 241-7510
fax: (613) 241-5923
http://www.cacc-acssc.com

Alberta

Alberta Long Term Care Association
#509, Centre 104
5241 Calgary Trail South
Edmonton, Alberta
T6H 5G8
tel.: (780) 435-0699
fax: (780) 436-9785
www.longtermcare.ab.ca

Home Care and Support Association Alberta
#410, 1111 11th Avenue
Calgary, Alberta
T2R 0G5
tel.: (403) 229-2888 or
       (780) 482-3370

Provincial Health Authorities of Alberta
44 Capital Boulevard 200-10044
108 St. NW
Edmonton, Alberta
T5J 3S7

British Columbia

British Columbia Association of Private Care Facilities
#101, 1700 West 75th Avenue
Vancouver, British Columbia
V6P 6G2
tel.: (604) 263-4223
fax: (604) 263-4229

Health Association of B.C.
#700, 1380 Burrard Street
Vancouver, British Columbia
V6Z 2H3
tel.: (604) 488-1554
fax: (604) 488-3983

British Columbia Paraplegic Association
Gd 4 2525 Highway 97 S
Westbank, British Columbia
V0H 2A0
tel.: (250) 768-5345

New Brunswick

HomeSupport New Brunswick
Box 21004, 1715 Woodstock Road
Fredericton, New Brunswick
E3B 7A3
tel.: (506) 784-6300
fax: (506) 784-6306

**New Brunswick Association of
Nursing Homes**
197 Main Street
Fredericton, New Brunswick
E3A 1E1
tel.: (506) 460-6262
fax: (506) 458-9206

Newfoundland and Labrador

Beclin Building, Topsail Road
PO Box 8234
St. John's, Newfoundland
A1B 3N4
tel.: (709) 364-5203
fax: (709) 364-6460

Nova Scotia

**Associated Homes for Special Care,
Nova Scotia**
33 Ochterloney St. Ste. 260
Dartmouth, Nova Scotia
B2Y 4P5
tel.: (902) 453-2977
fax: (902) 464-3791

**CCANS (Continuing Care Association
of Nova Scotia)**
2786 Agricola Street, Room 119
Halifax, NS B3K 4E1
tel.: (902) 453-2977
fax: (902) 453-2967

Home Support Nova Scotia
Association
Box 1180
Wolfville, Nova Scotia
B0P 1X0
tel.: (902) 542-2595
fax: (902) 542-6118

**NSAHO (Nova Scotia Association
of Health Organizations)**
2 Dartmouth Road
Bedford, Nova Scotia
B4A 2K7
tel.: (902) 832-8500
fax: (902) 832-8506

Ontario

**Ontario Home Health Care Providers
Association**
19 Melrose Avenue South
Hamilton, Ontario
L8M 2Y4
tel.: (905) 543-9474
fax: (905) 545-1568

**Ontario Association of Non-Profit
Homes and Services for Seniors**
Suite 700
7050 Weston Road
Woodbridge, Ontario
L4L 8G7
tel.: (905) 851-8821
fax: (905) 851-0744
http://www.oanhss.org

**Ontario Community
Support Association**
Suite 104
970 Lawrence Avenue West
Toronto, Ontario
M6A 3B6
tel.: (416) 256-3010
fax: (416) 256-3021
http://www.ocsa.on.ca

Ontario Long Term Residential Care
Association
2155 Leanne Boulevard
Suite 218
Mississauga, Ontario
L5K 2K8
tel.: (905) 403-0500
fax: (905) 403-0502

Ontario Long Term Care Association
Suite 102-202
345 Renfrew Drive
Markham, Ontario
L3R 9S9
tel.: (905) 470-8995
fax: (905) 470-9595

Prince Edward Island

Community Care Facility Association
c/o Bayview Lodge
22 Washington St. Souris
Prince Edward Island
C0A 2B0
tel.: (902) 687-3122
fax: (902) 687-4419

Health Association of PEI
10 Pownal Street
PO Box 490
Charlottetown, Prince Edward Island
C1A 3V6

Nursing Home Association of PEI
c/o Dr. John Gillis Memorial Lodge
Belfast, Prince Edward Island
C0A 1A0
tel.: (902) 659-2337
fax: (902) 659-2865

Quebec

Confédération Québécoise des
Centres d'Hébergement et de
Réadaptation
1001 de Maisonneuve est, Bureau 1100
Montréal, Québec
H2L 4P9
tel.: (514) 597-1007
fax: (514) 873-5411

Saskatchewan

Saskatchewan Association
of Health Organizations
1445 Park Street
Regina, Saskatchewan
S4N 4C5
tel.: (306) 347-5500
fax: (306) 525-1960

Glossary

Abuse Harm to a victim caused by anyone upon whom the victim relies for basic needs or support.

Academic Skills Skills that provide the basic foundation to get, keep, and progress in a job.

Acquired Brain Injury Brain injury that occurs as the result of trauma, anoxia, hemorrhage, seizure, or toxins.

Acquired Immune Deficiency Syndrome A condition caused by the HIV virus in which the person experiences opportunistic diseases.

Acute Care The type of care provided in hospitals. Clients in an acute care setting are usually called patients.

Acute Care Facility A setting in which a person receives treatment for a specific medical condition on a short-term basis.

Adaptive Communication A form of communicating in which a group of techniques is used to adapt communication to the specific needs of the sender or receiver.

Adult Learning Changes in behaviour that result from new information.

Age-Related Changes The changes that are part of the aging process that happen to everyone if they live long enough.

Alignment The positioning of the body along a straight line.

Alimentary Canal The structure that links the organs of the digestive system.

Anatomy The study of the body's structure.

Antibacterial An agent that destroys bacteria and/or prevents bacterial growth.

Antibiotics Drugs that treat bacterial infections.

Anticipatory Grief The sense of loss, grieving, and preparing to move on that occurs before an expected loss happens.

Anxiety Disorders A group of conditions in which anxiety becomes extremely disabling over a long period of time.

Aphasia The complete or partial loss of language skills because of an injury to the brain.

Apraxia A condition that results from an injury to the brain, making voluntary, physical control of purposeful movement difficult.

Appearance Observations about body language, dress, and cleanliness.

Arthritis A condition that causes pain, stiffness and swelling in or around the joints. It can affect other tissues.

Assertiveness A technique that helps you respect others' views, concerns, and needs while not compromising your own.

Assessment The phase of support planning that determines the type of support needed.

Assisted Living A setting in which clients live in their own apartments or townhouses but receive services from an agency in the building.

Attendant A person who assists a client with physical disabilities where the client directs his or her own care.

Attire Clothing.

Augmentative Communication A form of communicating in which physical aids are used in communication.

Autism A condition that results from structural disorders in parts of the brain.

Autonomy Each person's right to have his or her decisions respected.

Bacteria Microscopic plant life that we commonly call germs

Barriers Things that prevent the message from getting across when communicating, such as language or hearing impairment

Behaviour Observations about actions, awareness and interest in surroundings, and awareness and interest in others

Beneficence The obligation to prevent or remove what is bad and to promote what is good.

Biodegradable A material that is easily broken down into chemicals that do not harm the environment

Bipolar Disorder A condition in which a person has alternating periods of hyperactivity and depression; also called manic depression

Blood Assists in nutrition and elimination, regulation, protection, and oxygenation of the body

Body Language Communication through posture, facial expressions, and movements

Body Mechanics Using your muscles correctly to move or lift objects properly

Bones Hard, rigid, living structures that provide support for the body

Buccal Tablet A dose of medication that is dissolved in the mouth and absorbs through the mucous membrane of the mouth

Canada's Food Guide A guide that is based on nutritional needs and provides an easy way to ensure that people obtain the nutrients required to build and maintain a healthy body

Cancer A disease in which cells grow abnormally and out-of-control

Carbohydrates Substances formed of starches and sugars that provide energy

Care Plan A written document that outlines the support a client is to receive. This document often describes client needs, support goals and includes names and contact information for family members and other services involved in the client's support.

Caregiver A person who assists the client.

Cell The basic element of the human body and all living things

Centre of Gravity The point where mass is equally distributed

Cerebral Palsy A condition that results from an anomaly or injury to the brain as it develops

Chain of Infection The process of transmission of an infection

Chronic Care The type of care provided to people whose condition is stable, but who need more professional care than residents of long term care facilities.

Chronic Obstructive Pulmonary Disease A group of irreversible lung diseases

Chronological Resume A resume that organizes the information in each section by date

Circumcision The surgical removal of the foreskin of the penis

Clarifying Describing things clearly so that others understand or asking questions so that you understand

Clean Technique A method of destroying pathogens to prevent transmission of infection

Cleft Lip A fissure or opening in the upper lip

Cleft Palate A condition in which there is no passageway between the naso-pharynx and the nose

Client A person who uses community support services.

Client Teaching The instruction given to a client by a support worker

Club Foot A malformation of the bones of the foot, causing it to twist inward or outward

Code of Conduct A statement that is intended to guide support worker practice. It is often made up of ethical principles, support worker qualities, and skills. It is sometimes called a code of ethics.

Cognition The ability to process information; includes six cognitive processes

Cognitive Impairment A condition that disrupts the way the brain works to think, use language, remember, and coordinate movements

Cognitive Processes The six factors that contribute to cognition: perceiving, recognizing, interpreting, and organizing information; judging; and reasoning

Communication The ability to share your ideas, explore others' ideas, and resolve conflicts. In reporting, it refers to observations about messages.

Community A setting in which a person lives in her or his own home (house or apartment) without support services located in the same building.

Conditional Offer of Employment An offer of employment that is conditional upon you providing certain documents before you can be hired

Confidentiality A term that describes privacy of a person's information

Congenital Hip Dysplasia A condition resulting in partial or total hip dislocation

Connective Tissue The tissue that forms bones, tendons, and cartilage

Consumer A person with temporary or permanent disability who uses support services.

Continuing Care A type of care provided on a long-term basis.

Continuum Range

Content Facts communicated through words

Cycle of Abuse A term used to describe the three phases of abuse; abuse, remorse, and anger escalation.

Day Program Programs that provide clients an opportunity to take part in activities and be with others in a secure setting.

Decubitus Ulcers Sores caused when tissue is trapped between a hard surface and a bony prominence; also called pressure sores

Delirium A reversible cognitive impairment often related to extremely high fever

Dementia A term used to describe the types of cognitive impairment.

Depression A range of conditions from a feeling of sadness to a clinical syndrome

Diabetes A disease resulting from the pancreas' inability to produce enough insulin or to properly use the insulin that is produced

Disability A limitation to a person's functioning, caused by an impairment, that affects things the person needs or wants to do

Disinfection The process of destroying pathogens

Distress Stress that prevents us from functioning in the way we would like.

Do Not Resuscitate Orders A document that states a person is not to receive life-sustaining measures

Documentation Written reports such as notes, reports, and checklists

Dossette A container that holds individual doses of medication

Down Syndrome A genetic condition produced by an abnormality in chromosome 21

Drug An agent that alters the body's mechanisms

Dysarthria A condition that results from a weakness or lack of coordination in some of the muscles involved in speaking

Early-Onset Dementia Dementia that occurs in younger people

Empathy The ability to sense what others are feeling while respecting that you will never fully understand their emotions

Employability The ability to do the tasks of a job

Engorgement A painful overfilling of the breasts.

Epithelial Tissue The tissue that covers the internal and external body tissues

Ethics The principles that guide how people behave.

Ethnicity A person's ethnic origin

Evaluation The phase of support planning that reviews the client's situation, needs, and preferences

Facility A setting in which a person lives that has shared dining and recreational facilities. Support services are housed in the same building.

Failure to Thrive A condition of abuse that causes a child to fail to grow and develop.

Fat The substance that allows fat-soluble vitamins to be used by the body

Feelings Emotions communicated through words and body language

Fetal Alcohol Effect (FAE) A disorder that can occur when a woman drinks alcohol during pregnancy; milder than FAS

Fetal Alcohol Syndrome (FAS) A disorder that can occur when a woman drinks alcohol during pregnancy; more serious than FAE

Filters Things that affect how we communicate including body language, mood, and stress

Fire Hazards Things in the environment that pose a risk of fire or could make a fire spread

Flexibility The ability to adapt to changes in a relationship, setting, or situation.

Fragile X Syndrome A genetic disorder caused by a weakness or break in a portion of a child's X chromosome

Functional Impairment The way in which a particular condition affects a client

Functional Resume A resume that groups skills and experiences gained from a variety of employment situations

Fungi Bacteria that use spores to reproduce

Generic Name The name of the active ingredient in a drug

Goal Setting The phase of support planning in which client goals are identified along with the methods that will be used to attain the goals

Grief Work Tasks associated with moving through the phases of grieving

Group Home A home in which a small number of people live; in most cases no more than eight people. The group home has round-the-clock staff members and usually located in residential neighbourhoods.

Habilitation A process by which a person chooses to gain or regain function, or to adapt to a change in function in order to attain self-fulfillment

Handicap Commonly used to refer to a disability or activity limitation; not as widely used as it once was

Health "A state of complete physical, social, and mental well-being, not merely the absence of disease or infirmity" (WHO, 1998)

Health Condition Something that causes a change in a person's health status

Hemiplegia Partial or total paralysis of one side of the body

Herbal Medications Substances that contain naturally occurring chemicals

Heterotopic Ossification Abnormal bone growth in joints after a brain injury

Home Care Services provided to clients through a provincially-funded program.

Home Management The process of taking care of the client's home.

Hospice A residence where terminally ill people receive support and care

Human Immunodeficiency Virus The virus that causes AIDS

Huntington's Disease An inherited neurological disease

Hydrocephalus A condition related to an increase intracranial fluid in the brain that causes increased head size and pressure in the brain

Impairment   A change in a person's functioning that differs from that expected of others of the same age or sex

Implementation   The phase of support planning in which the methods identified in the goal setting phase are put into practice

Independence   The ability to do things for oneself

Infantilize   The treatment of an adult like a child

Infectious Agent   Microorganism capable of causing disease

Integument   Another term for skin

Interdependence   The reliance we have on others to help us do things.

Irreversible   Not curable or capable of being restored to a previous state.

Isolation Precautions   Techniques used to prevent transmission of serious and highly contagious diseases

Jaundice   A condition that causes yellowing of the skin

Joints   The points where two or more bones meet and move

Lateral   Side-lying

Laundry Symbols   Symbols that indicate the type of care a garment should receive

Life Satisfaction   Being content with our lives

Life Span   The length of time a person is alive

Life-Threatening Illness   An illness that is likely to cause death

Living Will   A document that gives specific instructions as to the care and treatment a person wants; also called an advance directive

Long-Term Care Facilities   A setting in which a person lives and receives assistance with routine activities of living as well as some nursing care.

Matrix   The substance found between cells and tissues from which a structure develops

Means of Transmission   The method of transfer of a causative agent from a reservoir to a susceptible host

Medical Asepsis   The destruction of pathogens to prevent transmission of infection

Mental Health   The ability to deal with the conditions of life effectively

Mental Health Conditions   Conditions that affect a person's self-concept, behaviour, thoughts, or feelings to such an extent that they interfere with the person's ability to deal with situations effectively

Mental Health Facility   A facility designed to provide service to people with mental health concerns.

Microorganisms   Organisms that are microscopic, including bacteria, viruses, protozoa, rickettsia, fungi, and parasitic worms

Milestones   Sets of abilities that a child is expected to attain by a certain age

Minerals   Inorganic materials that the body requires

Mobility Aids   Aids that are designed to improve a person's stability by expanding his or her base of support

Mental Health Facility   A facility designed to provide service to people with mental health concerns.

Multidisciplinary Teams   A support team made up of members from different professions or backgrounds.

Multiple Births   The births of more than one baby during one pregnancy

Multiple Loss   The loss of more than one thing at a time

Multiple Sclerosis   A central nervous system disease caused by the inflammation and scarring of the myelin sheath that protects nerve fibres

Muscle Tissue   The tissue that can contract and relax; may be smooth, striated, or cardiac

Muscles   Part of the musculoskeletal system that helps maintain posture, movement, and body heat

Muscular Dystrophy   A condition that causes muscle tissue to degenerate and be replaced by fatty and connective tissue

Mutuality   The ability to see how both people in a relationship benefit from it.

Narcotics   Drugs that dull the senses to provide pain relief and are very addictive

Need   Something we must meet in order to survive or feel satisfied with our lives

Neglect   The intentional or unintentional failure to provide the essentials of life

Negotiating   The give-and-take used in problem solving

Nerve Tissue   The tissue made of nerve cells that transmits electrical signals from the central nervous system to various parts of the body

Nonmaleficence   The obligation to do no harm to another person.

Nosocomial Infections   Infections acquired after admission to a facility

Nutrients   Vitamins, minerals, proteins, fats, carbohydrates, and water that your body needs to be healthy

Omnipotent   The state of being above all harm

Osteoporosis   A condition that causes bones to become less dense, brittle and weak

Organs   Groups of tissues working together with a specific purpose

Ostomy   A surgical opening in the body

Outreach Services   Services that are provided to clients in their own home, not in facilities, assisted living or supportive housing.

Over-the-Counter Medications   Drugs that can be purchased and used without a prescription

Overlapping Tasks   Tasks that are started and allowed to continue while another task is finished or begun.

Palliation   Providing care, support, and comfort to a client whose condition cannot be cured

Palliative Care   Active and compassionate care with the purpose to provide comfort and control pain

Paranoia   A range of conditions in which a person has delusions and believes that he or she is being persecuted or threatened.

Parasitic Worms   Multi-celled organisms that live within the human body and obtain nourishment from this host

Parent   A person who has the primary responsibility of caring for a child

Parkinson's Disease   A neurological disorder that affects the ability to initiate movement

Pathogens   Microorganisms that cause infection

Patient   A person who is in an acute care facility (hospital).

Personal Culture   The mix of many factors including ethnicity, religion, race, and experiences that make a person unique.

Personal Management Skills   The combination of skills, attitudes, and behaviours required to get, keep, and progress in a job

Personality   The psychological traits that each person has

Personhood   The characteristics, attributes, and strengths of an individual

Phenylketonuria   A disease caused by the absence of a liver enzyme

Physiology   The study of the body's functions

Police Record Check   A check done to provide proof that a person has not been convicted of a crime that would affect that person's employability

Polypharmacy   The use of more than one medication

Portal of Entry   The path into the body through which the infectious agent enters the host

Portal of Exit   The path by which the infectious agent leaves the reservoir

Post-Polio Syndrome   A condition that can occur in people who have had polio; causes further weakening of the muscles injured by the virus

Postpartum Depression   A depression in women who have recently had a baby

Posture   Position of the body

Presbyopia   A condition in which vision changes due to increasing age

Prescription Drugs   Drugs that are prescribed by a doctor for the treatment of specific conditions

Prevention   Avoiding the creation of unnecessary illness, impairment, or disability

Priorities   Goals that you want to attain before others

Probationary Period   A trial period of employment

Professional Appearance   All aspects of how you appear, including clothing, cleanliness, and the attention paid to the details of grooming

Professional Behaviour   Conducting yourself in a polite and business-like manner

Progressive   Worsens over time

Prone   Stomach-lying

Proprietary Medications   Drugs that a person can buy to treat minor conditions or symptoms of a condition

Protein   The substance essential for growth and tissue repair

Protozoa   Parasitic, single-celled organisms that thrive in areas of poor sanitation

Pulse   The rate at which blood is pumped through the heart; heartbeat

RIDICUPS   An acronym describing the eight principles of personalized care: Respect, Independence, Dignity, Individuality, Communication, Understanding, Privacy, and Safety

References   People who have agreed to give information regarding your abilities to potential employers

Rehabilitation   A process that helps people regain desired activities and levels of participation when these things have been affected by an impairment

Rehabilitation Centre   A facility which provides rehabilitation services to patients to help the patient recover from surgery, illness or injury.

Reservoir   The place where the infectious agent survives

Resident   A person who lives in a long-term care facility, retirement, or rest home.

Respect   The ability to recognize and accommodate others' thoughts, opinions, behaviour, needs, preferences, and decisions.

Respiration   The rate at which air is inhaled and exhaled; breathing

Respite Care   A type of service provided to a client and the client's caregiver, so that the caregiver can be relieved from the responsibilities of caring for the client and has the opportunity to take a break.

Retirement Homes or **Rest Homes**   Settings in which older adults live where some laundry and homemaking services are provided.

Reversible   Curable or capable of being restored to a previous state.

Rickettsia   Microscopic organisms that can only live inside cells and are almost always transmitted by insects

Right   Something we have the authority to do

Risk Factors   Factors that put a person's mental health at risk

SMART Goals   Criteria for describing the effectiveness of goals

Schizophrenia   A chronic mental health condition that affects a person's ability to take part in everyday activities. The condition may cause delusions, hallucinations, and disordered thinking.

Sense of Home   The feeling that a person has about where they live

Sensory Loss   Changes in the senses that result in a loss of hearing, smell, touch, taste, and sight

Service Agreement   A document that spells out the services to be provided, but does not usually include goals or client needs.

Social Role   Activities that are grouped together because of the expectations of a group or society

Spina Bifida   A condition caused by a defect in the way the spinal column has formed

Spinal Cord Injury   A condition caused by damage to the spinal cord, usually as a result of injury to vertebrae

Status   Observations about a client's condition, function, and any change that was seen.

Stress   A psychological and physiological condition that arises when we respond to stimulation or adjust to changes and demands.

Stressor   A particular source of stress.

Sublingual Tablet   A dose of medication that is dissolved under the tongue and absorbs through the mucous membrane of the mouth

Substance Abuse   The intentional misuse of medications, illicit drugs, or alcohol

Supine   Back-lying

Support Worker   A worker who provides personal support.

Support Plan   The foundation for all services that a client receives

Support Planning Process   The process used to identify the goals and preferences of the client

Susceptible Host   A person lacking resistance to a particular infectious agent

Syringe   A hollow tube that can be filled with a medication for administration

System   Groups of organs working together with a specific purpose

Team   The term used to describe the group of people who work together (and depend upon one another) to provide support to a client.

Teamwork Skills   Skills that are needed to work with others in a job

Temperature   The measurement of body heat

Therapists   Professionals who help the client regain ability or adjust to changes.

Time Management   Making the most of the time you have, in light of your priorities

Tissues   Groups of cells linked together by a matrix

Traumatic Brain Injury   Brain injury caused by traumatic events such as motor vehicle accidents, gunshot wounds, and falls

Tuberculosis   A bacterial disease affecting the lungs

Universal Precautions   A set of procedures used to prevent the spread of a communicable or contagious disease

Viruses   Microscopic organisms that grow in living cells and use the cells to sustain themselves

Vital Signs   Measurements of temperature, pulse, and respiration

Vitamins   Organic compounds that provide elements that the body needs to function

WHMIS   The Workplace Hazardous Materials Information System used to provide information about the proper use, handling, and storage of hazardous materials

Index